How to Do Everything with

ACT!

MW00905685

Douglas J. Wolf

Osborne/**McGraw-Hill**

New York   Chicago   San Francisco   Lisbon
London   Madrid   Mexico City   Milan   New Delhi
San Juan   Seoul   Singapore   Sydney   Toronto

Osborne/**McGraw-Hill**
2600 Tenth Street
Berkeley, California 94710
U.S.A.

To arrange bulk purchase discounts for sales promotions, premiums, or fund-raisers, please contact Osborne/**McGraw-Hill** at the above address. For information on translations or book distributors outside the U.S.A., please see the International Contact Information page immediately following the index.

How to Do Everything with ACT!

1234567890 FGR FGR 01987654321

ISBN 0-07-213370-8

Publisher	**Acquisitions Coordinator**	**Computer Designer**
Brandon A. Nordin	Tim Madrid	Kate Kaminski
Vice President & Associate Publisher	**Technical Editor**	Happenstance Type-O-Rama
Scott Rogers	Chris Lagarde	**Series Design**
Editorial Director	**Copy Editors**	Mickey Galicia
Roger Stewart	Erin Milnes	**Cover Series Design**
Project Manager	Lunaea Weatherstone	Dodie Shoemaker
Deidre Dolce	**Proofreader**	**Cover Illustrators**
Freelance Project Manager	Kelly Marshall	Tom Willis
Laurie Stewart	**Indexer**	Joseph Humphrey
	Jack Lewis	

This book was composed with QuarkXPress 4.11 on a Macintosh G4.

I dedicate this book to my grandmother Pearl Ida Wolf. She is an octogenarian who has hardly ever missed Lutheran church on Sunday and other mandated attendance dates. She has shown grace under pressure and lived life with a realistic optimism that inspires me and her many descendants.

About the Author

Douglas J. Wolf started writing computer how-to books in 1986. His first work, *Quick and Easy Guide to Lotus 123*, sold exceptionally well. Thinking he could get rich writing books, he has since authored over 30 other books, including the first book on ACT!, *The Authorized Insider's Guide*, and subsequently three more ACT! books. He did not get rich or learn to touch-type. He is a business and journalism graduate of the University of Minnesota at Mankato and has been an ACT! Certified Consultant for ten years. He lives in San Diego, California, is married to the luscious Gloria, and has two exceptional children, Alexander and Ilsa. Their wonder dog, Nietzsche, contributed nominally to this work.

Contents

viii   Contents

x Contents

Foreword

In 1985, Mike Muhney and I decided that there had to be a better way to use computers to help salespeople keep control of their time and not miss sales opportunities. What we found was software that was hard to use or had so many shortcomings it was not worth it. So we made a great leap of faith and decided to do it ourselves. After lots of trial runs and coming close to starving, we were showing ACT! at a trade show when an investor offered us a million dollars for the rights to the product. At that point, we knew we were on the right track. We turned down the offer and had to slug our way every day until we sold ACT! to Symantec in 1993.

But I never lost the desire to keep building tools for salespeople. In 1995, I started SalesLogix to make a software product similar to ACT! but for large companies. We were a success, and then in 1999, Symantec decided to divest itself of ACT! and I was there to buy back my original product. In May 2001, we partnered with Sage as a wholly owned subsidiary and we plan to integrate ACT! with their accounting software to synergize our relationship. We have already started by linking ACT! to MAS-90.

Today, ACT! is the dominant software product in sales force automation. With a 70 percent market share, and well over 3 million users worldwide, it is the product of choice for salespeople everywhere.

I met Doug Wolf in 1991 when we needed to have a manual written in a hurry, for our 2.0 DOS version of ACT!. In a week's time, most of the manual was written, even though I was still tinkering with the program interface at the same time. It drove Doug nuts, but he is a better man today thanks to me! Doug then went on to write the first published book on ACT!, *The Authorized Insider's Guide to ACT!*, and has written four more ACT! books, all of them a superb way to help you learn the essentials and the tricks to making ACT! the best tool a salesperson can have. I recommend that you make this book an essential part of learning ACT!. It will reward your effort may times over.

Patrick Sullivan
CEO and Founder, Interact Commerce Corporation

Acknowledgments

The folks behind the scenes who deserve a big thank you and a "well done" are, in no particular order: Matt Wagner, my agent at Waterside Productions; Roger Stewart, the editorial director of this tome; Chris Lagarde, my tardy technical editor; Laurie Stewart, punctilious project manager; Erin Milnes and Lunaea Weatherstone, copy editors; and Kate Kaminski, layout specialist.

A special thanks to Pat Sullivan and Mike Muhney, who had the vision to create ACT! and have revitalized the software in the past two years, Winton Churchill, who got me involved with ACT! eleven years ago, and Ted Cooper at Interact Commerce for his help. Also, thanks to David Church and all ACT! Certified Consultants who have answered my questions over the years.

Finally, to my tennis buddies, Mike Kelly, Harlan Reese, Robert Howe, Jerry von Teuber, Eric Hyberstsen, et al, who kept me in shape during the production of this book.

Introduction

When I was writing my first book on ACT! in late 1991 and early 1992, Windows 3.0 had just become a bestseller and Contact Software was working furiously on the Windows version of ACT!. In the summer of 1992, the product shipped and became the best-selling contact management software in the world. Why? Because the preponderance of users of ACT! are salespeople who hate paperwork, cannot type, and always manage to lose that crucial phone number when it's most needed. ACT! made it easy for them to get their schedule under control, make the phone calls they were supposed to, and remember their anniversary.

How to Use this Book

The purpose of this book is to take you through the various components of ACT! in the same way I teach my clients. In the beginning chapters, I focus on the aspects that get you productive immediately. Then, as you become more comfortable with ACT!, you can read the chapters on more advanced ACT! tools, such as reporting. If you are brand new to ACT!, read the first several chapters in order, up to Chapter 9. Then look to the chapters you need to fill in your knowledge.

A Short History of ACT!

Pat Sullivan and Mike Muhney founded Contact Software in 1986. They are both dynamic salespeople who were continually frustrated by the lack of a good software tool for sales-related tasks. For example, there are many database programs that are very good at retrieving reams of data, but the average user doesn't have the time or sophistication to learn how to use such a tool. Besides, the other features that Pat and Mike felt were necessary, such as alarms for important events, word processing, and so on, weren't available in database programs. So they sat down and drew up their ideas for a software program. (At that time, the term "contact management" had not yet entered the computing vocabulary.) With the help of a couple of programmers, version 1.0 of ACT! was written. It took time, but by bootstrapping and a little luck, ACT! became recognized as the contact management software tool of choice. Then in June of 1993, Symantec Corporation purchased Contact Software and all its products. Symantec then produced versions 3.0, 4.0, and 2000.

But the story continues. After Pat Sullivan sold ACT!, he started a new publicly traded company called SalesLogix to make an ACT!-like software product for very large databases with hundreds of thousands of records. In 2000, Symantec got a new president who decided that ACT! did not fit the product line that he intended to pursue and so cast about for a buyer for ACT!. Pat Sullivan immediately recognized the opportunity to marry ACT! to his new product and bought ACT! back from Symantec. In March of 2001, in order to connect contact management software with accounting software, Pat decided to merge his company with Sage Software, the makers of MAS 90, Business Works, and a number of other accounting programs.

My Story

I was introduced to ACT! for DOS version 1.0 by a friend in 1989. He was insistent that ACT! was the best software on the market for managing all the names, phone numbers, meetings, and tasks that any busy person must keep track of. At that time, I was a mortgage broker and writing books, generally going crazy trying to juggle all I was supposed to do, so I started using it. I too had searched for a program such as ACT! to aid me in my business endeavors. I had just written a book on Agenda, the Lotus product, and had decided that, though it was very powerful, it was difficult to master the conceptual nature of the product. I also had used Sidekick, but it wasn't a very robust product and it too required a little too much thinking on the part of the user. So ACT! was a pleasant surprise. It was obviously designed by real salespeople. I've used it continuously since.

When version 2.0 of ACT! for DOS was ready to ship, Contact Software asked me to assist them in preparing the documentation. On a very tight schedule, we managed to get the product out. I have written three other books on ACT! and since 1995 I have been busy installing, training, customizing, and troubleshooting ACT! for my clients, as part of the Interact ACT! Certified Consultants program. I also was the founding editor of *Easy ACT!*, the monthly newsletter for ACT! users.

In addition to this book, I've created training videos and CD-ROMS that cover ACT! and follow the same outline as this text. To order, contact me directly at (800) 449-9653, or visit my web site, www.howtosoftware.com. All of my customers can call or e-mail directly for help.

Time Management, Goals, and ACT!

Goal-setting is crucial to success in any endeavor, yet it's amazing how many people set out upon their lives each day with little thought as to the result. The best book on the market for goal-setting and life management is Steven Covey's *The Seven Habits of Highly Effective People*. In it, he extols the absolute necessity of defining your life principles so your goals and priorities are in harmony with your overall life mission. I highly recommend this book as part of your effort to become more organized and efficient.

Time management means that you've planned what you're going to do and when you're going to do it. The earliest proponents of time management taught that people should sit down at the end of the business day and list the important things they had to do the next day, by using the previous day's list of tasks as a guide. Those tasks that weren't accomplished would be carried over to tomorrow's agenda. The next evolution in time management was the idea of prioritizing those tasks, so the most important items received immediate attention.

ACT! facilitates the execution of the tasks you've decided to undertake, implementing the best ideas in time management. By recording calls to make, meetings to go to, and things to do, you've created your task list. After a business day, you can sit down with ACT! and review your task list, erase those tasks that have been accomplished, and add new tasks for tomorrow, prioritizing or reprioritizing as you go. ACT! automatically reminds you of activities you didn't complete the day before and asks you if they should be rescheduled for the current day. Computers are supposed to simplify your life, and ACT! is one of the tools that can do that for you.

Terminology

Each person or company you enter in ACT! is a contact record. The terms *record* and *contact* are used interchangeably. A set of contact records constitutes an ACT! database. The designers of ACT! took the view that people do business with other people, not with companies. Ergo, ACT! is a person-centered database. Also, ACT! has your scheduled activities with those other people, but then those activities are placed on, among other places, the Task List. They could have called it the Activity List, but that would make it too easy.

Contacting Interact for Help

If you really get stuck on a problem and can't find the answer in my book or the ACT! manuals, here are the resources to contact for help:

- Customer service: (877) 386-8083

- 800 Technical support, charged at $29.95 per incident: (800) 927-3989

- 900 Technical support, charged at $2.95 per minute including hold time: (900) 225-2205

- Web site: www.actsoftware.com

Program Updates

Interact now provides a way for you to get no-fee upgrade releases of ACT!. In other words, when they go from release 2000 to 2000.01 you can get it free. In ACT!, open the Help menu and select the Check For Updates option.

ACT!'s Update Wizards will walk you through the process. (Of course, you have to have an Internet connection.) You can get the same update files via the Web site, but you have to apply the install yourself.

www.theactbuzz.com

As soon as you can, browse to this web site and sign up for the free, twice-a-month ACT! newsletter. I am the editor.

Certified Consultants Program

If you or your company need specialized help for customization, synchronization, or custom programming, you can call upon a Certified Consultant for help. They do charge for their time, but you will likely save money and frustration if you call upon their expertise. Go to www.act.com and look for Certified Consultants.

Here are some of my favorites:

Geoff Blood	San Francisco, CA
Judy Bragg	Dallas, TX
Dwight Carlson	San Carlos, CA
Kevin Chieff	Red Bank, NJ
Steve Chipman	San Rafael, CA
Rich Heimann	Orange, CA
Scott Holmes	Houston, TX
Chris Legarde	Austin, TX
Lance McLean	Irvine, CA
Mike Moldofsky	Burbank, CA
Lon Orenstein	Dallas, TX
Bobby Saxon	Alpharetta, GA
Rich Spitz	New Rochelle, NY

Chapter 1

Installing and Creating a New Database

How to...

■ Work with the Install Wizard

■ Start ACT!

■ Open the ACTDEMO5 database

■ Create My Record

ACT! can be the tool that gives you control of your time and your life if you make the commitment to use it the way it is supposed to be used. If you work at a desktop most of the day, it should be running in one of your Windows. If you are mobile, the Palm Pilot or Windows CE device should be your constant companion. If you are accustomed to a paper system, such as a Franklin Planner or Day Timer, you should begin to wean yourself away, gradually and inevitably. Why? Because no matter how good your memory is, ACT! is better.

Where to Start?

If you are an experienced ACT! user and have an existing ACT! database, skip to the section later in this chapter on converting from 1.0, 2.0, 3.0, or 4.0. If you're starting from a brand-new installation and you have never used ACT!, start reading the next section.

Adding Your Installation Preferences

The installation program of ACT! includes a series of dialog boxes that ask questions, called the QuickStart Welcome Wizard. This wizard is not at all like the man from Oz (but pay no attention to the man behind the curtain!), in that these questions guide you to correctly set up ACT!.

After you install ACT!, you may be asked to restart your computer. After you've rebooted, click the ACT! icon to start ACT! or click the Start button, select Programs, choose the ACT! 2000 group, and then click the ACT! 2000 icon. The next thing you see is the QuickStart Welcome dialog box. Click the Next button. The second dialog box asks whether you want to connect to Interact's web update server. This option is a way for you to get the most recent version of ACT! directly from Interact to your desktop. If you choose this option, your computer's modem dials a number (or starts your Web connection) that connects to an Interact computer. The Interact computer checks the version of ACT! that you have and, if it is out-of-date, sends and installs the update automatically. I suggest that you take a few minutes and click the Connect button to make certain you are working with the latest release. After the sequence of QuickStart wizards, the next dialog box tells you a bit about ACT! and its capabilities. Click Next to see the advertising, and then click Next again.

Word Processor and Fax Software

Move on by clicking the Next button. ACT! gives you the opportunity to select the word processor you want to use and, if installed, the fax software, as shown in Figure 1-1. Most computers have a word processor, most likely Microsoft Word. Select the word processor you prefer. For faxing, I recommend that you use WinFax, made by Symantec, because it is tightly integrated with ACT!. In fact, you can edit an ACT! contact record directly from WinFax! If WinFax is installed on your computer, ACT! finds it automatically and, when you click Next, displays a path to any existing ACT! databases. Move to the next dialog box by clicking Next.

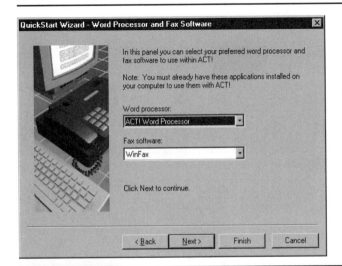

FIGURE 1-1   The QuickStart Wizard lets you select your word processor and fax software.

E-Mail

Again, ACT! searches for installed versions of Lotus Notes, Eudora, or Outlook 98 programs that ACT! can use for e-mail. ACT! lists any e-mail software found on your system. If you have none of these programs, I suggest that you select Internet Mail. ACT! has built-in e-mail software that can work with virtually any Internet service provider (ISP) that uses the POP3 universal standard. Avoid America Online, because it uses a proprietary e-mail system, and MSN, because it has recently changed its security standards. Click the box preceding the name of the e-mail software you have, and then click the Set Up E-Mail Now option button to begin setting up e-mail. At this point, the dialog box for your e-mail settings should look like the one shown in Figure 1-2. (If you don't intend to use e-mail, skip to the next section.) Click Next.

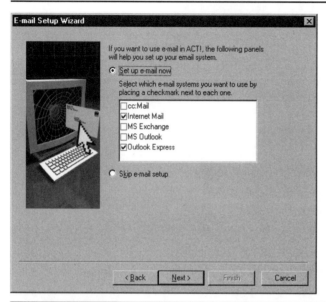

FIGURE 1-2 The ACT! E-Mail Setup Wizard enables you to configure your e-mail account.

In the resulting wizard, click the New Account button. You can now supply your account information as provided by your ISP. Table 1-1 shows how to make the entries.

Field Name	Information to Enter
Default Account (User Name)	Enter the first part of your e-mail address only. My e-mail address is dwolf@howtosoftware.com, so my entry is simply **dwolf**.
Outgoing SMTP Server	This information is provided by your ISP. Type it in exactly as given to you.
Incoming POP3 Server	This information is provided by your ISP. Type it in exactly as given to you.
Real Name	Enter your proper name, such as **Douglas J. Wolf**.
Organization	If appropriate, make an entry, but this information is not required.
Reply To Address	Enter your own e-mail address.

TABLE 1-1 Account Information to Supply

The next check box involves passwords. You can choose to have ACT! remember your password so that you are not required to type it every time you send or receive e-mail. Or, you can elect to enter your e-mail password every time you use e-mail. In an office, you may want to require the password, so that you are the only person who can read your e-mail.

The next option, Leave Retrieved Messages On Server, requires a bit of thinking. Usually an ISP deletes your e-mail from its server when you download it. However, you can select this check box so that the e-mail remains on the ISP's computer. You may want to do this if you access your e-mail from two locations—say, from office and home—and you want to leave messages on the ISP's computer so that you can read the messages from either location, regardless of whether they have been downloaded already at another location. My suggestion is that you turn this option off so that your e-mail isn't deleted.

If you connect to the Internet by modem, you may want to disconnect automatically from the phone line when all your messages have been sent and received. This option is particularly useful if you use ACT! in a home office and have a single phone line for e-mail and faxing.

You can also select the way you connect to the Internet, with the Connect To The Internet Using option. The default setting is via a direct network connection, which shows the bias of the programmers, who are of course connected to a network themselves. But most ACT! users are still dialing via a modem. Chances are, you already have your ISP's dial-up information configured. In that case, it appears on the pull-down list, so you can just select your ISP from this list.

The Advanced button is used to test your e-mail connection. Click it and you see a dialog box that allows you to indicate the authentication style used by your ISP, (usually passwords) and provides a button you can click to run a test. I suggest that you test the connection at this point. If it works, you see a message to that effect.

Click OK after the test. You'll return to the wizard. Now, click Next to get to the big enchilada, setting up your database.

Setting Up Your Database

The following sections apply only to users who do not have an existing ACT! database from any version. If you already have an existing ACT! database, skip to the section on converting from 1.0, 2.0, 3.0, or 4.0. The QuickStart Wizard asks you to create a name for the database. ACT! recommends *contacts,* but I suggest that you use your company name or your own name. For example, Wolf's Byte or Doug's Contacts. Click Next after entering a name.

The QuickStart Wizard is ready to complete the process. The dialog box shows you the choices you have made. Click Finish and ACT! starts creating the database.

My Record

After ACT! finishes creating the database, it presents the My Record dialog box (shown in Figure 1-3). You'll see My Record whenever you start ACT! My Record is a key component of ACT!. The information you enter is used in many places in ACT!, as you can see in the dialog box. When you start ACT! on a single-user database, the first record you will always see is My Record. If you are working on an ACT! database that is to be used on a network with multiple people accessing the database, each person will have their own My Record and they will see it every time they start ACT!. With the My Record dialog box, ACT! knows which activities belong to which user. For example, if I have scheduled four phone calls, two meetings, and six things to do for today, ACT! displays those activities. Other users see their own activities.

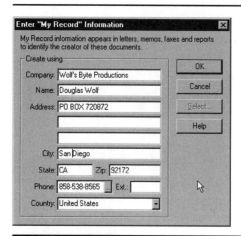

FIGURE 1-3   ACT! presents this dialog box for entering My Record information.

My Record Myopia

Another important concept about My Record, which I will repeat ad nauseam, is that whenever you think of scheduling a call, meeting, or to-do, always do so for the contact with whom the activity will be scheduled. Many times, I have been asked to come to a company and fix ACT!. Actually, ACT! was working fine. It was the way it was being used. The customer had been putting all his activities on his My Record. So, I erased all the activities one by one, and as I did, I located the contact record for the person with whom he was planning the activity, and scheduled the activity there.

Enter your information carefully. The most important field is the Name field. All the other fields can be changed later, but the Name field can cause problems if not completed properly.

After you enter the information, click OK. ACT! asks whether the information is correct. Click Yes.

Congratulations! You now have a brand-new ACT! 2000 database.

Converting Existing 1.0, 2.0, 3.0, or 4.0 Databases

ACT! is such a popular program that it is likely that many of you already have an ACT! database that was created in a former version. It is easy to convert the old database, but before you do, you need to know from which version you are converting.

ACT! 1.0 and 2.0

If you have an ACT! 1 or 2 database, follow these steps to convert it:

1. Open the File menu and choose Open. The Open dialog box appears, as shown in Figure 1-4.

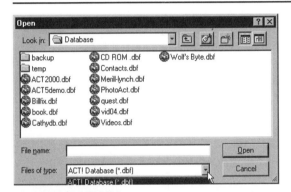

FIGURE 1-4   The Open dialog box is your first step in converting an existing ACT! database.

2. Select the ACT! 1.0 - 2.0 Database (*.dbf) option from the Files Of Type drop-down list.

3. You must know where the old database is stored because it probably is not in the folder that you see in the Open dialog box. To browse to the correct folder, click the Up One Level button (arrow pointing up on top of a folder) at the top middle of this dialog box. Doing so moves you up a level. You can continue to move up until you locate the folder in which the old database resides.

4. Click the filename of the old database.

5. Click the Open button.

    ACT! alerts you with a dialog box that the file you are about to open is from a previous version of ACT! and asks whether you want to back up the file before it is converted. Click Yes. Depending on the number of records and the speed of your machine, this process will take some time. Now might be a good time to check out the sports section.

ACT! 3.0 and 4.0

Converting an ACT! 3 or 4 database is also fairly simple. Just follow these steps:

1. Open the File menu and choose Open. The Open dialog box appears.

2. Select the database type you have from the Files Of Type drop-down list.

3. You must know where the old database is stored because it probably is not in the folder that you see in the Open dialog box. To browse to the correct folder, click the Up One Level button (arrow pointing up on top of a folder) at the top middle of this dialog box. This moves you up a level. You can continue to move up until you locate the folder in which the old database resides.

4. Click the filename of the old database.

5. Click the Open button.

   ACT! alerts you that the database you are trying to open was created in an older version of ACT! and asks whether you want to create a backup and whether you want to move the converted database to the default folder. Select the check box for creating a backup— unless you have already backed up the database yourself. In addition, you should select the check box for moving the database to the default folder.

If all goes well, your old database should appear in an updated database.

Starting and Exploring ACT!

You might think this section should be first. As you can see, it isn't. Installation comes first, and, as you've seen, installing ACT! involves a number of configuration issues. But now all that is behind you, and you're ready to go. The following steps show you how to start ACT!:

1. Click the Start button.

2. From the menu, select Programs.

3. From the submenu, select ACT! 2000.

   A second submenu appears, with ACT! 2000 listed again, as shown in Figure 1-5.

4. Click ACT! 2000. You'll see the ACT! startup screen, as shown in Figure 1-6.

   ACT! opens the same database you had open when you last exited the program. So, if you were working in an existing database, that database appears. If you haven't yet created a database or converted one as described in the preceding section, you will see the Database Wizard. Follow the prompts to create a new database.

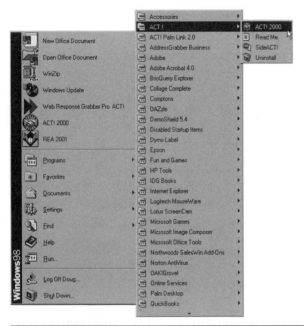

FIGURE 1-5   Choose the ACT! 2000 icon from the ACT! program group on the Start menu.

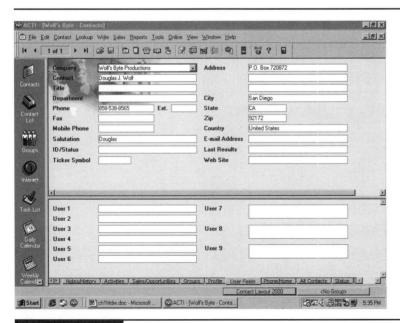

FIGURE 1-6   You'll see this ACT! opening screen whenever you start ACT!.

The ACT! install program also puts a pair of shortcut icons on the desktop: one to start ACT! and another to start its cousin, SideACT!. You can start ACT! by clicking the ACT! icon or by using the Start menu.

SideACT! Briefly

Before the arrival of ACT! 4.0, one of the criticisms of ACT! was that it did not include an easy way to create a simple list of to-dos. The ACT! thinking has always been that everything you do should be attached to a contact record. But customers disagreed, and they have the gold. So following the golden rule (those that have the gold make the rules), ACT! now includes SideACT!. This application offers you an easy way to enter your grocery list, a series of stops you have to make after work, or your personal goals for the next year. The list can be easily printed and thrown on the dashboard. To find out more about what you can do with SideACT!, read Chapter 20.

The ACT! Demo Database

To learn ACT!, you need to have some contact records with which to work. Anticipating this, ACT! includes a database that has a number of records you can use to follow the examples in this book.

Opening the ACT! Demo Database

Open the demo database as follows:

1. Open the File menu and choose Open. The Open dialog box appears, as shown in Figure 1-7.

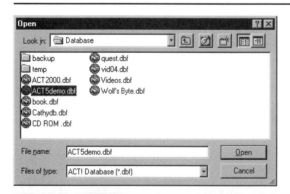

FIGURE 1-7   You can open the ACT! File menu by clicking the menu bar or by pressing ALT-F.

2. Select ACT5demo.dbf.

3. Click the Open button.

   If all goes according to plan, the first record you see is Chris Huffman. Chris is the My Record for this demonstration database. That is why it is the initial record on the ACT! screen.

Network or Standalone Database Creation?

The ACT5demo database allows you to consider the difference between a standalone and a network database. If you are working with ACT! on your desktop or laptop computer and are not connected directly to a network, then you are a standalone user and do not need to create a place for the database that other users can access. Also, a single My Record will be in the database because only you will be entering records, scheduling activities, and so on. It is possible to allow multiple people to use ACT! as a standalone. For example, you might have an administrative assistant who enters names for you. If you plan to have that sort of arrangement, read the next section on networks.

Network Databases

The only differences between ACT! on a standalone system and a network are where the database is located and who can use it. The first consideration is who is going to be using ACT!. This process is called defining the users of the database. Unless a person is defined as a user, none of the information he or she enters will be identified as coming from that person. Let's take a look at defining a user of a shared database.

1. If you have not done so, open the ACT5demo database.

2. Open the File menu and select Administration. The submenu appears, as shown in Figure 1-8.

3. Select Define Users. The Define Users dialog box appears, as shown in Figure 1-9.

This demonstration database has several predefined users. Chris Huffman is automatically defined as the Administrator because he created the database. The other users have standard security, which means that they can open the ACT! database and add new records, edit existing records, and delete records.

Yikes! You might be thinking that you don't want all the users of your ACT! database to be able to delete records, but there's no other choice. It is your responsibility to make backup copies (see Chapter 22) and train the users not to delete contact records except under specific circumstances. However, you can assign users the Browse level of security—that way, all they can do is look at contact records, and none of the changes they make are saved.

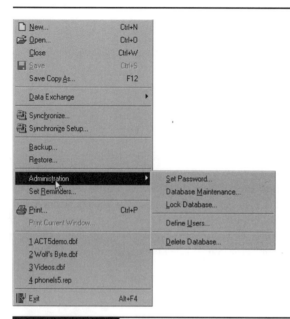

FIGURE 1-8 You access the Administration option from the File menu.

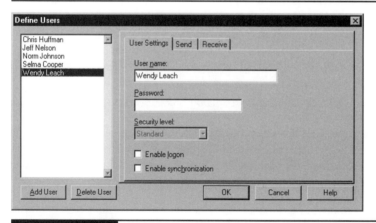

FIGURE 1-9 You define the users of the database in the Define Users dialog box.

1

Defining Users on a Shared Database

Adding a new user of a database is easy. Just follow this procedure:

1. In the Define Users dialog box, click the Add User button. ACT! inserts the placeholder, User1, into the User Name field.

2. Type a new name.

3. Add a password if desired.

4. Set the Security Level.

5. Select the Enable Logon check box.

6. Click OK. ACT! responds with a dialog box asking you to create the My Record for the new user, as shown in Figure 1-10.

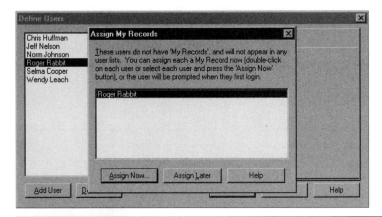

FIGURE 1-10   The Assign My Records dialog box asks for the My Record for a new login user of the database.

You have two options at this point:

- If the user already has a record in the database, click Assign Now. Use the Select button to locate that person's record, and click it to use the information.

- If that person is not in the database, click Assign Later. When the new user tries to access the database, ACT! asks him or her to complete a My Record.

In Search of Login History

The term *login* has nothing to do with forestry. The term originated in computer parlance many years ago to keep a track record—a log—of when, for how long, and where users went on the system. ACT! uses the login on a multi-user database to connect the activities, notes, and other items to the person logging in.

A Simple Login Test

To test the way ACT! tracks the login, click the name Jeff Nelson in the Define Users dialog box and select the Enable Logon check box. Then, click OK to close the dialog box, and follow these steps:

1. Close the ACT5demo database by opening the File menu and selecting Close.

2. Open the File menu again and select Open.

3. From the Open dialog box, double-click the ACT5demo filename. The Login To ACT5demo.dbf dialog box appears, as shown in Figure 1-11. As you can see, ACT! thinks you are Chris Huffman because he was the last person to open this database from your computer.

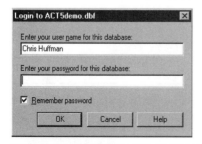

FIGURE 1-11   ACT! launches and prompts Chris Huffman to log on.

4. Change the user name by deleting Chris Huffman and typing **Jeff Nelson**.

5. No password was assigned to Jeff, so click OK.

    You will be asked to enter the My Record information, as this is the first time that Jeff has logged into the database. Because this is a demonstration database, I know there is an existing record for Jeff so I simply select it.

6. Click the Select button. ACT! opens a dialog box with the contact names and company names of existing records. Scroll the list until you locate Jeff Nelson.

7. Click Jeff Nelson.

Voilà! You are now logged in to the ACT5demo database as Jeff Nelson and his My Record appears on the screen.

Locating the Network Database

Now that you know how to set up a new database and add users, you must think about where you want the database stored. When you installed ACT!, it created a series of folders. One of those folders is named Database and is located on your C drive. If you are using Windows 98, the folder is located in the C:\My Documents\ACT\ path. You can see this arrangement in the Open dialog box, as shown in Figure 1-12, which you can access from the File menu.

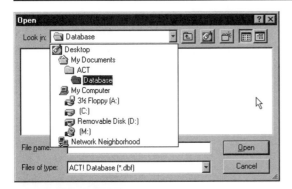

FIGURE 1-12   The Open dialog box shows your folder hierarchy.

You probably don't want the other members of your team accessing your C drive to use ACT!. After all, that is the purpose of a network server—having the data on a fast computer that can be easily accessed by everyone. Talk to your network administrator about setting up a folder on the network drive for the shared ACT! database. In Chapter 23 I'll provide more information on using ACT! on a network.

> **NOTE** *Frequently, smaller companies try to share an ACT! database on a peer-to-peer network as a means of saving money. This strategy is counterproductive. A peer-to-peer network is designed only to let others share hardware, such as a printer, or to copy files from one computer to another. It is not designed to have multiple computers actively accessing a shared, dynamic database. So, be smart and spend the money for an NT workstation, at minimum, to host the ACT! database. To put all that together, you will need to understand a few key concepts about putting an ACT! database on a network drive. Chapter 23 covers the needs of each user and the information for the network administrator.*

Summary

■ On a standalone system, your database is located on your C drive and after creating a new database, you are ready to go.

■ On a multi-user system, the database is located on a network drive and before using ACT! each user has to be defined by the ACT! administrator.

How to...

■ Work with the menus and toolbars

■ Display different layouts

■ View the tabbed information

At this point, your database might contain many records, or it might not. ACT! has a demonstration database with lots of records that you can use for learning purposes. If you do have a database that contains more than five records, you can use it for the examples in this chapter. If not, open the ACT5demo database as follows:

1. Start ACT!.

2. Open the File menu.

3. Select Open. The Open dialog box appears.

4. Click the ACT5demo database name.

5. Click the Open button.

If you changed the login to Jeff Nelson following the directions in Chapter 1, you will see the Login dialog box, with Jeff Nelson's name.

1. Type **Chris Huffman** as the login name.

2. Click OK. The Chris Huffman My Record appears, as shown in Figure 2-1.

 *At various times in this book, you will see both the terms contact record and record. They mean the same thing. The term record is a conventional database term whereas contact record is ACT! specific.*

Familiarizing Yourself with the ACT! Interface

Take a tour of the ACT! interface. Begin at the upper-left corner of the screen. Across the top is the name ACT! and the name of the database. Directly below them is a series of menus, beginning with File and ending with Help. Beneath the menus is the toolbar, which includes a series of icons that perform ACT! functions. Figure 2-2 shows each of the icons with a short description of what each does.

At the left side of the screen, running from top to bottom, is the view bar, a series of graphics labeled Contacts, Contact List, and so on. (If you are an ACT! 3.0 or 4.0 user, you'll note that these icons used to be in the lower-right corner of the screen.)

At the bottom right are two buttons: No Group and Contact Layout 2000r.

FIGURE 2-1   When you log on as Chris Huffman, the appropriate My Record appears.

Did you know?

ACT! Was Designed to Imitate a Recipe Card?

Before computers, most salespeople had a card file with the name and address of their customers on the front of a 4"×6" card and the details jotted on the back. It was primitive, but it worked.

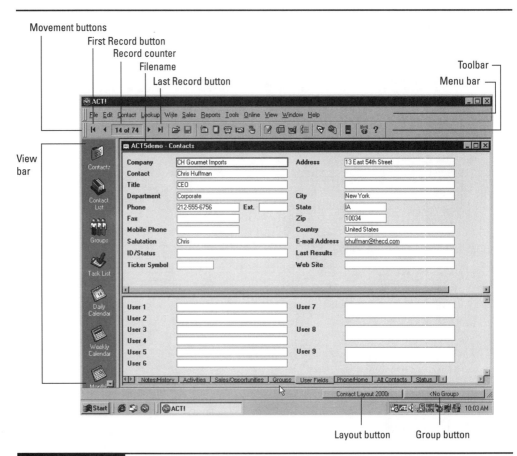

Movement buttons
First Record button
Record counter
Filename
Last Record button
Toolbar
Menu bar

View bar

Layout button   Group button

FIGURE 2-2   The ACT! toolbar provides instant access to common functions and tasks.

Moving from Record to Record

You can easily navigate from record to record using ACT!'s toolbar buttons or your keyboard. Before you decide where you want to go, however, you must know where you are. The ACT! toolbar includes a record counter, located between the first four buttons on the left of the toolbar, which indicates the total number of records. In Figure 2-2, it reads 14 of 74. This means that there are a total of 74 records in the database. Note that the 14 does not mean that the Chris Huffman record has been assigned record number 14.

To see a different record, click the First Record button (the one with the triangle pointing left to a solid vertical line) at the far left of the toolbar. When you click this button, you'll see the first record in the database. ACT! sorts the contact records by company and then by last name. All the records that lack a company name, as the one shown in Figure 2-3 does, appear at the beginning of the sort order.

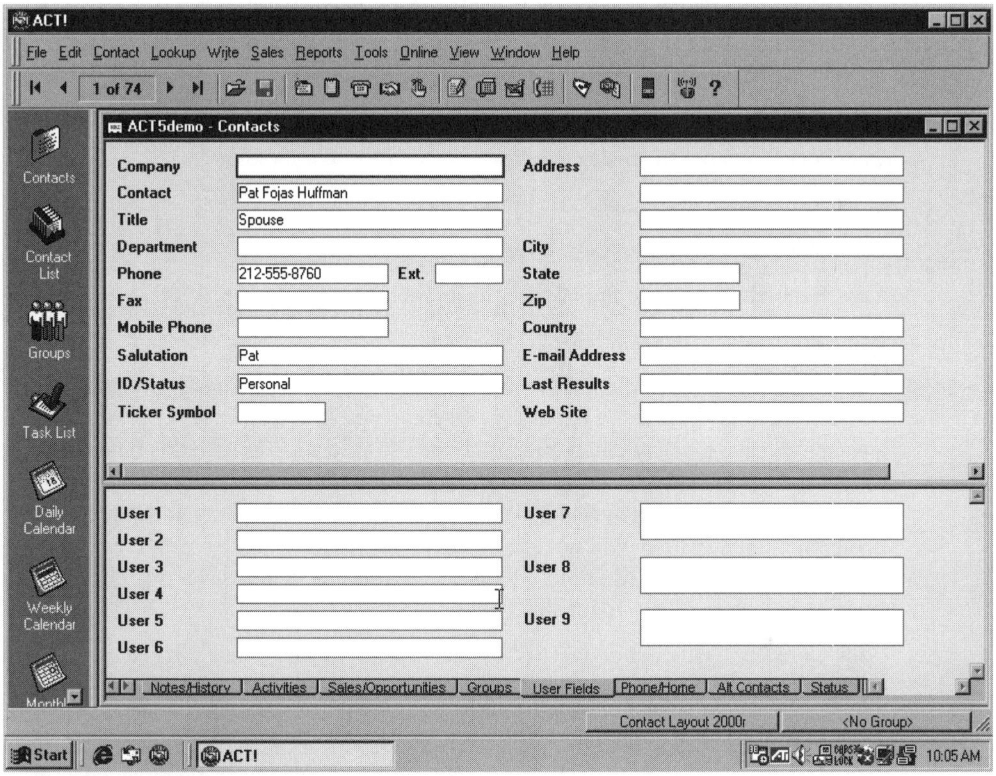

FIGURE 2-3 Your initial contact record will look something like this.

Next, click the Last Record button (the one pointing right to a vertical line). This button takes you to the final record in the database. The Previous and Next buttons (which display only a triangle, on either side of the record counter) move you from record to record, one at a time. Try clicking either one to see how it works.

If you want to use the keyboard to move through the records, PGUP takes you to the previous record and PGDN takes you to the next record. Holding down CTRL and then pressing HOME moves you to the first record in the database, and CTRL-END moves you to the final record.

The movement buttons are particularly useful after you have performed a lookup. For example, let's say your database has 1,000 records and you want to find all contact records in the city of San Diego. ACT! finds 12 records. The movement buttons enable you to flip from one record to another among these 12. This notion will be clearer when you perform a lookup, which I'll cover in Chapter 4.

The Toolbar

When you move your cursor on top of a toolbar button, a pop-up window appears, revealing the name of the button. At the bottom left of the screen, ACT! displays a short message telling you what the button does. Each of the buttons on the toolbar is discussed below, listed from left to right as they appear on the toolbar.

First Record   Moves to the first record in the current lookup.

Previous Record   Moves to the previous record in the lookup.

Record Counter   Total number of records in the current lookup.

Next Record   Moves to the next record in the lookup.

Last Record   Moves to the last record in the lookup.

File Open   Opens a different ACT! database.

Save   The beauty of ACT! is that it saves information automatically when you move to a different record or close the database. So, you never have to worry about reminding yourself to save a newly entered record or edited information. Use this button to actively save information entered into a record. One common use of this button is when you are editing a record on a network database. If someone else is looking at the same record on a different computer, they will not see any new information you have entered unless you move to a different record or close ACT!. Clicking this button saves any changes so that other users can see them immediately.

New Contact   This button is used to enter a new contact. When clicked, the ACT! fields are blanked out, ready for new information.

Insert Note   Use this button to add notes easily to a contact record.

Schedule Call, Schedule Meeting, and Schedule To-Do   These buttons open the Schedule Activity dialog box. You can set up different defaults for each activity; for example, you can block five minutes on your calendar for calls but reserve two hours for meetings.

Letter   This button fires up the word processor and sends the information from the current contact record to a letter as the inside address and salutation. This feature is every lazy typist's dream. No excuses now not to write Mom!

Quick Fax   If faxing software is installed on your system and the current contact record has a fax number, you can send a fax to him or her automatically. This method does not provide a cover sheet. More on faxing in Chapter 11.

E-Mail   Click this button to open a new e-mail message.

Dial Phone   The Dial Phone button not only dials the number you want, but also automatically starts the process of logging the call. That is, a dialog box appears and asks you what happened—was the call completed? Did you leave a message? The dialog box also includes a button for starting the call timer.

SideACT!   This button opens the SideACT! window. Use it to jot down a shopping list or a reminder to pick up the dry cleaning. More on SideACT! in Chapter 20.

Synchronize with Palm Handheld   Click this button to set up or review the options you need to synchronize ACT! with your Palm.

Check for Updates   This is your most valuable tool against software problems. The Check for Updates button connects your computer to Interact and downloads and installs any new free updates of ACT!. This feature is particularly useful when Interact finds a problem with ACT! and fixes it. You don't have to wait for a disk from them to fix the problem.

?   This button opens the Help Topics dialog box. ACT! will search for help text on the topic you enter in the dialog box.

The View Bar

On the left side of the ACT! screen is a set of large buttons for some popular ACT! features. These features are accessed more frequently than others, which is why they have an elevated status. The list that follows describes each button in detail, listed from top to bottom as they appear in the view bar.

Contacts   This button opens the view at which you are looking.

Contact List   This button changes the view of your ACT! records from one record at a time to many, as shown in Figure 2-4. Contact List view allows you to compare your contact records or scan them quickly for specific information. See Chapter 6 for more information.

Many ACT! users prefer to work in Contact List view. That way, they can easily scroll to the record they want to see, or type the first few characters of the first, last, or company name to view a specific record.

Groups   This button opens the Groups window, where you can create, edit, or delete groups. A group is a way to identify contact records by an affiliation you have determined. For example, you might create groups identifying your golfing foursome or purchasers of your new cure for male pattern baldness. See Chapter 15 for more information.

Task List   This button opens the Task List window, which displays all your scheduled activities. See Chapter 8 for more information.

Daily, Weekly, Monthly Calendars   Display your calendars quickly by clicking the appropriate button. See Chapter 9 for details about the calendars.

E-Mail   E-mail is so important that it gets a button on more than one toolbar. Click this button to open a new e-mail message to the current contact. More about e-mail is found in Chapter 13.

FIGURE 2-4   Contact List view allows you to review many records at once.

Keep Track of All That E-Mail!

Sending e-mail through ACT! creates a copy of the e-mail that is attached to the contact record on the Notes/History tab. This makes it very easy to review what messages you have sent to a client. Without this handy feature you would have to search your e-mail program's outbox for any correspondence you sent to that client, wasting lots of your precious time.

Menus

The menus in ACT! can be opened by clicking on them or by pressing the ALT key and then typing the underlined letter in the menu name. For example, ALT-F opens the File menu, as shown in Figure 2-5.

New...	Ctrl+N
Open...	Ctrl+O
Close	Ctrl+W
Save	Ctrl+S
Save Copy As...	F12
Data Exchange	▶
Synchronize...	
Synchronize Setup...	
Backup...	
Restore...	
Administration	▶
Set Reminders...	
Print...	Ctrl+P
Print Contact List	
1 ACT5demo.dbf	
2 Wolf's Byte.dbf	
3 Videos.dbf	
4 Contacts.DBF	
Exit	Alt+F4

FIGURE 2-5   You can open the File menu by clicking the menu name or by pressing its keyboard shortcut, ALT-F.

With any menu open, you can press the RIGHT or LEFT ARROW keys to open the adjoining menus. Note that many menu items can be activated by a combination of keystrokes. For instance, you can print the current document by pressing CTRL-P. These keystrokes are listed next to the corresponding menu item.

I'll describe many of the menu commands as you need them throughout the book. For now, you can cruise through and try a few by opening a menu and clicking an item or two.

The Tabs

The release of version 3.0 of ACT! brought with it a major improvement: the addition of tabs to access more information on a particular contact record. Figure 2-6 displays these tabs. You'll notice that each tab has a name that briefly describes its purpose. Click each tab to see the kind of information it holds. The section that follows describes in detail what the various tabs are used for.

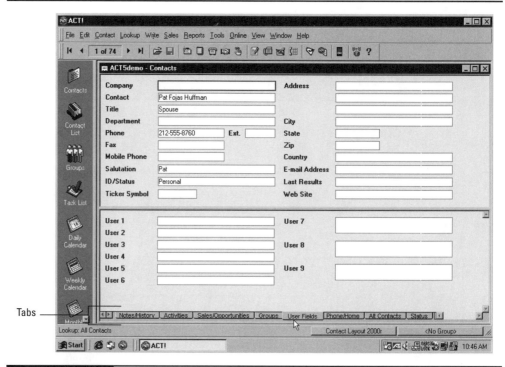

Tabs

FIGURE 2-6   The information tabs in ACT! provide easy access to additional contact information.

Notes/History   This tab contains four pieces of information: notes, history, letters, and e-mail. Notes are text entries that you add. History entries are added automatically by ACT! When you schedule an activity and then later record the disposition of the activity, the result is written to the tab as a history entry. For example, if you changed the ID/Status field from prospect to customer, the history entry reads Field Changed ID/Status Prospect. When you send a letter to a contact, you can save it as a word processor file and then attach it to the contact record. Later, when you want to see exactly what you sent to the contact, click the attachment icon, and ACT! will open the letter for you. E-mail works the same way. When you send an e-mail message, the action is recorded automatically by ACT!. You can also attach the entire e-mail message if you like.

Activities   The Activities tab lists your scheduled activities with a contact. Each activity appears on its own line. You have a variety of options for filtering the information displayed, such as Today's Activities Only or Today And Future. The filtering process is discussed in detail in Chapter 8.

Sales/Opportunities   This tab is new to version 2000. ACT! now makes it easy to keep track of your sales pipeline. All good sales people and sales managers need this information, but even if you aren't in sales, you also can use it. For example, if you use ACT! to track the progress of grant proposals, you can create a report that shows where each application stands. Chapter 18 discusses the Sales/Opportunities tab in detail.

Groups   When you click this tab, you see to which groups the contact record belongs. ACT! allows for an unlimited number of groups, and a particular contact record can be in any number of groups. Groups are covered in detail in Chapter 15.

User Fields   You can customize this tab for your own use. A series of fields are already available that you can modify. Chapter 16 discusses various customization techniques.

Phone/Home   This tab includes several more fields for the seemingly unending stream of phone numbers we all now have. There also are fields for the home address of the contact.

Alt Contacts   In many cases, a contact will have an assistant or perhaps a financial advisor—someone who does not need to have a complete contact record, but requires a few fields. If you anticipate no need to schedule activities or to track history with that person, this tab provides a place for you to store simple contact information.

Status   The Status tab has a number of system fields—that is, fields in which non-editable information is generated for you by ACT!. An important field on the Status tab, if you are on a network, is the Public/Private field. Because ACT! is the tool for your time management, you will want to include your personal activities, and yet keep them private. So, if, for example, you put your proctologist's record in the database, be certain to make it a Private record! If you subsequently schedule an appointment, it will show up on the network calendar as "private activity," not "Harry is getting his hemorrhoids removed." To complete the process of making activities private, you will need to click the Advanced Options tab in the Schedule Activities dialog box and check the Private Activity box. See Chapter 7 for more on this feature. You can also modify other user fields on this tab as you see fit. I will discuss these options in later chapters.

The Scrollbars

Scrollbars are located on the bottom and on the right side of the ACT! record screen. Your use of them depends on the screen resolution setting of your monitor. If the resolution is set to 800×600, you will have to use the scrollbars to see all the contact record. At 1024×768, all the information is visible.

In Windows, you can change the screen resolution by clicking the Adjust Display Properties button in the lower-right corner of the screen (if a small icon of a computer monitor is visible), or right-click on the desktop, select Properties, and click the Settings tab. Remember, in Windows you can maximize an individual window to see more. If you cannot see the Notes/History tab and so on, maximize the ACT! program window and the contact record window.

Summary

■ Navigating the records in ACT! is easy with the movement buttons or the keyboard.

■ Display different layouts in ACT! to view the information you want the way you want it.

■ You can see more information regarding each contact record by clicking the appropriate record tab.

Chapter 3

Creating Records

How to...

- Enter information into a new record
- Use the ID/Status field to organize records
- Edit drop-down lists
- Add notes

Whether you open a new database when you start ACT!, or one with many records, the first record you will always see is My Record. In a new database, with only My Record entered, the record counter will read "1 of 1," as shown in Figure 3-1. In a database with many records, the record counter will read "*YY* of *XX*." The *YY* number tells you My Record's current position in the database. The *XX* number tells you the total number of records in the database.

The My Record in the figure is mine—Douglas Wolf. I'll use this new database to show you how to enter a new record. Open your own database and follow along.

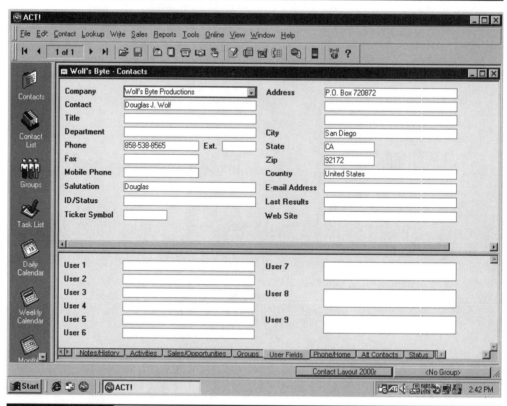

FIGURE 3-1   A new database opens to My Record and shows it as record 1 of 1.

Creating a New Contact Record

3

The first step to entering a new record is to click the New Contact Record icon, or open the Contact menu and select New Contact. Take a look at the opened Contact menu shown in Figure 3-2.

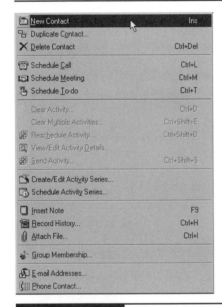

New Contact	Ins
Duplicate Contact...	
Delete Contact	Ctrl+Del
Schedule Call	Ctrl+L
Schedule Meeting	Ctrl+M
Schedule To-do	Ctrl+T
Clear Activity...	Ctrl+D
Clear Multiple Activities...	Ctrl+Shift+E
Reschedule Activity...	Ctrl+Shift+D
View/Edit Activity Details...	
Send Activity...	Ctrl+Shift+S
Create/Edit Activity Series...	
Schedule Activity Series...	
Insert Note	F9
Record History...	Ctrl+H
Attach File...	Ctrl+I
Group Membership...	
E-mail Addresses...	
Phone Contact...	

FIGURE 3-2 Select the New Contact item from the Contact menu to begin entering a new contact record.

Did you know?

ACT! Has Multiple Access Points

ACT! is designed so that virtually anything you want to accomplish can be achieved in multiple ways. While some people prefer to open menus and make a selection with a mouse, some prefer to click an icon, and others prefer to press an assigned key. For example, you can begin creating a new contact record in three ways: by clicking the New Contact button on the toolbar, by pressing INSERT, or by opening the Contact menu and selecting the New Contact command. When you perform any of these actions, ACT! presents a blank contact record, as shown in Figure 3-3.

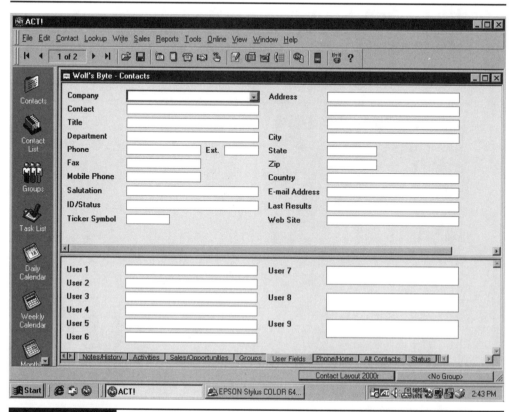

FIGURE 3-3   Creating a new contact record begins with opening a blank record.

> **TIP**
>
> *It often happens that you are all set to enter information for a new record, you have pressed INSERT or clicked the New Contact button, and the phone rings. On the other end of the line is one of your key clients. You immediately forget about entering the new record and look up the key client. When you do, ACT! saves the blank record you started! When you decide to enter that new contact later, the blank record is still around. In a perfect world, you would go to the blank record and enter the new contact. But, what usually happens is that you start over and click the New Contact button again. After a time, this process will result in several empty records at the beginning of your database. This causes no problems. Once a week or so, you should use the movement buttons to go to the first record of the database and delete any blanks you see. To do that, open the Contact menu, select Delete Contact, and then click Yes.*

From Company to Department

At this point you are ready to begin typing. If the person works for a company, go ahead and enter that information. I have included sample text for your new record in the instructions that follow.

1. In the Company field, type **ABC Company**.

2. Press TAB to move the insertion point to the next field, which is Contact.

3. Type **Sam Wells**.

ACT! does something different with names than almost every other database program. It requires both the first and last name in a single field, the contact field. It then assumes that the first set of characters is the first name and that the characters following the space constitute the last name. ACT! is smart in that it both recognizes and ignores honorifics such as Dr., Frau, or Monsieur or suffixes such as Ph.D., MBA, or Jr. See the "First, Last Name?" section later in this chapter for more information.

4. Press TAB to go the Title field.

    Because ACT! is designed by non-typists for non-typists, many fields have drop-down lists that contain the most likely entries for the field.

5. At the right end of the Title field is a gray box with a down arrow. Click it. The drop-down list appears with a set of common options, shown in Figure 3-4. (You can edit these options; see "Editing the City Drop-Down List" later in this chapter for details how.)

    As you can see, you can select a title from the list, eliminating a typing chore. The list is sorted alphabetically, so scroll to get to the President entry.

6. Select President. ACT! inserts President into the Title field for you.

7. Press TAB. The insertion point is now in the Department field.

    You might not need this field. If not, you can skip it. If you find that you never use this field, or any other, it easily can be deleted from the layout. Chapter 16 covers modifying the layout.

    For this example, enter a department, using the drop-down list. But, instead of opening it and looking for the entry you want, assume that you want the word "Corporate" in this field.

8. Type **C**.

    When you type C, ACT! searches the drop-down list for the first entry that has the letter *C* as its first letter. It finds Corporate and enters it into the field. If there was a Cost Accounting entry in the list, and that was what you wanted, typing Cos would cause ACT! to insert that department name into the field. You can use this type of shortcut in all fields with drop-down lists.

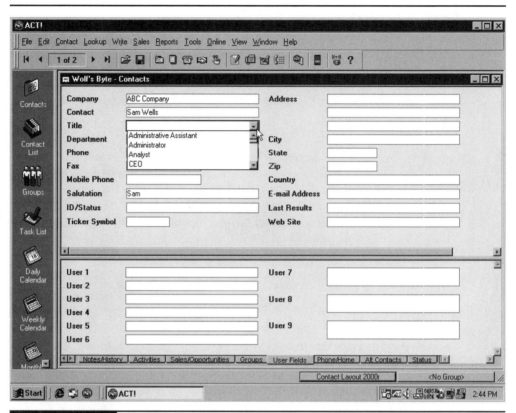

FIGURE 3-4 A drop-down list or "pick" list makes it easy to enter data without typing.

From Phone to Salutation

1. Press TAB to move the insertion point to the Phone field. This field has special formatting capabilities. At the right end of the field is a gray box. Click it to reveal the Country Codes dialog box, shown in Figure 3-5.

   If you are entering phone numbers for the United States and do not intend to make phone calls out of the country, the default settings for phone numbers are fine. However, if you are not in the United States, you can select the name of your country and the phone format will match. The pound sign (#) determines where a number must be entered, and ACT! automatically inserts the appropriate parentheses or dashes for you. After choosing the country, select the Apply This Format For Country Code option.

   For our purposes, select the U.S. format.

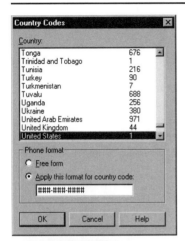

   Country codes can be entered for individual contact records.

 *The Phone field is formatted on a per-record basis. That means you can make calls to phone numbers all over the world and each one will be formatted appropriately for its country.*

2. Enter a phone number by typing **858-555-1212**.

3. Press TAB. The insertion point jumps to the Ext. field. Use this field if the contact has a phone extension.

4. Press TAB. The active field is now Fax. The same rules apply to this field as to the Phone field.

5. Press TAB. The Mobile Phone field is active and the same rules apply as they did for Phone and Fax.

6. Press TAB. The Salutation field is filled automatically. The default in ACT! is to enter the first name of the contact. This default can be modified, as explained in Chapter 10.

ID/Status to Address

ACT! allows for three street or box entries, so you have room for special address information such as a mail stop number.

1. Press TAB. The insertion point is now in the ID/Status field. For this example, type **PR** and ACT! enters Prospect into the field.

Remember to enter your own phone/fax/mobile numbers in the My Record, or ACT! will add the country code to the Phone and Fax fields of each of your contact records.

The ID/Status field is important because it is one of the choices on the Lookup menu and works with several of the reports in ACT!. Let me offer a few suggestions on how to use this field. ACT!'s drop-down list suggests that you identify your contacts by category—as a vendor, shareholder, competitor, and so on. This arrangement may work for you. Some companies use this field to enter the customer account number. Other companies use this field to separate different kinds of contact records such as prospect and customer. Using the prospect and customer designations can give you an idea of the conversion time of a customer—that is, how long it takes for a prospect to buy. The key is to think through how you want to use this field before entering many records. Chapter 15 focuses on groups, which is another category you can use to organize contact records. The ID/Status field can be used in concert with groups to help you organize your contacts in the most efficient manner.

2. Press TAB to move to the Ticker Symbol field. This field is used to enter the symbol for this contact record's stock, assuming he or she works for a publicly traded company. This entry comes in handy when using the Internet links, covered in Chapter 13.

3. Press TAB to go to the Address field. ACT! provides three fields for the address, even though you cannot see the labels Address 2 and Address 3. For this example, there is no need to make entries at this point.

The City Field

The next stop is the City field.

1. Press TAB three times to go to the City field.

Editing the City Drop-Down List

The City field is good place to learn how to add or delete an entry in a drop-down list. You can use the steps you'll perform here to edit any drop-down list you find in ACT!.

1. Open the drop-down list by clicking the arrow at the right end of the field.

2. Scroll down the list until you reach the bottom and click Edit List. The Edit List dialog box for the City field appears, as shown in Figure 3-6.

3. If your city is already in the list, you can just read along. If not, click the Add button. This opens the Add dialog box.

4. For this example, type **Poway**.

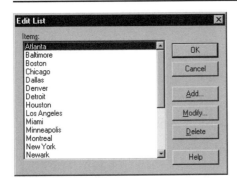

3

FIGURE 3-6   Add a new entry to a drop-down list via the Edit List dialog box.

There's no need for a description (despite Poway's reputation!). Descriptions can be helpful for other types of information, however. If you were entering codes for salary levels, for example, you could add that as the description. On a network, the administrator can prevent other users from editing the drop-down list to any field, thereby stopping them from seeing the description field.

5. Click OK. Poway is added to the list.

6. Click OK again. Poway appears in the City field.

TIP

ACT! can automatically add new items to a drop-down list if you have activated that feature for the field. See Chapter 17 for more information.

Finishing the New Record Entry

The State and Zip fields are straightforward.

NOTE

You can use an add-on program to fill in the City and State fields automatically when you enter the Zip code. See Appendix A for information on that product and others.

The Country field may be superfluous in your business. Use it if needed.

From E-Mail Address to Web Site

The E-Mail Address field is special—similar to, but not quite the same as, the Web Site field. You can enter an e-mail address by typing it in. Once entered, the field becomes active, and when you click it, ACT! opens the E-Mail window, assuming that you want to create an e-mail message. Web site addresses do not change much, but e-mail addresses do, and many people have multiple e-mail addresses. Fortunately, ACT! enables you to edit the address and to save several e-mail addresses for the contact.

To see how this process works, enter an e-mail address:

1. Press TAB to move the insertion point to the E-Mail Address field.

2. Type **swells@pabell.com**.

3. Press TAB. The E-Mail Address field displays in color and is underlined, alerting you that it is an active field.

4. Press SHIFT-TAB, which moves the insertion point back to the E-Mail Address field. You can't click to do this because clicking opens the E-Mail window.

You can also right-click in the E-Mail Address field to edit it just as you can in the Web Site field to make changes.

5. Add a second e-mail address. To do this, click the arrow at the right edge of the E-Mail Address field, and select Edit E-Mail Addresses, which opens the dialog box shown in Figure 3-7.

FIGURE 3-7 Opening this dialog box allows you to add multiple e-mail addresses for a contact.

6. Click the New button. The New Address dialog box appears.

7. Type **swells@bugfoot.com**.

8. You have the opportunity to make the new address the primary address—that is, the address that shows in the field and is used by default when you create an e-mail message to this contact. Click OK twice to leave it as is.

The next field is Last Results. In a way, it is a holdover from the DOS version of ACT!—before it was easy to enter a note in a contact record. Consider it a shorthand way of entering an update to the record. The field includes a drop-down list that contains a series of selections general enough for every business. The Last Results field also includes the History attribute.

That is, when you make an entry into the field, a copy of the entry is entered automatically on the Notes/History tab.

The final field on the top half of the contact record screen is the Web Site field. Press TAB to enter the Web Site field. For this example, enter a useful web address such as **www.act.com**. Note that the entry displays in a color, and is underlined, alerting you that this is an active field. Assuming that you can connect to the Internet from your computer, clicking the entry in this field starts your web browser and opens the Internet site you have entered. This is handy because companies often post their latest product announcements, financial reports, and other important news on their web site. So, when you view a contact record, you can click the Web Site field and go directly to his or her company web site and find out the latest on your customer's business.

 *If the web address for the company changes, a special trick is required to edit the field. Instead of clicking the field, right-click it. A menu appears; choose Select All. The entire web address will be highlighted and your browser will not fire up. Now, select Delete to erase the old address and enter the new.*

Does this Contact Need a Record?

In deciding whether to create a new contact record for a person, you must know whether you will need to

- Look up the person
- Schedule activities
- Keep a running history of what has occurred with that person

If not, then perhaps the person can be added as an alternate contact on another contact record. Or, you could go to My Record and enter the person's name and phone number as a note.

Entering a Duplicate Record

You do not want to save duplicate records in your database! Why, then, this section title? Because many of your contact records may be very similar—that is, you may be doing business with a number of people from the same company. The main difference between records for people from the same company is probably the name and phone number. As a result, you can create a duplicate record, change just a few pieces of information, and save yourself a lot of time. To speed up the entry of new contact records that are virtually identical, do the following:

1. Look up the contact record that is the most similar to the new one you plan to enter. For more information on locating the record you want, see Chapter 4.

2. Click the Contact menu. Figure 3-8 shows the opened menu and the concomitant items.

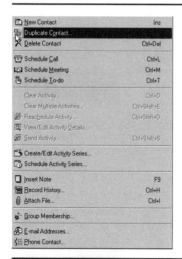

FIGURE 3-8 The opened Contact menu includes the Duplicate Contact command.

3. Select Duplicate Contact. The Duplicate Contact dialog box appears, as shown in Figure 3-9. •

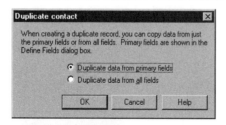

FIGURE 3-9 The Duplicate Contact dialog box lets you copy some or all of a contact's data.

There are two options. One is to grab the information from all the fields (excepting the contact name) and the other is to get the information from only the primary fields. The primary fields are the Company field and all the address-related fields.

4. Select the option that works best for your purposes.

5. Enter the contact name and phone number to complete the new record.

NOTE

You can designate which fields are the primary fields for purposes of creating new contact records as described above. Chapter 17 provides details on this process.

First, Last Name?

As pointed out earlier in this chapter, ACT! is a bit unusual in that both the first and last names of contacts are entered into a single field. So, it is important to understand how ACT! reads the entry in the Contact field.

If you enter a name, such as Sam Wells, ACT! easily identifies the first name as Sam and the last name as Wells. ACT! also identifies honorifics such as Dr., Mr., Ms., and suffixes such as Ph.D., M.D., and Sr., not as names but as what they are—additions to the name. It also correctly identifies last name prefixes such as Von, de, da, and St. But names that have more than two significant parts can cause trouble, including hyphenated names, such as Gloria Wheeler-Wolf; three-part names, such as Gabriel García Márquez; and names with initials, such as T. S. Eliot. ACT! tries to guess which of the parts of the entry are the last name that you would use to look up the contact. Sometimes it may be right and other times wrong. Plus, you may prefer to look up a contact by the last name with which you are most comfortable—"I never call her Gloria Wheeler-Wolf, just Gloria Wheeler. Why she married that Wolf idiot, I'll never understand." In such an unhappy case, you would want to look up Gloria by the last name Wheeler, not Wolf. Anyway, follow the steps here to see how ACT! identifies the name parts.

1. In any contact record, click in the Contact field.

2. Press F2. The Contact Name dialog box appears, as shown in Figure 3-10.

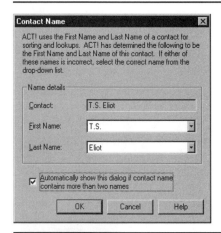

FIGURE 3-10   The Contact Name dialog box indicates which name ACT! regards as first and which as last.

If you can look up a contact record by company or phone number, but ACT! refuses to find the same record when you use the Lookup menu's Last Name option, click the Contact field and press F2 to check out what ACT! thinks is the last name. If it is wrong, use the drop-down list and select the correct part.

 *The Contact Name dialog box opens automatically when you enter names that include more than two parts if the check box is selected in this dialog box.*

A final thought on entering contact records. If you imported your records (for more on importing records, see Chapter 21) and the names came in formatted last name first (as in Wolf, Douglas), ACT! assumes that the last name is Wolf and the first name is Douglas, saving you the trouble of editing all the records. The comma between the names does the trick. However, if the names came in like Wolf Douglas, with no comma, you have work to do—unless you use an add-on tool to fix this problem, as detailed in Appendix A.

 *A product called AddressGrabber makes it easy to convert the name and address information in an e-mail message to an ACT! contact record without typing! See Appendix A to see how to obtain this product and more details.*

Inserting a Note

In early incarnations of ACT!, it was a bit of a chore to add a note to a contact record. Version 3.0 made the task very easy, and this ease continues in ACT! 2000.

Follow these steps to add a note to a contact record:

1. Press F9 or click the Notes/History tab. (Make sure there is a check mark in front of the word "Notes" to the right of the Filter.)

2. Click the Insert Note button.

3. For this example, type **This is an example note**.

4. Click anywhere in the contact record, and the note appears, as you can see in Figure 3-11.

When a note is created, the date and time are inserted for you, plus the type of entry. To the right of the note, there is a column labeled Record Manager. On a standalone system, your name appears. On a network, the Record Manager entry is taken from the My Record of the person entering the note. Usually, this is your name. But, suppose you are out of the office, playing golf. If your best client calls to leave important information, and one of your coworkers goes to the client's contact record and inserts the important information as a note, the coworker's name is inserted as the record manager for that note. When you toddle in from the 19th hole, you can see who talked to your client and thank him or her for entering the note.

You can enter a note of any length that you need. At the right margin, ACT! wraps the text. You can modify the display of the note in several ways. For example, you can make the note field longer by positioning the mouse pointer on the right border, holding down the mouse button, and then dragging the border to the right. You also can change the font of a note, the current size being 8 teeny-tiny points, to whatever size your failing eyesight enables you to read. See Chapter 10 to learn how to edit this setting.

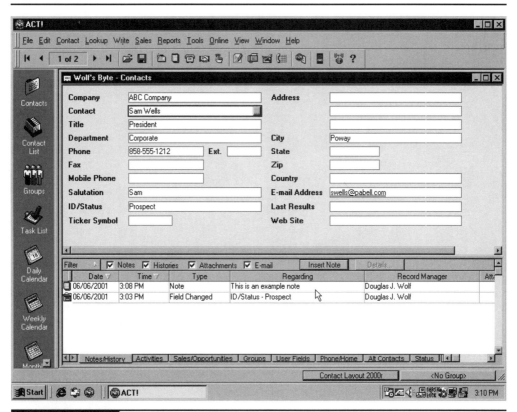

FIGURE 3-11   Your example note appears on the Notes/History tab.

Summary

- Enter a new record by clicking the New Contact button, then opening the Contact menu and selecting New Contact, or by pressing INSERT.

- Use the ID/Status field to identify and categorize contact records at a top level, such as prospect or customer.

- Edit drop-down lists by scrolling down to the bottom and selecting Edit List.

- Add notes to a contact record by clicking the Insert Note button or by pressing F9.

Chapter 4

Looking Up Records

How to...

- Execute a keyword search
- Look up a contact record by the contents of a specific field
- Add to a lookup to create a larger subset of records
- Narrow a lookup to search by several criteria
- Perform a lookup for empty and non-empty fields

In this chapter, you will learn how to locate the contact records that you have entered. The Lookup menu includes easy ways to look up contact records and several ways that require detailed explanation. This chapter covers the easy methods, and Chapter 5 covers the esoteric.

The Lookup Menu

After entering hundreds and possibly thousands of records into ACT!, the next logical step is to find a particular record. You could use the movement buttons to flip from record to record, as described in Chapter 2, but that becomes impractical when hundreds of contacts are in your database. The movement buttons work best when used after you create a lookup that narrows the number of contacts.

You find a record by using the Lookup menu, which is shown in Figure 4-1. Now, I'll discuss this menu's components in some detail.

FIGURE 4-1   The Lookup menu is where you go to find records in your database.

My Record

When you open the Lookup menu and select My Record, ACT! finds and displays the My Record contact screen. Now, try the following steps:

1. Select My Record. The contact record appears. Notice that the entry in the status bar under Lookup reads "My Record." This is to remind you how the contact was found. Also, the record counter now reads "1 of 1."

2. Click the Next Contact button. ACT! beeps at you!

This short example serves to illustrate an important concept in ACT!. That is, when you execute a lookup, ACT! creates a subset of contacts in the database based on the lookup criteria you specify. In this example, there is only one contact record that can be put into the My Record subset, so you can't move to the next or to a previous record. Expanding this idea a little further, suppose that you want to work only with contacts in a specific city. Using the Lookup menu and the City option, ACT! creates a subset of the database containing only contacts who live in the city you specified. This is a subset of the entire set of contacts in your database.

Even though a lookup creates a subset of the records in the database, you do not have to execute an All Contacts lookup to access the rest of the database. In this way, ACT! is unlike most databases, which require you to release a "query" before executing another lookup.

All Contacts

As you might suspect, the All Contacts option accesses the contacts in their entirety. In other words, if you click the Next and Previous buttons, you can walk through every contact in the entire database, one at a time. This is a good item to select when you want to find out the total number of contacts in your database.

Keyword Search

The keyword search method has been changed dramatically in ACT! 2000. Because ACT! includes many user-definable fields, has a note-taking facility for each contact, stores e-mail addresses, and records sales opportunities, information can be stored in many places. The keyword lookup is the catchall for information you need but whose location you've forgotten. For example, in a conversation two years ago a contact mentioned a hot stock pick and you entered the ticker symbol and type of business into the Notes tab for that contact. This morning you saw a news story on a technology that promises to be a big winner for companies in that field. You remember that your contact said the same thing about this hot stock pick, but you have long forgotten the name of the contact or anything to do with it except that it is somewhere in Notes. Relax! ACT! will find the stock information for you. Here's how:

1. Open the Lookup menu and select Keyword Search. The Keyword Search dialog box opens, as shown in Figure 4-2.

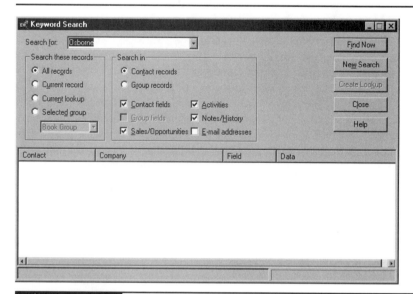

FIGURE 4-2   The Keyword Search dialog box is your first step to find records based on the information they contain.

2. In the Search For text box, enter the word or phrase you want to find.

3. Click Find Now.

While taking a moment to look at your search options, consider that a keyword search is a brute-force method for locating the contact record or records. ACT! looks at every piece of information in each record to match the entry you make. So, if you have 20,000 records with five years of Notes/History, this search could take some time. That's why ACT! includes search parameters that you can use to reduce the scope of data to be searched. You can control these settings in the Search Keyword dialog box. For example, you could have ACT! search the Current Lookup in Notes/History only, by making the appropriate selections.

These are the options in the Search These Records section of the Keyword Search dialog box:

All Records   Searches all records in the database

Current Record   Searches only the record that was onscreen when the dialog box was opened

Current Lookup   Searches the records you have selected from a previous use of the Lookup capability

Selected Group   Searches in the specific group you select from the drop-down list

In addition to choosing what records to search, you can select which fields, tabs, or even groups you want to search. Here are your options as presented in the Search In section of the Keyword Search dialog box:

Contact Records   Searches in the contact records, not groups

Group Records   Searches in the groups, not the contact records

Contact Fields   Searches in the contact fields

Group Fields   Searches the group fields

Sales/Opportunities   Searches the information on the Sales/Opportunities tab

Activities   Includes activities in the search

Notes/History   Includes Notes/History in the search

E-Mail Addresses   Includes e-mail addresses in the search

Performing a Keyword Search

Use the ACT5demo database that was shipped with ACT! to perform the following search. The assumption is that you have entered the word "product brochure" in the notes of several records, but you cannot remember which ones.

1.   Open the ACT5demo database.

2.   Click the Lookup menu and select Keyword Search.

3.   Select All Records.

4.   Select Contact Records.

5.   Select the Contact Fields check box.

6.   Clear the E-Mail Addresses and Activities check boxes that it has deselected.

7.   Click the Notes/History check box, so that a checkmark appears.

8.   In the Search For text box, type **product brochure**.

9.   Click the Find Now button. ACT! responds with a list of the records something like the one shown in Figure 4-3.

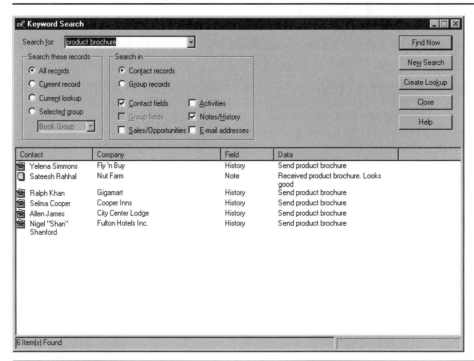

When you perform a keyword search, ACT! displays a list of matching records.

The result of the lookup shows the contact, company, and field in which ACT! found the matching data. The search also shows the search text with some surrounding text.

After performing this lookup, you have several choices. You can click the Create Lookup button to see the records in Contact view. You can select a single record by clicking part of it. You can then select multiple adjacent records by clicking the first record, holding down SHIFT, and clicking the last record. To select records that aren't adjacent, click the first record, hold down CTRL, and then click on the other records you want. After selecting a record or records, right-click one of your selections. A menu appears with three options:

- Click Go To Record to see that single record.

- Click Lookup Selected Records when you have selected multiple records.

- Click Lookup All In List to see the records in Contact view. (You can achieve the same result by clicking the Create Lookup button.)

After you create a keyword lookup, ACT! saves the lookup's settings. The keyword you entered is stored on a drop-down list so you can access it later. Because the settings are saved, you can easily tweak the parameters of your first search and run another. Sticking with our example, follow these steps to broaden the keyword search to include Activities:

1. Click the Lookup menu and select Keyword Search.

2. In the Keyword Search dialog box, select the check box in front of Activities. Leave all other settings the same.

3. Click the Find Now button.

One additional record should appear in the results. Remember, the earlier exercise assumed that all the matches could be found on the Notes/History tab. But, this example should teach you not to trust your assumptions and to try several settings before being satisfied with the result.

Looking Up by Field Contents

The next section of the Lookup menu includes a variety of options for looking up records by the content of their fields. One thing all these options have in common is the Lookup dialog box (described next and in "Lookup Options" later in this chapter).

Company

Use this option to find a contact or contacts that are identified with a certain company or with companies that have specific letters in their names. ACT! assumes that you are entering the name of the company in the Company field of the contact record. To look up by company, click the Lookup menu and select Company. The Lookup dialog box appears with the Company criterion selected, as shown in Figure 4-4.

FIGURE 4-4   The Lookup dialog box lets you search for information by company name.

ACT! prompts you to enter the company name in the Search For section of the dialog box. What ACT! doesn't tell you is that you don't have to know the exact spelling of the name. For example, if you know that the company name you're looking for begins with the letters *MULT*, you can type those letters into the field and click OK. ACT! finds all contact records that include company names beginning with *MULT*:

Multiplexing Systems

Multiple Sources

Multimation

Multiplying Inc.

Multisource

In this example, five contacts were found. When you look at the first record in Contact view the record counter will indicate "1 of 5." But if you entered only the letter *M* as the text to match, ACT! will return all records that include companies whose name begins with *M*, This lookup will probably result in a much longer list.

Lookup Subsets

An ACT! concept that sometimes confounds new users is that despite the fact that the previous lookup assembled matching contacts into a subset of the database, you don't have to use the Lookup | All Contacts command to "deselect" the contacts before you can execute another lookup. So, after finding the MULT subset, you can immediately execute a lookup for contacts whose last name is Smith, and ACT! dutifully finds that group of contacts from among your entire contact list. (For details about last name lookups, see "First Name, Last Name" later in this chapter.)

The Lookup command was designed to create subsets because that enables you to easily locate specific contacts for form letters, mailing labels, or a list of calls that you want to direct to a smaller portion of the entire database. You can perform these actions on your subset without affecting the larger contact list.

Lookup Options

The Lookup dialog box includes settings that allow you to refine the lookup. After you create a lookup, you can add more records or reduce the number of records using the settings described below:

Replace Lookup   This is the default setting in ACT!. That is, if you run a lookup and then decide to run a second lookup, ACT! assumes that you want to select an entirely different set of contact records from the entire database. So, all you have to do is type in a new lookup entry in the field to execute a new lookup.

Add To Lookup   After executing a lookup, you may find that you want to keep the set of contact records you have found and then add another set of records. Select this option to do so.

Narrow Lookup   After executing a lookup, you may find that you want to narrow the scope of the lookup. When you do this, ACT! uses only the first set of contacts to look for the next batch.

Adding Records to Your Lookup

One useful and timesaving feature of ACT! 2000 is the ability to combine lookups to create lists matching multiple criteria. Here's how you do it.

Suppose that in your database, you have entered the customer's product interest in the ID/Status field, and you look up all contacts that are interested in Product A. Then, you decide you want to see the customers who are interested in Product D, but you want both sets of records to be included in the same lookup. All you have to do is execute a second lookup to add the contacts interested in Product D, like this:

1. Click the Lookup menu and select the field you want to search (in this case, ID/Status).

2. Enter the first value and click OK.

3. After ACT! performs the lookup, open the Lookup menu again and select the field you want to use for the second lookup (ID/Status again).

4. Before clicking OK, select Add To Lookup in the Lookup dialog box.

The lookup now contains both sets of contacts. There's no limit to the number of subsequent lookups you can perform to get the set of contacts that you want.

This is a great way to create groups of contacts that you will need to use in the future. After the lookup is complete, create a permanent group so that you do not have to repeat the steps. See Chapter 15 for more on groups.

Narrowing Your Lookup

Sometimes you will run a lookup that returns more records than you need, possibly because there's something extra the records you really want have in common that you haven't specified. For example, suppose that you used the Lookup command to find all your contacts in San Diego. But you really want to find all your contacts in San Diego who are interested in a specific product, which is listed in the ID/Status field. You would then narrow your lookup results like this:

1. Click the Lookup menu and select the field you want to search. In this case, it's City.

2. Enter the search criteria (San Diego) and click OK.

3. ACT! responds with a set of contacts that meet the criteria. In this example, you looked up all contacts in San Diego.

4. Click the Lookup menu again and select the second field on which to search. For this example, choose the ID/Status field, which contains the name of a product in which your contact is interested.

5. Enter the next criteria (Product A) for the search.

6. Select Narrow Lookup.

7. Click OK.

In the second lookup, ACT! searches only those contacts that were identified by the first search criteria. So, it will find all the contacts in San Diego with an ID/Status indicating interest in Product A.

First Name, Last Name

I'm going to discuss these two lookup methods in the same section because they work in exactly the same way.

Selecting either the First Name or Last Name option from the Lookup menu opens the Lookup dialog box. As in the Company lookup, you do not have to enter the entire name to find the contact. If you know the exact spelling, all the better, but it isn't critical. You can use just the first few letters.

Name Order and Honorifics

When you enter a name in the Contact field, you may enter it as **John Smith** or as **Smith, John**. The operative distinction is the comma. When ACT! sees a comma between two entries in the Contact field, it assumes that the first entry is the last name of the contact. So, it doesn't matter how you enter the first and last name—as long as you have the comma between them when you use the second method, ACT! recognizes the first and last names. If you enter **Smith John**, though, ACT! assumes that the last name of the Contact is John. The key is to be consistent in the way you enter names. Choose one method or the other.

You may include a courtesy title such as Mr., Ms., or Professor with your contact names, because ACT! recognizes those entries for what they are: prefixes and not a first or last name. You can add your own prefixes for recognition as described in Chapter 14.

CAUTION   *If you import data from another database, and the first name is in one field and last name is in another, you can map both the names to the Contact field. ACT! provides the field names First and Last as target fields, even though the contact records do not have separate fields for each. See Chapter 21 for the exact steps.*

Phone

It's happened to you; it's happened to everyone. You get a message on voice mail or from a temporary secretary, and the name is so mangled that you cannot make out who it is. Never fear! ACT! saves the day by enabling you to look up the entire phone number or just the first few digits and returns the matching contact record from your database.

City

The City lookup finds contacts on the same match criteria as the other lookup options. If you enter the first three letters, such as **San** then ACT! finds all city names that begin with "San," such as San Francisco, San Antonio, Santa Fe, or Santiago.

The Add To Lookup feature works great in conjunction with this lookup. You can add cities or whatever you need on-the-fly.

Using the Drop-Down List

Instead of typing the data into the field, you can use the drop-down list to select a city. Click the drop-down arrow in the City list of the Lookup dialog box and you will see the same drop-down list that appears when you enter data into a new contact record, as shown in Figure 4-5. Select the city you want from the list, and click OK. The city is inserted into the City field of the Lookup dialog box. Click OK to execute the lookup.

FIGURE 4-5   The City list with both the field drop-down and the previous Lookup entries.

Because ACT! tries to guess what you want to type, it fills in the previous entry. This is good and bad. If the previous search entry was wrong, you have to edit the entry. When this happens, the best way to handle it is to press SPACEBAR after you type the characters that you think are correct. The SPACEBAR erases everything after the letters you type.

State

You can enter the state name into your contact records as an abbreviation or as a full name and be able to look it up equally well. But be consistent. Don't enter Texas as both **TX** and **Texas** and expect that ACT! will easily find all your contacts from Texas. ACT! uses the two-letter postal abbreviations for its list of states. Using the drop-down list to enter the state when creating the contact record means that you can easily use it again in the Lookup dialog box to find the contact.

Try this lookup example. To do so, you need to open the ACT5demo database that is shipped with ACT!.

1. Open the ACT5demo. It's My Record is displayed, as shown in Figure 4-6.

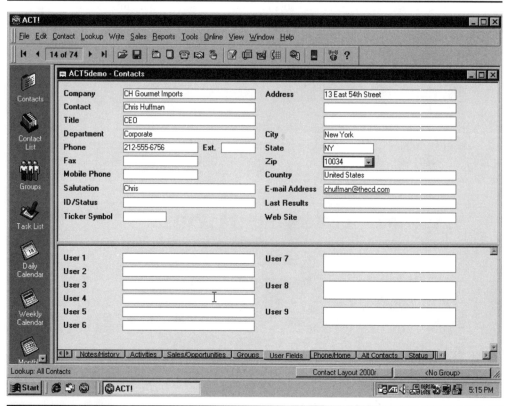

FIGURE 4-6   The ACT5demo database opens to Chris Huffman's My Record.

2. Open the Lookup menu and select State.

3. The Lookup dialog box appears. Click the drop-down arrow. The list of state names appears.

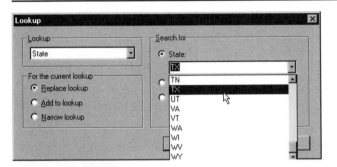

4

FIGURE 4-7   You can choose a state's abbreviation from the State list in the Lookup dialog box.

4. Select TX, as shown in Figure 4-7.

5. Click OK. ACT! inserts the abbreviation TX into the State field of the Lookup dialog box.

6. Click OK.

ACT! locates the contacts that meet the lookup criteria. In the demo database, four contacts hail from the Lone Star State.

Remember, the Add To Lookup feature enables you to add another state if needed to build the set of records you want. The Narrow Lookup feature works great in conjunction with the State option in that you can then specify a city within the state as a further search. Or, as I pointed out previously, you can use the ID/Status field as the next level of the search.

Zip Code

Looking up contacts by Zip code is a powerful option for a number of reasons. Imagine being able to group all of the contacts in your database that live in a certain Zip code. The capability to target a market or to plan trips based on a tight geographic region is yours with this lookup. Even though this entry is numeric (in the United States, anyway) you enter the matching data the same way as in the other lookup fields. For example, for all the contacts in Zip 92*XXX*, enter **92** only. But, if you want to find all of the contacts in Rancho Penasquitos (a suburb of San Diego) you would enter the full Zip code, **92129**.

Here again, the Add To Lookup or Narrow Lookup features make selecting exactly the records you want quite easy.

ID/Status

This option works the same way as the other lookups. Enter the first couple of letters or the entire entry. A drop-down list is available in this dialog box, too. This is probably the most important field in each record because you can use this field with the Group feature to locate contacts in specific ways. For example, you can enter the level of interest the contact has in a purchase by ranking him or her with numbers 1, 2, 3, or with words such as suspect, prospect, and likely customer. Combine this ranking with grouping and you can create a group of contacts interested in a specific product, ranked by interest level. Or, you can reverse the process and use the ID/Status field to indicate the product and then create groups by interest level.

E-Mail Address

Use this lookup to locate records by the entry in the E-Mail Address field. It works in the same manner as the other lookup fields. Enter a partial or full entry, and ACT! tries to make a match.

Sales Stage

Every sales opportunity in ACT! must have a sales stage. With that attribute, ACT! can search the database for the records that have sales opportunities in a specific stage. So, you might want to locate all the records that have opportunities that are close to being consummated in order to determine if you can get that new Porsche next quarter.

Other Fields

When software developers started creating database programs, one of the first problems they ran into was being able to locate a particular record quickly. Imagine trying to locate a record in a database consisting of thousands of records, where each record contains hundreds of pieces of data. It would be similar to having to read every word of an encyclopedia to find the topic you needed! Even a fast computer chokes. The solution was to create an index of selected fields in the record.

When you open the Lookup menu, the fields such as Company, City, ID/Status, Phone, State, and Zip Code are indexed fields. In addition, ACT! creates an index for the Contact's first and last names. So, when you ask ACT! to locate records with a Zip code of 92129, it skips all the other data in the records, goes to the Zip Code Field index, reads the index until it finds the number 9, and then finishes the lookup.

The Other Fields lookup gives you easy access to the fields not on the Lookup menu. Because the other fields are not indexed, this is a slower search, especially if you are working in a large database—10,000 records or more. But, if you want to look up a record by, say, the Referred By field, this is the fastest way. Follow these steps to look up records by a field not listed on the Lookup menu:

1. Open the Lookup menu and select Other Fields. The Lookup dialog box opens.

2. Open the drop-down Lookup list, as shown in Figure 4-8.

3. Select the field you want to use from the list.

4. Enter the text you want to find and set any other options, such as Add To Lookup or Narrow Lookup.

5. Click OK.

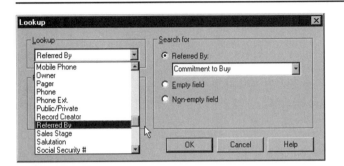

FIGURE 4-8   Select a field in the Lookup list to search the content of fields not listed on the Lookup menu.

Notice that almost all the fields appear in the Lookup drop-down list. This list is available every time you open the Lookup dialog box. If you start the lookup by using the Company option and then decide that you really need the State field, you can easily change the field you want to use in the search by pulling down this list and selecting the field.

If you have customized a field and need to look up information in that field on a regular basis, you can create an index for a user field. This process is covered in Chapter 17.

If you want to search on the ACT! system fields found on the Status tab, such as Last Attempt, Last Meeting, Create Date, or Edit fields, you must use the Lookup By Example option.

Previous

Often, you will want to toggle between lookups. ACT! provides the Previous item to do that. You can perform a lookup to get the records you want, execute another lookup, and then select the Lookup | Previous command to view the first set of records. This tool is useful when used with the Narrow Lookup and Add To Lookup options in the Lookup dialog box. Let's say you ran a lookup and then executed a second lookup selecting the Add To Lookup option. Then you realized that you did not want to add the second set of contacts after all. Fortunately, you can use the Previous command to return to the original set of records.

The next four topics are covered in greater detail in the next chapter on advanced lookups.

Looking Up by Empty or Filled Fields

New to ACT! 2000 is the capability to locate records that have any entry in a particular field or records in which a particular field has no entry. In other words, records in which a certain field is blank or is not. This type of lookup used to require a high level of query expertise in ACT!. No longer. The best example of the use of this type of lookup is for e-mail addresses or fax numbers. When you want to send an e-mail message or fax to many recipients, the job is easier if you eliminate records that lack an entry in the requisite field.

Lookup for Empty Fields

To search for records that have an empty field, follow these steps:

1. Open the Lookup menu.
2. If the field that you want to find empty is one of the ones listed, select it. If not, use the Other Fields option.
3. In the Lookup dialog box, select Replace Lookup.
4. Select Empty Field.
5. Click OK.

   ACT! responds with the records that have no entry in that field.

Lookup for Non-Empty Fields

Follow these steps to perform a lookup for filled fields:

1. Open the Lookup menu.
2. Select the field that you want to ensure is filled. If the field is not on the menu, select Other Fields and use the drop-down list to select the field.
3. Select Non-Empty Field.
4. Click OK.

   The records that have an entry in the field chosen are displayed.

Summary

- When you have an ACT! database with hundreds of records, you can find the one you want using the Lookup menu.
- You can search for records using the information that you remember about the contact, including field contents such as company, contact name, and phone number or a keyword that appears somewhere in the record.
- You can combine lookups to create new groups of contacts with common criteria.
- The entry does not have to match the record for which you are searching exactly, but the letters you do use as your search criteria must match the first letters of the contact field contents for which you are looking.

Chapter 5

Advanced Record Lookups

How to...

■ Find records by example

■ Modify the Lookup menu

■ Find records by sales stage

■ Use the Internet directory

In Chapter 4, you looked up records by a single criterion at a time, narrowing or adding to the records found by repeating lookups. Fortunately, ACT! enables you to streamline this process by allowing you to ask for records matching multiple criteria at once. With this capability you can then create targeted mail, e-mail, or phone campaigns that have the most likely chance of converting prospects to customers or customers into repeat buyers.

Looking Up Contact Records by Example

A *query* is a question you want to ask of the database. When you need to make a complex query of your database, you can use the By Example option on the Lookup menu to perform your search. The previous lookup options, discussed in Chapter 4, were simple queries because they examined only a single field at a time. The By Example option enables you to create complex queries with multiple variables.

ACT! records can be located by using Boolean search techniques. This means that you are limited only by your own creativity in constructing sophisticated search criteria and the type of data you have entered into your database. Customizing your user fields and properly entering data into the ID/Status field makes ACT! a data mining tool. However, the Boolean searches only apply to ACT!'s default fields and will not work on any new fields you add.

The By Example lookup, when converted to an Advanced query, also allows for the use of Boolean logic. That is, you can include arithmetic operators in the queries and specific words such as AND, OR, NOT, and CONTAINS to combine or exclude criteria. Suppose that you want to find all your contacts identified as prospects whose Zip code is 92000 or greater. In Boolean terms, the operators would be >=92000 (greater than or equal to 92000). So, ACT! would find 92000, 92001, 93000, and so on. For all the details about operators, see "What Those Operators Mean" later in this chapter.

A Simple Lookup By Example

Let's create an example query using the By Example option. In this exercise, I'll use the ACT5demo database to illustrate the query. It contains 14 records in the state of New York. The query example locates the contact record(s) in New York that have a Zip code greater than 10300.

To begin your By Example lookup, follow these steps:

1. Open the ACT5demo database.

2. Open the Lookup menu and select By Example. The Query window appears, as shown in Figure 5-1.

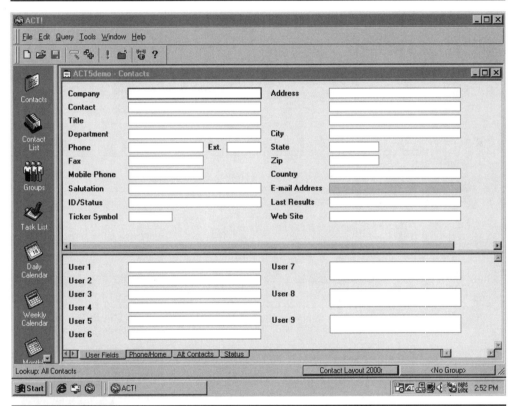

The blank Query window lets you specify criteria for one or more fields.

3. Click the State field.

4. Press F2. From the resulting list, select New York. NY is entered as the first search criteria in the Query screen.

5. Click the Zip field.

6. Type **>10130**. The completed query looks like Figure 5-2.

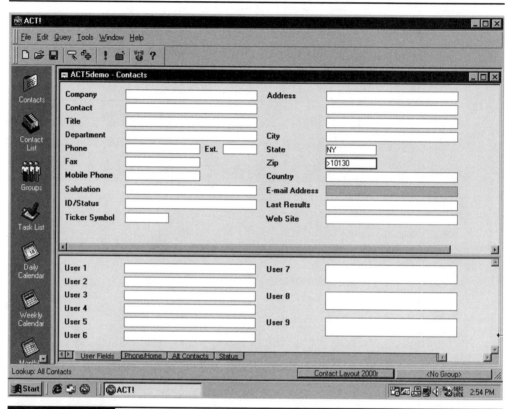

FIGURE 5-2 This query includes entries in the State and Zip fields.

This query translates into plain English as Find all the contacts whose State entry equals New York and whose Zip code is greater than the number 10130.

7. Open the Query menu and select Run Query by clicking the green exclamation point.

   A pop-up message appears asking whether you want to replace, add, or narrow the lookup.

8. Select Replace.

   ACT! carries out the lookup and finds the single contact in this database that matches the query.

By combining the State field entry with the Zip entry, you can be certain that if there is more than one record, all of the contacts found will be located near each other.

If your database has a custom field called Gross Sales and you entered the gross sales for each customer, you could easily locate the customers whose sales are less than or greater than a certain number. Suppose that your company sells several products and you entered the type of product that the customer purchased into the ID/Status field. You could execute a By Example lookup that located the customers who purchased a certain amount of a particular product.

Advanced Queries

Let's take this query idea a step further by adding another logical operator (another term for a Boolean operator) to the search expression.

You can begin your advanced query in the same way you began the simple query: by entering data in the fields of the Query window. You are not required to enter data; you can skip directly to the Advanced Query window. Follow these steps to continue with the example using the ACT5demo database:

1. Open the Lookup menu and select By Example.

2. Open the Query menu and select Clear (it may appear dimmed already).

    This option removes any previous query data. It's a good practice to do this because you might have entered data into a field that is not visible. If so, you may get strange results when you run the query.

3. In the State field, type **NY**.

4. In the Zip field, type **>10010**.

5. Open the Query menu and select the Convert To Advanced Query command, as shown in Figure 5-3.

| FIGURE 5-3 | The Query menu lets you generate an advanced lookup request. |

The Advanced Query window appears, as shown in Figure 5-4, featuring the Query Helper dialog box.

As you can see in the window, ACT! converted the entries in the query screen into the logical expression (("State"="NY"*)) AND(("Zip">"10010")).

No, you haven't opened a window into ACT!'s program code. This obscure-looking formula is simply how ACT! represents the criteria you entered into the nice, friendly dialog box. As such, it just means that the State field must contain NY and the Zip field must be larger than 10010. Not too difficult, is it?

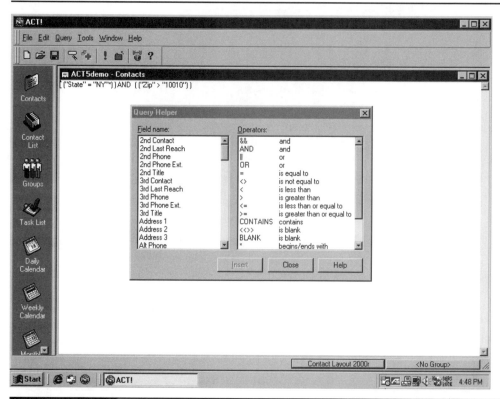

FIGURE 5-4 The Advanced Query window includes a dialog box that helps you build queries.

Now it's time to add a third variable. Suppose that you want to find the contacts in New York that have a Zip code greater than 10010 and whose last names begin with A or B.

There are two ways to enter a new variable. You can go back to the Lookup dialog box and enter the variables in the respective fields. But, if you want to use a Boolean operator, you must do it in the Advanced Query window. To continue with the example above, follow these steps:

1. In the Advanced Query window, click to place an insertion point at the right end of the expression.

2. In the Query Helper dialog box, select the AND operator and then click Insert to paste it in at the insertion point.

3. Next you need the field name for ACT! to look in. In the Query Helper dialog box, double-click on the Last Name field. ACT! inserts the name of the field for you.

   Now you need to limit the lookup to last names that begin with A or B. In the context of the alphabet, ACT! understands less than to mean "comes earlier in the alphabet" and greater than to mean "comes later in the alphabet." So the expression "Last

Name" < "C" will restrict the search to last names that begin with a letter that comes before *C* in the alphabet.

4. In the Query Helper dialog box, double-click the Is Less Than sign (<) to insert it into the expression.

5. Type **"c"** (including the quotation marks). You may have to press the SPACEBAR to see the quotation marks. If they do not appear, add them. Figure 5-5 shows the completed query.

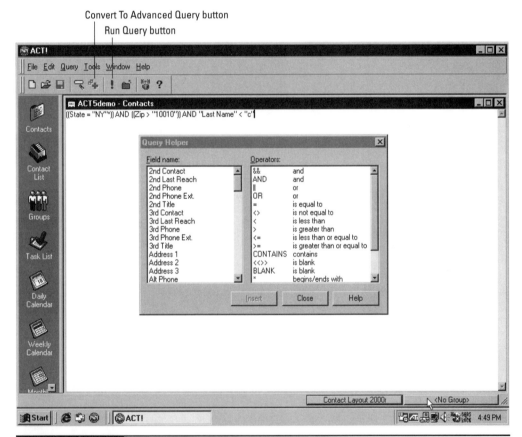

FIGURE 5-5 You can use a three-criteria query to further limit your lookup.

Now the search expression reads, "Find the contacts that have a State entry of New York and a Zip code that's greater than 10010 and a Last Name that begins with the letter A or B."

6. Open the Query menu and select Check Query Syntax to make sure you've formatted your query properly.

If you have followed the directions, you will get the message "Query Correctly Formatted." If not, a message will indicate at what character position you have made a mistake. ACT! is *very* picky, and everything has to be in exact order for queries of this sort to work.

7. When your query syntax checks out, click the Run Query button (the one with the green exclamation point).

8. ACT! Asks whether you want to save the query. Click Yes. The Save As dialog box appears, as shown in Figure 5-6.

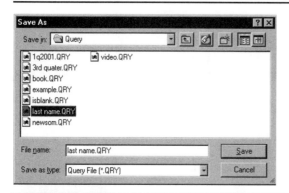

FIGURE 5-6   Save your query so you can run it again later.

9. Type a name for the query, such as **last name**, and click Save.

The Run Query Options dialog box appears.

10. Select Replace Lookup and click OK.

Complex queries take longer than the simple lookups we've done so far (particularly in a large database) because of the complexity of the query. In advanced queries, each contact must be searched for the matching data, whereas in simple lookups, only the indexed fields are searched.

More on Advanced Queries

This next example cannot be duplicated using the ACT5demo database unless you modify a record. If you decide not to, follow the steps outlined and look carefully at the figures, so that you can re-create this type of query in your database. (If you want, you can use the File menu and Save As command to save a copy of your demo database before making any changes.)

The Advanced Query window includes a way to insert not only logical operators, but also field names and Boolean operators. One of those Boolean operators is CONTAINS. Let's say you are in the executive search business (okay, a headhunter), and you specialize in computer programmers. Rather than enter the languages that the prospects are trained to use in several different fields, in each of their records, you enter all their abilities in the User 1 field. The entries in that field could be C+, Basic, Visual Basic, COBOL, and SQL. Plus, you need to enter a range of Zip codes so you can determine whether the job seeker is within a reasonable commuting distance of the potential new job.

To enter multiple items from a drop-down list, open the drop down, press F2, and click the first item. Press and hold CTRL to click as many other items as you want.

5

You need to find someone who can program SQL in the New York City area. In English, the search is Find the contacts that can program in SQL and live in the 10000 to 10034 Zip code area.

To duplicate this example, you must add an entry to a record in the ACT5demo database (or the copy you just made). Follow these steps to do so:

1. Open the Lookup menu and select Last Name.

2. In the Lookup dialog box, type **Newsom**.

3. Click OK. The record with the name Joshua Newsom should appear.

4. Click the User 1 field.

5. Type **SQL**.

6. Open the Lookup menu again and select My Record. Moving to another record saves the changes you have made.

   The record has now been altered so that the example advanced query will have the results you want.

Obviously, you know which record has the information you are trying to find, but follow these steps to see whether you can make the lookup work:

1. Open the Lookup menu and select By Example.

2. In the blank Query window, go to the Zip code field and enter the lower Zip number by typing **10000**.

3. Click the Convert To Advanced Query button (the one that shows a green plus sign and two small windows).

4. In the Query Helper dialog box, select Range (the two dots) from the Operators list.

5. Place the insertion point after the number 10000 and then click the Insert button.

6. Type the second value: **10034**.

7. Place the insertion point to the right of the parentheses.

8. In the Query Helper dialog box, select AND from the Operators list.

9. Click Insert.

10. Remember, the field in which you entered the programming skills is User 1. Select User 1 from the Field Name list and click Insert. The field name is added to the expression.

11. In the Query Helper dialog box, click the operator CONTAINS.

12. Click Insert and then Close to close the Query Helper dialog box.

13. Type **"SQL"** (including the quotation marks).

    Entered correctly, the expression will look like the one shown in Figure 5-7. If an asterisk (*) appears in the expression, be sure to delete it.

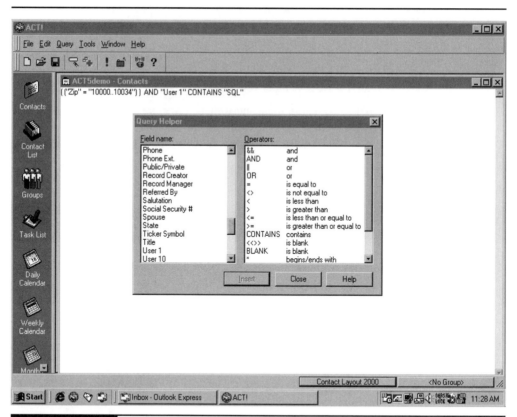

FIGURE 5-7   With an advanced query, you can search for records that contain data within a specified range.

14. Click the Run Query button.

Joshua Newsom should be the single record returned by the query.

The foregoing example query would find the contact assuming it had been entered into ACT!. Using the Range operator made it easy to select the series of Zip codes, and the CONTAINS operator allows you to search for the matching text string *anywhere* in the User 1 field. This example should give you an idea on how the Advanced Query feature can be effectively used.

What Those Operators Mean

They might look complicated, but the logical operators and the Boolean operators really aren't. Take a look at Table 5-1 and you will discover how easy they are to use.

Symbol	Meaning and Use
=	Equals. An exact match: 2=2
>	Greater than. 3 is greater than 2 (3>2); B is greater than A (B>A)
<	Less than. 2 is less than 3; A is less than B
<>	Not equal to. 4 is not equal to 3 or 5
>=	Greater than or equal to. 3 is greater than 2 and equal to 3
<=	Less than or equal to. 2 is less than 3 and equal to 2
CONTAINS ...	The field contains a sequence of characters. "Software" contains "war"
*	Begins/ends with. *PET (ends with "pet") might yield "carpet"; PET* (begins with "pet") might yield "petunia"
&&	Same as AND
AND	The contact must have both matching words or values. The contact is a dealer AND requested more information
II	Same as OR
OR	The contact must have at least one matching value. The contact is a dealer OR requested information
NOT	Contact does not have a matching value. Contact is NOT from Omaha
Blank	Field has no entry, is blank
<< >>	Same as Blank
..	Range: Field has a range of values. 5..9 means the contact has 5, 6, 7, 8, or 9
!	Same as NOT

TABLE 5-1   Boolean Operators

5

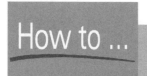

Find Records in a Range of Dates

A range query can be used many ways. An example is trying to find contacts that were entered into the database in a specific time period, such as last year. To run such a query, click the Status tab, open the Lookup menu, and select By Example. In the field named Create Date, enter the date this way: **01/01/1999..12/31/1999**. Click the Run Query button (the exclamation point) to run the query and any records created in that time period are located. Also, you can find records that have been imported (Merge field) or edited in the same way. If the date range you desire is in this millennium, you can drop the four-digit year: **01/01/01..12/31/01**.

Checking a Query for Precision

As I've mentioned, ACT! is notoriously picky about how you create queries. Even though you think you have correctly created a complex query, you may have missed a nuance. ACT! can give you a hand by checking the query for you before you run it and receive an error message.

After creating a query, open the Query menu and select Check Query Syntax. ACT! processes the query, stopping if there is incorrect syntax. The most common error is "Value Expected." Check to see whether quotation marks enclose each of the matching values. This feature can save you plenty of headaches when you're creating complex queries!

Sorting on a Query

ACT! sorts the contacts that match your query in ascending alphabetical order by the entry in the Company field, and if there is no entry in the Company field, the results are sorted by the Last Name in the Contact field. ACT! uses this rule by default, but changing the sort order is a snap! Before selecting the Run Query command on the Query menu, select Specify Query Sort. The Sort Contacts dialog box opens, as shown in Figure 5-8.

As you can see, you can specify up to a three-level sort and specify the order within each sort level. This does not affect the sort order of the entire database—only the lookup results. I describe how you can change the sort order for the database in Chapters 6 and 12. One practical use of the sorting is by Zip code when you anticipate doing a bulk mailing to the contacts found by the lookup.

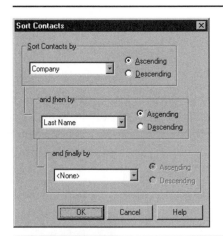

FIGURE 5-8   The Sort Contacts dialog box lets you change the default order of the lookup results.

In a database with more than 5,000 records, you may find that the time to execute a query becomes too long. An inexpensive add-on product, Turbo-Lookup, reduces the processing time by 90 percent—a 30-minute lookup using ACT! alone can be reduced to 2 minutes. This tool is available from J L Technical at www.jltechnical.com. I describe an example query using this utility in Appendix A.

Executing a Saved Query

You'll probably find yourself executing certain queries repeatedly. For example, you might want to create an e-mail list by finding contacts' e-mail addresses or by finding all contacts that were edited last week. Fortunately, you don't have to create these queries from scratch; you can save a working query and use it any number of times. That's why you saved the query in this chapter's first example.

To access and execute a saved query, use the following steps:

1. Open the Lookup menu and select By Example.

2. Open the File menu and select Open. The Open dialog box appears.

3. Double-click the name of the saved query. The search criteria are inserted into the Advanced Query window.

4. Click the Run Query button to execute the query.

That's all there is to it! Now you can update your lists as your database grows by performing the same query at different times.

Modifying the Lookup Menu

In a previous example, you used a By Example lookup to create a highly specialized query and then saved it as a file. The designers of ACT! anticipated that you might want to have a faster way to access a saved query. So, the program lets you add a saved query to the Lookup menu. Here's how to do it:

1. Save a query as a file.

2. Open the Lookup menu and select Modify Menu. The Modify Menu dialog box appears, as shown in Figure 5-9.

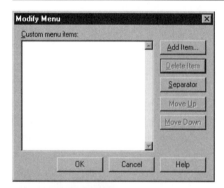

FIGURE 5-9   The Modify Menu dialog box lets you add a useful query to ACT!'s Lookup menu.

3. Click the Add Item button. The Add Custom Menu Item dialog box appears, as Figure 5-10 shows.

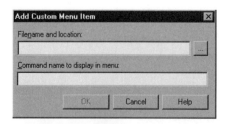

FIGURE 5-10   Use this dialog box to add a query to your menu.

4. If you know the exact name of the query file, type it into the Filename And Location box. If you don't know the name of the file, click the Browse button (the mysterious gray box with three tiny dots to the right of the field), which invokes the Open dialog box listing the saved query files. Double-click on the filename, and ACT! inserts it into the Filename And Location field of the Add Custom Menu Item dialog box.

5. Type a description of the query in the Command Name To Display In Menu box. You must add a name for the process to work.

6. Click OK. The description name appears in the Custom Menu Items list in the Modify Menu dialog box.

If you plan to add several items to the Lookup menu, use the Separator button in the Modify Menu dialog box to separate them so that each query is easy to read. You can also click on an item and move it to a different position on the menu by using the Move Up and Move Down buttons.

5

7. Click OK to close the Modify Menu dialog box.

8. Click the Lookup menu to see your new query in place, as shown in Figure 5-11.

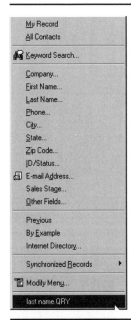

FIGURE 5-11 I've added the last name.QRY query to the Lookup menu.

 *If you are using ACT! on a network and others would like to have a query on their Lookup menu, someone must modify the menu at each workstation. Put the saved query in a folder on the network drive so that it is easy to locate.*

Lookup by Sales Stage

Essentially, this lookup lets you determine at what point your sales contacts are in your sales process. Imagine the power of combining this lookup with ID/Status! You could lookup the prospects in ID/Status and then use the Sales Stage lookup to check the sales pipeline. To use this lookup to its fullest, please take the time to learn how to enter the sales stage information needed, as described in Chapter 18.

At its most basic, you can look up contact records using Sales Stage as you have defined the stages.

1. Open the Lookup menu and select Sales Stage.

2. Select the records that are to be included in the lookup.

3. Enter the sales stage you want to match.

4. Click OK.

Internet Directory

ACT! 2000 provides an exciting feature that can bring you contacts from around the world. No longer do you have to enter your contacts and search only the records you've entered. Now you can go online to find people via the Internet!

In other words, this Lookup option connects your computer to popular Internet search engines such as Bigfoot or Yahoo!. When you want to find a person's phone number, physical address, or e-mail address by searching the Internet, you can do so—provided you have an account with an Internet service provider (ISP) or your company has a direct Internet connection.

This lookup is most useful when the contact is not already in your database. However, if you want to look up information on a contact in your database, you can use an option on the Online menu and Internet Links called Yahoo! Person Search. If you access the Internet that way, the name of the contact is transferred automatically to the search engine fields.

To get information on a person not in your database, follow these steps:

1. Open the Lookup menu and select Internet Directory.

   The Internet Directory Lookup dialog box appears, as shown in Figure 5-12.

2. Enter the name of the person you want to find.

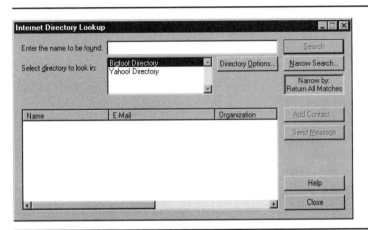

FIGURE 5-12   The Internet Directory Lookup dialog box lets you search online for contact information.

3. Select the directory you want to search. You may have to try both search engines to locate the target—and remember, not *everyone* is in a directory.

4. Click Search.

If you use a dial-up connection (via a modem), your browser is started, the modem dials your ISP, and the search begins. Figure 5-13 shows the results of searching for a certain famous author's name in the Bigfoot directory.

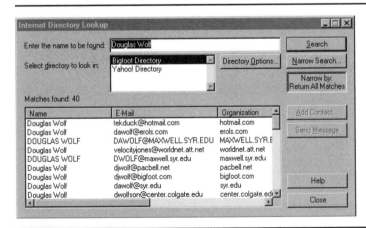

FIGURE 5-13   This is the result of a Bigfoot directory search for the name of your curmudgeonly author.

As you can see, there are many names that match the search criteria. If you recognize the correct name when you run the search, click the name to select it. Then, create the new contact record by clicking the Add Contact button, which opens the Add Contact dialog box, shown in Figure 5-14.

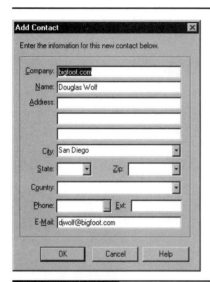

FIGURE 5-14   Click the Add Contact button to open the Add Contact dialog box.

Whatever information was included with the name from the directory automatically appears in this dialog box. Most of the time you will get only the city, state, country, and e-mail address. Click OK to add the new record.

Narrowing the Search

Depending on the name you're looking for, it's possible that the search returns so many names that it's impractical to look at them all. You can narrow the search provided you have some data on the contact. To narrow the search, click the—you guessed it—Narrow Search button. Figure 5-15 shows the Narrow Search dialog box that appears.

To restrict the search to a specific state, for example, select State and enter the full name of the state. Click OK to close the Narrow Search dialog box, and then click the Search button again.

Sending E-Mail

You may also send an e-mail message immediately to someone your Internet search found by selecting the name in the Matches Found box and then clicking the Send Message button. The e-mail message window you see depends on which e-mail system you use. Chapter 13 covers the different e-mail systems that are compatible with ACT!

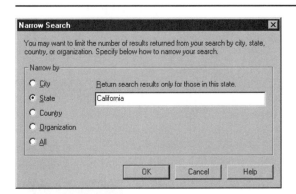

FIGURE 5-15   The Narrow Search dialog box restricts the names returned by the Internet name search.

Adding Other Search Directories

Although ACT! provides two directories, you can add as many as you like to the list, provided you have the technical information from the directory service. To add a new directory, follow these steps:

1. In the Internet Directory Lookup dialog box, click the Directory Options button. The Directory Options dialog box appears.

2. Click the Add button. The Add Directory Service dialog box appears, as shown in Figure 5-16.

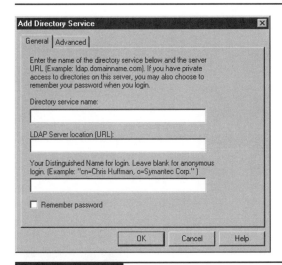

FIGURE 5-16   The Add Directory Service dialog box lets you send your Internet search to other search engines.

To add a directory, you need the name of the service, the LDAP, and perhaps a logon name if it is a private directory. You may also have to go to the Advanced tab to limit the search scope and port. These settings will likely require the assistance of your network administrator.

3. Click OK twice after entering the information to save the new directory service.

Lookup by Synchronized Records

If you are synchronizing records, this option allows you to see several things. When you synchronize, you receive records from other ACT! users. Some of the records may be new and others may be modified versions of records you already have in your database. So, selecting this option after synchronizing creates a lookup of those records that were received in the most recent synchronization file, giving you the opportunity to review those records. The second option, Deleted By Remote Users, is intended for the administrator of a master database that is synchronized. Remote users cannot delete records without the agreement of the administrator. This lookup allows the administrator to monitor and decide which records get deleted. These two topics are covered in more detail in Chapter 25.

Summary

- Advanced lookups (also called queries) are not that complicated as long as you think through the process when you begin entering the lookup criteria.

- To create an advanced query, open the Lookup menu and select By Example. Enter the characters you want to match in as many fields as you want, and then click the Run Query button.

- After you create a complex query, it can be saved and added to the Lookup menu for easy access.

- Records can be located by sales stages in sales opportunities.

Chapter 6

Working in the List View

How to...

■ Open the List view

■ Customize columns

■ Work with the Edit and Tag modes

■ Print the List view

If you started reading this book from the beginning, you have been working in what ACT! calls the Contact view. You may have heard this presentation style referred to as the single-record-at-a-time view or as the *form* view because data is laid out in a predesigned form. Underlying all databases are *tables*—columns of information with headers that tell you what the data is in the particular column. If you have worked with database programs such as Microsoft Access or FoxBASE or a spreadsheet such as Excel, you are familiar with columns of information. ACT! uses tables of data, too. You can look at your contact records as tables of data using the List view. In fact, many users of ACT! prefer the List view for a variety of reasons. Try it; it may be a more efficient way for you to work.

Opening the List View of Contact Records

To see how to work in the List view in ACT!, open the demonstration database. Or, if you have a database with more than five or six contacts, you can use your own database.

Follow these steps to open the demonstration database and see the contact records in List view:

1. Open the File menu and choose Open.

2. From the Open list, select the ACT5demo database.

3. Click Open. The demonstration database should open with Chris Huffman as the My Record.

4. Click the Contact List icon at the left of the record form. ACT! displays your contacts in list format, as shown in Figure 6-1.

When you switch to List view, the contact record you were viewing when you switched is highlighted on the screen. Note the column and row format with the field names as headings to each column.

It is important that you understand what the buttons do in both the Edit and Tag modes. Each has a distinct purpose, as described below:

Edit/Tag Mode Toggles between Edit and Tag modes (see "Edit vs. Tag Mode" later in this chapter for more information)

Tag All Selects all records (see "Changing to Tag Mode" later in this chapter for more information)

Untag All Deselects all records (see "Changing to Tag Mode" later in this chapter for more information)

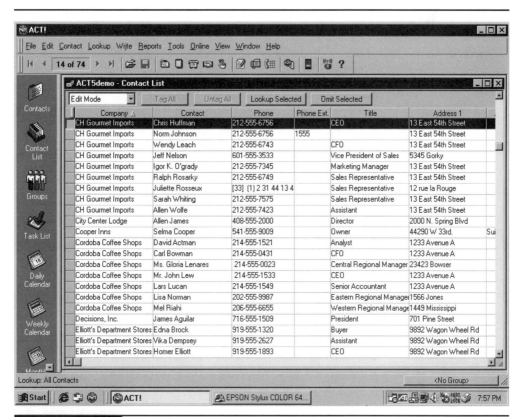

FIGURE 6-1 You can look at contact records in List view.

Lookup Selected Performs a lookup based on the records tagged (see "The Lookup Selected and Omit Selected Buttons" later in this chapter for more information)

Omit Selected Removes the tagged contact records from the List view (see "The Lookup Selected and Omit Selected Buttons" later in this chapter for more information)

Scrolling the List

You should see two scrollbars in the List view: the vertical and horizontal. The vertical scrollbar moves the list so that you can view the previous or next records. The horizontal scrollbar shifts the view so that you can see the columns to the right or left.

Scroll the list so that the first record in the database, Pat Huffman, is visible. That is the first record, because by default, ACT! sorts records in ascending alphabetical order by company. If no company name is in the contact record, ACT! displays those records at the top of the list, using the Last Name field to sort them. The Pat Huffman record is the *only* record without a company that appears in the first position.

Sorting Records

To sort the list, click any column header. For example, the list is currently sorted by the Company name. Click the Contact header, and ACT! sorts the list by last name, as shown in Figure 6-2.

FIGURE 6-2   You can sort the List view by contact last name.

Now, click the Contact header again. Doing so *reverses* the sort order to descending alphabetical order. The sort order is indicated by the tiny triangle in the column header. Pointed up is ascending and pointing down is descending.

You can sort the list using any field in the view. This is particularly handy for sorting by Zip code for bulk mail or form letters. The sorting in the List view does not affect the Contact view, so you can sort your list as often as necessary.

Customizing Columns

You can resize, rearrange, and otherwise customize the columns in the List view to suit your needs. The rearranged list view is sticky, which means that if you close ACT! and start again, then switch to List view, the changes you made appear again. If you are on a network, the change only affects your workstation.

Resizing the Columns

Each of the columns can be resized—made wider or narrower. To change the width of a column, move the mouse pointer to the line that separates the names of the columns. The pointer changes from a pointer to a line with arrows pointing left and right. Click and hold the mouse button, and then drag the mouse to the left to narrow the column, or to the right to lengthen the column. In Figure 6-3, I have narrowed the Phone field so that only the area codes are visible.

6

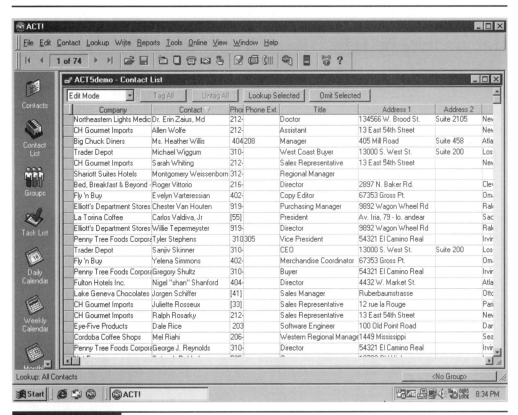

| FIGURE 6-3 | The Phone column has been narrowed to show only the area code. |

The process can be repeated to designate the column widths, as you want them to appear. When you close the List view and then reopen it, the list appears as you last customized it.

Rearranging the Columns

Not only can you resize a column, you can drag the columns around to create the order you want. Suppose you want the Title column next to the Company column. Just follow these steps:

1. Click and hold the left mouse pointer on the Title column header and drag it to the right of the Company column header and on top of the Contact column header. While you drag the column header, the mouse pointer appears as a small hand.

2. Release the mouse button. The columns are rearranged, as shown in Figure 6-4.

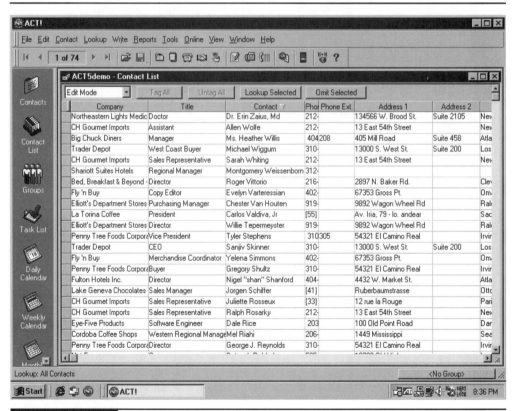

FIGURE 6-4   You can rearrange the column order in List view.

 *If you click the column header and do not begin moving the column immediately, ACT! may think you want to re-sort the database. If it looks as though nothing is happening, it might mean that ACT! has begun to re-sort the list. If your database contains more than 5,000 records, the re-sort could take a while.*

Adding New Columns

The columns that you see in List view may not include the field or fields you want to see. Suppose you wanted to see the date that each of the records in your database was created. The field that has that date is not included in the default List view. To add a column or columns to the view, follow these steps:

1. Scroll the List View window to the left until you have plenty of white space.

2. With the mouse pointer in the white space of the window, right-click the mouse. When you do, the shortcut menu appears, as shown in Figure 6-5.

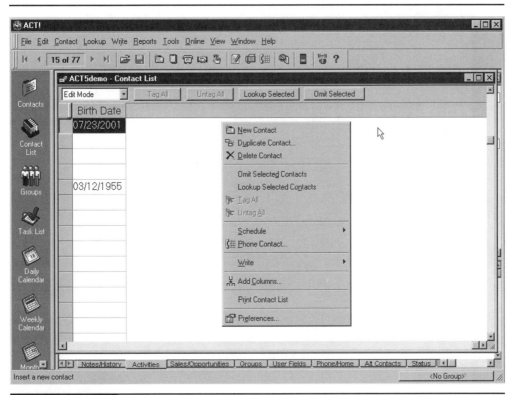

In the List view, this shortcut menu enables you to add columns.

3. From the menu, select Add Columns. The Add Columns dialog box appears, as shown in Figure 6-6.

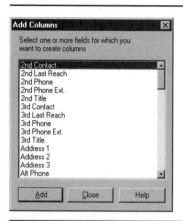

FIGURE 6-6   The Add Columns dialog box is your key to displaying more fields in List view.

From this dialog box, you can scroll the list to find the field or fields you want to add to the List view. The fields are listed in ascending alphabetical order.

4. Select the field you want to add, and click Add. To add a second column, select it and click Add again. In this example the field you want as a column is the Create Date field. The result of adding the new field as a column is shown in Figure 6-7.

A new field always appears at the far right. Because you already know how to move columns, you can reposition the column anywhere in the List view. Just click the column header and drag the field to the desired location.

Any changes you make to the List view appearance have no affect on the contact record data or on the fields.

Deleting a Column

Deleting a column from the List view may seem a little disconcerting, but rest assured that doing so does not affect the database in any way. The data for that field is simply not visible, but it's still recorded. To delete a column, click the column header and drag it toward the top of the screen. When the mouse pointer turns into a small trash can, release the button and the column is deleted. It's that simple!

If you accidentally delete a field you want displayed, follow the procedure in the previous section to replace it.

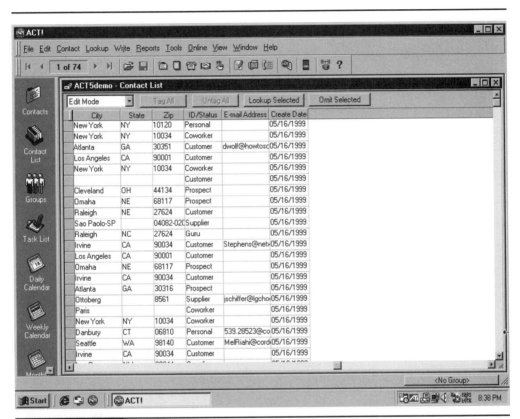

FIGURE 6-7   Presto! You've added a new field to the List view.

Locking Columns

If you have used a spreadsheet program such as Excel, you have encountered the column locking feature and probably wished ACT! could do it too. Well, it can. When you have many columns in the List view, you can lock the names so that if you scroll the window to the left, you will still be able to see one or several columns at the left edge. The trick to getting this feature to work is pointing your mouse on exactly the correct spot: the column anchor. Notice the position and shape of the mouse pointer in Figure 6-8.

To lock columns, click the column anchor and drag it to the right edge of the column you want to anchor. Figure 6-9 shows two columns locked at the left; the column anchor appears as a heavy border on the right edge.

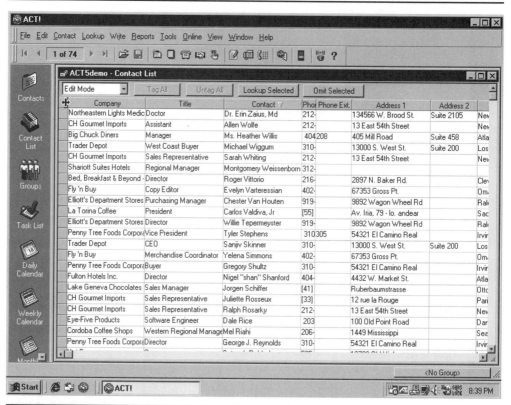

FIGURE 6-8 When the mouse pointer is located on the column anchor, it takes on a new shape.

Edit Mode

When you initially open the List view, the window is in Edit mode. That is, you can click a particular record and make changes. For example, if you click the Title field on a record, a drop-down list appears, as shown in Figure 6-10.

A benefit of being able to see the records in this fashion is the speed of editing. If the area code ever changes for a series of records (that *never* happens!), you can create a lookup by phone number using only the area code as the match, and then go to the List view and change each record. (In Appendix A, I'll discuss a software product that keeps the area codes in your database up-to-date.)

You can also use the Edit mode when there are duplicate records in your database. Creating a lookup of the duplicates and then viewing the records in a list side by side makes it easier to decide whether the records are truly duplicates (or merely similar), and if so, which one to keep.

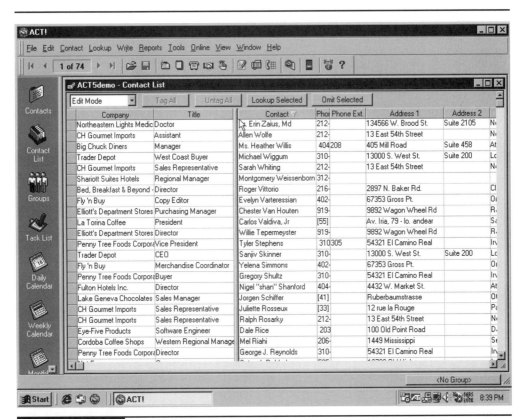

FIGURE 6-9 The column anchor appears as a heavy border on the right side of the locked column(s).

Searching in Edit Mode

In addition to scrolling the list or using the Lookup menu to find a record, you can type the initial letters pertaining to the data in the field and ACT! scrolls the list to that record for you. Click the column header of the column you want to use for the search. (Remember, ACT! sorts the list by that column when you do this.) Assuming that the records have been sorted by Company, typing the letters **LA** opens the Look For box at the top left of the columns, and the list scrolls so that the first record that has a company name that begins with *LA* appears at the top of the list. This record is also highlighted. If you continue typing, ACT! continues to scroll the list to match what you type. An example showing the Look For box appears in Figure 6-11.

Note that when you are in Edit mode, if you click in a single field in a record and then type, you will be entering the keystrokes into that field (editing it), rather than searching. Make sure the cursor doesn't appear in any fields before you start typing for your search.

FIGURE 6-10 You can easily edit fields via a drop-down list.

Lookup Selected and Omit Selected

With a record or records selected, you can create a lookup by one of two methods while in Edit mode. If you want to keep the records you have selected as the lookup, click the Lookup Selected button. Conversely, to get rid of the records selected and keep the others, click the Omit Selected button.

If you select a record by accident, click the mouse in white space and select again. Or, press CTRL and click the record.

NOTE *Incidentally, all the Lookup menu methods discussed in Chapters 4 and 5 work identically in the List view.*

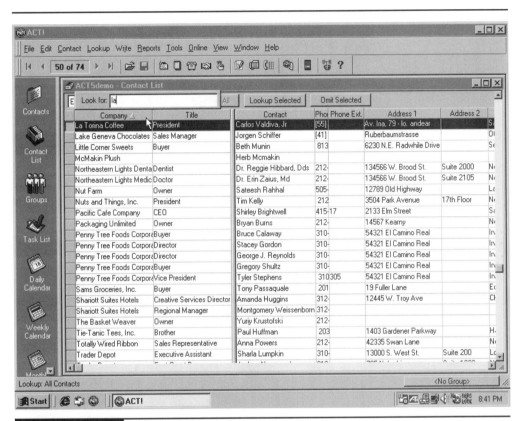

FIGURE 6-11 You can type the first few letters of a record in the Look For box to find the contact in the List view.

Tag Mode

The Tag mode offers an easy way to mark records. Usually, the reason for marking the records is to generate form letters, create groups, or delete specific records from the database. Tagging is the best way to create ad-hoc lists of contact records because it's easy to select the records randomly.

   To switch from Edit mode to Tag mode, move your mouse pointer to the drop-down list in the upper-left corner of the List View window. You should see Edit Mode selected in the list. Click the drop-down arrow and select Tag Mode. The List view changes to resemble what you see in Figure 6-12.

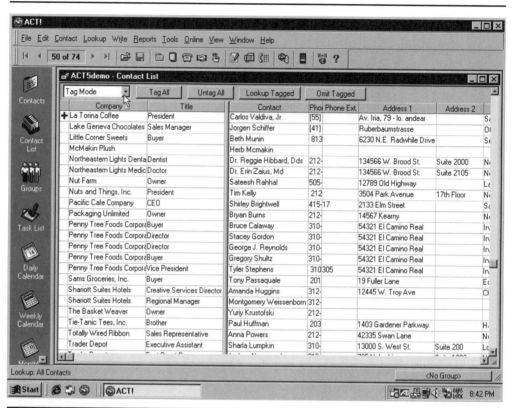

FIGURE 6-12   You can use Tag mode to select records in the List view.

One record will likely be tagged by default—the record you were looking at before you switched to the List view. The tag is the big plus sign (+) to the left of the record. The buttons on the top of the List view change, too. The Tag All and Untag All buttons are self-explanatory. The other buttons are described below.

To tag a record, click anywhere on the record's information. ACT! adds the plus sign (+) and draws a frame around the record. The purpose of the frame is to let you know which record was the last selected. To tag a series of contiguous records, click the first record, hold down SHIFT, and click the last record. To untag a record, click it again.

Lookup Tagged and Omit Tagged

With a record or records selected, you can create a lookup by one of two methods in Tag mode. If you want to keep the records you have selected as the lookup, click the Lookup Tagged button. Conversely, to get rid of the records selected and keep the others, click the Omit Tagged button. Pretty easy, as is everything in ACT!.

Other Actions in the List View

You can undertake several other actions in the List view, in either Edit mode or Tag mode. One way to access several options is to right-click a record. The shortcut menu that appears depends on whether you have selected records and whether you are in Edit mode or Tag mode. What commands are available also depends on which mode you are in. Figure 6-13 shows the shortcut menu for a selected record in Tag mode. As you can see in the figure, some of the commands are not available. For example, you cannot enter a new contact or duplicate an existing contact in Tag mode. But you can delete the contact, schedule activities with the contact (covered in Chapter 7), as well as have ACT! dial the selected contact's phone number; or write a letter, fax, or e-mail to the selected contact. You can also add columns as well as print the contact list per your design.

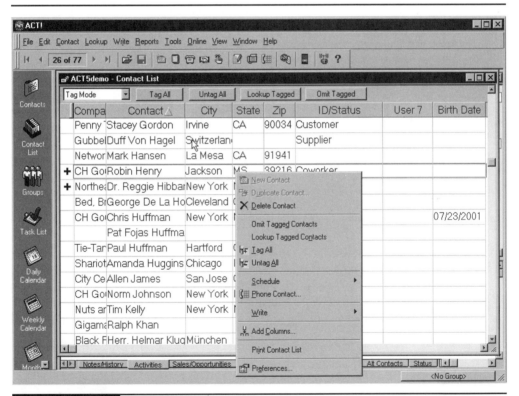

| FIGURE 6-13 | Right-clicking a record in the List view produces a shortcut menu with handy options. |

Printing the List View

ACT! includes many ways to print your contact records: address book form, Filofax, Day Runner, and so on. Several reports are also available, such as the phone directory, which prints the company, contact, and phone number. The List view also gives you the ability to print an ad-hoc list with the exact columns and names that you want included. For example, one handy list is a phone and fax list. You can create a lookup, delete the columns you don't want, keep the phone column, add the fax column, and print the resulting list.

To print a contact list, follow these steps:

1. Right-click the mouse in any blank space. The shortcut menu appears.

2. Click the Print Column List command. The Windows Print dialog box appears. Click the Print button. If the columns fit on a single page, the file is sent to the printer. If they don't fit, the Print List Window dialog box appears, as shown in Figure 6-14.

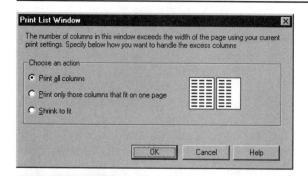

You can choose Print All Columns, which will print the list across more than one page. Or, you can choose Print Only Those Columns That Fit On One Page. The last choice, Shrink To Fit, may work best if you don't have many columns. Shrink To Fit allows ACT! to shrink the type font so that all the text fits. If you have many columns, however, the resulting list will be too small to read.

 *If you're facing a spacing crisis, you can also try to get the columns on a single sheet of paper by changing the page orientation from portrait to landscape.*

Summary

- Changing from the single record Contact view to the List view is as easy as clicking the Contact List view button at the left of the ACT! program window.

- You can sort, resize, add, and delete columns in the List view without affecting your database.

- You can use the List view to make ad hoc sets of records for mail merging, creating groups, editing fields, or deleting records.

6

Chapter 7

Scheduling Activities

How to...

- Schedule calls, meetings, and to-dos
- Deal with alarms
- Modify scheduled activities
- Create a series of activities

Procrastination is one of the salient qualities of human beings. With that in mind, the next aspect of working with contacts I'll tackle is the scheduling of activities. ACT! categorizes activities into three areas: telephone calls, meetings, and to-dos (any other type of task).

 *The key to successfully using ACT! is to proactively schedule activities with other people. After you complete the activity, close the loop by clearing the activity.*

The My Record contact that was created when you installed ACT! is for scheduling those activities that do not warrant entering a contact, such as stopping at the dry cleaners. However, remember this key concept of ACT!—always schedule your activities by going to the contact record of the person with whom you want to interact. One of the most common mistakes new ACT! users make is to schedule everything in My Record. Don't make that mistake—only use My Record to schedule tasks that you need to do apart from any contact in your database.

The steps to schedule activities are nearly identical whether for calls, meetings, or to-dos. As I describe each, I'll highlight the differences.

Scheduling an Activity

As is true with most actions in ACT!, there is more than one way to schedule an activity. In fact, there are three ways to schedule an activity: you can use menus, the toolbar, or a combination of keys. The toolbar is the fastest, so I'll concentrate on that method in the following sections.

1. Use the Lookup menu to find the contact with whom you want to schedule a call, meeting, or a to-do.

2. With the contact on screen, click the Schedule Call button in the toolbar. ACT! opens the Schedule Activity dialog box, displaying the General tab, as shown in Figure 7-1.

ACT! assumes that you want to schedule a call for the current day at the current time. You use this dialog box to change these assumptions. Let's look at the various settings in the General tab of this dialog box.

Activity Type   ACT! inserts the type of activity you have selected from the toolbar. If you decide that a call is not appropriate, click the drop-down arrow and select the activity you want.

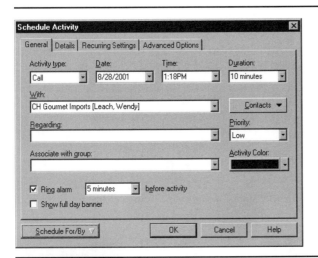

FIGURE 7-1   You can schedule an activity with any contact in your database.

7

Date   By default, ACT! inserts the current date. Click the drop-down arrow to see a calendar, as shown in Figure 7-2.

FIGURE 7-2   You can use this calendar to pick a date for your activity.

Time   By default, ACT! inserts the current time as the time for the call. Click the drop-down arrow to select a time from the list of times presented. Or, you can select the Timeless option at the bottom of the list, as shown in Figure 7-3.

TIP

Selecting the Timeless option means that the activity is scheduled for a specific date, but not a specific time. So, if an alarm is set, it will appear at 8 A.M. on that date, or whatever daily start time you have selected for the Daily Calendar in the Scheduling Preferences.

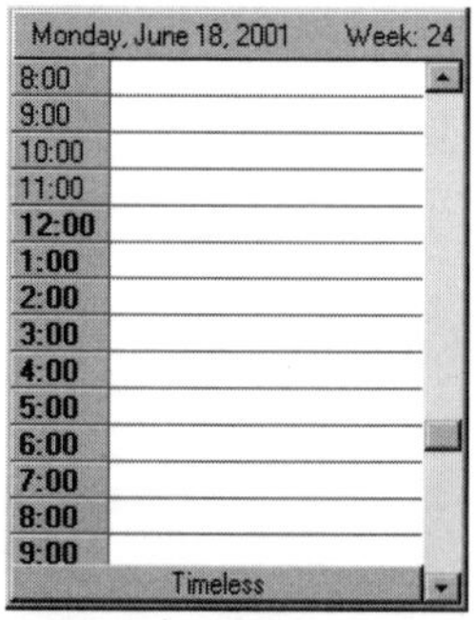

Monday, June 18, 2001	Week: 24
8:00	
9:00	
10:00	
11:00	
12:00	
1:00	
2:00	
3:00	
4:00	
5:00	
6:00	
7:00	
8:00	
9:00	
Timeless	

FIGURE 7-3   You can specify a time for your activity by selecting from this list.

Duration   In this box, you can select a single time period (15 minutes by default), or you can select the start time, hold down the mouse button, and drag down through the time periods until the correct amount of time is blocked. The Duration box reflects the time period that you have blocked. ACT! has default settings for each activity—15 minutes for a call, 1 hour for a meeting, and 0 minutes for a to-do.

With   ACT! inserts the name of the contact you were viewing when you selected the activity button. If you decide that you want to schedule the activity with a different contact in the database, you can do it through this setting without having to close the Schedule Activity dialog box. Here's how:

1. Click the drop-down arrow at the right end of the With field.

   The Contact/Company list appears, from which you can select another contact in the database, as shown in Figure 7-4.

2. In the list, scroll to and click the contact name you want, or begin typing the letters of the last name, and ACT! will jump to the nearest match. Or, if you want to schedule an activity for yourself, select My Record, which appears as a button below the list.

Regarding   Enter a note to yourself as to why you have scheduled this activity. For example, you might designate some calls as first contacts and others as follow-ups. A drop-down list is available with a series of standard entries. You can also add your own by editing the list. Simply scroll the list to the bottom, and select Edit List. In the Edit List dialog box, click the Add button and type your entry. Click OK to complete the editing process.

Priority   With each activity, you can determine its priority. The chief importance of priority is that you can then locate activities by that designation. You can designate certain activities as high-priority items, and then narrow your Task List so that it only displays these items. The default for all activities is low priority.

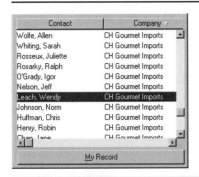

Contact	Company ▽
Wolfe, Allen	CH Gourmet Imports
Whiting, Sarah	CH Gourmet Imports
Rosseux, Juliette	CH Gourmet Imports
Rosarky, Ralph	CH Gourmet Imports
O'Grady, Igor	CH Gourmet Imports
Nelson, Jeff	CH Gourmet Imports
Leach, Wendy	CH Gourmet Imports
Johnson, Norm	CH Gourmet Imports
Huffman, Chris	CH Gourmet Imports
Henry, Robin	CH Gourmet Imports
Chan, Jane	CH Gourmet Imports

My Record

FIGURE 7-4   You can plan your activity with someone else by making a selection from this list.

Associate With Group   Creating and working with groups is covered in detail in Chapter 15. At this juncture, if you want an activity to be attached to a group, you can select a group from this drop-down list.

Activity Color   If you want to associate a specific color with the priority of an activity, you can select the color you want from this pull-down palette.

Ring Alarm   One of the outstanding features of ACT! is the way it nags you until an activity you have scheduled is completed, deferred, or erased. A prime component of this nagging process is the alarm. Adding an alarm to a scheduled activity causes ACT! to open a dialog box on top of your ACT! screen at the appropriate time. When you select the Ring Alarm check box, the Before Activity field becomes active. You then decide how long before the activity you want to be alerted to the activity. Later in this chapter, I'll discuss the options for handling alarms. If you scheduled an activity with the Timeless attribute, the alarm appears as soon as you start your computer, or at 8 A.M., whichever is the later.

TIP   *Although I am enthusiastic regarding the alarm feature, it becomes too easy to rely on alarms as a way to use ACT!. Do not fall into the trap of having 20 alarms sound off every time you fire up ACT!. Be judicious, and use alarms for the high-priority items of your day or for future items for which you need time to prepare.*

Show Full Day Banner   If you have a full-day activity, this option makes it very apparent by placing a banner across the day on the calendar. You can also use the banner for activities that you want to stand out on your calendar, though they might not consume an entire day. Suppose you schedule a partial lobotomy for early morning—you might need the rest of the day to recover, so select this check box, and ACT! will place a banner on the day in your calendar. An example is shown in Figure 7-5.

7

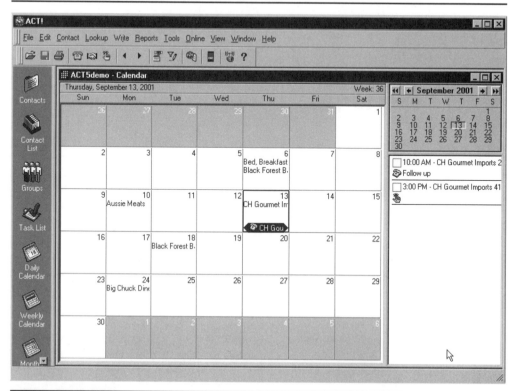

FIGURE 7-5   This calendar shows a full-day event scheduled for the 13th.

Schedule For/By   Clicking the Schedule For/By button expands the bottom of the Schedule Activity dialog box. This expanded area is for scheduling activities for other users on a network. You might decide that one of your coworkers needs to have a meeting, make a call, or tackle a to-do with a contact in the database. So, you look up the contact, open the Schedule Activity dialog box, and enter the requisite information. Finally, you click Schedule For/By, and then select the coworker's name from the Scheduled For field, as shown in Figure 7-6, and your name automatically appears in the Scheduled By field. The meeting then appears on the coworker's calendar and Task List. Imagine the time you can save with this one aspect of ACT!, especially if you are the sales manager parceling out leads to the sales team.

TIP   *When you use the Schedule For/By method to hand over activities, the person to whom the task is assigned has no way of knowing from whom the activity originated. So, I advise you to enter your initials after the Regarding entry, for example, "Call this guy for a possible sale/DW." That way, the recipient of the task can track the sender.*

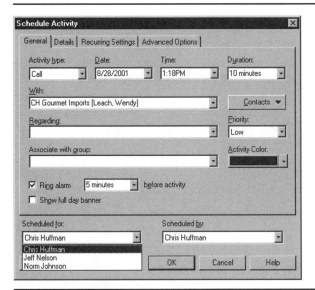

FIGURE 7-6   Clicking the Schedule For/By button expands the dialog box to show other users on the network, whom you can select from the drop-down lists.

The foregoing are the basic steps for creating any of the three kinds of activities with a single contact. Remember, you determine whether the activity is a call, meeting, or to-do by making a selection from the Activity Type list. Clicking OK adds the activity to the Activity tab of the contact and to your Task List and calendars. If you included an alarm as part of the scheduling process, the alarm will appear at the appropriate time on your desktop.

ACT! must be running for your alarms to be triggered. If you exit the program, you might miss a reminder.

Scheduling a Phone Call

Try scheduling an activity for yourself in the demonstration database.

1. Open the ACT5demo database.

2. Look up the Gloria Lenares contact record (if you need a reminder on how to do so, see Chapter 4).

3. Click the Schedule Call icon on the toolbar.

4. In the Schedule Activity dialog box, accept the default date, time, and the duration.

5. In the Regarding field, type **Example Activity with an Alarm**.

6. Accept the Priority and Activity Color settings.

7. Select the Ring Alarm check box.

8. The Before Activity field is activated. Accept the 5 minutes default.

9. Click OK.

In a few moments, the Alarms dialog box appears. (If it doesn't, make certain that the clock in your computer is set to the correct date and time. To do so, double-click the time indicator on the right side of your Windows taskbar and make any necessary adjustments in the resulting dialog box.) Read on to the next section, where I discuss how to handle alarms.

Handling Alarms

At the time you specified, ACT! pops up a dialog box alerting you that one of your scheduled activities is impending. Plus, ACT! plays the default alarm sound, in case you aren't looking at the screen at the moment (ACT! can't help you if you've stepped out of your office entirely, though). Now, I'll describe the options you can select when the alarm appears, as shown in Figure 7-7.

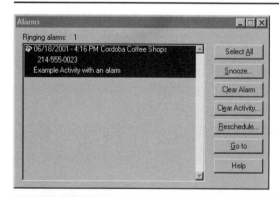

| FIGURE 7-7 | ACT! presents the Alarms dialog box when one of your scheduled activities is coming up. |

Select All   If more than one alarm appears, click the Select All button to select all alarms. After the alarms are selected, you can use any of the other options to affect all the alarms at once.

Snooze   If you want to handle the alarm at a later time, click the Snooze button, and the Snooze Alarm dialog box appears. It works kind of like the snooze alarm you might have on your alarm clock, but it gives you more choices, as shown in Figure 7-8.

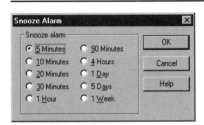

FIGURE 7-8 ACT!'s Snooze Alarm dialog box lets you defer action on a scheduled event.

Select the time period you want, and then click OK to close the dialog box.

Clear Alarm If you want the alarm to go away, click the Clear Alarm button. ACT! closes the alarm, but the activity remains on your calendar and Task List.

Clear Activity To remove the activity from your calendar and Task List, click the Clear Activity button. ACT! opens the Clear Activity dialog box, shown in Figure 7-9, prompting you to enter a disposition for the activity.

7

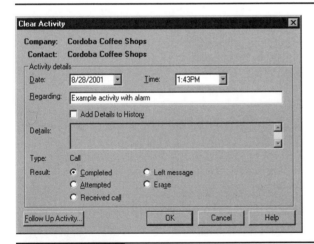

FIGURE 7-9 The Clear Activity dialog box asks you how you want to dispose of the event.

In clearing the activity, you can choose the correct Result option, and if you prefer, enter a message that is recorded with the History of that activity, or you can click the Follow Up Activity button, which takes you back to the Schedule Activity dialog box, in which you can schedule a further activity.

If you select the Result option for erasing the activity, no History record is kept.

Reschedule   Clicking the Reschedule button opens the Schedule Activity dialog box, allowing you to re-enter the parameters of the activity.

Go To   Click the Go To button to move from the current contact to the one with which the activity is scheduled.

Scheduling a Meeting

The steps to scheduling a meeting are identical to those for a call, except for the starting point. Click the meeting button to begin. Doing so automatically adds the default settings you have created as preferences for your meetings. You also can use the Contact menu to schedule the meeting. Those of you using a laptop on an airplane or who otherwise prefer the keyboard, press CTRL-M to open the Schedule Activity dialog box with Meeting as the default.

Scheduling a To-Do

The steps to schedule a to-do are identical to scheduling a call or meeting, except for the starting point. To-dos can include a variety of tasks that you perform for yourself or for your contacts, such as send a fax, send a letter, send apologies, and so on. Start scheduling a to-do by clicking the To-Do button (a finger with a string tied around it) and make your entries. You also can schedule a to-do from the Contact menu, or by pressing CTRL-T. The Schedule Activity dialog box appears with To-Do as the default.

Advanced Scheduling

Scheduling an activity with a single contact is straightforward. As you might expect, ACT! adds a plethora of options for scheduling. Taking advantage of these options not only can streamline your business day, but can make you a power user of ACT!

Adding a New Contact from the Schedule Activity Dialog Box

The Contacts button comes in handy when you need to add a new contact record while in the Schedule Activity dialog box. Suppose that you're on the phone discussing a possible meeting date with someone who isn't already in your database. This button allows you to add the basic contact record information without closing the Schedule Activity dialog box, which makes scheduling the meeting a quick next step. Figures 7-10 and 7-11 illustrate this process.

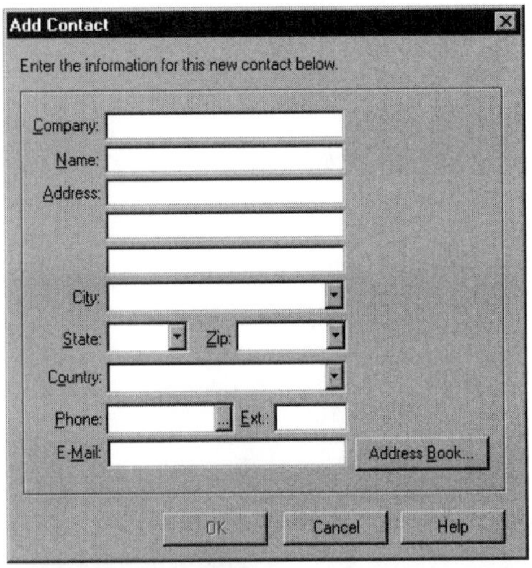

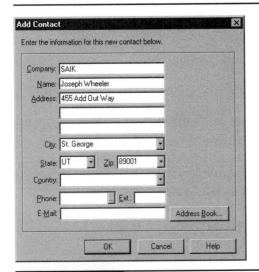

FIGURE 7-10   Select the Contacts button in the Schedule Activity dialog box, and pick New Contact to display the Add Contact dialog box.

FIGURE 7-11   Enter the contact's information in the familiar Add Contact dialog box.

Enter the new contact record information. If you suspect that you already have the e-mail address of the new contact—this often happens—you can add it to the record immediately. Click OK to save the information.

Selecting Multiple Contacts from the Schedule Activity Dialog Box

You might suppose that the only way to schedule the same activity with multiple contacts is to look them up one at a time and go through the scheduling process. Not so! After selecting a contact with which you want to schedule an activity, click the Contacts button, and then choose the Select Contacts option. The Select Contacts dialog box opens, as shown in Figure 7-12.

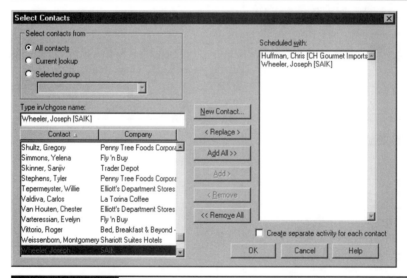

FIGURE 7-12 You can open the Select Contacts dialog box from the Schedule Activity dialog box.

To add other contacts to your activity, set the following options in this dialog box:

Select Contacts From Your first choice is to decide whether the universe of contacts from which you can select is All Contacts, those in the Current Lookup, or from a Selected Group. All Contacts means that you can scroll your entire database and select several contacts to be included in the activity. To add a contact to the activity, click the contact's name and then the Add button. ACT! inserts the name into the Scheduled With list box.

If you click Current Lookup as your source for names, only those contacts that were in the lookup before you opened the Schedule Activity dialog box are available for inclusion.

If you click Selected Group, ACT! lists the names of the groups that you have already created. By selecting a group, you have scheduled the activity with all members of that group. (See Chapter 15 for information about creating groups.)

Contact/Company   Depending on the selection you made above, this list includes the contact and company names for your entire database, for the contacts in the current lookup, or for the contacts in the selected group. The default sort order is alphabetical ascending based on company name, as indicated by the upward-pointing gray triangle at the end of the word Company. Change the sort order of the Company field by clicking Company. Or, click Contact to sort the list by contact name.

To move to a specific name, you can scroll the list (or lists) or type the first letter of the contact's name in the Type In/Choose Name box. For example, for Wolf you type **W**. When you type **W**, the first contact with a last name beginning with *W* is highlighted. This search method is progressive—typing a second letter scrolls the list to and highlights the next match. Typing **Wo** highlights the first record that has a last name that matches both letters, such as Womack or Woolworth.

If you want to select several names at the same time, click the first name, press and hold SHIFT, and then click the names to select names that are sequential. If you click a name and press and hold CTRL, you can jump around the list selecting names.

New Contact, Replace, Add All, Add, Remove, Remove All   You can use these buttons to add or subtract names from the Scheduled With list. They're pretty much self-explanatory, but let's take a quick look at them.

> **New Contact**   Click this button to add a new contact to the database.

> **Replace**   Click this button to replace the contact or contacts in the Scheduled With list with the selected contacts in the Contact/Company list.

> **Add All**   If you have selected multiple contacts in the Contact/Company list, click this button to add them to the Scheduled With list.

> **Add**   Select a name in the Contact/Company list, and then click this button to add it to the Scheduled With list.

> **Remove**   Click a name in the Scheduled With list, and then click this button to remove it from the list.

> **Remove All**   If you have selected several names in the Scheduled With list, click this button to remove them from the list.

Create Separate Activity For Each Contact   This check box requires some thought. If you schedule an activity with several contacts or a group, selecting this option creates an activity with each of the contacts separately. If this check box is not selected, an activity is scheduled with the first contact record *only*. The benefit of adding the activity to every contact is that you can see all the names associated with the activity in your Task List or in a calendar. The downside is that the Task List and calendars can start to overflow with names and activities scheduled for the same time—and, if you schedule reminders for each activity, the number of alarms can grow unmanageable.

Adding Details When Scheduling Activities

Although the Regarding field on the General tab of the Schedule Activity dialog box (see Figure 7-1) provides a short reminder of the activity, the Details tab opens a large field into which you can type an extended treatise of why you have to have to have this meeting at, oh, Las Vegas instead of the office.

On a practical note, the Details tab can hold your notes on a negotiating session, price lists, or product specifications. If the information is in another application—a word-processed file, for example—you could open that file, copy the text, and paste it into the Details field.

Scheduling Recurring Activities

ACT! has a specific tab in the Schedule Activity dialog box to handle activities that occur on a regular, or not so regular basis. Clicking the Recurring Settings tab, shown in Figure 7-13, reveals the following settings:

Once   This is the default setting for an activity.

Daily   Clicking this option lets you set the activity to recur every day, every two days, and so on until the ending date you specify in the settings area on the right of the dialog box, which becomes active when you select this option.

Weekly   Click this option to make the activity occur once a week, every two weeks, and so on, until the specified end date. ACT! also will make sure that the date is the correct day of the week, as specified by you.

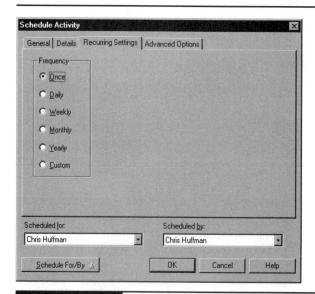

FIGURE 7-13   The Recurring Settings tab lets you handle repeating events.

Monthly   This setting allows for the scheduling of an activity that might be regular in terms of the time, that is, the third Thursday of every month, but not on a specific date. Figure 7-14 shows the tab with the monthly settings active. To use this option, first select a value in the Every box, which indicates every month, every two months, and so on. Enter the ending date in the Until box, and then select a time value under Repeat On The. Finally, select the weekday on which the event falls.

FIGURE 7-14   You can establish settings for an activity recurring on a monthly basis.

Yearly   The marriage saver! Yes friends, never again forget your spouse's birthday, anniversary, or other significant date. You also can use this setting to remind yourself of important dates for your contacts, a yearly company event, or whatever else you want to be reminded of.

Custom   This setting is used for activities that do occur on a specific date. That is, if your club meeting is always held on the 15th of the month, you can enter **1** as the value for Every, enter an ending date, and then click the date itself.

Advanced Options

The Advanced Options tab on the Schedule Activity dialog box adds the ability to send an e-mail message to the person or persons with whom you have scheduled the activity and to make the activity private.

The private activity works this way: If you are on a network system, and you have scheduled a job interview with another company, it's likely that you do not want the entire office to be privy to your plans. By making the activity a private meeting, the other users of the network can look at your calendar and only see that you have a meeting marked private. Be careful not to add too much information to the Regarding field—it appears along with the activity and may reveal your plans.

The e-mail options are to send, in ACT! format, the activity itself to another ACT! user, who can then apply it to his calendar. You also can e-mail an event in Outlook 98 format, and the Outlook user can apply the meeting to her calendar. You also can e-mail an event in both formats. When you complete the settings for the activity and click OK, ACT! immediately creates the e-mail and displays a message like the one shown in Figure 7-15.

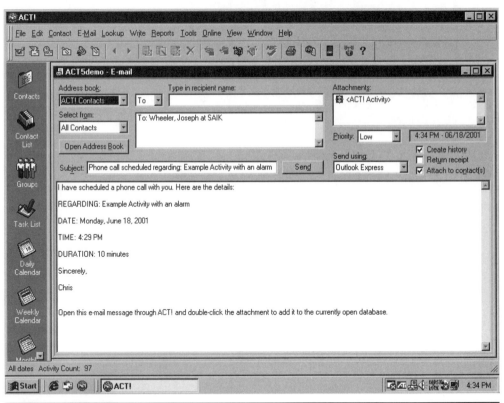

FIGURE 7-15   When you e-mail an activity to other participants, ACT! creates a message like this one.

You can edit the message, or send it as is by clicking the Send button.

Setting Activity Defaults

One of the virtues of ACT! is its flexibility. Each of the three types of activities in ACT! can have unique default settings. For example, you might want the Duration for all meetings to be set to three hours. Or you might want all your calls to be Timeless. Of course, when you actually schedule the activity, you can override these defaults.

To set the defaults for activities, open the Edit menu and select Preferences. In the Preferences dialog box, click the Scheduling tab. Select the activity type, and then select the defaults. These settings are user specific. That is, they can be unique for every user of the database, and ACT! recognizes your settings based on the name you enter when you log in to the database. Chapter 14 covers how to set all of ACT!'s preferences. Preference settings are computer specific with Windows 98. With Windows 2000, and NT, the settings are user specific.

Creating a Series of Activities

Suppose that your company has a booth at a trade show. At the end of the show, you have collected many business cards and each requires a series of follow-up activities. The hard way to add the activities is to create the lookup and then add the activities, one at a time. ACT!'s new series scheduling feature saves you this trouble. As another example, if your business has a project with a due date, you can schedule a series of activities with the same due date. In this case, each activity is scheduled moving backward from that date.

Follow these steps to create a scheduled series of activities:

1. Open the Contact menu and select Create Activity Series to launch the Activity Series Wizard, shown in Figure 7-16. The first page of the wizard presents two choices: create a new series of activities or edit an existing series.

2. Select Create A New Activity Series.

3. Click Next. The Series Date page asks whether the new series has a start date or a due date. Entering a start date means that all other activities occur after that date. Providing a due date schedules the activities working backward from that date. Select the Start Date option, and click Next. The First Activity page appears, as shown in Figure 7-17.

4. Select from the drop-down lists, or enter the Activity Type, Duration, Priority, and Regarding attributes for the initial activity.

5. Determine the number of days, weeks, or months *after* the start date for the initial activity to occur. Set an alarm if you like (see the caution in this section) and determine whether a weekend date is appropriate for the activity. Then click Next. The Series page appears, as shown in Figure 7-18.

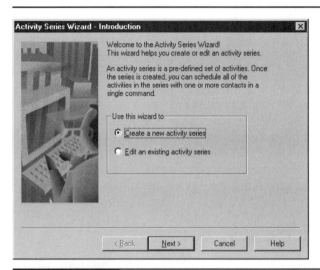

FIGURE 7-16   The Activity Series Wizard helps you to create a new series or edit an existing series.

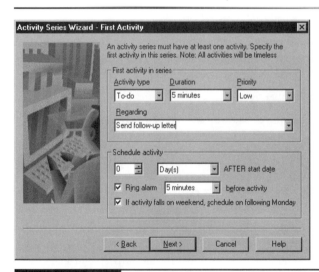

FIGURE 7-17   Use the First Activity page of the Activity Series Wizard to enter the initial activity in the series.

 *It is not a good idea to set alarms for activity series. Let's say you attend a trade show and have gathered the names of 200 people who should be contacted for follow-up. If you've set an alarm for this series, 200 alarms will go off when you start ACT!, which will take forever and slow down ACT! for everyone on the network.*

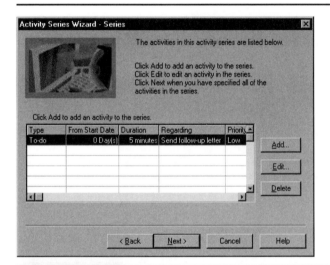

FIGURE 7-18   The Series page shows the initial activity that you have scheduled and the options to add, edit, or delete subsequent activities.

6. Add the subsequent activities to the series. To begin, click the Add button. The Add Activity dialog box appears, in which you can add a second activity. Enter the attributes for this activity. As you enter multiple activities, you can scroll down so that you can see the previous activities scheduled and determine the date spacing.

7. Add all the activities you want, and then click Next.

8. On the Finish page, shown in Figure 7-19, enter a name for the series and a description so that you can recall the purpose of the series. Click Finish to close the wizard.

Applying a Series of Activities to Contacts

With a series of activities created and saved, the next step is to apply the series to a contact or to multiple contacts. Here's how:

1. Look up a contact record or create a lookup if you want to apply a series to multiple contacts.

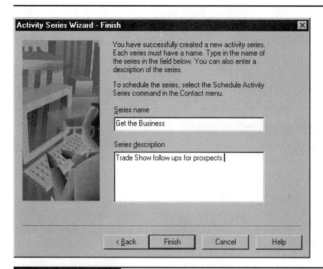

FIGURE 7-19 Add a name and a description for the series on the Finish page.

2.   Open the Contact menu and select Schedule Activity Series. The Schedule Activity Series dialog box opens, as shown in Figure 7-20.

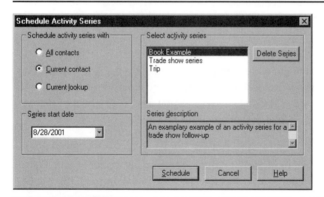

FIGURE 7-20 You can apply an existing series to a single contact or to multiple contacts.

3. Select the contacts with whom you want to schedule the activity series: All Contacts, Current Contact, or Current Lookup. Enter a start date, and then select the activity series.

4. Click the Schedule button, and ACT! begins adding the activities to the contact records you have chosen.

ACT!'s series scheduling ability is an extremely powerful tool and should save you many hours.

If you select many contact records to add a series to, and the activity series includes several activities, ACT! could take quite a while to add the activities to each record. You might want to take a tea break while this occurs.

Editing an Activity

7

After creating an activity, you might need to make adjustments to it. The activity record is stored in several places. It can be found on the Activity tab for the contact record or listed in your Task List. It can also be found on your calendars. Changes to the activity can be made from any of these locations.

Editing an Activity from the Contact Record Activity Tab

Let's start with the most direct method—editing an activity from the contact record. To do so, follow these steps:

1. Open the Lookup menu to locate the contact record that includes an activity you want to modify.

2. Click the Activity tab. If the activity is listed, you can edit it. If it isn't, then you must check the filter settings. The filter is used to customize the view of the activities on the list.

3. Click the Filter button in the upper-left of the Activities tab and check the following settings:

   Types To Show   Be sure that all the types of activities are selected.

   Priorities To Show   Be sure that all priorities are chosen.

   Dates To Show   Be sure the setting is All dates.

   Select Users   If you are on a network, be sure your name is selected.

4. Click the gray box that precedes the activity you want to edit and then right-click. A shortcut menu appears, as shown in Figure 7-21.

Schedule ▶
Reschedule Activity...
View/Edit Activity Details...
Send Activity...

Clear Activity...
Clear Multiple Activities...
Erase Activity

Go to Contact
Create Lookup

Phone Contact...

Filter Activities...
Add Columns...

Print Activities

Preferences...

FIGURE 7-21 Right-click an activity to display this shortcut menu.

5. There are a plethora of choices. For this example, choose Reschedule Activity. The Schedule Activity dialog box appears.

6. Make the change you want to the activity.

7. Click OK.

The dialog box closes, and the activity is changed.

Editing an Activity from the Calendar

Chapter 9 focuses on the ACT! calendars. However, take a moment to look at the Daily Calendar to see how you can modify an activity.

1. Open the Daily Calendar by clicking its icon in the view bar. The Daily Calendar appears, as shown in Figure 7-22.

2. Right-click the activity you want to modify. The shortcut menu appears, identical to the one you saw in the previous section.

3. Select Reschedule Activity. The Schedule Activity dialog box appears.

4. Make the changes you want to the activity.

5. Click OK.

The activity is modified in the calendar and on the Activity tab of the contact record.

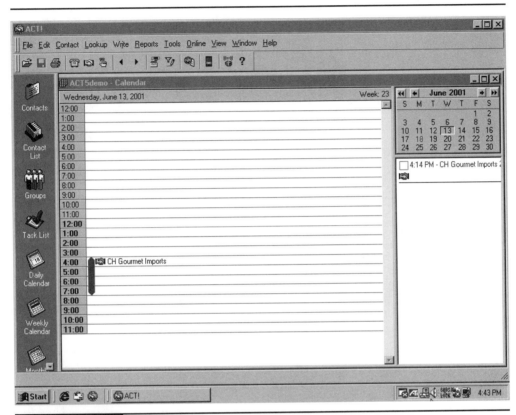

FIGURE 7-22   You can modify activities in the Daily Calendar.

Editing an Activity from the Task List

ACT!'s Task List is where you should begin your business day! Chapter 8 is entirely devoted to it for that reason. But, because you can modify an activity by using the Task List, let's take a look at this quick example:

1. Open the Task List by clicking the Task List icon in the view bar.

    All the activities, for all contact records, appear in the Task List, as shown in Figure 7-23.

2. Click the gray box that precedes the activity you want to modify.

3. Right-click your mouse to open the shortcut menu.

4. Select Reschedule Activity. The Schedule Activity dialog box appears.

5. Make the changes you want to the activity.

6. Click OK to save the changes.

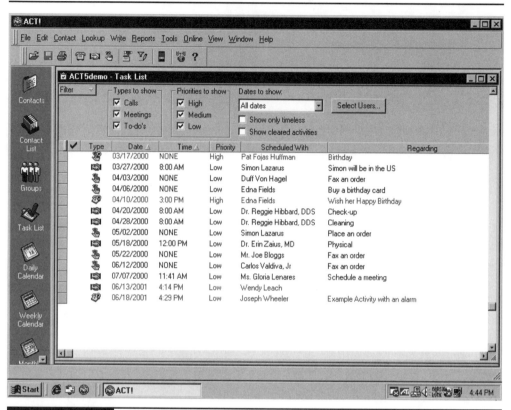

FIGURE 7-23   The ACT! Task List includes all your scheduled activities.

Summary

■ The process for scheduling activities is identical for a call, meeting, or to-do, except for the starting point.

■ You can establish alarms at various intervals to remind you of appointments, and you can dismiss or defer them when they appear.

■ If your business involves a predictable series of activities, create an activity series that you can apply to a single contact or multiple contacts.

■ You can modify a scheduled activity from the Activity tab of the contact record, from your calendars, or from your Task List.

Chapter 8

Tackling Activities

How to...

- ■ Work with the Task List
- ■ Clear tasks
- ■ Check task history
- ■ Add notes to a record
- ■ Print Task List and Notes/History reports

Your contacts are entered, the activities are scheduled, and now the time has come to tackle the activities. ACT! is intuitive, which makes it easy to understand how to access the activities you've scheduled and execute them. ACT! offers a condensed format, called the Task List, for viewing your scheduled activities. In addition, ACT! allows you to customize and modify the Task List to best fit your working style. So, to best use ACT!, start your business day by checking your Task List.

Accessing Your Task List

The Task List can be accessed in three ways: from the View menu, by pressing F7, or by clicking the Task List icon located to the left of the contact record screen, second from the right. A Task List appears, as shown in Figure 8-1.

In Figure 8-1, a multitude of tasks appear because the date filter is set to All Dates. The default filter for the Task List is to have ACT! show you only those activities that are scheduled for today, as determined by your computer's system clock. So, if the computer says that today is January 16th, the activities for that date are going to appear. Of course, you can change this filter setting. Before you do, though, take a look at the components of the Task List window.

Right-click on an activity to open the shortcut menu, which has a host of options, one of which is Go To Contact and allows you to go directly to the contact record connected to the activity.

Customizing the Task List Window

In Chapter 6 I covered the array of possibilities presented by the column list format that is used to list contact records. ACT!'s Task List offers the same options. You can

- ■ Right-click and select from the shortcut menu to add columns to the Task List.
- ■ Click a column heading and drag it to a different position in the list.
- ■ Click a column heading and drag it up, and, in so doing, delete it from the Task List view. (Doing so only deletes the column from the view; no data is deleted.)

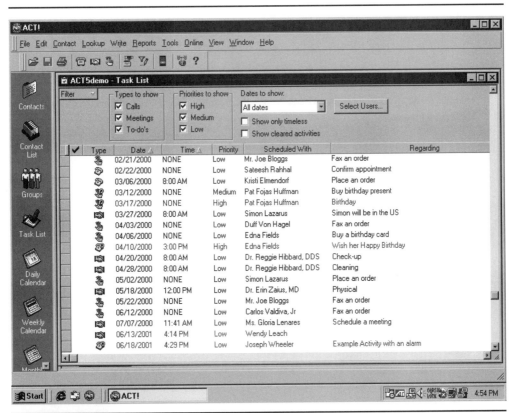

FIGURE 8-1   The Task List view looks like this.

- Click column headings to sort the list of activities. For example, if you want the list sorted by Priority, clicking that column heading re-sorts the list in Low, Medium, and High priorities. There is a visual cue in the column header to let you know which column the list is sorted by: a small gray triangle that points either up or down, depending on the sort order. The only column that will not sort this way is the Scheduled With column.

- Clicking a column heading again reorders the list. For example, if the list has been sorted by Priority in Low, Medium, and High order, the column will now sort in High, Medium, and Low order.

To see the step-by-step instructions on the foregoing tasks, turn to "Customizing Columns" and "Sorting Records" in Chapter 6.

Setting Filters

You can set various filters to get the kind of information you want to see, the date range, and if you are on a network, the tasks of other ACT! users. The ACT5demo database Task List is shown in Figure 8-2.

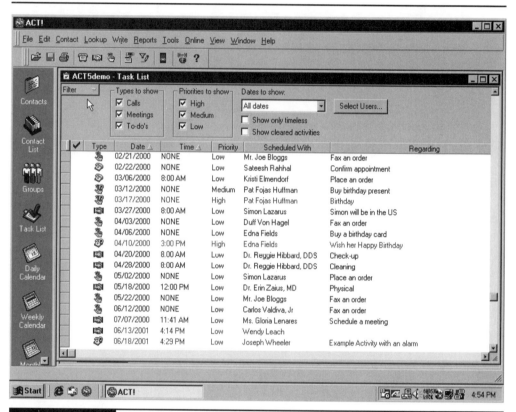

FIGURE 8-2
The Task List window looks like this when the filter is open.

Let's examine the filtering options.

Types To Show

Need to see only your calls that are high priority? The Types To Show settings work with the other settings so that you can get to exactly what you want. Select the check box(es) for the type(s) of activities you want to see.

 *You can also alter the filter settings from the toolbar by clicking the Filter button, or right-clicking the Task List to open the pop-up dialog box.*

Priorities To Show

Select the appropriate check box to see the level associated with each activity. This ability reinforces a key point: Whenever you schedule any type of activity, it is important to indicate a priority level. One of the greatest mistakes to make in time management is to assign every task the same weight. Not every call is equally important, so assign priorities and your Task List will be more useful.

Dates To Show

The default setting of the Task List is the current date. However, you can see activities in a variety of ways. The All Dates selection shows all activities scheduled and those cleared. (If the Show Cleared Activities check box is not selected, cleared activities will not be displayed.) The Today option shows the activities for the current date based on your computer's system date. Date Range allows you to select a range of dates for viewing. Past shows activities cleared and uncleared, depending on the Show Cleared setting. Finally, you can choose to view today's and future activities by selecting Today and Future.

When you select any of the options, that is the filter that will appear the next time you access the Task List. ACT! keeps the filter settings pane open, so that you can make further changes if necessary.

Show Only Timeless

This setting is particularly useful when you have lots of activities that have been rolled over from previous days. It gives you an idea of what you have been missing and how to better schedule. On a network, it also might tell you who has been playing golf too much.

Show Cleared Activities

Time management experts suggest that you clear your activities by drawing a line through them, which is the default setting in ACT!. No one has a good enough memory to keep track of what they have done, so combining this option with the Date Range gives you a tool to see what exactly happened on a specific date or dates. Including cleared activities every time can result in a pretty crowded list, so I suggest that you exclude them except when you need to review a series of events.

Select Users

The Select Users button will be used by those of you on a network. You can select the public activities of a single user, of selected users, or of all users on the network. Click the button to open the Select Users dialog box. There you can select names in the list to see the public activities of those users. The default setting is that all (everyone's) activities are shown.

If you are working in a network database, the first thing to do in the Task List is to change the setting in the Select Users dialog box to only your own name. (Unless you are the boss and you want to know whether the staff is [1] using ACT! as it should be used and [2] as busy as they say they are!)

Creating a Task List Lookup

After making the filter settings, the next step is to create a lookup based on the settings. Doing so gives you the list of records that have the activities you want to take on. It's easy:

1. Make the filter settings to give you the list you want.

2. Right-click the mouse.

3. From the shortcut menu that appears, select Create Lookup.

ACT! returns the contact records based on the filter settings. Your record counter will read "1 of XX," where XX is the total number of records that have activities scheduled that meet the filter criteria. Your next step is to begin calling, or whatever the activity is for that first record. Then clear the activity and move to the next one.

Making a Call

Now that you have seen the ways in which you can look at the activities in the Task List and how to make changes, let's select a scheduled call and see how to execute that task. In the ACT5demo database Task List, a call is scheduled to Tony Passaquale. So, the first thing to do is to click the activity; ACT! takes us to his record. Follow these steps to carry out the task:

1. Click the gray box to the far left of the Task List. The entire line is highlighted.

2. Right-click the mouse to see the shortcut menu, as shown in Figure 8-3.

    As you can see, one of the options is Go To Contact, which takes you to the record. Once there, you can click the Dialer button to start the call. If, instead, you would rather make the call while viewing your Task List, you can do that from this menu by selecting the Phone Contact option. In either case, you will be using the Dialer dialog box, shown in Figure 8-4, which displays a list of phone numbers.

FIGURE 8-3   The shortcut menu is displayed over the Task List.

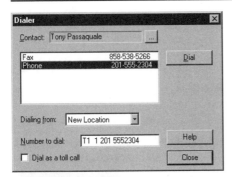

FIGURE 8-4   The Dialer dialog box lists the contact's phone and fax numbers.

3. Select the number you want to dial. You also can select a location from the Dialing From list, so if you make calls from a home and office location, you can record the steps to dial from either. See the sections that follow for setting other dialing preferences.

4. Click the Dial button.

   Depending upon the type of phone set you have, ACT! dials the number and a new dialog box appears.

5. When you hear the called party answer, click the Speak button. If you have the advantage of having a TAPI (Telephony Application Programming Interface) phone system, ACT! uses its software to handle the call.

(The foregoing assumes that you have a modem in your computer and you have configured it for ACT!. If you have not done so, read the next section on installing the modem and dialing preferences.)

The Timer dialog box appears, as shown in Figure 8-5 (unless you have turned it off).

FIGURE 8-5 The Timer dialog box appears after the called party answers.

You can start and restart the timer at will.

6. When you have completed the call, click Stop.

ACT! opens a dialog box, shown in Figure 8-6, for creating a history record that includes the length of the call.

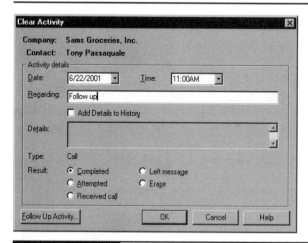

FIGURE 8-6 The Clear Activity dialog box allows you to record the results of a call.

7. Enter text and adjust the settings in this dialog box to document your task and click OK.

ACT! creates a history entry in the contact record. Figure 8-7 shows the Notes/History tab for the contact we called in the example. The record for the call is the first in the list.

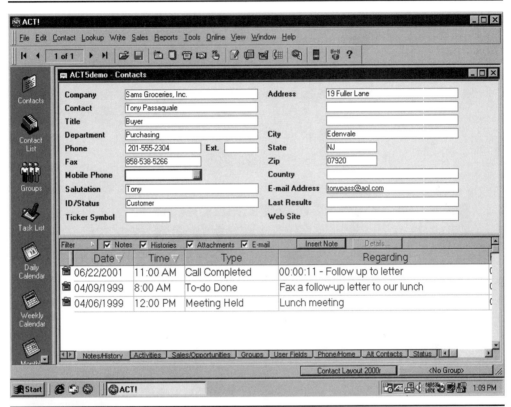

FIGURE 8-7   The History entry for a phone call with duration added for you by ACT!.

So, if you are a consultant or attorney who bills by time, this record can be invaluable documentation for creating invoices.

Dialing Options

When you start the dialer, ACT! assumes that you want to call the contact onscreen. However, you can select a different contact. In the Dialer dialog box, click the gray box with three dots in it to the right of the person's name, and select another name. Or, you can have ACT! dial any number you want, by entering it into the Number To Dial field. You must include all area codes or country codes if you choose to make a call in this manner, as ACT! will not know whether the number is long distance or international.

The Dial As A Toll Call check box is for calls that are local—that is, in the same area code, but require a 1 before dialing.

Installing the Modem and Setting Modem Preferences

One of the joys of Windows 95/98/Me is that it looks at what hardware is installed on your system and configures itself accordingly. With NT or Windows 2000 Professional, you will need the assistance of your computer support technician.

To activate the modem and set dialing preferences in Windows 95/98/Me, follow these steps:

1. Open the Edit menu and select Preferences.

2. Click the Dialer tab, as shown in Figure 8-8.

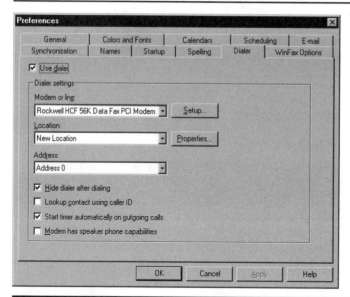

FIGURE 8-8   You can set all your dialing preferences on the Dialer tab of the Preferences dialog box.

Click the Use Dialer check box and Windows *should* insert the name of the modem it found installed on your machine. If not, click the drop-down list box in the Modem Or Line field and select the name of the modem and the model.

3. Click the Setup button. The Modem Properties dialog box appears, as shown in Figure 8-9.

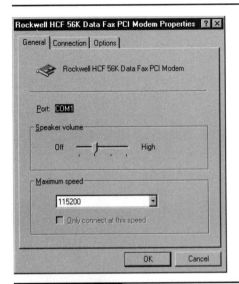

FIGURE 8-9   Use this dialog box to set the properties for your modem.

The dialog box has three tabs, which you can select to add more setup data for the modem. Normally, the modem uses COM 1 unless you have selected a different port. You also can select the speaker level and the modem's maximum speed.

To see the other options, click the Connection tab, which allows you to specify the time out setting. The Options tab has more settings. However, you should not have to change any of these settings if Windows 95/98/Me has recognized the modem.

4. Configure the Modem Properties dialog box, and click OK to return to the Dialer tab of the Preferences dialog box.

Dialing Properties

You may use ACT! from several different locations: home, office, and so on. To configure the individual dialing settings for each, follow these steps:

1. In the Dialer tab, click the Properties button. The Dialing Properties dialog box appears, as shown in Figure 8-10.

2. Configure the settings to match your circumstances.

    The I Am Dialing From setting allows you to create multiple locations from which to call. That way, if your office and home dialing conditions are different, such as the area code or code for accessing an outside line, you can create the settings. Simply click New, add a location name, and fill in the blanks.

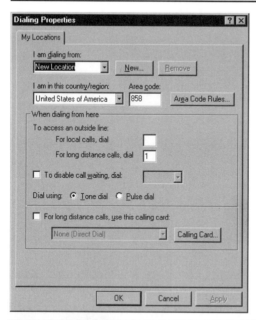

FIGURE 8-10   Specify the dialing location in the Dialing Properties dialog box.

The For Long Distance Calls, Use This Calling Card setting allows you to select a card (and the concomitant dialing instructions) that you have already input, or create an entirely new set of calling card directions. Click the Calling Card button to input the new information.

You also can designate what number to call to turn call waiting off if you use the modem to dial; otherwise, the interrupt feature of call waiting will disconnect your phone conversation if another call comes in. To turn off call waiting, click the check box and enter the prefix numbers that your local phone company supplies for that purpose.

3. After making these entries, click OK to go back to the Preferences dialog box.

Other Dialer Preferences

There are a few more dialer settings of which you should be aware:

Hide Dialer After Dialing   Unless you are TAPI enabled, you will want this dialog box to close after dialing is completed.

Lookup Contact Using Caller ID   If you use your modem on a phone system that allows caller ID, ACT! can automatically retrieve a contact record by identifying the number as the phone rings!

Start Timer Automatically On Outgoing Calls   If you make a call with the dialer, this option starts the timer for you. I recommend you activate this option.

Modem Has Speaker Phone Capabilities   For those of you with a speaker phone built into your modem, this setting allows you to speak via that system when calling or receiving a call.

Once you have configured the Dialer tab to your liking, click OK to close the Preferences dialog box. ACT! will now use those settings when you dial.

By using the dialer every time you make a call, you begin to build a history of your business activities that is invaluable for charting the future. After all, how can you decide where you are going if you do not know where you have been?

You can purchase a TAPI phone that ACT! can use as the dialer, which is much faster than using the modem. The phone is connected to your PC via a serial cable. Comdial, Mitel, and Xinex all make this kind of phone. Check with your telephony (love that word!) consultant to see if one can be added to your setup.

Clearing an Activity

Even if you use the dialer to make a call, you need to take the steps to clear the activity from your schedule, as ACT! has no way of knowing the final disposition of the call. This is true for all activities, not only calls.

There are four ways to clear activities: one from the Task List and three from the contact record. Follow these steps to clear an activity from the Task List:

1. Click the gray box at the left of the activity you want to clear.

2. Right-click the mouse.

3. From the shortcut menu, select Clear Activity. The Clear Activity dialog box appears, as shown in Figure 8-11.

    In this dialog box, you can accept the defaults, or you can modify the date and time that the activity was cleared as well as the Regarding field. Select Add Details To History, and the Details box is activated, allowing you to enter the exact disposition of the activity.

4. Finish configuring the Clear Activity dialog box and click OK.

To clear an activity from the contact record, look up the record, click the Activities tab and right-click the activity. From the shortcut menu, select Clear Activity.

The third way to clear an activity is from an Alarm. Click the Clear Activity button. ACT! opens the Clear Activity dialog box. Configure it as you did above.

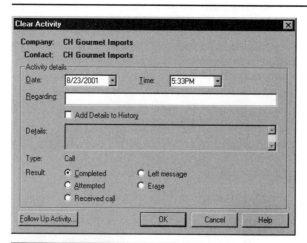

FIGURE 8-11   Use this dialog box to clear a task.

Finally, you can click the column underneath the check box in the Activities tab of the contact record in front of the activity to open the Clear Activity dialog box.

If you truly desire to become a better manager of your time and more productive at your job, following the process of scheduling and appropriately clearing activities is absolutely necessary. If followed, this process will leverage your investment in ACT! at least ten-fold.

Creating a Follow-up Activity

If the result of clearing the current activity is that you need to schedule another activity, open the Clear Activity dialog box and click the Follow Up Activity button. The Schedule Activity dialog box appears, allowing you to do so. Power users of ACT! habitually clear their activities and always schedule a follow-up.

Erasing an Activity

Instead of clearing an activity, use the same right-click procedure and select Erase Activity from the shortcut menu. When you do, it is as if the activity was never scheduled, and no history is created.

Modifying an Activity

All the aspects of an activity are subject to modification. Click the particular aspect that you want to change. ACT! opens a drop-down list and allows you to make any change you want. Here in Figure 8-12 you can see the drop-down list for the Time value.

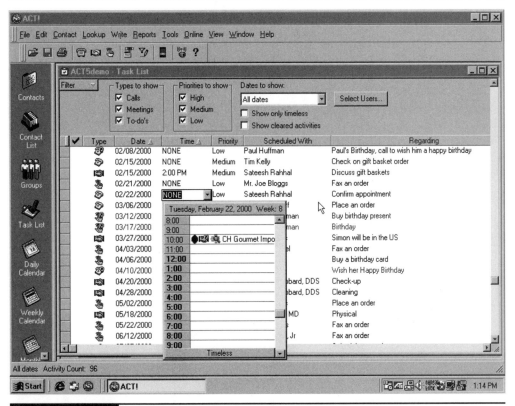

FIGURE 8-12   The Time setting drop-down list in the Task List view is ready for modification.

Printing the Task List

There are two ways to print your Task List: by using the File menu or the Reports menu. The first way is WYSIWYG—ACT! prints the columns in an identical fashion as you see them on the screen. The second way is via a report that provides more options.

Printing the Standard Task List

To print the list via the File menu, follow these steps:

1. Filter the Task List so that the types, priorities, date range, and so forth are set the way you want them to appear.

2. Open the File menu and select Print Task List. The Print dialog box appears.

3. Click OK and the Print List View dialog box appears onscreen. This dialog box gives you the choice of printing the information in a variety of ways. The most interesting choice is to print the columns to fit. If you have many columns, the information may be too tiny to read because ACT! will fit it all on one page. The best advice is to try several of the settings and see what works best.

4. Click OK again. ACT! prints your Task List.

 *If you wish to include many columns on a single page, you can change the page orientation from portrait to landscape.*

Printing a Task List Report

The second way to print the Task List is to print via the Reports menu. Follow these steps:

1. Open the Reports menu and select Task List. The Run Report dialog box appears, as shown in Figure 8-13.

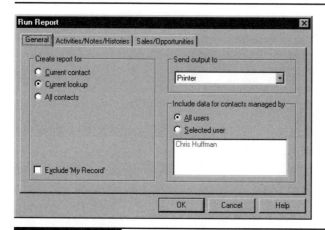

FIGURE 8-13   The Run Report dialog box

Again, you have a range of options in terms of what to print, and to what output device. If you desire, you can print to a fax (provided you have fax software configured) or as an e-mail message. The Preview option, under Send Output To, prints the report to the screen so that you can view the report before printing.

2. Click the Activities/Notes/Histories tab to set more parameters. Figure 8-14 shows the filters I've selected.

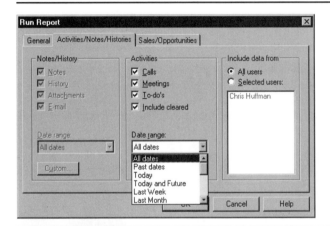

FIGURE 8-14   Use the Date Range list to select what activities will be included in your Task List report.

The salient option here is Date Range. Clicking the drop-down list offers you a wide variety of date settings, or you can click the Custom button to choose a special range from the calendar that appears.

If you are on a network, you can select the users to be included in the report.

3. Once you have configured the Run Report dialog box as you want it, click OK.

Working with Notes/History

The following sections show you how to create a history entry, take notes, and print your history and notes, among other handy tasks.

Creating a History Entry

Suppose that you are working away clearing scheduled items from your Task List, and one of your contacts calls. You could enter a note, but a better method is to create a history entry. Here is the process:

1. Look up the contact.

2. Open the Contact menu and select Record History.

    The Record History dialog box appears, as shown in Figure 8-15.

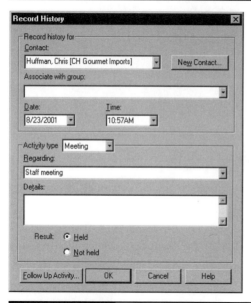

FIGURE 8-15   The Record History dialog box is for unexpected activities that need to be recorded.

3. When you open the Record History dialog box, the current contact record's information is entered for you. If the History entry pertains to a new contact, click the New Contact button and create the contact record. Enter the details that you want included in the History entry, and if necessary, click the Follow Up Activity button to create a new activity. Most of the time, you will use the Record History capability for incoming phone calls, which leads to a follow-up meeting or to-do.

4. Click OK after entering the data you need.

Taking Notes

Another feature of ACT! that I appreciate more and more as I use it is the fact that I can see my notes on a contact without having to open a window. Simply clicking the Notes/History tab presents the notes to me. The combination of notes and history together creates a synergistic tool for keeping track of projects. To add a note to a contact, follow these steps:

1.   Look up the contact to which you want to add a note.

2.   Click the Notes/History tab.

     Like the List view, the Notes/History window is a columnar report, which means that the myriad of column options is in effect. You can resize the columns, move the columns, and add new columns. You can also sort the entries by clicking the column name or re-sort by pressing shift and clicking the column name.

     The Notes field is dynamic, which means that you can type a note as long as you want, and ACT! wraps it into the space allowed.

3.   Click the Insert Note button. ACT! inserts the date and time for you and the type of entry it is. The Regarding field has a visible outline and you can begin typing. The text is editable, the same as any word processing document.

4.   Moving to another record or exiting ACT! automatically saves the note.

You can copy information from a customer's web site and paste it directly into a note. The text can be of any length. This is a good idea for those bits of information that you want to refer to without opening your web browser.

Other Stuff You Can Do in Notes/History

By right-clicking in the Notes window, you open a shortcut menu, shown in Figure 8-16, that allows you to add columns, attach files, and so on.

FIGURE 8-16   You can open this shortcut menu by right-clicking in the Notes window.

Do not clear any of the filtering check boxes—Notes, Histories, Attachments, or E-Mail—except to change the view of the current record. Why? ACT! is optimized for speed to include all four and shutting them off slows down ACT! unacceptably.

Printing Notes/History

There are two options when it comes to printing notes and history. You can print the information exactly as it appears on the tab, or you can use a formatted report from the Reports menu. In the previous section, you were shown how to add or delete the columns on the tab. So, before you print using the first method, you may wish to make adjustments to the columns.

Standard Printing

The fastest way to print the notes only is as follows:

1. Look up the contact for which you want to print the notes.

2. Click the Notes/History tab.

3. Clear the check boxes for Histories, Attachments, and E-Mail. That way, ACT! prints only the Notes. (Or leave them selected if you want to print one or more of the other types of information stored on this tab.)

4. Open the File menu and select Print Notes/History.

5. The Print dialog box opens. Click OK. The Print List Window dialog box appears, as shown in Figure 8-17.

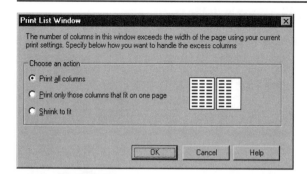

FIGURE 8-17 Use the Print List Window dialog box to determine how your columns will fit on the printed page.

6. Configure as needed and click OK.

To print history only or attachments or e-mail, follow the same steps, making sure the appropriate check box is selected in step 3.

 *When you print the notes via the File menu all notes on the record are included; you cannot define a date range.*

Printing a Notes/History Report

If printing the information directly from the Notes/History tab does not give you what you want, try a Notes/History report. The report is designed to offer the most likely options you would need. To access the report, follow these steps:

1.   Open the Reports menu and select Notes/History.

The Run Report dialog box appears, as shown in Figure 8-18.

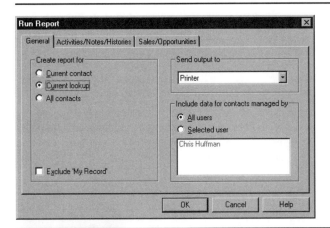

FIGURE 8-18   Use the Run Report dialog box to modify report options.

In this dialog box, you have the option to include more than the current record in the report, whereas in the prior method, only the current record could be included.

2.   Select the records you want to include, and then click the Activities/Notes/Histories tab and select the settings that you desire.

3.   Click OK to print.

 *For more details on reports, including information about customizing them, refer to Chapter 19.*

Attaching a File to a Contact Record

In many business situations, you need to have crucial information at your command. An example might be a spreadsheet that has been used to generate a quotation on a development project. Or it could be a contract that was not created via ACT! that you want to be able to open with a mouse click while speaking to the contact.

To attach a file to a particular contact, follow these steps:

1. Look up the record to which you want a file attached.

2. Open the Contact menu and select Attach File. ACT! opens the Attach File dialog box.

3. Locate the file by using the dialog box's built-in file navigation system.

4. Click OK.

When you create an attachment, you might not see it listed (a small icon appears) until you turn the attachment option off, and then back on, or until you move to another record and then return. If you still don't see the attachments, make sure the filter shows Attachments as selected. Otherwise, the attachments are there but you cannot see them.

Changing Fonts

The font size and style can be modified for both notes and history records. The default size is quite small and might be okay for a desktop computer, but on a laptop, it's tough to read. Follow these steps to change the character style:

1. Open the Edit menu and select Preferences.

2. Click the Colors And Fonts tab, as shown in Figure 8-19. Notes/History Tab should appear in the Customize list.

3. Click the Font button. The Font dialog box appears, as shown in Figure 8-20.

4. Select the size and style you desire. ACT! gives you a preview (in the Sample box) of how the font will appear as you make your choices.

5. Click OK.

6. Select the color of the text and the background for the Notes/History tab, if you like. You can also select the Show Grid Lines option, which makes it easier to see each individual entry.

7. Click Apply to see the effect of the changes you have selected. If you are satisfied, click OK.

Figure 8-21 shows the text enlarged to 14 point and grid lines selected.

As you may have guessed, you can make the same sorts of changes to text in all the tabs, in e-mail, and in the contact list.

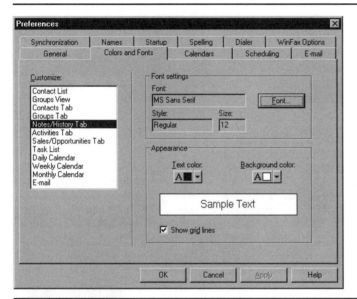

FIGURE 8-19   The Colors And Fonts tab allows you to select a personalized scheme.

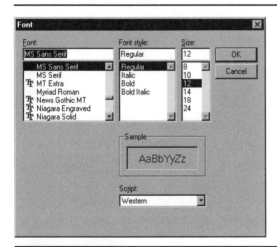

FIGURE 8-20   Select the font type and size in the Font dialog box.

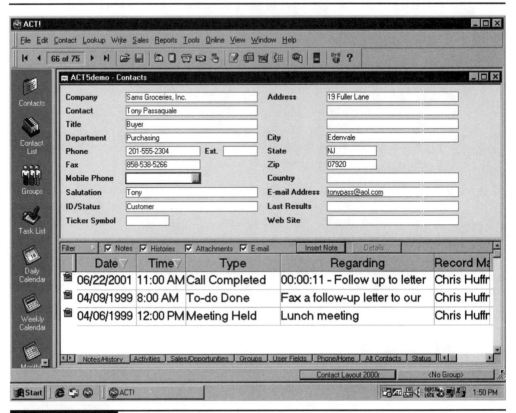

FIGURE 8-21   The Notes/History tab appears here with enlarged text.

Summary

■ To see all of your activities with every contact record, open the Task List by clicking
the Task List button in the view bar to the left of the contact window.

■ After viewing the Task List and making filter settings, click the Create Lookup button
to start completing each task.

■ Clear the activity when a resolution occurs. This makes you a power user of ACT!

■ Adding notes to a contact record is a powerful way to keep yourself and everyone on
your team up to speed on the contact.

■ The Task List can be printed as you see it on the screen or in a report format that has
more filtering options.

Chapter 9

Customizing and Using the Calendar

How to...

■ Customize the calendars

■ Add or modify an activity while in a calendar

■ Print calendars

■ Filter calendars

ACT! provides three main calendars—Daily, Weekly, and Monthly—and a special calendar called the Mini-calendar, which is a nostalgia feature from the DOS days of ACT!. The Mini-calendar still has some use, but it no longer holds its position as an important feature of ACT!. The Daily, Weekly, and Monthly Calendars can be printed in a variety of formats, and activities can be scheduled or modified directly in any calendar.

If you read Chapter 8, you know all about the Task List, and you probably have a good idea of how ACT!'s calendars and Task List might be interrelated. The Task List and the calendars contain all the activities in the database (depending on your filter settings), whereas a contact record shows the activities for solely that contact. Read on to learn more about how you can best use ACT!'s calendars to organize your schedule.

Viewing a Calendar

To open a calendar, click the appropriate icon (Daily, Weekly, or Monthly) in the view bar. To return to the contact record, close the calendar by clicking the X in the upper-right corner of the window, or click the Contacts icon. Or, you can open the Window menu and select *XXX* Contacts, where *XXX* is the name of the database. If you are working in the ACT5demo database, the window is listed as ACT5demo-Contacts.

List Activities Under the Company's or Person's Name?

One of the disputes that arises among users of ACT! is whether a person primarily deals with a company or a person at that company. This dispute is not an academic exercise. Because ACT! is oriented toward people, the default setting for displaying activities on your calendar is by name of the person with whom you have scheduled the activity. This is fine for most, but the argument is made that it is just as important to know which activity pertains to which company. ACT! does not show both, so you are going to have to make a choice. I suggest that you try the default of having the contact name and see if it is effective.

To view an example, open your database or the ACT5demo database and take a look at the Monthly Calendar shown in Figure 9-1.

To see the difference the company name makes, follow these steps:

1. Open the Edit menu and select Preferences. The Preferences dialog box appears, as shown in Figure 9-2.

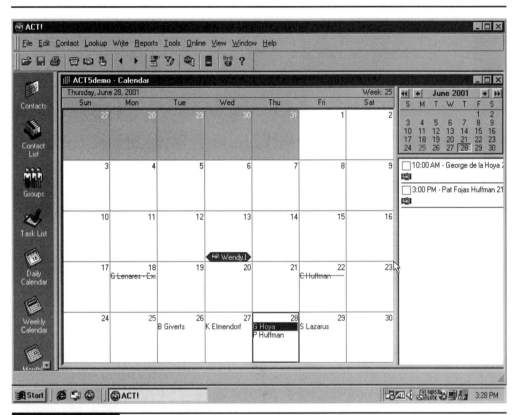

FIGURE 9-1   The monthly calendar display in ACT! shows the contact name and scheduled activities.

2.   Click the Calendars tab.

3.   Under On Calendars Show, select Company Name.

4.   Click OK to close the dialog box.

Figure 9-3 shows the results of the change. (Note that activities with contacts whose record shows no company name are listed under the contact name.) You may find this view works better for you; it is a matter of personal preference.

NOTE   *If you are using ACT! on a network, the calendar setting you make here affects only your view of the calendar—no one else's.*

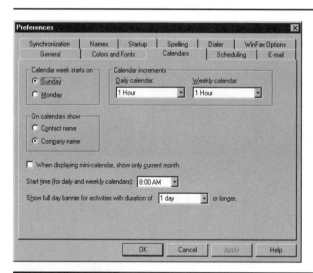

FIGURE 9-2   Use the Calendars tab in the Preferences dialog box to make changes to your calendar settings.

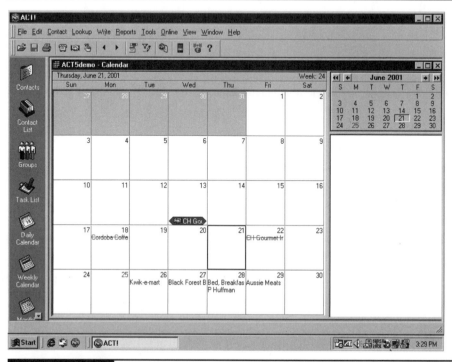

FIGURE 9-3   You can display the Monthly Calendar with the company name and activities displayed.

The Monthly Calendar

The Monthly Calendar view is the one I prefer. I can look at it and it reminds me of upcoming meetings or events for which I have to plan and makes it easy to schedule new activities because I can easily see where I have free time.

 *If you schedule many activities for a particular day, when you select that date on the calendar, you may have to scroll to see all your activities.*

The Weekly Calendar

The Weekly Calendar is shown in Figure 9-4. As you can see in this figure and the ones preceding, the calendars have a very similar design. The Weekly Calendar assumes that your working week begins on Monday. The start date for the week can be changed to Sunday by using the Preferences dialog box (shown in Figure 9-2). Under Calendar Week Starts On, select Sunday.

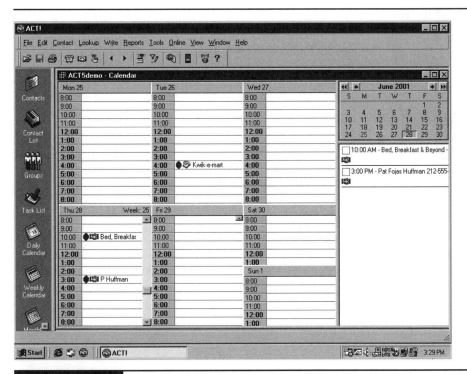

FIGURE 9-4   The ACT! Weekly Calendar looks like this.

The Daily Calendar

Take a moment to look at the Daily Calendar. If the Monthly Calendar is open, you don't have
to close it. Simply click the Daily Calendar icon in the view bar and ACT! replaces the current
calendar with the selected calendar, as shown in Figure 9-5.

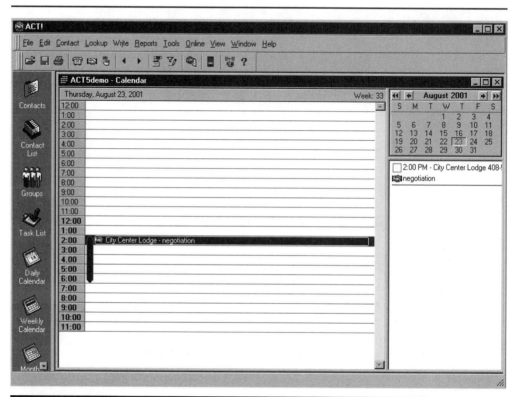

FIGURE 9-5   This Daily Calendar lists company names with activities.

The length of the colored vertical bar preceding the activity indicates the time duration that
has been allotted, a feature not available on the Monthly Calendar (unless the activity has a full
day banner). To see a specific date, click it on the small month calendar in the upper-right
corner of the calendar window.

You can change the time increment that is displayed on the Daily Calendar by right-
clicking in the calendar and selecting Preferences from the shortcut menu. Your choices are 5
minutes to 1 hour.

Scheduling an Activity in a Calendar

Though Chapter 7 covers scheduling activities in detail, the important thing to remember from the calendar perspective is that you can use the shortcut menu to schedule and reschedule your activities. To schedule an activity, follow these steps:

1. Click a date and then right-click to open the shortcut menu, as shown in Figure 9-6.

2. Select Schedule from the menu and then the type of Activity (call, meeting, or to-do) from the pop-up list.

    ACT! responds with the Schedule Activity dialog box, and the current contact record is inserted into the With field, from which you can select a different contact record.

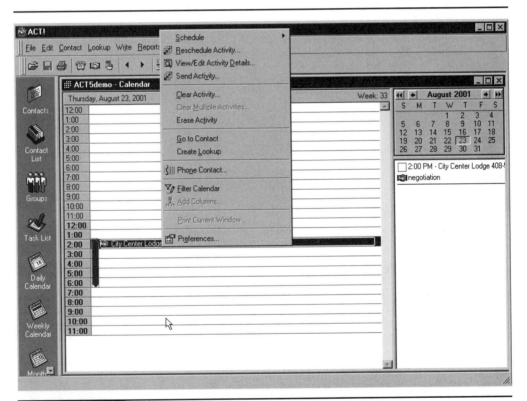

FIGURE 9-6   When you right-click an activity, this shortcut menu appears, allowing you to schedule or reschedule the activity.

Modifying an Activity in a Calendar

In all of the calendars, you can change a scheduled activity. For example, you can click and drag an activity from one date to another to change the date on which the activity is to occur. When your mouse pointer is poised on an activity, the pointer is transformed into a four-headed pointer. When you see that icon, pressing and holding the left mouse button allows you to drag the activity from date to date.

- In the Monthly Calendar, dragging an activity to a different day maintains all the other activity settings, such as time of the activity.

- In the Weekly Calendar, the activity can be dragged to a new date and time within the same week.

- In the Daily Calendar, the activity can be dragged to a new time.

To further modify an activity, you can use the shortcut menu to make the additional changes. To do so, follow these steps:

1. Right-click the activity you want to modify. The shortcut menu appears.

2. Select Reschedule Activity. The Schedule Activity dialog box appears.

3. Make the changes as needed. (See Chapter 7, for more information on scheduling.)

4. Click OK to finish the change.

 *Clicking and dragging is the easiest way to change the date of an activity. I use this technique all the time when speaking to clients who need to change a scheduled appointment.*

Viewing and Editing Activity Details

If there are any details attached to an activity, you see a small magnifying class that indicates the presence thereof and you can edit, delete, or append those details by clicking the activity and then right-clicking to open the menu and selecting this option.

Sending an Activity to Another Person

ACT! has the ability to send an activity that is scheduled with a person to that person if he or she is another ACT! user or is a Microsoft Outlook user. The activity is attached to an e-mail message and added to the receiver's database. To send an activity, follow these steps:

1. Right-click the activity. The shortcut menu appears.

2. Select Send Activity. The Format Options dialog box appears.

   The choices in this dialog box, shown in Figure 9-7, are straightforward. It helps to know which application the receiver is using, but it is not crucial.

3. Select the format.

4. Click Continue. The ACT! E-Mail window appears, as shown in Figure 9-8.

5. Complete the e-mail and send it, or cancel. Even if you have selected a different e-mail system such as Outlook, the message is created in ACT!'s E-Mail window and then sent to the Outlook outbox for the actual send.

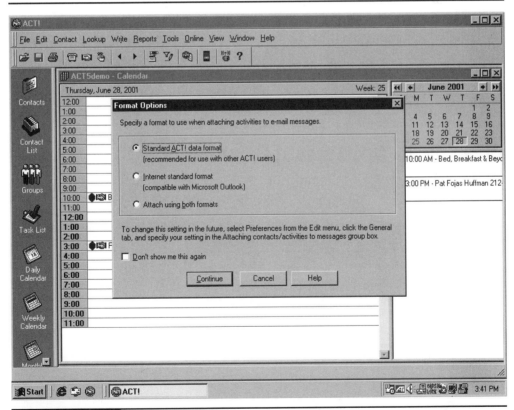

FIGURE 9-7   The Format Options dialog box appears when you are sending an activity to an ACT! or Outlook user.

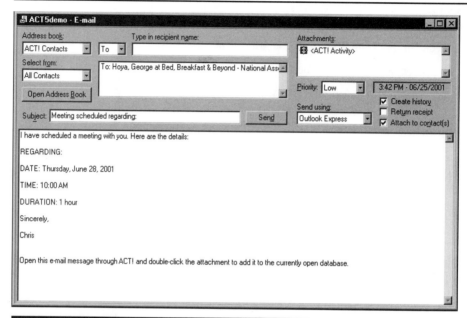

FIGURE 9-8 The ACT! E-Mail window with an activity ready to send.

Clearing an Activity in a Calendar

To clear an activity from any of the calendars, right-click the activity and select Clear Activity from the shortcut menu. Figure 9-9 shows the Clear Activity dialog box.

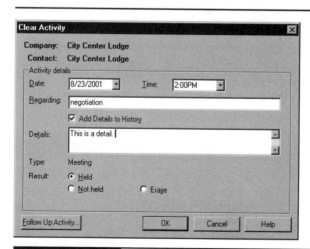

FIGURE 9-9 The Clear Activity dialog box is for disposing of an activity.

The clearing action you can take depends on the activity and what has happened. All of the choices add the results of the activity to the History tab, *unless* you choose the Erase option. To add a new activity, click the Follow Up Activity button and ACT! displays the Schedule Activity dialog box.

Clearing Multiple Activities

The Clear Multiple Activities command on the shortcut menu is not active in any of the calendar views. The only way you can clear more than one activity at a time is to go to the Activities tab of the contact, or via the Task List.

Erasing an Activity

The Erase Activity command on the shortcut menu eradicates an activity leaving no trace. No history record is created, so it is as if the activity was never scheduled. Use this only if you are certain that you need not track what happened to the activity.

Going Directly to a Contact Record

This is a very handy option on the calendar shortcut menu—especially if you have forgotten why you have an item on your calendar. From any calendar, right-click an activity, and from the shortcut menu, select Go To Contact. ACT! closes the calendar and displays the contact record for whom the activity is scheduled.

9

Creating a Lookup from the Calendar

There might be times when you want to create a lookup of contact records that have activities scheduled for the day displayed, the displayed week, or displayed month. Right-click the activity and select Create Lookup. ACT! closes the calendar view and shows you a lookup of those contact records. So, if 15 activities appeared on the calendar, your lookup should read "1 of 15"— unless you have scheduled multiple activities with the same contact.

Phoning the Contact

The Phone Contact command is covered in detail in Chapter 8. Select this option if you want to start the dialer and place a call to the person with whom the activity is scheduled.

Filtering the Calendar, or How to Legitimately Snoop on Your Coworkers

This topic is important if you are using ACT! on a network. Because multiple users are logging into the ACT! database, each user has his or her own set of activities with various contacts. When you look at any of the calendars, the default setting is to show all the activities that have been scheduled (or someone has scheduled for you). But, suppose that you are an administrative assistant and you schedule activities for your boss. When you schedule an activity, you will not see it on your calendar—because it is not for you. But by changing the filter setting, you can see your boss's activities. A second instance when you may need to look at other people's scheduled activities is when you are trying to schedule a meeting with people who are perpetually in and out of the office. By using the filter, you can select the people with whom you want to meet and scan for an open date and time. If you are lucky, they might even come to the meeting—but that's a different problem.

Follow these steps to change the filter settings for a calendar:

1. Click the Filter Calendar button in the toolbar. It's the fifth button from the right; the one with the small funnel and pencil on it. The Filter Calendar dialog box appears, as shown in Figure 9-10.

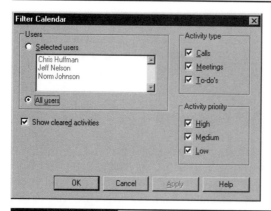

FIGURE 9-10   You can choose what kind and whose activities are displayed with the Filter Calendar dialog box.

2. Under Users, select Selected Users. If you are on a network it should already be selected.

3. From the list of logged on users, click the names of the people whose calendar items you want to view.

4. If you want, choose which activity types and the level of priority you want displayed.

5. Click Apply to see the effect of the changes without closing the dialog box.

6. If the results are what you expected, click OK. Otherwise, make changes and then click Apply until you are satisfied, and then click OK.

The filter settings remain in place until you change them. If you close ACT!, and then restart, the default setting of showing you just your calendar returns.

Printing Calendars

ACT! prints to many formats that are identical to paper planners, such as Day Runner or Franklin. You purchase the blank paper from your handy-dandy stationery store (the one that is not moving) and insert it into your printer.

To print a calendar, follow these steps:

1. While viewing a calendar, open the File menu and choose Print. Right-click to open the shortcut menu and choose Print Current Window, or click the Print button on the toolbar.

   The Print dialog box, shown in Figure 9-11, opens. On the right of the dialog box, ACT! displays a graphical preview of the printout. On a slower machine, you can speed up the redrawing of this dialog box by clearing the Show Preview check box.

9

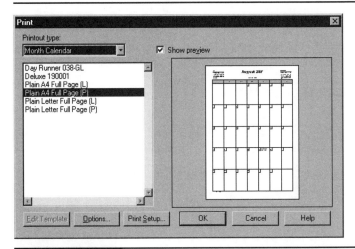

FIGURE 9-11   Monthly Calendar printing options are shown in this Print dialog box.

2. Select to print the Day Calendar, Week Calendar, or Month Calendar from the Printout Type list. It doesn't matter which calendar was displayed when you opened the Print dialog box, you will be able to print the calendar you want.

3. Select the form of printout you want from the list below.

4. To modify other settings for your printout, click the Options button.

   The Calendar Options dialog box appears. Figure 9-12 shows the Calendar Options dialog box for a Monthly Calendar.

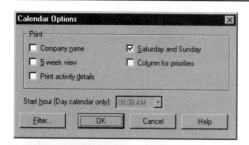

FIGURE 9-12   The Calendar Options dialog box offers a variety of ways to print the calendar information.

5. For even more control over your printing, click the Filter button in the Calendar Options dialog box. The Filter Calendar Printout dialog box appears, as shown in Figure 9-13.

   You can use this dialog box to print a Monthly Calendar for a selected set of users, to print only the activities desired in a restricted date range, and, yes, even to print a Monthly Calendar.

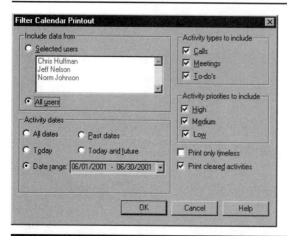

FIGURE 9-13   The Filter Calendar Printout dialog box offers many ways to further customize your printout.

6. Click OK to close the Filter Calendar Printout dialog box, and click OK again to close the Calendar Options dialog box.

7. Click OK to close the Print dialog box and in the Windows Print dialog box, click OK to start printing.

Using the Mini-Calendar

The legacy of DOS lives on in ACT!. In the olden days before Windows, the only way to see a calendar pop up in ACT! was by using the Mini-calendar, shown in Figure 9-14. Now, the Mini-calendar remains in ACT! for those antediluvian users who cannot let go of the F4 key. The thing most users like about the Mini-calendar is that they can display it anywhere in ACT! except the word processor.

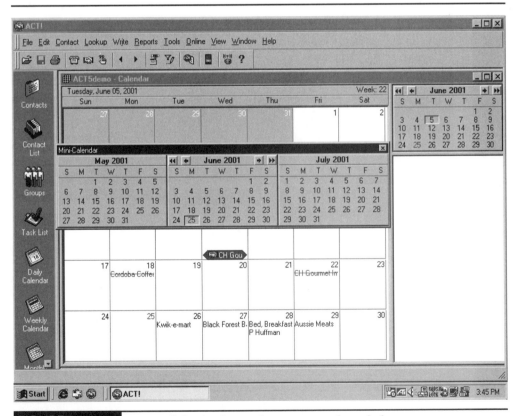

FIGURE 9-14   The Mini-calendar can be seen over other windows.

The Mini-calendar is in synch with any calendar you display. So, if the Monthly Calendar window is open and you press F4, the Mini-calendar reflects the same date. Moving to another date in either calendar moves both displays. The Mini-calendar can be set to show three months at a time or only one month by using the Preferences dialog box, as described in Chapter 10. Right-click a date in the Mini-calendar and ACT! displays the schedule of activities for that date.

Close the Mini-calendar by pressing F4 again!

Summary

- To see your calendar, click the icon in the view bar for the calendar type you want to view.

- You can customize the ACT! calendars to display daily, weekly, or monthly time spans.

- You can filter calendars to display only appointments with certain contacts, a certain date range, or other restrictions and to view other people's scheduled activities if you are using ACT! on a network.

- Print any of the calendars to fit the format of your paper planner, and select options and filters to see exactly what you want.

Chapter 10

Creating Documents

How to...

- Create letters and other documents
- Edit documents
- Save and re-open documents
- Print documents
- Attach documents to a contact record

In the early 1980s, the business gurus were boldly predicting that the paperless office was just around the corner. They believed that sending electronic messages and files on disks would obviate the need for printed material.

As is true with most predictions, however, the experts were wrong. Computers have actually *increased* the amount of paper generated by businesses. Successful people consistently keep in touch with their clients, customers, fellow workers, friends, and prospects by sending thank you notes, update memos, and other pieces of printed information.

That is what successful people do. The less than successful do not regularly communicate with their clients and prospects. The problem is the process. First, you have to write the letter or memo, then you have to dig through an address book to find the recipient's address, and finally you have to find an envelope and a stamp and get it in the mail. ACT! makes it easy to do the first two parts: writing the letter or memo and getting the correct address. (You still have to supply the envelope and stamp.)

ACT! can generate letters, personalized form letters, memos, fax covers, e-mail messages, and documents that you design. ACT! can then print any necessary mailing labels or envelopes. In short, ACT! can be used as a mass-mailing machine that one person can easily operate. This chapter is devoted to the word processor and the enhancements that make it easy to send 1 or 100 letters.

 *Although most companies have standardized on Word as the word processor of choice, I recommend the ACT! word processor because it has 95 percent of the features that most people need and it is not resource intensive.*

Creating a Letter

Creating a standard business letter in ACT! is simple. Just follow these steps:

1. Look up the contact record to which you want to send a letter.

2. Open the Write menu and select Letter, as shown in Figure 10-1.

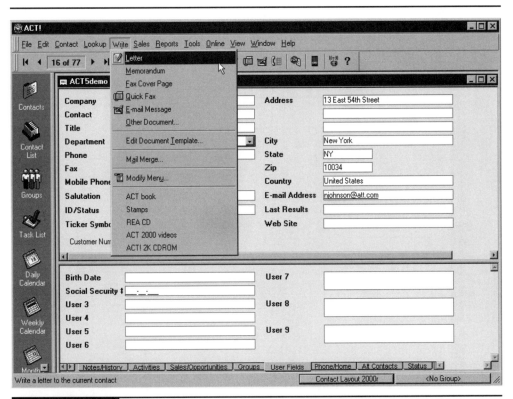

FIGURE 10-1   Choose Letter from the Write menu to begin a letter to your contact.

ACT! opens the word processor—either ACT!'s or Microsoft Word—that you selected when you installed ACT! and then inserts the inside address information from the contact record, as shown in Figure 10-2. Also, ACT! includes the date, a salutation based on the entry in the Salutation field of the contact record, and a closing based on the name entered in the My Record dialog box. (Remember, you entered your name in My Record when you installed ACT!.) If you want a particular contact record to have a different salutation, you can edit it in the record. To change the default salutation that ACT! enters,open the Edit menu and select Preferences and the Name tab.

You may have selected ACT!'s word processor or Word as your word processor, but the instructions in this chapter relate primarily to ACT!'s word processor. Instructions for ACT! working with Word are later in this chapter.

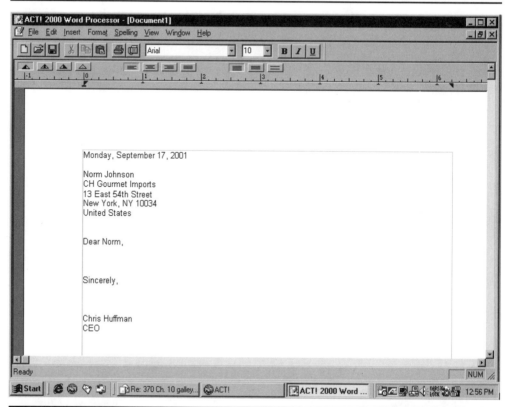

FIGURE 10-2   ACT! inserts the contact record information to complete the inside address.

The insertion point is the vertical flashing bar that indicates where characters appear as they are typed. The mouse pointer is no longer shaped like an arrow, but is an oversized capital *I*. Note too, that the letter body is surrounded by an outline that indicates the borders of the text in relation to the paper dimensions.

When you are in word processing mode, the menu names and icons change to reflect word processing functions. In the border at the top of the window is the title of the letter. At this point, however, there's no title (because you haven't saved the document), so the document is titled Document1. Had you retrieved a saved letter, the title would appear. ACT! enables you to have many word processing windows open at the same time and switch among them, and even move back and forth between the contact record window and the word processing windows.

At the top of the word processing window, underneath the border, is the ruler. Look at the position of the scroll boxes in the scrollbars. Click the horizontal scroll box and drag it to the far right edge of the scrollbar. Click the vertical scroll box and drag it to the bottom of the scrollbar. This gives you an idea of the electronic sheet of paper concept. The default left margin is 1.25 inches and the top margin is 1 inch.

Entering Text

The word processing window is an electronic sheet of paper that is extremely long—infinitely long, in fact. The words you type are stored temporarily in memory, and you can manipulate them by cutting and pasting. When you type a line of text, ACT! automatically determines the number of characters, including spaces, that can fit on a single line and "wraps" any word that won't fit onto the next line, creating what's known as a soft carriage return. So you don't have to (and shouldn't) press the ENTER key when you come to the end of a line. Pressing the ENTER key creates a hard carriage return, which you should use only when you want to create a new paragraph.

If you are new to word processing, try entering the following practice letter. Several intentional errors are included to illustrate the spell checker and editing functions. Use any contact record you want, from the sample database, if necessary. The insertion point should be beneath the salutation. Type the following:

> Thank you for taking the time to meet with me today. As you requested, I will be sending you a sample of my product, prior to our next meeting. You should recieve it shortly.
>
> I would like to invite you to visit our booth at the Consumer Electronics Show. It is booth #333, and we will be exhibiting all of our new products. I have enclosed a guest pass for your use.
>
> I hope your dog is feeling better!

Saving a Letter

Before editing or enhancing the letter, it's best to save it. That way, if you decide the original text was superior, it's retrievable. ACT! won't let you exit the program if you haven't saved a letter, but computers do shut off accidentally or crash when you least expect it, so it's a good idea to save a letter periodically, even before finishing it. To do so, follow these steps:

1. Open the File menu and select Save.

    If this is the first time you've saved the document, the Save As dialog box appears, as shown in Figure 10-3.

2. In the File Name field, ACT! inserts the current name of the letter. In this case, the default entry is Document1 because the letter doesn't have a name yet. By default, ACT! saves letters in the ACT\DOCUMENT folder.

    At the bottom of the dialog box is the Save As Type field. By default, ACT! saves the document as an ACT! Word Processor Document with the three-letter file name extension .wpa. If you would like to save the document in a different format, click the drop-down arrow to see a list of other choices.

3. Press DELETE. ACT! erases the Document1 entry from the File Name field.

4. Type **Thanks** in the File Name field.

5. Click Save.

10

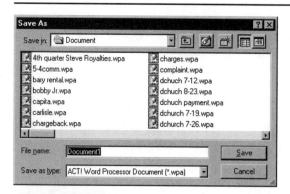

FIGURE 10-3   The word processor's Save As dialog box looks like any other in ACT! or Windows for that matter.

Unless you've saved a different letter under the name "Thanks," ACT! saves the letter and returns you to the word processing window. Notice that the name Thanks now appears in the window border at the top.

*Note that the ACT!'s word processor uses the filename extension .wpa, whereas Microsoft Word saves its documents with the extension .doc. You can use the extension to help you locate documents. If you create a letter in ACT! and then cannot locate it, use the Find File (Windows 95/98) or Search File (Windows Me/ NT/2000) method to locate the document. Type ***.wpa** to find all ACT! documents.*

Creating Other Documents

All other documents you create in ACT! follow the same steps as used to create a letter. The only difference is sometimes you create a document for single use and other times you create a document template that is used repeatedly, such as the FAX template.

Checking Spelling and Editing a Document

After you've created a draft of your document, you'll want to edit it. ACT! makes it easy to check spelling, replace text, style the type as bold or italic, and perform pretty much any editorial task you might think of.

Using the Spell Checker

Let's start editing by checking the spelling. First, open the Spelling menu, which is shown in Figure 10-4.

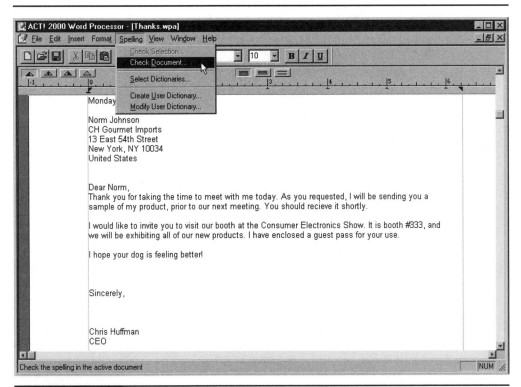

FIGURE 10-4 The Spelling menu allows you to begin checking a document and to create or modify user dictionaries.

Select Check Document, and ACT! starts checking both spelling and basic grammar from the beginning of the document. Figure 10-5 shows the ACT! Spell Check dialog box.

ACT! begins by checking and stopping on the names and addresses in the inside address. To avoid this, you can click and drag over the body of the letter before starting the spell checker and then select Check Selection from the Spelling menu. The spell checker then checks the spelling only in the material you have selected.

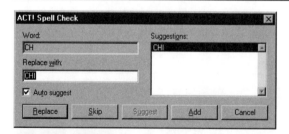

FIGURE 10-5 The ACT! spell checker finds suspect words and suggests an alternative spelling.

In the example letter, the first word that is questioned is one that has bedeviled school children (and adults) forever. *Receive* is one of the words whose spelling is governed by *the i before e except after c rule*. Well, ACT! has correctly identified it as being misspelled in the letter.

ACT! suggests what it believes to be the correct spelling in the Replace With box, and also displays a list of other possible correct spellings. The list is provided because the Auto Suggest check box is selected, which is the default.

Click the Replace button. ACT! inserts the corrected spelling and continues the spell check. When it reaches the end of the document, a dialog box appears indicating the total number of words checked and the number of questionable words. Click OK to end the spell check.

Checking the Spelling of a Word or Group of Words

If you want to check the spelling of a particular word, double-click the word so that it's selected and then open the Spelling menu and select Check Selection. Or select a phrase, sentence, or paragraph, and click Spelling | Check Selection. ACT! checks the selected word or words only.

Adding Specialized Words to the Dictionary

Many businesses have specialized language, or jargon, that might violate the normal rules of the spell checker. You have two choices on how to deal with this situation. You can add your specific words to the main dictionary of ACT!, or you can create a new dictionary with specialized terms.

To add words to the main dictionary, when you come to a word that the spell checker doesn't recognize but that you want to be in the dictionary, simply click Add in the ACT! Spell Check dialog box. The word is now part of ACT!'s main dictionary.

To create a new dictionary, follow these steps:

1. Open the Spelling menu and choose Create User Dictionary.

2. Type a name for the dictionary. ACT! adds the .usr extension.

3. Click Open.

   Now that the file exists, the rest of these steps enable you to add your terms.

4. Open the Spelling menu and choose Modify User Dictionary. The User Dictionary dialog box appears, as shown in Figure 10-6.

FIGURE 10-6   The User Dictionary dialog box is for adding specialized words to the spell checking process.

5. Click Add and type the word that's special to your industry in the dialog box shown in Figure 10-7. In the figure, I'm adding an uncommon name to the user dictionary.

10

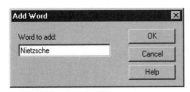

FIGURE 10-7   You can add words to or remove them from the user dictionary with the Add Word dialog box.

6. Click OK to close the Add Word dialog box.

7. When you've finished adding or removing words from the user dictionary, click OK to close.

   There's no limit to the number of entries you can make to a user dictionary, nor to the number of specialized dictionaries you can create. If you mistakenly added a word to the user dictionary, use the Modify User Dictionary option to open the dictionary and the word list and remove or edit the word.

Turning Off Auto Suggest

If you're running ACT! on a laptop, as I often do, you'll find that the Auto Suggest feature slows down the process of spell checking significantly. With it turned off, you can still check spelling. ACT! locates a questionable word and you can either figure out the correct spelling or click the Suggest button in the dialog box and ACT! dutifully responds with what it thinks to be the correct word. To turn off Auto Suggest, follow these steps:

1. Open the Edit menu and choose Preferences.

2. Click the Spelling tab.

3. At the bottom, clear the Auto Suggest check box.

4. Click OK.

   From this point forward, Auto Suggest is off. You can turn it on manually when you run the spell checker by selecting the check box in the ACT! Spell Check dialog box.

Erasing an Entire Line of Text

You may decide that the final line of the text of the letter is a little too cute, so you want to cut it. To do so, click and drag so that the entire line of text is selected. Press DELETE, and the line is erased. (You could have used the Edit | Cut command too.)

Undoing a Mistake

If you make a mistake while deleting, you can retrieve the deleted text if you immediately access the Edit menu and select Undo. Let's give it a try to see how it works:

1. Click and drag so that the body of the letter is selected.

2. Open the Edit menu and select Cut. Your screen should be blank.

3. Open the Edit menu again, and it appears as shown in Figure 10-8.

4. Select Undo Cut. ACT! replaces the deleted text. The text remains selected so that you can further manipulate it if necessary.

5. Click anywhere to deselect the text.

The important thing to remember about using the Undo Cut command is that only the text most recently deleted can be retrieved. So if you delete the first line of a letter, and then delete a paragraph at the end of the letter, you can retrieve only the paragraph.

You can use the Undo command to undo almost any action. The specific name of the command changes on the Edit menu, depending on what action you just completed. For example, if you type some text and then decide you don't want it after all, open the Edit menu. You will see Undo Typing as the Undo command. Select it, and the text you typed is removed.

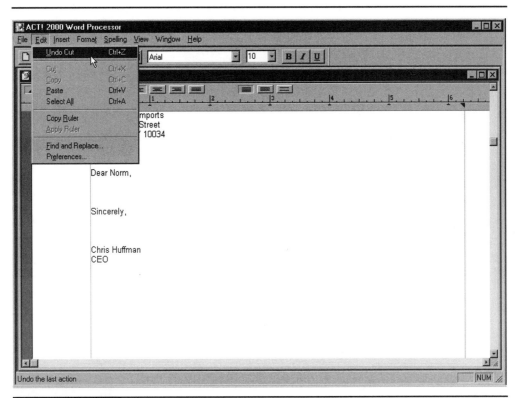

FIGURE 10-8   The Edit menu appears with Undo Cut as the first option after you have used the Cut command.

Finding and Replacing Text

Suppose your company changes the name of a product that you've mentioned repeatedly in a long document. Sure, you could sit down, read through the document, and try to find every instance of the change, but that's what computers are supposed to do! To automate the replacement of text, follow these steps:

1. Open the document you want to change.

2. Open the Edit menu and select Find And Replace. The Find And Replace dialog box appears, as shown in Figure 10-9.

    The options that appear can be used as described below:

    Find   Enter a word, phrase, or just a couple of characters for the match you want to find.

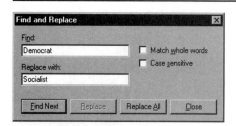

FIGURE 10-9 The Find And Replace dialog box lets you make global changes to your documents.

Replace With This is an optional entry. If you want to find only a certain piece of text, skip this entry and click OK. If you're certain of the replacement, enter the text or characters here.

Match Whole Words If you want ACT! to locate only characters surrounded by spaces or punctuation, click this box. Otherwise, if you enter the letters *act* as the match, words such as "active," "action," and "tract" will be found as possible candidates for replacement.

Case Sensitive This is a great feature for finding and replacing words that should or should not be capitalized. When this check box is selected, ACT! matches not only the characters in the Find box, but the capitalization, too.

3. Click the Find Next button. ACT! locates the first matching entry and highlights it. Now you can choose to replace the text or move on to the next occurrence. Click Find Next to move on; click Replace to make the change. Or you can click Replace All to replace every occurrence of the Find text.

4. If you mess up, open the Edit menu and select Undo. All the changes made in the Replace All operation will be reversed.

5. When you are done replacing, click Close.

Changing Text Styles

Because of the capabilities of Windows, changing the format of text is as easy as can be. You can change the style (regular, bold, italic, and so on) of a word, sentence, or paragraph, or change the font for the entire letter. ACT! always leaves the text selected after you make an adjustment, allowing you to make as many changes as you want without having to click and drag the same text over and over. Follow these steps to change specific text:

1. Click and drag over the text that you want to change. In the sample letter shown in Figure 10-10, the words "Consumer Electronics Show" are selected.

2. Open the Format menu and select Font.

3. Choose 14 pt.; the words are increased in size to 14 points and remain selected.

4. You can make other text enhancements as well. For instance, you may decide to make the words bold, too—click the Bold button on the toolbar.

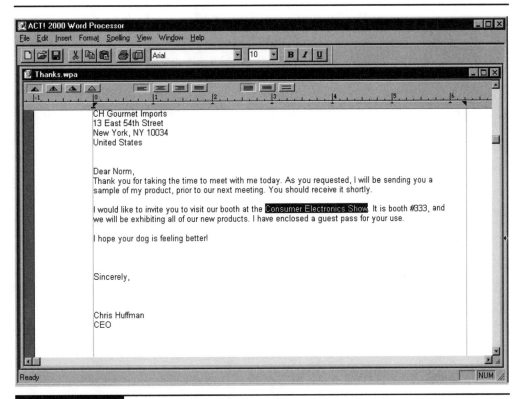

FIGURE 10-10   To make the words bold, choose Bold from the Style submenu or click the Bold button on the toolbar.

10

For display purposes, you can also change the color of specific text. (And someday, when we all have color laser printers, it will print in color.) Figure 10-11 shows the reformatted text.

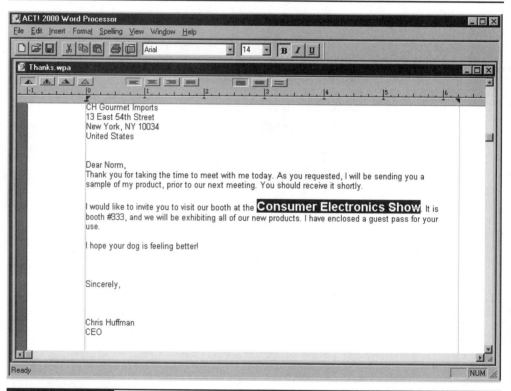

FIGURE 10-11   The reformatted text is shown here.

Resaving an Edited Document

You can save the letter so that you can recall it later. Open the File menu and choose Save. ACT! assumes that you want to save the letter under the same filename. If you want to save under a different name, open File | Save As, and enter a different filename.

Saving a Document to a Different Drive or Directory

ACT!'s installation program creates a multitude of folders for different file types. One of those folders is called ACT\Documents; it is the default folder for all your documents, including letters. To save a document to a drive or folder other than the default, follow these steps:

1. Open the File menu and select Save As.

2. At the top of the dialog box is a small folder icon. Every time you click the folder icon, you move up directories and you see different folders, until you get to the main directory, which lists My Computer, and any disk drives you have.

3. Click the folder to which you want to save the file, or click the disk drive.

4. Click Save.

On a network setup, the default folder for saving documents may be located elsewhere. You can select Network Neighborhood (or, My Network Place) in the Save As dialog box to save the document to a network drive if needed.

Saving a Document as an RTF File

Every Windows-based word processor can open a Rich Text Format (RTF) file. This format removes some complex document formatting, such as tables and embedded graphics, but retains boldface, underlining, font color, and so on. So, if you want to share a document with users of other applications, save it in the RTF format. Follow these steps to save a document as an RTF file:

1. Open the File menu and select Save As.

2. If you need to save the file to a different drive or folder, make the necessary entries.

3. Type in a filename.

4. Click the drop-down arrow in the Save File As Type box.

5. One of the types listed is Rich Text Format (rtf). Select the option you want.

6. Click Save.

NOTE

If you have saved a file in RTF, the extension is now .rtf instead of .wpa (the extension for ACT! documents) or .doc (the extension for Word documents). If you want to open the document again in ACT!, you must change the file type by changing the extension to .rtf.

10

Modifying Default Document Templates

You can change the default settings, including type size and style, paragraph formatting, and many other attributes, for ACT!'s document templates. One modification I recommend is to change the default font size and perhaps type for the letter template. It is simple and another change for the presbyopic that make reading easier. I make the default font size 14, knowing that I can reduce it when I am ready to print the actual letter. To change the letter template, follow these steps:

1. From the Contact view, open the Write menu.
2. Select Edit Document Template.
3. From the list of templates, select letter.tpl.
4. Click Open. The empty template appears with the placeholders for the field data that comes from the ACT! record.
5. Open the Edit menu and select Select All. The entire letter is highlighted.
6. On the toolbar, select the font you want from the drop-down menu, and/or select the size.
7. Open the File menu and select Save.
8. Close or minimize the word processing window.
9. Test the new template by opening the Write menu and selecting Letter. If you are unhappy with the results, repeat the process. Remember, you can always modify the size and font when you actually create a letter.

The procedure is the same for modifying other document templates. The next chapter goes into more detail in its discussion of creating multiple document templates.

Opening a Saved Document

I strongly urge that you always attach a document to the contact record so that you can retrieve it without having to search your hard drive. (For details, see "Attaching a Document to the Contact Record" later in this chapter.) But, there may be times that you want to open a document that was not saved as an attachment. It helps a great deal if you have an idea where the document has been saved. Follow this procedure to find it:

1. In ACT! (not in the word processor), open the File menu.
2. Select Open.
3. ACT! thinks you want to open a database. Change that by pulling down the Files Of Type list.

4. Select the type of word processor you are using, either ACT! (.wpa) or Word (.doc).

5. Use the Look In field at the top of the Open dialog box to browse to the folder in which you suspect the document is located. One thing that may aid in your search is to click the Details button at the far right of the Open dialog box toolbar. Several columns appear that may aid in the search, such as the modified date.

Changing Margins, Tabs, and Paragraph Formatting

Using the Thanks letter, let's look at how we can change the page layout features. Open the Format menu, shown in Figure 10-12, to begin.

FIGURE 10-12   The Format menu includes options for setting page margins, paragraph attributes, and more.

10

Along the top of the ruler are symbols that are used to adjust tabs, justification, and line spacing. You can also adjust these settings from the Format menu, but it's easier in most cases to use the mouse and the ruler. When you click one of the buttons, text you subsequently type is affected by the new setting. Or, you can click and drag text and then click the appropriate button to make the change.

Setting Page Margins

Selecting Page Margins from the Format menu opens a dialog box in which you can set the margins for the top, bottom, left, and right edges of the document. The default measurement unit is inches, but you can change that by opening the Edit menu and selecting Preferences. In the Preferences dialog box, select the measurement unit you prefer. You can also access this dialog box by right-clicking anywhere in the window and selecting Preferences from the shortcut menu.

Changing Page Margins

Under the 0 and the 6.5 on the ruler is a triangle. This symbol represents the left and right margin settings. To adjust the margins, click the triangle, drag it along the ruler to the position you want, and release the mouse button. If the insertion point is in a paragraph when you make the change, the text in the entire paragraph is reformatted to the new margin.

Setting Tabs

The symbol on the far left is the left tab, which is the default tab setting. The next symbol is the center tab, which centers text on the tab. The next symbol is the right tab. This aligns text on the right.

The last button is the decimal tab. Use this to build columns of numbers that are lined up based on the position of the decimal point. The decimal tab is great for aligning a column of numbers in a letter. Figure 10-13 shows an example of a decimal tab.

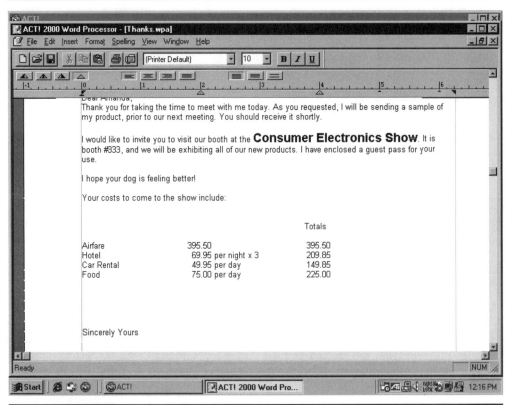

FIGURE 10-13 A decimal tab lines up each item in a list based on the position of the decimal.

Follow these steps to set a decimal tab:

1. Click the decimal tab button.

2. Position the mouse pointer on the ruler where you want the tab set.

3. Click the mouse button. The decimal tab symbol appears on the ruler line.

In the example letter, I inserted the numbers by pressing the TAB key and then typing the numbers with a decimal point. I continued to press the TAB key and add numbers. The tab symbol on the ruler line reflects the line in which the insertion point is positioned. After a decimal tab has been set, to have the tab (or any special tab format) carry over to the next line of the letter, you must press ENTER at the end of the line. If you use the mouse to move to a different line and then begin typing, the decimal tab is turned off. Any tab or paragraph formatting that you set continues as long as you press ENTER or continue typing so that ACT! wraps to the next line. You can see whether a tab has been set for a paragraph by placing the insertion point in that paragraph and looking at the ruler. If the tab icon appears on the ruler, you know it has been set for that paragraph.

Many people like to add a leader (dotted or dashed lines, for instance) in front of tab stops, especially on a column of numbers, so its easier to tell which number belongs to each category. Figure 10-14 shows the variety of leaders that you can select.

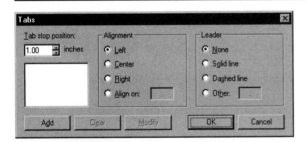

10

FIGURE 10-14   Select your tab stops and any leader in the Tabs dialog box.

Click the tab setting you want and click OK. In the example decimal tab setting, no leader type was included in the format. To add one, follow these steps:

1. Click and drag to select the lines of text that have the tab formatting.

2. Open the Format menu and select Tabs.

3. Select the Leader option you want.

4. Click OK. The Leader type should be applied, as shown in Figure 10-15.

NOTE

If you have set multiple decimal tabs, as in this example, you must select each stop individually at the left and then select the leader.

Removing a Tab Setting

Click the tab and drag it down and to the right, off the ruler. The tab is removed. Keep in mind that when a tab is removed, it's removed for only the active line—that is, the line in which the insertion point is located. No other existing tabs are affected. If you want to remove a tab setting from the entire document then select the entire document first, and then remove the tab. You can also use the Clear button in the Tabs dialog box to remove tabs.

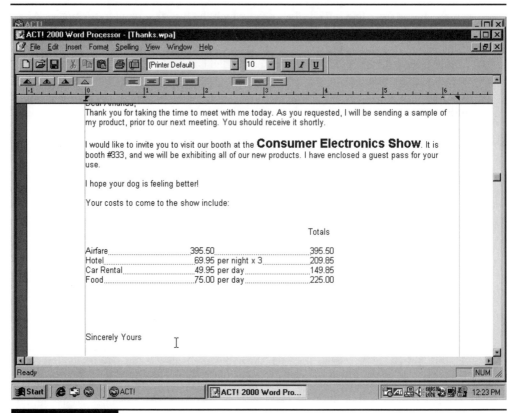

FIGURE 10-15 Decimal tabs with leaders are easy for your eye to follow.

Aligning Text

You can use the Format menu or the ruler buttons to change text alignment. Using the buttons is simpler, so let's take a look.

The three buttons in the center of the ruler are the text alignment buttons. The first button—Left Align—is the default. That means that the text is lined up on the left edge of the document and ragged on the right. The second button centers text on the page. The third button right-aligns the text so that the right edge is lined up with the right margin and the left edge is ragged. The last button is the Full Justification button. Full justification adjusts the text as it appears in a newspaper column, lined up on both margins, and should be applied before typing in the text for the best results.

Using the Thanks letter, let's apply some of the text alignments:

1. Click and drag over the inside address to select it.

2. Click the Center Align button. The text moves to the center of the page, as illustrated in Figure 10-16.

To use the Format menu to change alignment, select the paragraph you want to align, open the Format menu, select Paragraph, and choose the alignment you want from the Paragraph dialog box, as shown in Figure 10-17.

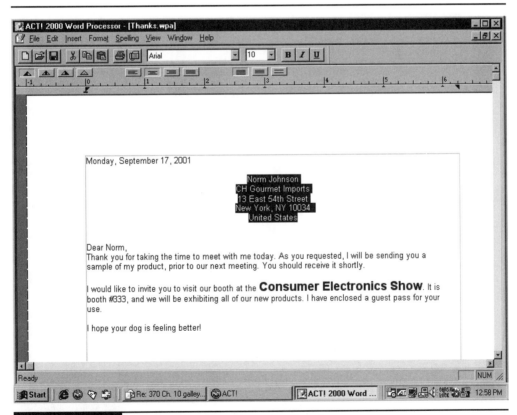

10

FIGURE 10-16   The inside address is center aligned.

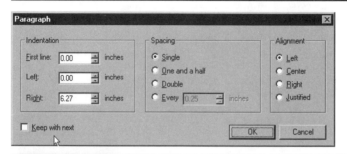

FIGURE 10-17   You can make changes to paragraph line spacing, indentation, and alignment by using the Paragraph dialog box.

Changing Line Spacing

The last three buttons on the ruler are for changing the spacing of lines in the document. The default is single spacing, indicated by the left button. You can change the line spacing by opening the Format menu and selecting Paragraph. From the Paragraph dialog box (shown in Figure 10-17), select the line spacing you want.

The other way to change the line spacing is to type the text, then select the paragraph(s) that you want to change, and click the appropriate line spacing button. Using the example Thanks letter again, try these changes:

1. Select the first paragraph of the letter.

2. Click the One And A Half Line Spacing button on the ruler. ACT! inserts the extra half space between the lines of text.

3. Click the Double Line Spacing button. The text is separated further, as shown in Figure 10-18.

4. If you don't like the way the text looks, click the spacing you want.

Changing Paragraph Indent

If you prefer to indent the initial line of a paragraph, ACT! allows you to apply such a style. On the ruler at the left margin marker is a symbol that looks like an upside down *T*. Position the mouse pointer on the bottom of the symbol and drag it to the indent position. If the insertion point is positioned in a line of text, the text is reformatted.

You can also use the Format | Paragraph command to change paragraph indentation.

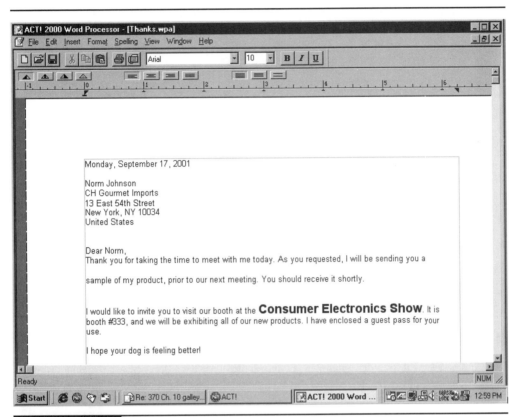

FIGURE 10-18   The text of the first paragraph is double-spaced.

Inserting the Date or Time

If you need a date and/or time stamp when a document is printed, open the Insert menu and select the appropriate option. If you also select Always Update, every time you print the document, ACT! updates the stamp. That way, you can create several drafts of a document and be confident that you're working with the latest draft.

Adding a Header or Footer

The default top margin in ACT! letters is 1 inch. When you add a header, rather than using part of the margin space for the header, ACT! adds an additional $1/2$ inch at the top of the document for the header. The insertion point moves to the header space, allowing you to enter the text you want printed on every page. The $^1/_2$ inch of space is good for three lines of text in the default type size of 10 points. You can use the date/time stamp in the header, too.

To insert a header or footer, follow these steps:

1. Open the Format menu and select Header And Footer.

2. From the dialog box, select Header or Footer or both. ACT! adds the header/footer outline.

3. After you've finished making the header entry, click the body of the letter to resume writing or editing.

All the formatting features, such as boldface, different fonts, and type size, can be used in the header the same way they are used in the body of the text.

You can also add a header or footer to a document to print text or page numbering. To add page numbers to a header or footer, open the Insert menu and select Page Number. You can format the position of the page number with the alignment buttons.

To delete a header or footer, open the Format menu, select Header And Footer, and clear the Header or Footer check box in the dialog box.

Inserting a Hard Page Break

As you type a long document, ACT! automatically breaks the pages at the standard 66 lines per page. A gray bar appears on the screen and the insertion point jumps to the next page, allowing you to continue typing. With some documents, however, you might want to end a page before the automatic page break.

To insert a page break, position the insertion point where you want the new page to begin, open the Insert menu, and select Page Break. The break is inserted.

To insert a page break quickly, just press SHIFT-ENTER. This only works in the ACT! word processor, not Word.

To delete a page break, point to the page break in the text and press DELETE.

Keeping Paragraphs Together

If a page break occurs within a sentence or paragraph that you want to keep together on one page, you can tell ACT! to format the document so that the items are kept together:

1. Select the sentence or paragraph that you want to keep with the following page.

2. Open the Format menu and select Paragraph. The Paragraph dialog box appears (shown in Figure 10-17).

3. Select the Keep With Next check box.

4. Click OK.

Printing Documents

After creating the letter, memo, or other document, printing it is a snap. Because you're working in the Windows environment, any document you want to print is sent to the Windows Print Manager. The Print Manager not only controls the printing, but acts as a buffer, allowing you to designate a long document for printing and then continue working while the Print Manager takes over the printing chore.

With the printer set up, turn your printer on and follow these steps to print your document:

1. Open the File menu and choose Print. The Print dialog box appears, as shown in Figure 10-19.

2. If you want to print selected pages in a document, select Pages and enter the beginning page number in the From box. Then specify the ending page number in the To box.

3. If the document is a draft, you can reduce the print quality and thereby the printing time by clicking the Properties button and specifying a lower dpi (dots per inch) setting or, depending upon your printer, switching from Final to Draft output.

4. If you want to print multiple copies, enter the number you want in the Number Of Copies box.

5. Click OK.

10

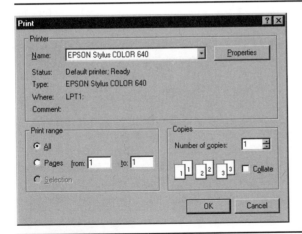

FIGURE 10-19   Decide how many copies you need in the Print dialog box.

Attaching a Document to the Contact Record

After you click OK in the Print dialog box, ACT! prompts you to record a History for the letter and asks whether the letter should be attached to the contact record. The Create History dialog box appears, as shown in Figure 10-20.

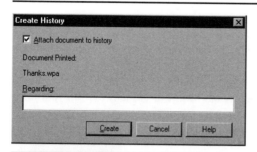

FIGURE 10-20 This dialog box appears after you print a document.

Creating a history is always a good idea. Let ACT! remember what you have sent and when by typing a short note in the Regarding field. Attaching the letter to the contact record takes a further step: Clicking the Create button requires that you give the letter a name to save it as a file. The document is saved in the Documents folder, and the link is added to the Notes/History tab.

After recording the history and perhaps creating the link, ACT! prompts you to print an envelope for the letter. Insert an envelope into the printer and click Yes. The Print dialog box appears from which you select the size of envelope you wish to print. Select the envelope and click OK. You are now presented with the Windows Print dialog box from which you can select a printer if it is different from the one you use for letters. Click OK again and depending upon your printer, you may be asked to select the feed direction for the envelope. Make a choice and away the envelope goes. If you do not want ACT! to prompt you to print an envelope, open the Edit menu and select Preferences and on the General tab, remove the check in the check box labeled When Printing Letters, Prompt To Print An Envelope.

If you are using Word to process documents and the Create History dialog box fails to appear after you print, you may have either a corrupted database, in which case you need to open the File menu and select Administration | Maintenance and then reindex the database. Or, the template could be damaged (more likely), in which case you will have to re-create the Letter template. This procedure is covered in the next chapter.

The attach capability and using long filenames to name a document obviates the need to create multiple folders for different types of documents, as the link automatically finds the document for you.

Double-clicking the link opens the word processor and the document. If you are using Word to create a letter, the link is a small Word icon. Figure 10-21 shows the link as it appears for an ACT! word processor document.

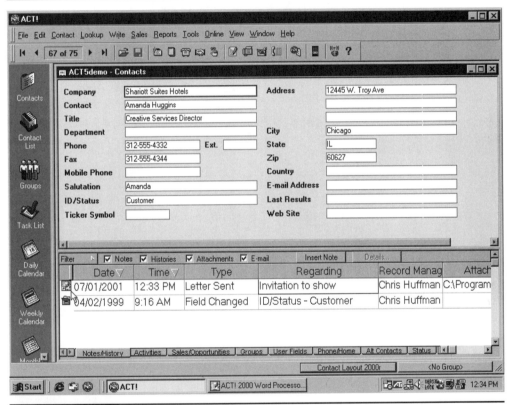

FIGURE 10-21   Clicking this link to a saved ACT! word processor document opens the word processor and the document.

Summary

- To create a letter, open the Write menu and select Letter.
- Check the spelling in a document with the Spelling menu.
- Use the Edit menu to find and replace text and make other modifications.
- Modify the appearance of your document, including paragraph alignment, tabs, and headers and footers, with the Format and Insert menus.
- Track your correspondence by attaching documents to the contact record.
- To use Word, rather than ACT!'s word processor, as your default, open the Edit menu and select Preferences.

Chapter 11

Form Letters, E-Mail Messages, Memos, and Faxes

How to...

- ■ Create a mail merge to a letter, e-mail message, memo, or fax
- ■ Print labels and envelopes
- ■ Modify templates
- ■ Add templates to the Write menu
- ■ Use Word for word processing

Computerized form letters are one of those tasks that are supposed to make our lives so much easier. But for all their power, with many word processors you still need to jump through lots of hoops before printing a batch of form letters. Because ACT!'s word processor is part of the program in which you keep your database, however, the process is fairly simple. In this chapter, you'll see how to create form letters, faxes, and mass e-mail messages that look personalized. I have also included some tips to create forms and to solve some common problems if you use Microsoft Word.

Creating a Mail Merge

If you've ever tried to create form letters with a word processor and a database, you know that you almost have to be a computer programmer to do so. Creating and printing a form letter using ACT! is the same as creating any other type of letter, except that you first create a form letter template, and then select the contacts to be included in the mailing. You can start a form letter by using an existing template or start completely from scratch. Take the following steps to use an existing template as a model:

1. Open the Write menu and select Edit Document Template. The Open dialog box with document templates appears, as shown in Figure 11-1.

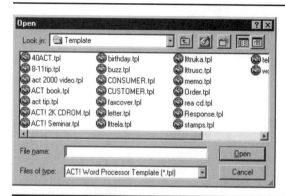

FIGURE 11-1   Choose a document template from the Open dialog box.

2. From the list of templates displayed, choose letter.tpl and click Open. The template appears, as shown in Figure 11-2.

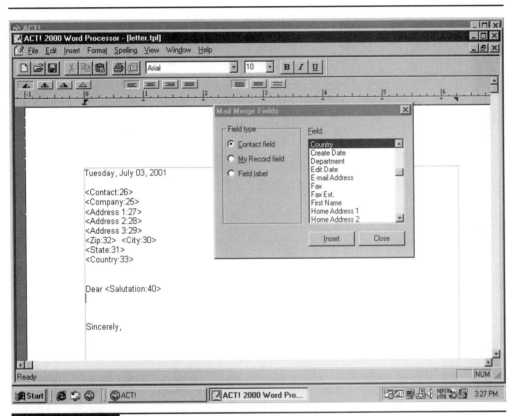

FIGURE 11-2 The letter template lets you whip up a quick form letter.

As you can see, ACT! inserts the current date and the names of the fields from which data will be pulled from the contact records. The default letter template includes fields for the contact's name, company name, address, salutation, and closing. You can then type the content you want right into the body of the form letter.

The Mail Merge Fields dialog box allows you to add a contact field, a field label, or My Record field into the letter. For example, if you were a participant at a trade show and wanted to send a letter to all the contacts you met, you could easily do so. The letter would be much better if you included the product or service that the contact was interested in (this process is called inserting a variable). Using the Mail Merge Fields dialog box, you can specify that information from a field in the contact record be inserted when the letter is printed. Scroll through the field names in the dialog box to locate the field name that has the information you want inserted into the letter. For example, if you want the name of a product that the prospect was interested in, and the product name was typed into User 1, click User 1. The field name appears at the insertion point in the form letter. Figure 11-3 presents a sample form letter.

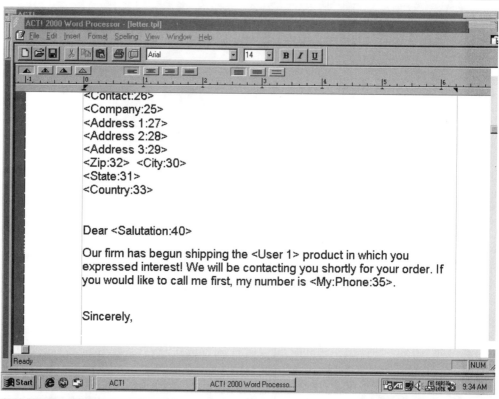

FIGURE 11-3 Sample letter with variables inserted for the contact, address, product (User 1) and the phone number from the My Record. The text has been enlarged to 14 point.

When you change a field name, for example, User 1 to Product, ACT! shows you the new name in the Mail Merge Fields dialog box. This makes it easy to find the field you want. Read more about this in Chapters 16 and 17.

Body text and a variable have been added. The information in User 1 is the product the client expressed interest in. When the letter is printed, the name of the product is inserted and properly formatted. In addition, the phone and fax numbers of the sender are inserted. To add information from the My Record, select My Record in the Mail Merge Fields dialog box, and select the field for insertion.

When you type the form letter, you might want to move the Mail Merge Fields dialog box or remove it from view. You can drag the dialog box out of the way by the title bar. Or click the Close button in the upper-right corner of the dialog box to remove it completely. Reopen the dialog box by choosing Insert and then selecting Mail Merge Fields at the bottom of the menu.

Saving the New Template

Before saving the new letter template, take a moment to spell-check the text. ACT! stops on the user field variables you've inserted and then checks any text you have entered.

Important: Save the template using a new filename! If you save the template as letter.tpl, you will be replacing the default letter template, and every time you want to write a letter, this document will appear, with the same body text and variables. To save the template under a different name, follow these steps:

1. Open the File menu and choose Save As.

2. In the Save As dialog box, enter a name, **customer**, for example.

3. Click Save.

ACT! automatically adds the .tpl extension. The original template, letter.tpl, is undisturbed because you saved the modified template with a different filename. When you're ready to actually print the form letters, the customer.tpl file is available, too.

If you are using Word, when you save the new template, simply type the new name without any quotation marks or an extension. ACT! automatically adds the .adt (ACT! document template) extension for you.

11

Testing the Form Letter

Before you actually print all the form letters, give the template a spin around the block by merging it with the current contact record. To test your new form letter, follow these steps:

1. In the word processor, open the File menu.

2. Select Mail Merge. The Mail Merge dialog box appears.

3. Select the Current Contact under Merge With.

4. Select the template you just created.

5. In the Send output to choices, select Word Processor.

6. Click OK.

ACT! inserts the field information from the current contact into the template. Read the letter. If it is acceptable, you are finished. If not, use the Edit Document Template command on the Write menu to select the template and make changes. Do not forget to save it again!

Printing a Form Letter

You've already created the template. The next step is to look up those contacts to whom you want to send the form letter. Follow these steps to find the appropriate records:

1. Use the Lookup menu to create a subset of contacts.

2. Open the Write menu and select Mail Merge. The Open File dialog box appears with Templates as the file type.

3. Select the template you want to use and click Open.

4. In the Mail Merge dialog box, click Current Lookup and select Printer for the output.

5. Click OK.

Printing a Form Letter to a Word Processor

Selecting the Word Processor output option in the Mail Merge dialog box allows you to preview each individual document before sending it. After clicking OK, the word processor appears and shows each individual document, one after another, so that you must scroll down to see them.

Printing Mailing Labels

To print the mailing labels for your form letters, you must first return to the contact screen. Assuming that you still have the same lookup of contacts selected, follow these steps:

1. Open the File menu and select Print. A dialog box appears that gives you the opportunity to print address books, labels, and reports.

2. Choose Labels from the Printout Type drop-down list. When you do, ACT! lists the label templates available. The most common is the three-up Avery 5160 label, but you can chose whatever label type you have.

3. Click OK.

4. Next, ACT! presents you with the Run Labels dialog box, which you can use to filter the labels. Two things to note at this point: If you are printing labels to go with a mail merge, you should have created the same lookup as when you created the letters. So, you would naturally choose the Current Lookup as the report to print. Second, you can begin printing the labels at any position on the paper. To set the start position, click the Position tab and select where ACT! should begin.

Creating Mass E-Mail

Mass e-mail is the most effective new means of communication with very little cost. Imagine, sending e-mail to 500 or 5,000 customers to notify them of a price change! Normally, the cost to contact customers in any volume is prohibitively expensive. The hucksters of Viagra and other dubious money-making schemes have discovered this and inundated our inboxes. So, many people automatically delete any e-mail that is not personalized. This is where ACT! comes in! By utilizing a word processing template in ACT!, the e-mail message appears to the receiver to be personalized in the same way a letter does.

Your ISP (Internet service provider) may block large e-mail packages—usually 2 MB is the limit. So, unless you do want to send 5,000 individual e-mails, you will have to use an e-mail service company.

To send mass e-mail, prepare the document template just as you did for a letter. I would advise that you not include the inside address, as that is not common in e-mail communication. The only difference between preparing a mass e-mail and a form letter is at printing time. In the Mail Merge dialog box, select E-Mail for the output. The following options then become active as well:

Return Receipt   This option lets you know the e-mail message was delivered, an option that rarely works anymore because most e-mail system administrators turn off this feature in order to reduce the traffic on their system.

Attach To Contacts   This option actually attaches the entire text of the e-mail message to each contact record, which is not a good idea. Because you are sending a template, you can always open it at a later time to see the content.

Create History When Sent   This option records that the e-mail message was sent.

Subject   The entry in this field is perhaps the most important aspect of the e-mail message. It appears in the Subject line of the receiver's e-mail inbox and is your *hook* to get him or her to read the message. So, be creative and get your message read!

As versatile as ACT! is, the e-mail portion cannot send live HTML (hypertext links) or graphics. Sending mail-merged e-mail with an attachment cannot be done either. To do that, you need to buy third-party software. Two vendors have products in this category: Northwoods Software Corporation at www.nwoods.com and Fortune Flow at www.fortuneflow.com.

Creating Mass Faxes

To print mass faxes, you must have faxing software installed—preferably WinFax. I recommend 200 faxes as the top limit for mass faxing because of the time involved with sending that many. A form letter fax ties up your computer for the entire process. A third-party service, listed in

Appendix A, can send faxes in greater quantities at an affordable price, using the document you create and your list of contact records. WinFax reports back to ACT! which faxes did not go through, so that you can follow up on those by resending or eliminating them from the fax list.

When you select fax as the output, the WinFax option becomes active. Click the WinFax Options button to see the available options in the WinFax Options dialog box. Select a cover page if desired, and then click the Schedule button to choose a time for the send.

Schedule the faxes to begin sending about an hour after initiating the broadcast fax. This will allow WinFax to do a single activity—prepare the faxes—and later do another single activity—send the faxes. Otherwise WinFax starts sending faxes while still preparing other faxes to send, which can cause the application to lock up.

Adding a Template to the Write Menu

As you begin using ACT! in your work day, it is natural that you will send the same letter template to many people. Adding it to the Write menu makes sending a one-click affair. It's a simple task to add a template you've created to the Write menu:

1. Open the Write menu and select Modify Menu. The Modify Menu dialog box appears.

2. Click the Add Item button. The Add Custom Menu Item dialog box appears.

3. Type in a description for the document. The description is for your reference. In the example shown in Figure 11-4, I have typed **New Product**. The filename is CUSTOMER.tpl. If you forget the name of the file, click the Browse button to see a list of the template files.

4. Click OK. The Modify Menu dialog box becomes active again. If you want to, you can add a solid line to separate the custom items.

5. Click OK.

6. Open the Write menu. The new letter template appears at the bottom of the menu, as shown in Figure 11-5.

To test the newly added menu option, select a contact, open the Write menu, and then select New Product. The word processor opens, and the appropriate data is inserted into the letter. From there, print the letter.

This example of modifying an existing template barely scratches the surface of all the kinds of specialized documents you can design. Also, if you aren't satisfied with the templates that appear as the defaults, such as fax.tpl, the template for fax covers, you can edit the template and resave it. Then when you open the Write menu and select Fax Cover, for example, your new default template appears.

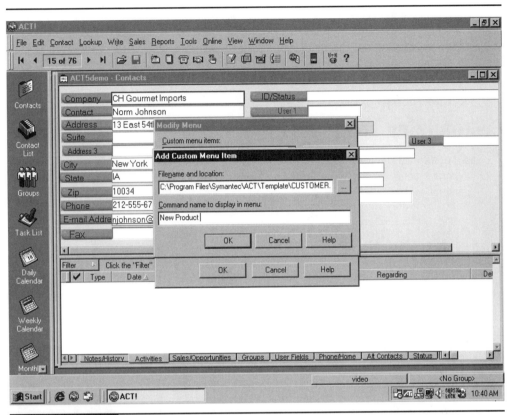

FIGURE 11-4 The filename of your new letter template appears in the Add Custom Menu Item dialog box.

11

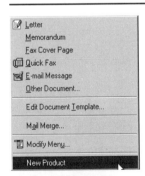

FIGURE 11-5 The name of your new letter template appears at the bottom of the Write menu.

Accessing Other Document Templates

If you have a multitude of document templates, you cannot put them all on the Write menu. To access other templates, open the Write menu and select Other Document. ACT! opens the Open dialog box with a list of existing templates.

Customizing Templates

All of the standard templates that come with ACT!—letter, fax, and memo—should be customized to reflect your company. The following sections provide direction on how to make ACT! a personalized tool.

Changing the Default Letter Template

If you have letterhead already printed, you may need to erase some of the data that prints as part of the letter template, or you may need to move the text up or down on the page. Or, you can add your company logo to the letter template and add any other static information such as your phone number and web address, obviating the need for expensive pre-printed letterhead.

The first change you should make is to increase the size of the type in the letter template to make it easier to read. To do so, follow these steps:

1. Open the Write menu and choose Edit Document Template.

2. Select letter.tpl.

3. With the letter template on screen, open the Edit menu and choose Select All, and then, from the toolbar, increase the point size to 14.

4. Open the File menu and choose Save. When ACT! asks whether you want to overwrite the file, click Yes.

Adding Your Company Logo to Letters and Faxes

Customize your documents with your company logo and eliminate the need for expensive stationery.

1. Use any graphics program to open your logo file. For example, you can use Microsoft Paint (found in Windows 98 or Windows 2000 under Accessories on the Start menu).

2. Once the graphic is open, select it (in Paint, you'll need to draw a box around it). Figure 11-6 shows my logo opened in Paint and selected.

3. Use the Copy command to copy the logo onto the Windows clipboard.

FIGURE 11-6   This logo is selected and ready for copying.

4. In ACT!, open the Write menu and select Edit Document Template.

5. Select letter.tpl. When the template is onscreen, move the insertion point to the place you want the logo to appear.

6. Click the Paste button on the toolbar, or select Edit | Paste.

I tried inserting my logo into the body of the letter above the inside address, which I moved down the page before placing the logo, but then I decided it would look better in the header. Placing the logo in the header is easy. Open the Insert menu and select Header/Footer. When the border indicating the header appears, click in the upper-left corner and then paste your logo. More likely than not, it won't fit, so you'll need to increase the size of the header. Open Insert and select Header/Footer again, and click the small up arrow until you have plenty of room. Another adjustment you will probably have to make is to decrease the size of the margin at the top of the page. Figure 11-7 shows the wolf logo and my business information in position.

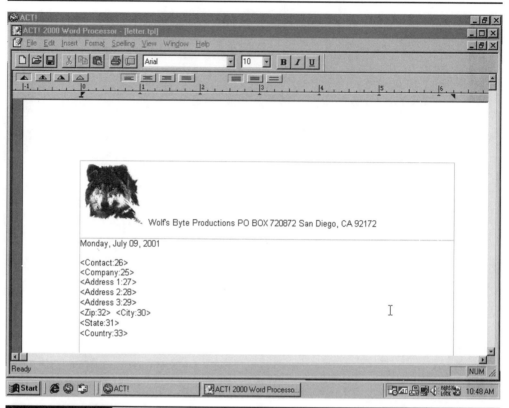

FIGURE 11-7 The wolf logo and the business address have been placed in the header of my template.

This technique works for all the templates and any documents you create. To add the logo to your fax cover, open the template and follow the same procedure.

If you want everyone in your company to have access to the templates, create a folder on the server and copy the templates there. Next, you must go to each workstation and open the Edit menu; select Preferences; and under Default locations, select Document Template from the list; and then Browse to the folder on the server.

Adding Your Signature to Documents

If you would like to be able to add a signature to your documents, you can do so. Sending your signature to www.sigfont.com with a check will get your signature into a TrueType font.

Modifying an Envelope Template

In all likelihood, you will need to customize ACT!'s default envelope template to better suit your needs. This default template prints the return address as derived from the My Record. Most companies use preprinted envelopes and, therefore, have no need for the return address to be printed on the envelope. You can easily rectify this problem by modifying the envelope template as follows:

1. Open the File menu and select Print.

2. From the dialog box, pull down the list and select Envelopes.

3. From the list of envelopes, select #10, and then click Edit Template. The underlying design is revealed with placeholders representing the actual data that is inserted at printing, as shown in Figure 11-8.

4. Remove all the fields in the return address portion of the envelope by selecting all the fields, right-clicking them, and selecting Cut from the shortcut menu.

    The fields are deleted.

5. Save the new template by opening the File menu and selecting Save.

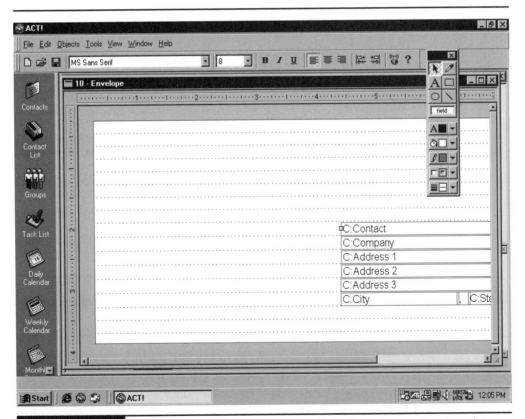

FIGURE 11-8   You can delete the return address fields from the envelope template.

 *There may be times when you want to create a modified template but need to save the original. If so, use the Files | Save As command and give the template a new name.*

Printing Envelopes

Many users of ACT! have problems getting envelopes to print properly. Envelopes are printed via a report that's created by, and can be modified by, the ACT! Report Writer. When you print a letter, ACT! asks you whether you want to print an envelope. ACT! then accesses the default envelope.env file. It should work with your printer. If it doesn't print the information you want or doesn't print on the envelope where you want it to, you need to modify the template. I advise that you print to a regular sheet of paper to see exactly where the information prints.

Follow these steps to print envelopes for your form letter:

1. Open the File menu and choose Print.

2. From the Print dialog box, pull down the Printout Type list and select Envelopes.

3. The most common envelope is a #10, so that is the report ACT! uses as its default to print an envelope following the printing of a letter. Select #10.

4. Click the Edit Template button.

   Figure 11-9 shows the #10 Envelope template. With the template on screen, adjust the margins by opening the File menu and selecting Page Setup.

Print the new format to a full sheet of paper. By comparing the printed output from the first envelope and the edited envelope, you should be able to get an idea of where the adjustments need to be made. Believe me, ACT! *does* print envelops properly; it just takes a little fiddling to get there.

Printing Envelopes from the Report Menu

I like to add the ability to print envelopes directly from the Report menu. It is much easier to print a single envelope this way. Follow these steps to add the Envelope Report to the Report menu:

1. Open the Reports menu and select Modify Menu. The Modify Menu dialog box appears.

2. Click the Add Item button. The Add Custom Menu Item dialog box appears, and you are asked to enter the filename and location for the new item.

3. At the far right of the Filename And Location field is a box with three tiny dots. That is (surprise) the Browse button—click it.

   The Open dialog box appears and displays the contents of the Reports folder on your C drive (unless you have changed the location under Edit | Preferences). No envelope templates are visible at this point.

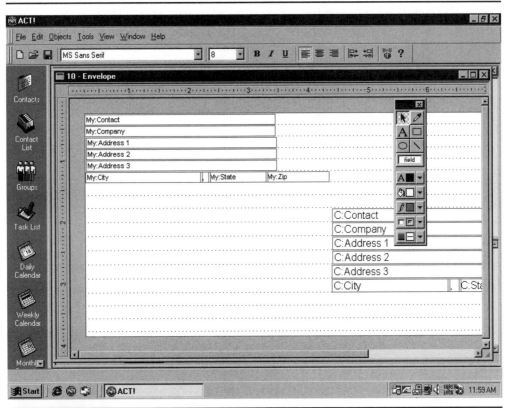

FIGURE 11-9 You can edit the #10 Envelope template to better suit your needs.

4. Click the drop-down arrow at the far right of the Files Of Type field.

5. Select Envelopes from the drop-down list. When you do, the envelope templates appear. Click the name of the envelope template you want on the menu and click Open.

6. The Add Custom Menu Item dialog box becomes active again, with the filename and location filled in. In the Command Name field, type the name for this command that you want to appear on the Reports menu, or accept the default.

7. Click OK twice.

8. Open the Reports menu. The new entry is at the bottom of the menu. Select New Envelope or the name of the file you wish to add to the menu, and the Run Envelope dialog box appears, from which you can print an envelope for the current contact, current lookup, or all contacts.

TIP *On a network installation of ACT! with a shared layout, you will have to configure each workstation's menu individually.*

Attaching a Document to a Contact Record After the Fact

Suppose you created a form letter, memo, or other document and forgot to attach it at the time. (In the case of memo, there is no "attach to contact" prompt when you create the document, so you will have to use the following method to attach it to a contact record.) You can attach the letter at any time later by following these steps:

1. Look up the contact record to which you want to create a link.
2. Open the Contact menu and select Attach File. The Attach File dialog box opens.
3. Browse to the folder that has the document. If you created the document with the ACT! word processor, the file can be found in the C:\ProgramFiles\ACT\Document folder. (If you have an older install of ACT! the path could be C:\Program Files\ Symantec\ACT\Document or C:\My Documents\ACT\Document, or for Windows 2000 users, C:\Documents and Settings*your user name*\My Documents\ACT\Documents.)
4. Double-click the filename.

ACT! creates the link on the Notes/History tab.

Opening a Document Attached to a Record

If you have created attachments to a record, the next step is opening the attachments. This process is simple:

1. Look up the contact record that has the attachment.
2. Click the Notes/History tab.
3. Check the Filter button to make sure that the Date Range includes the time the document was attached. If you still don't see the attachment, click the Select Users button to make sure your name (or the person who actually made the attachment) is selected.
4. Double-click the attachment's icon at the far left. The program that created the file starts, and the document is shown.

Creating a Memo

Creating a memo is identical to creating a letter. Look up the person to whom you want to send the memo, and then open the Write menu and select Memo. The word processor starts, and the memo template is filled in. To edit the Memo template, open the template with the Write menu, select Edit Document Template, and select Memo.

Creating a Fax Cover Page

In the past, everyone had standalone fax machines and it was deemed necessary to have a cover sheet that detailed the contents of the fax. Today this is archaic, but survives. When you want to send a fax in ACT!, open the Write menu and select Fax Cover Page. ACT! transfers the requisite information: the fax sender and addressee. Type the number of pages and the subject. If you have WinFax installed, you can fax directly from your desktop by following these steps:

1. Click the Fax button in the toolbar.

2. WinFax starts and takes over the process of actually sending the fax. The WinFax Send Fax dialog box appears when you begin to send, as shown in Figure 11-10.

3. Enter the information that you want recorded. If you choose to attach the fax to the contact record, it can be saved as a word processor file or as a WinFax file. If you save it as a WinFax file, it can be viewed later using the WinFax viewer.

4. Click Continue and the fax is sent.

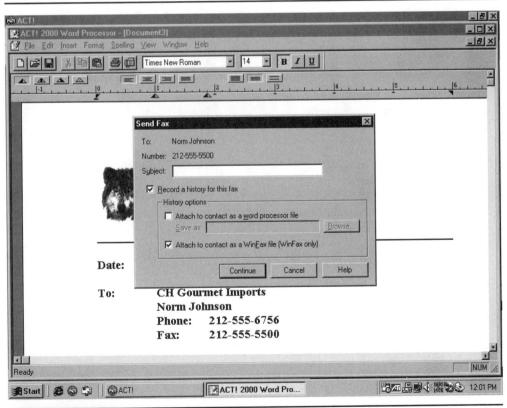

FIGURE 11-10   This is how WinFax looks when you start it from ACT!.

Creating a QuickFax

QuickFax is used to open WinFax and send a fax to the current contact, or to the current contact and others in your ACT! database. WinFax opens on the desktop. (You must have WinFax installed for this option to work.) Open the Write menu and select QuickFax. A screen similar to the one shown in Figure 11-11 appears.

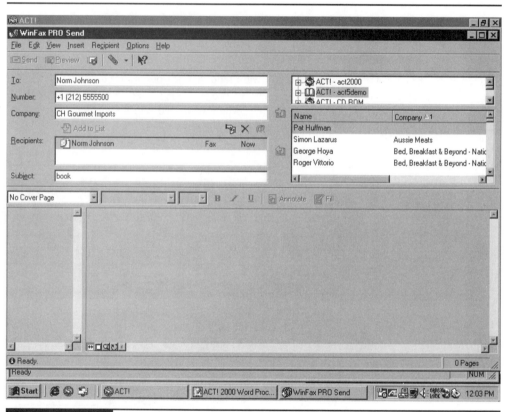

FIGURE 11-11 The current contact information appears in the WinFax window when you select QuickFax from the Write menu.

The current contact record's company name, contact name, and fax number are inserted. The list of the names and companies from the ACT! database appears on the right side of the WinFax window. Above the name and company is a list of the databases that ACT! can access as a phone book.

You can scroll the list to select additional recipients of the fax. The default sort order is by last name in ascending order (A, B, C, …). Re-sort the list of names and/or companies by clicking the column header.

To add an additional recipient:

1. Click the name or company and click Add To List above the Recipients field.

2. Type a subject line in the Subject field, and it is automatically added to the fax cover page.

3. Type the text of your fax. For easier viewing, right-click the text and select a lower percentage, such as 50%, from the shortcut menu.

   The word processor in WinFax includes a spell checker as well as different fonts so that you can edit and style your fax as you like.

4. Click the Send button to send your fax.

Using Microsoft Word as Your Default Word Processor

For various reasons, you might be required to use Word to create documents or you might simply prefer to use Word. Either way, a couple of considerations about using this word processor with ACT! are worth mentioning.

First, ACT! ships with Word-specific templates for letters, faxes, and memos. You cannot use your existing templates in Word and make them the default templates for letters, memos, and faxes. *You must use the templates that ACT! supplies as the starting point.* The reason is that ACT! uses hidden text in the template to identify the database to link to on the Notes/History tab in ACT!. If links are not being created for you in ACT!, the use of non–ACT!-supplied templates is usually the problem. So, if you already have Word documents that you want to use in ACT! as templates, use the Word letter template that ACT! provides, cut and paste your text into the template, and then use the Save As option on the File menu to create a new name for the template.

When you are editing a template in Word via ACT!, you can access the fields from the ACT! database. Follow these steps to do so:

1. Open the Write menu and select Edit Document Template. Word starts, and the template appears.

2. Open the Insert menu and choose ACT! Mail-Merge Fields at the bottom of the Insert menu. The Mail Merge Fields dialog box opens.

3. Insert the fields in the same way as you would for the ACT! word processor.

Microsoft Word Date Format Problems

If you are trying to write a letter in Word via ACT!, and the date field is printed as "day of week, month, day, year," you need to make the following change:

1. Close ACT!.

2. Click the Windows Start button, select Settings, and then select Control Panel.

11

3. From the Control Panel dialog box, double-click Regional Settings.

4. Click the Date tab.

5. Change the format to read "MMMM, dd, yyyy" in the Long Date Format, and then click OK.

6. Open ACT!.

7. Open the Write menu, select Edit Document Template, select the letter template, and then click OK.

8. Highlight and delete the date line from the template.

9. Open the Insert menu, and then select Date And Time.

10. Select the Update Automatically check box and choose the correct date format.

11. Click OK.

12. Open the File menu, select Save, and then exit the template document.

The History and Print Envelopes Dialog Boxes Do Not Appear

Have you written a letter from ACT! using Microsoft Word and printed it, only to find that the dialog boxes prompting you to create a history and print an envelope do not appear? Does this happen even though you have enabled the option to prompt to print an envelope in ACT!'s Preferences? But, both prompts appear when printing in the ACT! word processor, right?

Follow these steps in Word to correct the problem:

1. Open the Tools menu, select Templates And Add-Ins.

2. Under Global Templates And Add-Ins, clear any checked items.

3. Click OK. You should now see both prompts after printing a letter.

Creating Forms Using ACT! and Microsoft Word

Many users have asked how they can attach a form to a contact record. The idea is to create a form letter that includes spaces that the reader can use to fill in requested information. You may also want to print the form with the merge fields underlined. That way, if any fields in the records are blank, a space will be created for someone to write in the information after the form has been printed. An example would be an order form. First, make a paper and pencil outline of what should be on the form.

TIP

To Add underlining in a Word form, understand that there are two types of underlined fields: those that will be filled in by the customer and those that contain information from your database. You might want spaces for database fields underlined, so that if information is missing in your database, you or the customer can fill it in manually.

Once you've decided what you want in your form, follow these steps:

1. In ACT!, open the File menu and select New.

2. Select Word 95-2000 Template and click OK.

3. Save your new template using a unique filename.

4. Type any text that precedes a fill-in field.

5. At the point where a field begins, turn on underlining.

6. If you are inserting a field from your database, continue with steps 7 through 9 and stop with step 9. If you are inserting a blank line for the customer to fill in, skip down to step 10.

7. Insert the desired field from the Mail Merge Fields dialog box.

8. On the ruler, insert a tab where you want the underline to stop. Make sure you allow sufficient space for the information to be written in, if necessary.

9. Press TAB, and a line is drawn to the tab you just set.

TIP

If the field name is too long and you need to insert more than one database field on one line, delete only the field name from within the brackets. (Leave the brackets as well as the colon and field code.) For example: `[[City:30]]` `[[State:31]]` `[[Zip:32]]` *would look like* `[[:30]]` `[[:31]]` `[[:32]]` *when the field names are removed.*

10. (Remember: These steps are for inserting a blank line for the customer to fill in *only*.) On the ruler, insert a tab where you want the underline to stop. Make sure you allow sufficient space for the information to be written in, if necessary.

11. Press TAB, and a line is drawn to the tab you just set.

12. Turn off underlining. You are finished with this field.

13. Continue with additional body text, and return to step 4 if you want to add a new field.

14. Save your changes.

When you merge this template, the document creates either the merged fields underlined or a blank line extended to the tab.

11

Error Messages in Word

Several error messages can appear when ACT! tries to connect to Word. A common message is "Failed to connect to word processor or word processor is not installed." The problem lies in the attempts by Norton AntiVirus (NAV) to protect you from Word macro viruses. Follow these steps to correct the problem:

1.   Click Start and select Run. The Run dialog box appears.

2.   Type the following text. *Make sure that you include the quotes.* (The text shown assumes that NAV has been installed to the default location. If NAV has been installed to a different location, please substitute the correct path for your installation.)

```
"C:\Windows\System\Regsvr32" -U "C:\Program Files\Norton
AntiVirus\OfficeAV.dll"
```

If you installed Norton SystemWorks 2000 (which includes Norton AntiVirus 2000), please substitute the following path, correcting it as necessary for your installation:

```
"C:\Windows\System\Regsvr32" -U "C:\Program Files\Norton
SystemWorks\Norton AntiVirus\OfficeAV.dll"
```

3.   Press ENTER. You should receive the message "DllUnregisterServer in C:\Program Files\Norton AntiVirus\OfficeAV.dll succeeded."

Close ACT!, restart, and then try to create a document. Note that this plug-in is not necessary to protect your computer from viruses. The Auto-Protect feature of NAV, which is enabled by default, provides this protection. The plug-in was designed as a safeguard in case Auto-Protect is turned off. We strongly recommend that Auto-Protect be left on at all times. Please see your NAV documentation for information on how to do this.

Windows 2000 and Word

To run ACT! and Word on computers running Windows 2000 or Windows NT 4.*x* requires some special tweaking. These steps must be taken during install, so you may have to uninstall ACT! and then reinstall it. There are two basic requirements:

Install as Local Administrator   When installing ACT! 2000 on a computer running Windows 2000 or NT 4.*x*, the person installing the software must be logged in as that computer's *Local* (not network) Administrator—not as a Standard User or Domain Administrator.

Set program available to all users   During the install process, you must select the option to make the install available to all users. If you have not installed ACT! 2000 correctly on any Windows 2000 or NT 4.*x* machine, you will have to log in correctly and do the following:

1. Back up all ACT! data that resides on the computer.

If you can open ACT!, select Help/About ACT! and write down your serial number. You will need it when you reinstall. If you cannot open ACT!, you will need to have the CD sleeve available or the serial number you received via e-mail if you purchased and downloaded the product online. Please back up all database file sets and any custom templates and layouts you might have prior to the uninstall.

2. Uninstall, clean up, reinstall, and update while logged in as the local machine's NT Administrator.

3. While still logged in as the local NT Administrator, open ACT! for the first time. Set the default word processor by clicking the Edit menu, choosing Preferences, and selecting the General tab.

4. If you are using Microsoft Word, open the Write menu and choose Letter. Then, save (File | Save) and print (File | Print).

Now a standard user of the machine can log in and use ACT! 2000.

Word XP

If you have upgraded Microsoft Office to the XP version, you need to add a patch file to ACT!. Open your web browser and go to www.act.com and select Support and then Upgrades. You will have to download the compressed file to your computer and then open it to install the upgrade files.

Summary

■ Form letters, faxes, memos, or e-mail messages can be a huge timesaver in your marketing and sales campaigns.

■ You can print mailing labels or envelopes from your ACT! contact list.

■ For quick access, you can add frequently used templates to ACT!'s Write menu.

■ You can customize any of ACT!'s document templates to better suit your needs.

■ You have the choice of either using ACT!'s word processor or Microsoft Word.

■ Many administrators restrict user rights on the network drive. ACT! users need ALL rights—Read, Write, Create, and Modify—to the ACT! folders on the network drive. Otherwise, users will get a strange error message: Not an ACT! database, do you want to import?

Chapter 12

Printing Labels, Envelopes, Address Books, and Calendars

How to...

- Print envelopes
- Print mailing labels
- Print address books
- Print calendars

With the elusive promise of a wireless world still on the horizon, the need for printed material has not abated. We still need to use paper mail, and at times we need the ability to carry a printed version of our ACT! data. This brief chapter covers how to print to various forms.

Setting Up an Envelope

ACT! offers to print an envelope every time you print a letter. If you are lucky, the envelope prints as it should and you will not have to adjust the envelope template. However, there is a wide variety of printers and they each have their own software, called a driver, which instructs your printer to put the ink on the paper. So the first step in printing envelopes is to be certain the correct driver is installed on your computer. The best way to verify this is to check the web site of your printer manufacturer. But first, you'll need to know what version you are currently using. If you don't know, follow these steps:

1. Click the Start button.

2. Select the Settings item and from the submenu, select Printers. The Printers dialog box appears.

3. Right-click on the printer you use. From the shortcut menu, select Properties. Depending upon the printer, a variety of dialog boxes can appear. In Figure 12-1, the dialog box for the Epson printer I use is shown.

4. In the dialog box that appears for your printer, look for a button that is usually labeled About. Following the example of my Epson printer selection, I had to switch from the General tab to the Main tab to find the About button.

5. Click the About button. The version number of the printer driver appears, as shown in Figure 12-2.

Now go to your printer manufacturer's web site to see if your version is the most current one available. Enter the printer model you have and see if any updates have been posted. If the version numbers match, you are good to go. If not, you must download the printer driver and then run the installer. If you have never done this, the procedure I prefer is to create a folder in the My Documents folder and name it Download, then download the file. When you click the update, you are asked to choose between Run From Current Location or Save To Folder. Choose Save To Folder, then save to the folder named Download.

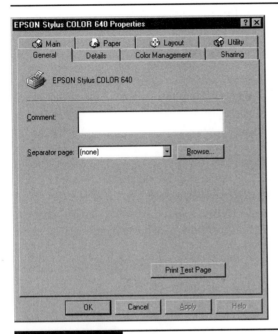

FIGURE 12-1   This is an example showing the Epson printer dialog box.

FIGURE 12-2   The About button reveals the version number of the printer driver.

After downloading, use Windows Explorer to locate the file in the folder in which it is saved (in this case, C:\ My Documents\Download) and double-click. The installer should start and update the driver. I recommend that you restart the computer after installing.

Testing the Envelope Template

In most cases, the envelope template works right out of the box. Nevertheless, I advise you to test-print to a full sheet of paper to determine if the envelope will print correctly. Start ACT! and follow these steps to run the test:

1. Open the File menu and select Print. The Print dialog box appears, as shown in Figure 12-3.

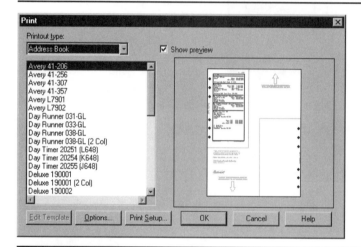

FIGURE 12-3   Print dialog box

2. Select Envelopes from the Printout Type drop-down list.

3. Select the #10 envelope type.

4. Click OK. The Run Envelope dialog box appears, as shown in Figure 12-4.

5. The default is to print for the Current Lookup, but for the test, select Current Contact.

6. The Send Output To field should be set to Printer.

7. Click OK and the Printer dialog box should appear. Click OK again. The Epson printer I use then presents the dialog box shown in Figure 12-5. As you can see, even though the printer driver is matched to this printer, I still have to select a Feed Method and Feed Direction. Your printer may not require this choice.

8. Print to a sheet of paper and set it aside. If no printing appeared, try it again and adjust the settings to get something on paper. For instance, change the Face Up setting to Face

Down (or vice versa) so you are printing on the correct side of the paper. Don't be too concerned about the format of the text; I'll cover that in the next section. At this point, you just need to make sure that your printer prints on the correct side of the paper.

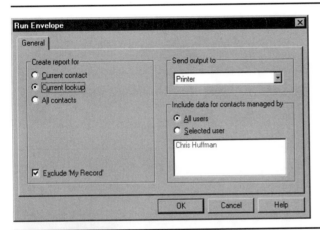

FIGURE 12-4   The Run Envelope dialog box presents printing options.

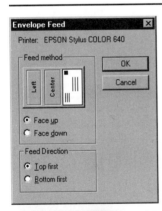

FIGURE 12-5   An Epson printer dialog box allows you to check the envelope feed.

12

9. Repeat the steps, but this time insert an envelope and see if the results are what you want. If not, compare the full sheet with the envelope output and try again.

Editing the Envelope Template

Assuming that you did get something on paper in the previous exercise and the results are not satisfactory, you need to adjust the page setup of the envelope template. To do so, first you need to open the Edit Template, as follows:

1. Open the File menu and select Print.

2. Select Envelopes from the Printout Type drop-down list.

3. Select the #10 envelope type.

4. Select Edit Template. The template appears as shown in Figure 12-6.

   The white area in this window represents the envelope, the gray is the background.

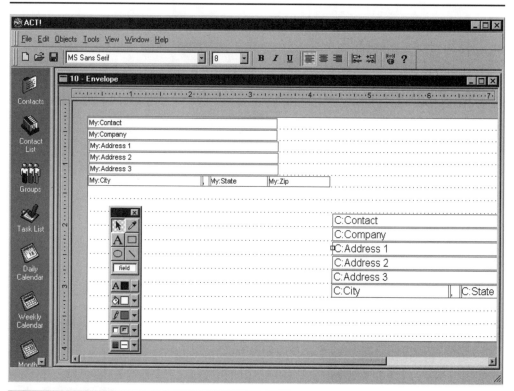

FIGURE 12-6   Template editing window

At this point, it's a little tricky to get exactly what you want, but with pluck and a little luck, ACT! will print your envelopes the way you want them to be printed. To make adjustments to where the information prints, do the following:

1.   Open the File menu and select Page Setup. The Page Setup dialog box appears, as shown in Figure 12-7. The margin setting that needs adjustment most often is Top, as the address often prints either below or above where the envelope feeds through the printer. Try reducing or increasing the setting.

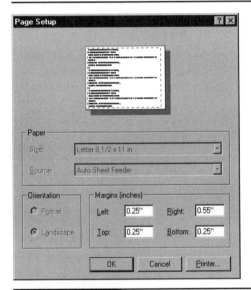

FIGURE 12-7   The Page Setup dialog box allows you to adjust the margin settings.

2.   Click OK once you have made your adjustments.

3.   Open the File menu and select Run. The Run Report dialog box appears.

4.   Select Current Contact and check that you are sending the output to the printer.

5.   Click OK. Check the printed output this time against the previous result. Keep adjusting the margins until the address prints as it should.

6.   Open the File menu and select Save. Now the default #10 envelope is the one you adjusted.

TIP
You can try using the File menu and Print Preview, but I have found that actually running the report is the best test.

12

Removing the Return Address

Many firms have spent the money to have envelopes printed with a fancy return address that includes a logo. The default envelope prints a return address and therefore would make a mess of the expensive envelopes. You can remove the fields that print a return address as follows:

1. Open the File menu and select Print. The Print dialog box appears.

2. Select Envelopes from the Printout Type drop-down list.

3. Select #10 and the envelope template appears.

4. Click under the bottom field on the return address, and hold down the mouse button. Drag the mouse up until all the fields are selected.

5. Right-click and select Delete from the shortcut menu. The fields are removed.

6. Open the File menu and select Save.

Adding a Logo to the Envelope Template

Perhaps you want a return address that reflects your business, but you have not yet had envelopes printed, or you've just decided to save money and print the envelopes using ACT!. In this scenario, you would not remove the fields for the return address, as described in the previous section. You can add your business logo to the envelope, provided the logo is saved in bitmap format. The first step is to copy the bitmap of your logo to the Windows clipboard. The following instructions use Windows Paint to copy the logo.

1. Open Windows Paint by clicking the Start button and selecting Programs.

2. Select Accessories and then select Paint from the submenu.

3. In Paint, open the File menu and select Open.

4. Locate the file that is a bitmap of your logo and select it.

5. Open the Edit menu and choose Select All.

6. Open the Edit menu again and select Copy. This copies the logo to the Windows clipboard.

7. Open ACT! and then open the File menu and select Print.

8. Select Envelopes from the Printout Type drop-down list. Select #10 (or whatever envelope you want to modify) and then click Edit Template. The template opens.

9. Right-click at the position you want the logo to appear. The shortcut menu appears.

10. Select Paste. The logo appears on the template. Figure 12-8 shows a logo on the envelope template.

11. Open the File menu and select Save.

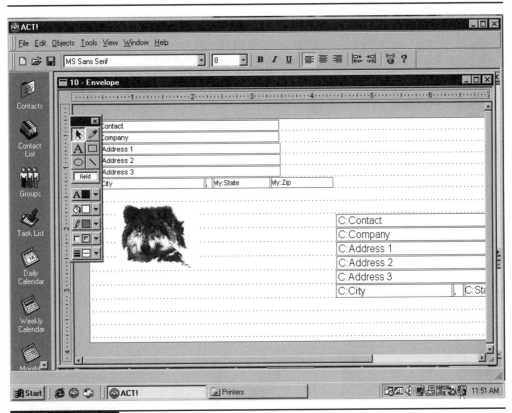

FIGURE 12-8   Logo added to the envelope template

TIP   *If you are sharing a database on a network and you want everyone to have access to the envelope template, create a folder on the network drive and copy the envelope file to it. To do this, instead of using File | Save, use File | Save As, browse to the network folder, and save your file there.*

Printing Labels

Printing labels is straightforward. Obviously, you need the correct blank labels in your printer. I strongly suggest that you not try to adjust the predefined label settings that come with ACT!. They are time tested and should print properly as is. To print labels, follow these steps:

1. Open the File menu and select Print. The Print dialog box appears.

2. Select Labels from the Printout Type drop-down list. The Print dialog box now lists the labels that can be printed, as shown in Figure 12-9.

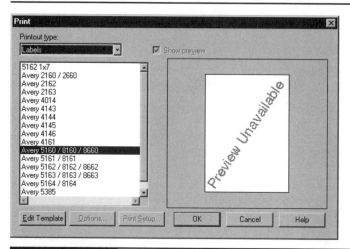

FIGURE 12-9 The Print dialog box lists a wide variety of labels.

3. The dominant player in the preformatted label market is Avery. Other makers use the Avery numbering system to match what you see in this dialog box. Select the label type you have and click OK.

4. In the Run Label dialog box that appears, select the range of contact records you want to print.

5. If you are printing less than a full sheet or have been printing a couple of labels at a time, you do not have to waste label sheets. Click the Position tab to set the Starting Position On options. Figure 12-10 shows you how to select the starting position.

6. Click OK.

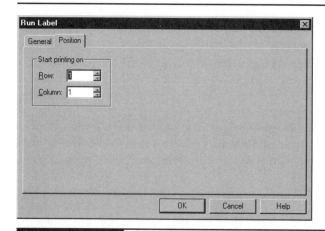

FIGURE 12-10 The Position tab allows you to select a specific label for the first address.

To print a set of labels for a group, before you start the printing process, select the group using the Group button. When you get to the Run Label dialog box, select Current Lookup. ACT! prints the records for the group. See Chapter 15 on creating groups for more information.

You can sort your ACT! database before printing labels. Open the Edit menu and select Sort. In the Sort Contacts dialog box, enter the fields you want ACT! to sort on—up to three levels and in either ascending or descending order. Click OK and then print the labels.

Printing Multiple Labels with the Same Address

Your business might need return address labels for packages that you ship. If so, you'll want ACT! to print multiple labels with the exact same information: your company name, address, and so on. ACT! does not print this label as a matter of course, a bit of legerdemain is required. In this example, the 5160/8160 label is our starting point.

1. Open the File menu and select Print.

2. In the Print dialog box, select Labels from the Printout Type drop-down list.

3. Choose the 5160/8160 label.

4. Click the Edit Template button. The template appears, as shown in Figure 12-11. As you can see, a single label is displayed. When the template is used, ACT! repeatedly prints the template and adds the address information from the various records.

5. Open the Edit menu and choose Select All. All the fields in the label should have little selection boxes on the borders.

6. Click the City field.

7. Right-click to open the shortcut menu. Select Properties. The Object Properties dialog box appears, as shown in Figure 12-12.

8. Click the Type tab.

9. Click the check box in front of Use My Record.

10. Click the Apply button. The fields should now show that the data is being pulled from My Record.

11. Save the new template by opening the File menu and selecting Save As.

12. Give the template a new name such as Return (for return address labels).

If you want to enhance the way a particular field prints, click it and use the tool palette to change the font color, border, or fill color. If the tool palette is not visible, open the View menu and select View Tool Palette.

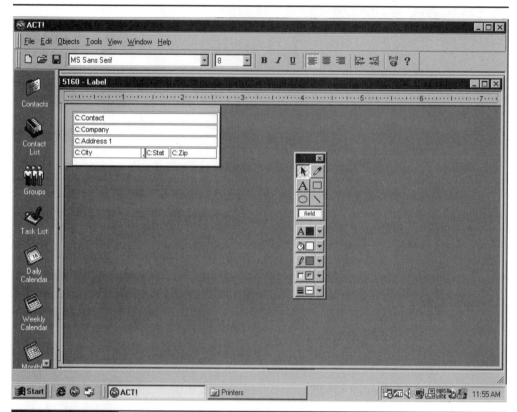

FIGURE 12-11   The 5160 Avery label template

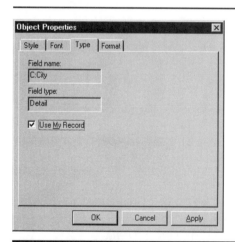

FIGURE 12-12   The Object Properties dialog box offers ways to format fields.

On the 5160/8160 label sheet, a total of 30 labels can be printed, so you need to create a lookup of 30 records. It does not matter which 30 records you choose: ACT! is going to print 30 labels with the information from My Record. One way to create the lookup is to open the List view and tag 30 names, and then click the Lookup Selected button.

To print 30 labels with a single address after creating the lookup:

1. Open the File menu and select Print.

2. Select Labels and then select the label template you created, such as Return.

3. In the Run Label dialog box, select Current Lookup.

4. Click OK and then OK again in the Print dialog box

You should get 30 identical labels with your return address.

Printing Multiple Labels for the Same Contact Record

Going a step further, you might need to send packages to the same contact record repeatedly. Rather than printing a label every time it is needed, a better solution is to print a full sheet of labels and keep them on hand. To do this, you can use the ACT! demonstration database or a new database that you create specifically for this purpose. Do not use your main database! Before following the steps below, you must have created the Return label as described in the previous section.

1. Assuming you are using the ACT5demo database, create a lookup that has 30 records. (To open this database, start ACT! and select ACT5demo database.)

2. In the My Record fields, erase Chris Huffman's information (he is the owner of the demonstration database) and replace it with the information of the contact record for which you want to print a full sheet of labels.

3. Open the File menu and select Print. Select Labels from the drop-down menu and then select the label template named Return.

4. Click OK, and in the Run Label dialog box, select the Current Lookup as the range to print.

5. Click OK. The printer should print 30 identical labels with the information you put into My Record.

6. To run another set of labels for a different contact record, look up My Record and edit the record by replacing the information with the next contact.

12

Printing Address Books

Although the advent of ACT! synchronizing with the Palm handheld has obviated the need in many cases to print address books and calendars, some ACT! users like to have a paper copy of their data to carry. ACT! can print to a wide variety of formats, such as Day Runner and Deluxe forms. Obviously, you must have purchased the forms in order to get the printed output. Let's take a look at the forms and the options presented.

1. Open the File menu and select Print.

2. In the Print dialog box, shown in Figure 12-13, select Address Book from the Printout Type drop-down list.

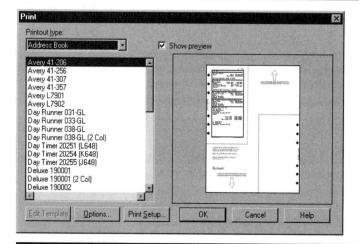

FIGURE 12-13   This is the Print dialog box with the Address Book list shown.

3. Select any of the formats and then click the Options button. The Address Book Options dialog box opens, as shown in Figure 12-14.

   The options are straightforward. You can mix and match the fields you want to include, plus how the information should print. The double-sided printing is pretty tricky unless you have great spatial sense. You can select to print all records or just a lookup. Remember, a group is considered the current lookup. Selecting a font determines the size of the text that in turn determines how many pages it will take to print all of the records you want.

4. Click OK after making your choices and OK again to get to the Printer dialog box.

5. Load the forms into your printer and away you go!

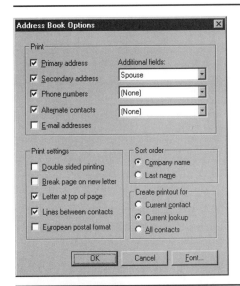

FIGURE 12-14   The address book has several printing options.

Printing Calendars

ACT! will print a daily, weekly, or monthly calendar. In our example, we'll look at a weekly calendar.

1. Open the File menu and select Print.

2. From the Print dialog box, select Week Calendar from the Printout Type drop-down list.

3. The options are limited to the forms you see in the dialog box. Select a form, and then click the Options button to see the Calendar Options dialog box, shown in Figure 12-15. The options found in the Calendar Options dialog box are described on the following page.

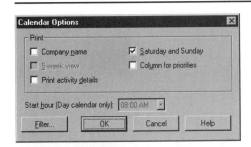

FIGURE 12-15   The Calendar Options dialog box has several options.

Company Name Select this option if you want the company name printed on the calendar in addition to the contact name.

5 Week View Select this option to print a full five-week monthly calendar, which means that partial weeks at each end of month are included.

Print Activity Details Select this to print the activity details text.

Saturday And Sunday Select this option to include Saturday and Sunday in the printouts. In a 24/7 economy, this may be essential.

Column For Priorities Select this option if you want activity priorities to be printed on your calendars.

Start Hour Choose at which hour you want the printed calendar to begin. Click the arrow to display the Start Hour drop-down list and select the hour.

Filter Click this button to set filtering options for printing your calendar.

4. Click the Filter button to open the Filter Calendar Printout dialog box (shown in Figure 12-16), which is a handy way to determine exactly what user information and activity type are to be printed. The options are discussed below:

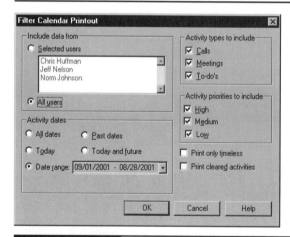

The Filter Calendar Printout dialog box

Include Data From

Selected Users Select this option if you want your printout to include activities from one or more of the users listed.

All Users Select this option if you want all users' activities to appear on the printout.

Activity Dates

All Dates   Select this option if you want the printout to include activities for all dates.

Today   Select this option if you want the printout to include only today's activities.

Date Range   Select this option if you want the printout to include activities for a specific range of dates. Select the date range by dragging through the dates you want and releasing the mouse on the ending date. Drag off the right side of the calendar to select more than one month. Click outside the date selector to apply the date range.

Past Dates   Select this option if you want the printout to include only past activities.

Today And Future   Select this option if you want the printout to include activities for today and future dates.

Activity Types To Include

Calls   Select this option to include calls.

Meetings   Select this option to include meetings.

To-do's   Select this option to include to-do items.

Activity Priorities To Include

High   Select this option to include high-priority activities.

Medium   Select this option to include medium-priority activities.

Low   Select this option to include low-priority activities.

Print Only Timeless   Select this option to include only timeless activities.

Print Cleared Activities   Select this option to include cleared activities.

Print Outlook Activities   Select this option to include Outlook activities.

5. After selecting the options, click OK to close this dialog box. Click OK again to close the Calendar Options dialog box and then OK again to open the Print dialog box and print away!

TIP   *Unfortunately, the filter settings are not printed on the calendar so there is no way to determine the settings after printing.*

Summary

- ACT! can print almost any data that is stored in the database.
- You need the correct forms to print address books and calendars.
- Label printing can be modified to print multiple labels for a single record.

Chapter 13

E-Mail and the Internet

How to...

- Set up ACT! to send e-mail messages
- Create, send, and read e-mail messages
- Use Internet links

While e-mail has grown geometrically as a means of communication, it can be a challenging part of ACT! to get working. This chapter covers the ins and outs of this tool and helps you troubleshoot connecting to the more popular e-mail programs. In addition, you can create your own links to specific internet sites and access them from with in ACT!.

Using E-Mail in ACT!

One of the most powerful features of ACT! is its ability to link with your e-mail program, allowing you to send messages to contacts instantly over the Internet. ACT! can send messages via its own e-mail program, Microsoft Outlook, Outlook Express, Qualcomm Eudora, and Lotus Mail. Most of the clients I work with use Outlook but send via ACT! so that they can automatically attach the e-mail message to the contact record, as described in this chapter.

Setting Up Your E-Mail Account

You might have configured ACT! to use an e-mail program during setup. If not, the steps to do so are easy—but you should have the information from your Internet service provider at hand, because you will need it. To set up your e-mail account, follow these steps:

1. Open the Edit menu and select Preferences. In the Preferences dialog box, click the E-Mail tab.

2. Next, click the New Account button. ACT! launches the E-Mail Setup Wizard, shown in Figure 13-1. You can now make the entries as provided by your Internet service provider.

3. Select the e-mail client(s) from the list of those that ACT! has located on your system. You can select more than one entry as an e-mail client. Figure 13-1 shows the e-mail programs on a typical system.

4. Click Next.

5. On the next page of the wizard, shown in Figure 13-2, complete the following Internet mail settings:

   Default Account (Username)   Enter the first part of your e-mail address only. My e-mail address is dwolf@howtosoftware.com, so my entry is simply **dwolf**.

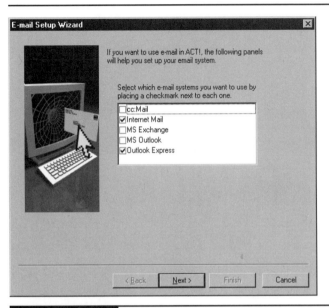

FIGURE 13-1   ACT! presents a list of the e-mail clients.

Using Outlook, Eudora, or Other Programs as Your E-Mail Client

You can choose Outlook, Outlook Express, Lotus Mail, Eudora, or other programs as your e-mail program. If you do, ACT! will read messages sent to the inbox and send messages to the outbox of that program. In short, you can check your e-mail by using either ACT! or the program you selected.

13

Outgoing SMTP Server   This is provided by your ISP. Type it exactly as given to you. An example is **mail.pacbell.net**.

Incoming POP3 Server   This is provided by your ISP. Type it exactly as given to you. An example is **pacbell.net**.

Real Name   Enter your proper name, like **Douglas J. Wolf**.

Organization   If appropriate, make an entry (like **Wolf's Byte Productions**); it is not required.

Reply To Address   Enter your full e-mail address: for example, **dwolf@howtosoftware.com**.

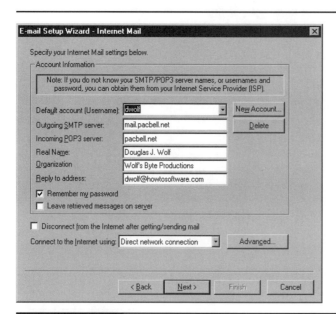

FIGURE 13-2   Enter your Internet mail settings on this page of the wizard.

6. Select or clear the Remember My Password check box. Your choices are these: Have
    ACT! remember your password so that you are not required to type it every time you
    try to send or receive e-mail, or not. In an office where someone else might gain
    access to your computer, you might want to require the password.

7. Select or clear the Leave Retrieved Messages On Server check box.

    This check box requires a bit of thinking. Usually, ISPs delete your e-mail from their
    server after you've downloaded it into your inbox. However, if you select this check
    box, your e-mail will remain on the ISP's server. You might want to choose this option
    if you access your e-mail from two locations—say, office and home—and you want to
    be able to read the messages from either location, regardless of whether they have
    been downloaded already in one of them. However, I suggest that you do not select
    this option.

8. Select or clear the Disconnect From The Internet After Getting/Sending Mail check box.

    If you connect to the Internet by modem, you might want to automatically disconnect
    from the phone line when all your messages have been sent and received—particularly
    if you use ACT! in a home office and have a single phone line for e-mail and faxing.

9. Select the way you connect to the Internet. The default setting is via a direct network
    connection, which is how most of us connect in an office setting. However, many ACT!

users are still dialing into their e-mail accounts via a modem. If you have a dial-up already created, it will appear on the drop-down list and you should select it.

10. Click the Advanced button to test your e-mail connection. A dialog box opens that allows you to indicate the authentication style used by your ISP (usually passwords) and contains a button you can click to run a test.

I suggest that you test the connection at this point. If it works, you will see a message onscreen that you have successfully communicated with the e-mail server. If not, go back and check the SMTP and POP3 settings—they must be entered exactly as the ISP directed. You're almost ready to begin sending and receiving all those e-mail jokes you have heard so much about!

Click OK to close the test.

> **NOTE**   *Although you cannot connect to the inbox or outbox of your America Online e-mail account within ACT!, a third-party product can accomplish it for you. Check out www.enetbot.com. Appendix A contains reviews of several third-party products for ACT!, including this one.*

11. Click Next. The setup page for Windows Messaging appears if you have this system on your network. You will need help from your system administrator to complete this page.

12. Click Next to access the final setup page. If you selected several e-mail clients on the first page of the wizard, ACT! asks you to select one as the primary e-mail client. For our purposes, Internet mail is selected, which means that ACT!'s e-mail client is in use.

13. Click Finish. Your e-mail account is now activated.

Creating and Sending E-Mail Messages

To create and send an e-mail message by using ACT!'s e-mail program, follow these steps:

1. Look up the contact record of the person to whom you want to send an e-mail message.

2. Open the Write menu and select E-Mail, or click the blue e-mail hyperlink in the E-Mail address field. Figure 13-3 shows the ACT! E-Mail window.

3. If the record has an e-mail address, it is automatically added to the message (although you will see the name of the contact, rather than the e-mail address, in the recipients list in the center of the window). Enter the subject of the e-mail, type the message you want to send, and click the Send button.

ACT! sends the message directly, or if you have selected another program as the e-mail carrier, the message is sent to the outbox of that program. If you use another e-mail program to send and receive messages and you are not always connected to the Internet, you will have to open that program, such as Outlook, to send the message.

13

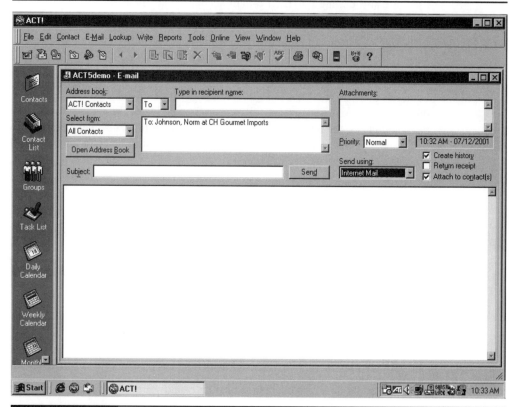

FIGURE 13-3 You can create e-mail messages in this view of the ACT! E-Mail window.

You do not have to send your e-mail message to the current contact—you can change the recipient. Follow these steps to do so:

1. Delete the name of the current contact in the recipients list (the large box below the To and Type In Recipient Name fields).

   The insertion point moves to the Type In Recipient Name field.

2. Enter the first couple of letters of the last name of the person to whom you want to send the message.

   ACT! searches its database for the record. If the person is in your database, ACT! inserts the name and the e-mail address. The data entry is reactive—type **W**, and the first contact record with a last name that begins with *W* appears. Type a second letter, **O**, and ACT! inserts the first last name it finds that begins with *WO*. You can scroll the list of names with the UP ARROW and DOWN ARROW keys.

3. When you find the name you want, press ENTER, and the name moves into the large field beneath the To field.

TIP *Make sure the name of the person to whom you are sending is in the address field. ACT! will not send the message until it is.*

Sending E-Mail Messages to Multiple Recipients

You can send your e-mail messages to more than one person at a time. For example, let's say you are responding to a customer query and you want your boss and the service department people to know what is happening. Or you are the sales manager and you want everyone on the sales staff to be aware of a price change.

Select either CC or, if you are using Outlook as your e-mail program, BCC. If you would like some of your contacts to receive the message as a courtesy or for their records, but don't necessarily need them to respond, addressing them with CC or BCC instead of To is your best bet. You can see these options by clicking the down arrow at the right of the To field.

The CC (carbon copy) abbreviation is an anachronism from the days of carbon paper. (Many people now spell out the abbreviation as "courtesy copy," since carbons are no longer used.) You can copy your e-mail messages to as many people as you like with CC.

When you send a message to multiple recipients using CC, everyone who gets the message will be able to see the list of To and CC recipients. If you would rather your recipients not know who else has been sent the message, you can use BCC (blind copy circulated or blind courtesy copy); the names of recipients who are sent a blind copy of the message will not appear in the recipients list. For example, let's say you are sending an e-mail message to a subordinate regarding an action you want taken, and you think your boss should know that the message was sent. You can add the boss to the address list as a BCC and your subordinate will not be aware that your boss got a copy.

To add a CC or BCC recipient to an e-mail message, follow these steps:

1. Click the down arrow in the To field and select CC or BCC.

2. Enter the beginning letters of the last name, or click Open Address Book and locate the recipient in the list in the Address Book dialog box, as shown in Figure 13-4.

3. Press ENTER if you used the type last name method to select the contact record, or click OK to close the Address Book dialog box.

13

TIP *If you are using both ACT! and Outlook, you can access the Outlook address book by pulling down the list in the Address Book field and selecting Outlook.*

If you select a contact who does not have an e-mail address, you can remove them from the recipients list, or if you have the e-mail address, you can add it on the spot, by clicking the Edit Address button in the Address Book dialog box. When you do, the E-Mail Addresses dialog box appears. You add the e-mail address by clicking the New button and entering the address in the New Address dialog box that appears, as shown in Figure 13-5.

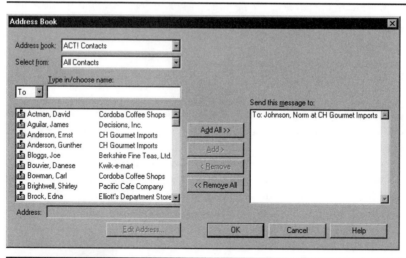

FIGURE 13-4   The Address Book dialog box appears when you click Open Address Book.

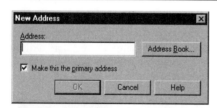

FIGURE 13-5   You can edit or enter a new e-mail address for a contact in the New Address dialog box.

Before sending an e-mail message to a large group (particularly if it is a sensitive or important message), send it to yourself so you can see how it looks at the receiving end.

If you can't find a contact's e-mail address, you can still keep the contact as a recipient. When ACT! actually tries to send the message, it reminds you that this record does not have an e-mail entry—at which point you can add the e-mail address if you've found it.

Before sending a mass e-mailing (an e-mail message addressed individually to many recipients), open the Lookup menu, select E-Mail, and search for Empty field. You can then remove the record(s) from the recipients list.

Indicating Priority Level, Creating a Record of the Message, and Getting a Receipt

When you create an e-mail message, you have some sending options to consider. For one, you can designate the priority you think the message deserves. The receiver sees the priority level with the summary information when opening his or her e-mail. Click the down arrow in the Priority list box to see your options.

You can also decide whether you want a history entry to be added to the Notes/History tab after the message has been sent. The Create History check box is selected by default, but you can clear it if you don't want a record of the message.

If you want a return receipt, you can get one by selecting that option. A return receipt is an automatic e-mail message that is sent to you from the recipient indicating that your message was received. Note that received doesn't necessarily mean that it has been read. Eudora offers return receipts that indicate whether your message has been read (or at least opened!).

 *Most e-mail systems no longer allow a return receipt, in an attempt to reduce e-mail traffic, but it is worth a try.*

Sending E-Mail Messages to a Group of Contacts

If you are the sales manager and want to send e-mail to all members of your team, you can use a group send to do so. Before you can create a group send, however, you must have created the group. Sending to a group is different from sending an e-mail message to a large number of recipients ("mass e-mailing"). See Chapter 15 for more information about creating and working with groups.

To send an e-mail message to a group, follow these steps:

1. Open the Write menu and select E-Mail. If you started in the e-mail window, no e-mail address is inserted in the recipients list (the large box beneath the To box). If you were in the contact record window when you started the message, delete the current contact from the recipients list.

2. Click the Open Address Book button. The Address Book dialog box opens.

3. Click the drop-down list in the Select From field.

4. Select Groups from the list.

5. Select the group to which you want to send the e-mail message from the large list on the left.

6. Click Add and then OK.

ACT! returns to the E-Mail window so you can continue your message.

13

You can send a mass e-mailing to hundreds of folks in which each recipient sees only his or her own name. To learn how, see Chapter 11.

Attaching a Contact, Group, or File to an Outgoing Message

If the person you are sending the message to is an ACT! user or Outlook user, you can send a contact record as part of the e-mail message. You only can send the contact records for groups to other ACT! users, but you can send a file to anyone.

To attach any of these items to your message, follow these steps:

1. After creating the message, open the E-Mail menu.

2. Select Attach To Message.

3. From the submenu, select the item you want to attach. You are not limited to a single attachment. If you select Contact, ACT! opens the Attach Contact(s) dialog box, as shown in Figure 13-6. If you want to attach a Group, skip to step 6. If you want to attach a file, skip to step 7.

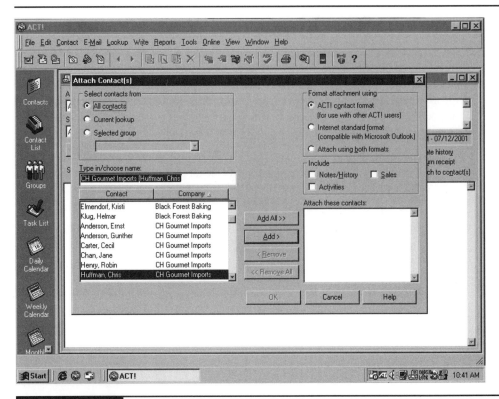

FIGURE 13-6   Choose which contact records to send with your e-mail message in the Attach Contact(s) dialog box.

4. Narrow the list of contacts by selecting either Current Lookup or Selected Group. Click the name/company record you want to attach, and then click the Add button. The record will appear in the Attach These Contacts box.

5. Now decide how to format the attachment and what else (if anything) to include with your message. Click OK to finish the attachment process.

Send a contact record to an Outlook or Eudora user with the International Standard (VCARD) format. The receiver gets only the information in the Company, Contact, Phone, and Address fields.

6. If you want to attach a group, select Group in the Attach To Contact submenu, ACT! opens the Attach Group dialog box, from which you can select the group(s) you want to send.

The following guidelines will help you make your selections:

Address Book   The address book can be pulled open and addresses from Outlook, Lotus Mail, Eudora, or another program can be accessed.

Select From   This choice works in concert with the Open Address Book button. If you leave the entry in this field as All Contacts, when you open the address book, every record is included. Or, if you limit the entry to the Current Lookup, whatever was selected is included.

Open Address Book   Opens the selected address book. The ACT! address book can be searched by last name. Type the first letters of the person's last name. Even if he or she does not have an e-mail address, ACT! responds with the person closest to what you have typed. At that point, if the contact does not have an e-mail address, you can add one.

Click Attach when you're done.

7. If you want to send a file, select that item in the Attach To Contact submenu. The Attach File dialog box appears. Depending upon the type of file you want to send, you might have to click the Browse button in order to locate the file. When you have located the file, click the Attach button.

Remember that an ACT! word processing file can only be opened by another ACT! user unless you have saved it as an RTF or ASCII (text) file.

Customizing Outgoing E-Mail Messages

Besides the message itself, you can customize a message by including text that has your "signature" on every e-mail message—in reality, a standardized message indicating who you are and possibly how to reach you. Veteran e-mail users often include their e-mail address; web page address; and phone, fax, or pager number as part of a signature—some people even include a quote. You can get quite fancy with your signature, enclosing the text in characters that resemble a frame or box, for example.

To customize your e-mail messages, follow these steps:

1. Open the Edit menu and select Preferences.

2. Click the E-Mail tab in the Preferences dialog box.

3. In the Signature Text field, type the signature you want on every outgoing e-mail message.

4. While you are in the Preferences dialog box, I recommend that you click Colors and Fonts tab, and make the e-mail text larger.

5. Click Apply, and then OK to make the change effective. Figure 13-7 shows an e-mail message with enlarged signature text.

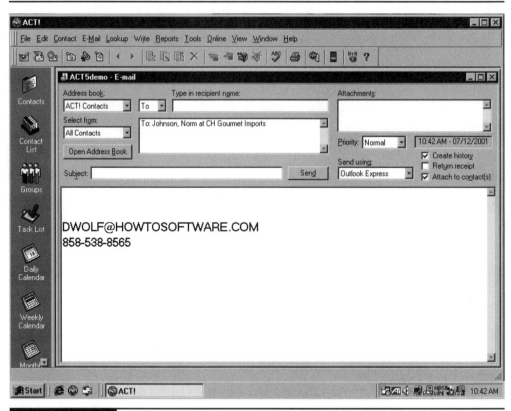

FIGURE 13-7   Signature text is automatically added to an e-mail message. This text has been enlarged.

After you click the Send button, if you are on network connection, the e-mail is sent immediately, either to the Internet or to your Outlook/Eudora/other outbox. If your modem has to dial up and connect to your ISP, the Connect To dialog box appears, at which point you click the Connect button. If you decide not to connect, ACT! alerts you that the message was not sent, and that it is being sent to the ACT! e-mail Briefcase folder and can be sent when a connection is established.

How to Receive E-Mail Messages

To see e-mail that has been sent to you, you either have to dial your ISP, or, on a direct network connection, refresh your inbox. On a network, you can have ACT! automatically refresh the inbox at a preset interval.

To set the refresh rate, follow these steps:

1. Open the Edit menu and select Preferences.

2. Click the E-Mail tab. On the left side, in the Inbox Settings section, select the Notify Me option and set a time interval.

3. Click Apply and OK to finish.

To view the e-mail inbox, click the View menu and select E-Mail. The E-Mail window appears, as shown in Figure 13-8, set up to display your messages.

This view of the ACT! E-Mail window shows you the incoming mail folders and any folders you may have created at the left, and message headers (sender, date, and subject) on the right.

> **TIP** *If you are on a network and are using Outlook as your e-mail client, ACT! opens your inbox and all other public folders on the network! This can result in extreme wait times for the individual messages to appear. See Chapter 22 on how to remove Outlook public folders using the ACT! Data Diagnostic program. Also to reduce wait times, keep the number of messages stored in your inbox to no more than 50. One more thing: do not create an e-mail folder named Inbox in Outlook.*

13

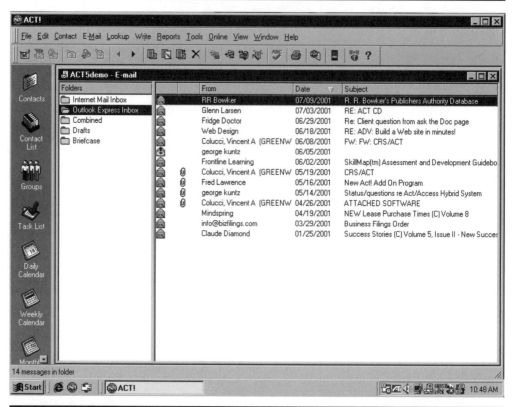

This view of the ACT! E-Mail window lets you check your incoming messages.

To refresh the inbox, right-click it and select Get/Send Mail from the shortcut menu. Any mail that was awaiting being sent in your outbox is sent, and ACT! queries your ISP for any new mail. The messages show up in the list on the right. When you receive e-mail, the entire message is not immediately visible; you must double-click the message header, or right-click it and select Read Message from the shortcut menu (shown in Figure 13-9).

After reading the e-mail message, you have several choices. You can print the message, delete the message, or move it to a folder that you have created for messages. Or, you can attach it to a specific contact record.

Printing E-Mail Messages

To print a received message, double-click the message to open it and then click the Print button located to the right of the Forward button.

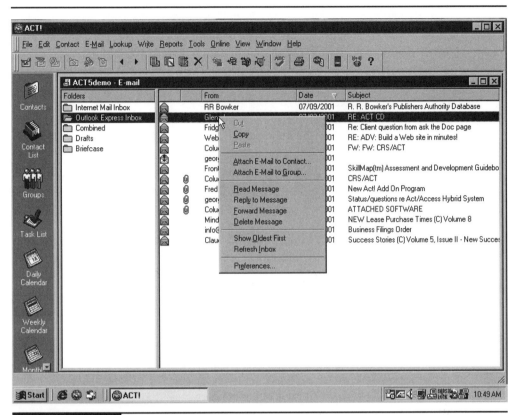

FIGURE 13-9 This shortcut menu appears after you right-click an e-mail message header.

Deleting E-Mail Messages

To permanently delete a received e-mail, right-click to open the shortcut menu and then select Delete Message.

Using Message Folders

You can use folders to organize the messages you've received. I recommend that you create several folders, so that you can keep messages for different projects or from different individuals separate. You cannot create folders for other e-mail systems, such as Outlook, this way; only for ACT!'s Internet mail.

To create a folder for incoming e-mail messages, follow these steps:

1. Right-click the Internet Mail Inbox in the Folders section.

13

2. From the shortcut menu, select Create Folder. The Add Folder dialog box appears, as shown in Figure 13-10.

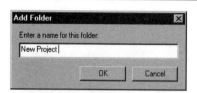

With the Add Folder dialog box, you can create new folders for incoming e-mail, making it easy to locate messages at a later time.

3. Type a name for the folder and click OK.

After creating the folder, you can move messages from the Internet Mail Inbox to the folder. Follow these steps to do so:

1. Click and hold down the mouse button on the message you want to move.

2. Drag the message to the folder in which you want to store it.

3. Release the mouse button. ACT! alerts you with a warning that moving the message causes it to be deleted from the current location.

4. Click Yes to complete the move.

You can move multiple messages at one time. Select the messages you want to move. (Click the first message and hold down SHIFT while you drag the cursor until the ones you want are highlighted.) Drag the messages to the destination folder. If the messages you want to move are not listed sequentially, hold down CTRL and select the individual messages you want to move.

When you receive e-mail messages, they appear in your inbox. The E-Mail window includes inbox icons for the e-mail systems you have set up to use in ACT!, such as cc:Mail, Internet Mail, or Microsoft Outlook. Unless you use more than one of these e-mail systems, your incoming e-mail messages will always appear in the same inbox. If you use multiple e-mail systems, you can view received e-mail messages in the individual inboxes for each system, or you can view all received e-mail messages for all systems in the Combined inbox. The Combined inbox appears only if you have set up multiple e-mail systems.

You also can move messages from your inbox to the Briefcase, which lets you read your messages when you are offline.

If you are using Internet Mail (ACT!'s e-mail account) and you have multiple e-mail accounts, you can retrieve mail for one or more of the accounts. When you choose the Get/Send Mail command, a dialog box appears in which all your Internet accounts are listed. Select the accounts to check for new mail, or select the Get Mail For All My Accounts option to check all accounts at one time.

How to Attach a Message to a Contact Record

You might prefer to attach a particular message to a contact in your ACT! database. That way, you can keep all the e-mail traffic with a particular contact with that contact. To attach an e-mail message to a contact record, follow these steps:

1. Right-click the record and from the shortcut menu select Attach E-Mail To Contact. The Attach E-Mail To Contact dialog box appears, as shown in Figure 13-11.

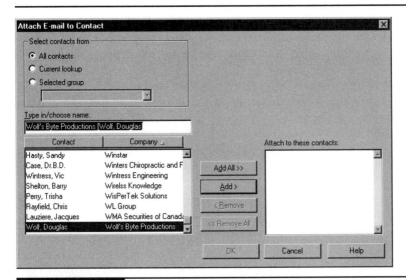

FIGURE 13-11   In this dialog box, you can attach a received e-mail message to a contact record.

2. Select the contact record, by scrolling the list and clicking the correct name, or type the first couple of letters of the contact's last name in the Type In/Choose Name box.

3. Click Add and then OK. The message is added as an attachment to the selected contact record, but is *not* removed from the inbox.

There is no way to automate this process. You must do it one message at a time.

Replying to an E-Mail Message

After opening an e-mail message, you can reply to the sender very easily. Right-click the message and from the shortcut menu, select Reply. A dialog box appears, asking if you want to include the message body from the sender. It is a good idea to do so, because that way the thread of

13

the messages is easy to follow. For example, if you send me a message, asking for an answer to a specific question, and I reply with the original text, I can be certain what you asked, if the question was clear, and if I supplied a congruent response. You, also, can be certain of what you asked, without having to look through your folders for your original message. On the other hand, if you have been sending me jokes, I might not want to reply with the joke included.

Forwarding an E-Mail Message

Forwarding an e-mail message is now the latest version of "fax-the-joke" (and uses less paper, to boot). Before e-mail became the standard, faxing was the way to spread the best jokes and cartoons—but the unintended consequence was that sometimes the wrong person read the fax. In the insane world of political correctness (and no sense of humor), this could cause a lawsuit and cost you your job. So, forwarding e-mail jokes is safer—if you are certain that your company does not prohibit it and the recipient is agreeable. Still, any e-mail message you send is like a postcard in that it can be read by any of the many administrative personnel that maintain the servers that process the messages.

 *According to industry sources, 60 percent of companies monitor e-mail using automated software tools that spot key words and phrases. Big Brother is not the government (yet)—it is your boss.*

To forward an e-mail message from your inbox or any folder, right-click the message and from the shortcut menu select Forward Message. The Address Book dialog box opens, from which you can select the recipients of the forwarded message.

 *E-mail etiquette is not well established at this time, but one good idea is to get an okay from every recipient before forwarding jokes and the like.*

Creating a Contact Record from a Received E-Mail Message

One of the terrific aspects of ACT! is the ease with which you can create a new contact record from an incoming e-mail message. Although ACT! does not enter everything, it does add the e-mail address for you. To create a record from a received message, follow these steps:

1. Open an e-mail message you received from a contact who is not in your database.

2. From the E-Mail menu, choose Create Contact From Sender. The Add Contact dialog box appears with the contact's e-mail address filled in.

3. Enter the contact's information and click OK.

4. The new contact is added to your database.

Navigating in E-Mail Messages

If you have more than one e-mail message in the inbox or a folder, use the left and right arrow buttons on the toolbar to move to the previous or next message. To return to the list view of your folder and see all the message headers, click the Inbox button on the toolbar.

Using Internet Links

ACT! includes a series of links to Internet web sites, which appears on the Online menu in the contact record window. When you open the menu and select ACT!, a submenu appears. In that submenu are links to the ACT! software web site; the ACT! Add-ons store, which has third-party products for ACT!; the list of certified ACT! consultants; and the ACT! Service and Support web site. Click one of the items and ACT! locates your web browser—such as Microsoft Internet Explorer or Netscape Navigator—and opens the Dialer dialog box (unless you are on a direct network connection) so that you can connect directly to the selected web site. The web site appears in a few moments and you can return to ACT! while being connected.

Customizing Internet Links

The real "oh wow" capability of this feature is being able to develop your own Internet or intranet links. This means that if you have favorite web sites that you want to visit frequently, you can do so directly from ACT!. Or if your company has an intranet, you can go directly to it to find out the latest on downsizing!

Creating your own Internet link is accomplished by opening a text file in Windows WordPad (a simple word processor that comes with Windows) and creating the linking text, and then saving the text as a file in the ACT\Netlinks folder. Here is an example:

1. Open Windows WordPad by clicking the Windows Start button and selecting Programs, then Accessories, and finally WordPad.

2. Type the name of the link, which will appear on the Internet Links menu, in brackets. So, for my web site, I type **[Wolf's Byte]**.

3. Add the URL (Universal Resource Locator). I type **http://www.howtosoftware.com**.

   The finished text should read [Wolf's Byte]http://www.howtosoftware.com.

4. Open the File menu and select Save As.

5. Make sure you are saving to the ACT\NetLinks folder.

6. The filename *must have quotes around it* and you must add the web filename extension (.web). So I type **"wolf.web"**.

7. Click the Save button.

13

8. Start ACT!.

9. Open the Internet Links menu and select Wolf's Byte.

With a little luck, the link worked, and you are propelled to the most informative, entertaining, and ACT!-enhancing web site of all. Thank you very much!

Checking for Updates

I cannot emphasize too much that you should, on a monthly basis, open the Help menu and select the Check For Updates command. Believe it or not, every software company ships products that have errors. They can cause problems, and Interact has developed the best way to solve these problems. Plus, new versions of ACT! are developed with enhancements, such as links to other programs, and the updates are free.

When you run Update, you are connected via your modem (or other connection) to an Interact computer. The Interact computer checks the file date of your version of ACT! and lets you know whether there is an update available and its size. At that point, you can decide to update ACT!, or if you do not have time to stay online to get the file, you can return later for the file. ACT! does everything for you; the file is downloaded from the Interact computer, and then applied to your program.

If you are on a network, your company probably has blocked this feature, so your Information Services person or network administrator must run Update from the server, and then send it to your computer.

Summary

- Create and send e-mail messages by opening the Write menu and selecting E-Mail.

- Send e-mail with contact records, groups, or files attached and send them to other ACT! users.

- With received e-mail, you can attach it to a contact or a group, forward it, or store in a folder.

- Open the Internet Links menu and browse to your destination. If you want to, add your own links.

Chapter 14

Setting Preferences

How to...

- Choose colors and fonts for display
- Customize scheduling
- Add words to the User dictionary
- Configure startup options

Preferences settings in ACT! allow you to customize many aspects of the ACT! program. As you'll see in this chapter, you can modify these settings via the Preferences dialog box to customize ACT! to your specific needs.

Network Versus Standalone Preferences

Most of the preference settings are particular to your login name—that is to say, on a network, you can log in on any machine and ACT! will remember your preferences. If you are the administrator of the ACT! database, you can modify some preferences, such as the location of the shared files, that affect all users of the database.

Working with the Preferences Dialog Box

To see the preferences settings, open the Edit menu and select Preferences. The Preferences dialog box appears, as shown in Figure 14-1. The Preferences dialog box contains 11 tabs, and each of these offers many options.

General Tab

The following sections describe the options on the General tab, which is displayed automatically when you open the dialog box.

Default Word Processor

Some of the preferences on the General tab were set when you installed ACT!. Most prominent is the selection of the default word processor. You have your choice of ACT!'s word processor or the popular, yet resource-hungry, Microsoft Word. The difference between the two programs is in scale: Word is the industrial-strength program with all the features, including the kitchen sink. ACT!'s word processor is very serviceable for 90 percent of the documents you are likely to create, and being more compact, is much faster. Any document you create in the ACT! word processor can be saved or exported to an ASCII or RTF file, allowing any word processor to open it. Many companies insist that you use Word; if yours is one of them, you might not have a choice.

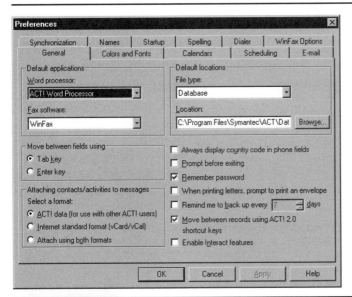

FIGURE 14-1 The Preferences dialog box displays the General tab by default when you open it from the Edit menu.

RTF Standard

RTF is short for Rich Text Format. This standard, developed by Microsoft, is a step up from ASCII. It allows special formatting, such as **bold** and *italic* text. RTF files are readable by almost all Windows-based word processors and many other programs. So, you can create documents in the ACT! word processor or Microsoft Word and save both as RTF files that can be opened by all word processors.

Default Fax Software

14

The next choice in establishing preferences is the default faxing software. ACT! was, at one point, produced by Symantec, and the best faxing software is WinFax, still produced by Symantec and tightly integrated with ACT!. In fact, it is so tightly integrated that you can edit an ACT! record directly from WinFax. If WinFax is installed, ACT! displays it as the default software. Chapter 11 describes how to send documents created in ACT! via WinFax.

Move Between Fields Using TAB or ENTER

Many DOS users are still wedded to the ENTER key as the one to press when moving between fields. Because of this, though the default setting for moving between fields is TAB (the Windows standard) you can switch it to ENTER. In Chapter 16, I discuss the way in which you can optimize your ACT! routine using both TAB and ENTER for data entry.

Attaching Contacts/Activities to Messages

ACT! allows you to send contacts and activities to other ACT! users, or to Outlook users, via e-mail. The recipient can then add the contact or activity to his or her own database. The default is to send in ACT! format, but if you are sharing data with Outlook users, you can use the vCard or vCal format. At the time you send the e-mail message, you can also change the format.

Always Display Country Codes in Phone Fields

This check box is found on the right half of the dialog box, beneath the Default locations section. If your firm deals with many companies or individuals that are from other countries, this setting specifies that the country code is displayed with the number. This feature is a timesaver when you are dialing the phone manually, as it eliminates the step of looking up the country code before you place the call.

If you do not enter your own phone number in your My Record, ACT! automatically inserts the country code prefix in every record. Entering the phone number in the My Record eliminates display of the country code.

If you enter a contact record without a phone number and you include a country entry that is different from the My Record, ACT! inserts the country code for you when you do enter the phone number.

Prompt Before Exiting

Select this option if you want ACT! to alert you that you are closing the program, at which point you can decide to keep it open. Frankly, unless you are prone to clicking the exit box in the upper-right corner of the ACT! program window, you can let ACT! assume you want to quit when you tell it to.

Unlike other programs, ACT! automatically saves your data when you move from record to record or when you exit ACT!.

Remember Password

The password entry (displayed in asterisks) will remain in the logon dialog box unless you clear this check box. You might want ACT! to require a password every time if your computer is in an area where others could gain access.

You are not required to have a password, but on a multi-user database you must enter your own user name.

When Printing Letters, Prompt to Print an Envelope

When you create and print a letter, you can have ACT! ask you if you also want to print an envelope. This check box is selected by default, which means that you will be prompted every time. If you are on a network, you'll probably want to turn off this feature. You can always print an envelope, label, or whatever you need from the File menu.

Remind Me to Back Up Every X Days

Turn this setting off if you are on a network unless you are in charge of making backups. Leave it on if you are a standalone user. The question is, how often to back up? Do it *every* day, and you'll never lose your data.

Although most of us have learned the hard way to make backups, virtually none of my clients ever test the efficacy of the backed files. I recommend that once a quarter you try to restore the backup data. You might be surprised.

Move Between Records Using ACT! 2.0 Shortcut Keys

The shortcut keys you can choose to invoke are PGUP and PGDN to move from record to record, and CTRL-HOME to go to the first record in the lookup and CTRL-END to go to the last record in the lookup.

Enable Interact Features

In version 2000 of ACT!, this option is available. It may or may not be in the version you have installed. If it is available, selecting the check box and then restarting ACT! adds a new tab, called Profile, to the bottom half of the contact record window between the Groups and User Fields tabs. The tab presents information on the company that is listed in the contact record such as current stock price and company media releases. It can also connect you to the wireless features of ACT!, such as browsing your ACT! database via a web-enabled cell phone.

14

Default File Locations

When you installed ACT!, it created the subfolders it needed for databases, documents, layouts, reports, and so on. For a standalone installation, the default choices should be quite adequate. With the release of Windows 98, Microsoft insisted that user-created files such as ACT! databases or documents must be stored in subfolders of the My Documents folder. So, if you use Windows Explorer to browse your computer files, you will see ACT\Database and ACT\Documents as subfolders of My Documents *and* as subfolders of Program Files.

On a network with a shared database, the default locations should be changed. Assuming that you are the person in charge of ACT!, you need to be able to create folders on the network server. This task is not difficult, but you might need the help of the network administrator. The folders must allow for read, write, and delete access or when someone tries to open the database he or she might get the message "Not an ACT! database. Do you want to import it?," which tells you that the folder permissions are not correct.

My recommendation is that you create a minimum of two folders, one for the database and one for customized layouts. If you want all ACT! users to use the same document, fax, and memo templates, then a folder for those is in order as well. (In addition, because ACT! allows you to attach sent and received e-mail messages to a contact record, a folder for shared e-mail should be created. Chapter 13 covers this situation in more detail.) After creating the folders, you need to go to each computer that will be accessing the database, open the Preferences dialog box, and make the changes as follows:

1. In the Preferences dialog box, on the General tab, click the drop-down arrow to select the file type.

2. For databases, select Database as the file type. Click the Browse button. Navigate to the folder that has or will contain the matching file. For example, if the file type is Database and you have created a folder on the network server named ACTDATABASE, navigate to that folder.

3. Click OK.

After doing so, when the user opens the File menu and selects Open, ACT! will look in this folder for database files. Repeat the steps for each type of file that you want shared by all ACT! users on the network.

Although the MIS department prefers that you map file locations using UNC (Universal Naming Convention), ACT! prefers mapping the drive. Use Network Neighborhood to browse to the server upon which ACT! is stored. If the entry in the field is something like \\server c\\act\\database, that is UNC data and you should change it.

ACT! is programmed to open the last accessed database every time you start. So, if you open the SALES database on your C drive, and then shut down ACT!, the next time you start ACT!, it opens the SALES database. To have ACT! open the shared database on the network, open the File menu and select Open. Because you have changed which folder ACT! is to look in when opening a database (by changing the setting in the Preferences dialog box), the shared database should be visible. Select the shared database and open it. Next, exit ACT!. Now, reopen ACT!, and the shared database is opened automatically. Several other preferences settings are integral to insuring that the user always opens the shared database. These settings are discussed in the "Startup Tab" section later in this chapter.

You must first log onto the network to access a shared ACT! database. Usually, to do so, you are asked to enter a user name and password when you start your computer. Of course, you can choose to log onto your computer without accessing the network, but if you aren't logged onto the network, you can't access the database files located there. After accessing the network, start ACT! and enter the user name and password specific to ACT!.

Colors and Fonts Tab

One of the first things I do for my clients is to change the display for Notes. Why? Because people refer to them almost every time they look up a record, and the default font setting for notes is so tiny (8 point) that eyestrain is inevitable. Making the font larger and adding grid lines will greatly increase legibility, and this change is easy to make on the Colors and Fonts tab of the Preferences dialog box, shown in Figure 14-2. The following instructions can be used to modify any of the items in the Customize list.

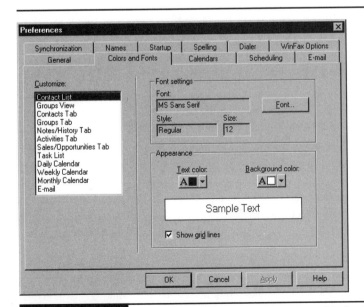

14

FIGURE 14-2 You can change text appearance with the Colors and Fonts tab of the Preferences dialog box.

To increase font size and add grid lines to the Notes/History tab, follow these steps:

1. Select Notes/History Tab in the Customize list.

2. Click the Font button. The Font dialog box appears, as shown in Figure 14-3.

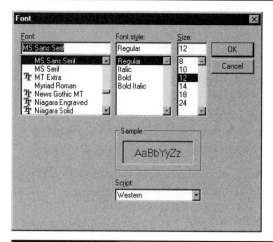

FIGURE 14-3   Select a new font in the Font dialog box.

3. If you suffer from middle-age presbyopia, as do I, 14-point type might be the choice for you. If you are so inclined, change the font style and the font, too. By customizing all the tabs in ACT!, you can tell at a glance which tab is selected by the fonts selected or by the presence of grid lines.

4. Click OK.

5. Select the Show Grid Lines check box on the Colors and Fonts tab, and click OK. Figure 14-4 shows the Notes/History tab with the larger font and grid lines.

The grid lines make it easier for the eye to follow the entries. However, the columns do not automatically expand to accommodate the new size, so you might have to move the mouse pointer to the column border and drag it to the right to make more room for the entries.

Color and font preferences are specific to the individual user. So, on a network, each person can have his or her own look and feel to ACT!.

Calendars Tab

The Calendars tab has one crucial setting, that being the choice to display the contact name or the company name on the calendars. The distinction is whether you want to see the name of the person with whom you have an activity scheduled or the name of the company. If you choose the company name, and the person with whom the activity is scheduled does not have an entry in the company field, the contact name appears.

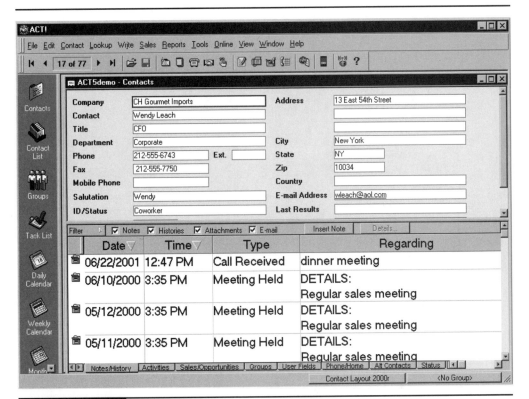

FIGURE 14-4   Using 14-point type and grid lines makes the Notes/History tab much easier to read.

The other settings on this tab are whether to have the week start on Sunday or Monday, what time increment to use for the daily and weekly calendars, and what time to show for the start of day. The full-day banner runs across the bottom of the individual day for any activity that meets the specified duration. The final setting is for the Mini-calendar, with three months being the default.

Scheduling Tab

The settings on the Scheduling tab control the defaults for scheduling an activity. To access the preferences for each type of activity (call, meeting, or to-do) select that activity in the Settings For list. The options for that type of activity are then available in the rest of the dialog box. It's a good idea to schedule a few different activities before you decide what the defaults should be. (Remember, you can always change any of the attributes for the particular activity at the time you schedule it.) Figure 14-5 shows the default settings for scheduling calls.

14

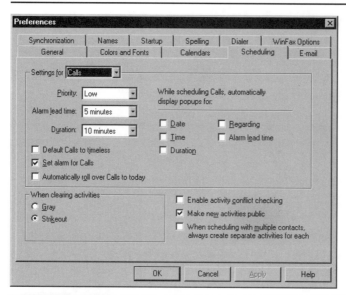

FIGURE 14-5   With Calls selected in the Settings For list, you can set the defaults that will be used when you schedule a phone call.

Automatically Display Popups For

For your activity defaults, the popup menu settings are among the most important. Popup menus are handy for speed in scheduling a new activity, but they can be clumsy when rescheduling an activity. For example, when you schedule a call, you might want to see the month calendar (Date option) pop up so as to pick a date, but you might not want the Time popup to appear. For meetings, you probably want the Date and Time popups to open.

Automatically Roll Over To Today

Even more important than popup menus is ACT!'s rolling over feature. I strongly urge that you have all calls and to-dos automatically roll over to the next day if you don't clear them. That way, ACT! continues to remind you of the activity. Also, you can make sure that an alarm is set for all your activities to remind you when the time approaches.

   *It is not a good idea to have activities rolling over in a synchronization environment. See Chapter 25 for more information on synchronization.*

The only drawback to rolling over is if you fail to clear completed activities. If you have been using ACT! for some time and have not been clearing activities, changing this setting causes ACT! to find any activities that have not been cleared and roll them over immediately.

If you have been negligent in closing out your tasks, you might find hundreds of uncleared activities—which can take hours to clean up. Proceed with caution.

When Clearing Activities

This setting lets you determine how to display completed activities. The best time-management experts recommend that a line should be struck through the item. In a world in which we mostly manipulate information rather than objects, it is satisfying to look at your Task List and see a series of scheduled activities crossed off. As you might expect, then, Strikeout text is ACT!'s default for displaying completed tasks.

Enable Activity Conflict Checking

If this option is selected, ACT! alerts you when you try to schedule more than one activity for the same time. When ACT! recognizes the conflict, a message alerts you to the fact, but you can ignore the conflict if you wish, or reschedule the new activity. I recommend leaving this option on, though it is not the default, so select this check box.

Make New Activities Public

This setting is for network use. The default is that all activities are public—that is, anyone using the shared database can see what you are up to. Any individual activity you schedule can be made private, so accept the default, and leave the check box selected.

When Scheduling with Multiple Contacts, Always Create Separate Activities For Each

This setting is handy when you are inviting more than one person to the same appointment. If you are scheduling a meeting with several people, you can have ACT! add the activity to your calendar separately with each meeting invitee, or with only the initial invitee. If you choose the latter, instead of your calendar being crowded with a host of names at the 2 P.M. time slot, only a single name will appear, followed by three dots indicating more folks are involved. The default, to create a single activity, is the superior way, so leave this check box cleared.

E-Mail Tab

Take a peek at Chapter 13 for the steps to set up e-mail. If you have already done the setup and are having problems, check the settings on this tab.

Synchronization Tab

Synchronization is the process whereby two or more databases are updated so that all data is identical in all databases. Let's say your company has a master database of all its customers

14

and you, as a sales representative, often have to modify records that are in the main database while you are on the road. How can the main database be updated to reflect all your changes without having to reenter all that data by hand? Easily. ACT!'s synchronization feature allows you to get the data in synch so that both have identical information.

This tab reflects the settings that have been made when synchronization is set up. Because of the complexity of the subject, see Chapter 25 for a complete discussion.

Names Tab

Because people's names vary widely, when you enter a person's name as part of a contact record, ACT! might have a hard time determining which text is the first and which the last name. You can help ACT! with this task by modifying the settings on this tab. Here you can see what ACT! recognizes as first name prefixes, last name prefixes, and last name suffixes. So, if you enter a name such Dr. Kris van Lom Sr., ACT! knows that the *Dr.* is not the first name and that the last name is not *Sr.*

If you commonly enter names with unusual prefixes, add them to the list. ACT! automatically opens the Definition dialog box for unusual names—but you can set this default to off.

American readers may want to remove the prefixes Don and Dona (the Spanish Mr. and Ms.) because if someone types in Don Lagarde then Don is considered a prefix.

If you import records that contain name prefixes and/or suffixes as part of the name, ACT! will not correctly recognize the first and last names, so you will have to manually identify them. I described this process in Chapter 3.

The Salutation setting also is determined on this tab. When you enter a name, ACT! selects the first name, last name, or no entry into the salutation field as directed here. You can always edit the entry you want in the salutation field, which is then used in the word processing letter template.

Startup Tab

The settings on this tab, shown in Figure 14-6, work with the settings for the default file locations found on the General tab. The Default Contact Layout setting is used to make certain that every user on a shared database has the same layout. To do so, click the gray box with the small dots to the right of the field. This opens the Browse window, from which you can locate the folder that has the layout you want the user to see. The group layout can be set up the same way. By making these entries, you can feel confident that the layout you have painstakingly designed is actually in use!

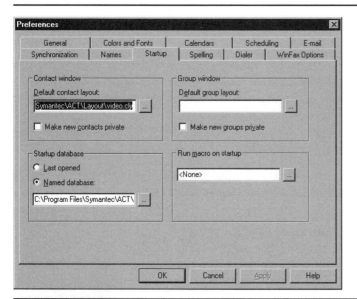

FIGURE 14-6   The Preferences dialog box Startup tab lets you assign which database opens automatically when ACT! is launched.

The last two settings of note are Make New Contacts Private and Make New Groups Private. Use these settings when you plan to enter multiple records into a shared database that you want marked as private. Do the same with group records. Suppose that you want to create several groups, like the tennis players from your club, your euchre partners, and your PTA roster, but you want the records to be private and the groups to be accessible by you only. Select both the Make New Contacts Private and Make New Groups Private check boxes and enter your data.

You also can run a macro when you open ACT!. You could also have ACT! download your e-mail when ACT! starts. See Chapter 16 for information on creating macros.

Spelling Tab

This tab pertains to creating documents. ACT!'s word processor has a built-in spell checker, but you may want to customize it with words that are specific to your profession so that ACT! does not stop on those words. Or, you can create industry-specific dictionaries that you can access when you are spell checking, thereby allowing words and spellings in one instance that would be incorrect in another.

ACT! also has choices for dialect—English being the common language that separates the British, Americans, and Australians—so you can select the dialect that fits your country.

To add a new word to the User dictionary, follow these steps:

1.   Click the User Dictionary field.

14

2. Click the Modify button. The User Dictionary dialog box appears atop the Spelling tab.

3. Click Add. The Add Word dialog box opens, as shown in Figure 14-7.

FIGURE 14-7   Add new words to the User dictionary with this dialog box, accessed on the Spelling tab of the Preferences dialog box.

4. Type the word that you want to add.

5. Click OK, twice.

The next time you spell-check a document using ACT!'s word processor, the new word is ignored and considered correct. If you are forced to use Word, you must modify its dictionary separately; changes you've made to ACT!'s User dictionary will not carry over.

The Auto Suggest Spelling feature is set to on by default. During a spell check, if ACT! runs into a word it doesn't recognize, a dialog box pops up that contains suggestions for the correct spelling. For example, if you typed **thier**, ACT! would suggest "their."

Dialer Tab

The dialer is a terrific feature in ACT! and can increase your productivity when used properly. You can use the settings on the Dialer tab, shown in Figure 14-8, to ensure optimum efficiency. For example, ACT! never misdials the number. Using the dialer starts the recording process for the call—automatically making an entry in the Notes/History tab and prompting you to record what happened in the call. You can also designate different locations from which to dial, home or office, for example, which can be handy if you use a laptop.

Enabling the Dialer

To enable the dialer, click the Use Dialer check box. This might be all you have to do, as ACT! looks at the Windows settings to determine whether you have a modem. If it finds one, then ACT! inserts the pertinent information into the fields.

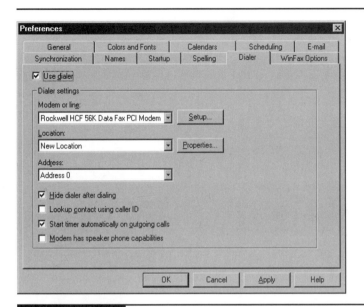

FIGURE 14-8   Configure dialer options on the Dialer tab of the Preferences dialog box.

Modem Setup

To change the settings for the modem, click the Setup button. Each modem has its own characteristics, so you might have to refer to the information supplied by the modem manufacturer to make changes. Usually, Windows handles all this for you.

Configuring for Multiple Dialing Locations

Suppose that you have a laptop and want to be able to use ACT! to dial from your office and also from home. Because the dialing sequence is likely to be different in each location, ACT! needs to know the differences. To set this up, follow these steps:

1. Click the Properties button. The Dialing Properties dialog box appears, as shown in Figure 14-9.

2. In the I Am Dialing From box, enter the name of the location, such as **Office**.

3. Open the drop-down list to select the country from which you are dialing.

4. Enter the area code, if appropriate.

5. Click the Area Code Rules button, and you see the Area Code Rules dialog box, as shown in Figure 14-10.

14

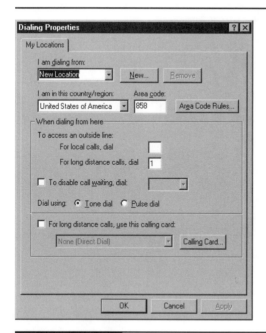

Use the Dialing Properties dialog box to create unique dialing
locations.

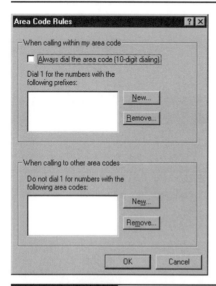

Use the Area Code Rules dialog box to establish whether certain area
codes require a 1 prefix.

The demand for new phone numbers has created a proliferation of new area codes. Ergo, the need for fancy ways to cram more numbers into an established area. Ten-digit dialing is one method and your area might be subject to this inconvenience. A refinement of the phone company dialing confusion is the requirement to dial a 1 for some prefixes, and not others! Use this dialog box to enter the rules for your area. If you are lucky, you will only have to do this once a year or so.

6. Click OK.

7. To create a second dialing location, such as home or a satellite office, click the New button on the Dialing Properties dialog box. Then enter the new dialing location in the dialog box that appears.

8. In the When Dialing From Here section of the Dialing Properties dialog box, enter the initial numbers for local calls and long distance.

9. Call waiting is next. You want to disable it if you have a dial-up Internet connection that uses the same line as your telephone, or you will be bumped off any time a call comes in. Select the check box and enter the code for disabling call waiting. (Consult your phone company for this code.)

10. Although long distance calling has gotten cheaper, it is not yet free, and many companies require that you use a credit/calling card to track calls. ACT! provides a painless way to use a calling card or alternative phone service. Click the long distance check box, and then open the drop-down list that includes many carrier access codes. For credit cards, click the Calling Card button, and then New, and finish by entering the numbers as required.

11. Click OK to close the My Locations tab.

Hide Dialer After Dialing

Use this option to close the dialer dialog box after ACT! completes the dialing process.

Lookup Contact Using Caller ID

Use this option if your phone system has caller ID. When you receive a call, ACT! attempts to match the phone number on the ID with any contacts in the database, and if it does, takes you directly to that record.

Start Timer Automatically On Outgoing Calls

If you are dialing via ACT! and need to time virtually all of your calls, this should be set to on.

Modem Has Speaker Phone Capabilities

Set this to on if it is true, even if you never plan to use the speaker phone.

Windows NT does not support speaker phone service.

WinFax Options Tab

If you have WinFax installed on your computer, the WinFax Options tab, shown in Figure 14-11, is available. First, you can make the ACT! database a phone book for WinFax, which means that all your contacts can be faxed directly from ACT! or directly from WinFax—even if ACT! is not running! The logging features are very valuable, and I recommend that you check all the boxes unless you fax to clients so frequently that history entries will become overwhelming. Particularly inviting is the option to have an activity created to resend a fax when a scheduled fax fails.

Finally, you can have a link created to the fax that is visible on the Notes/History tab. Click the link to open the fax itself, directly from ACT!

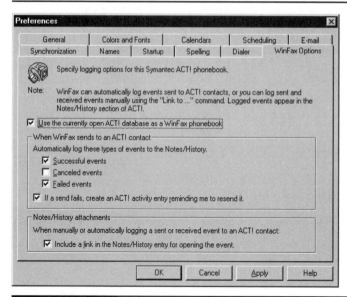

FIGURE 14-11 The WinFax Options tab appears with a variety of options regarding ACT!.

Sending more than 200 faxes as a mail merge is likely to overburden your system. When clients ask what to do, I point them to a third-party faxing service that will take your ACT! information and the document and send it for you. Check Appendix A for information on the fax service.

Summary

■   The Preferences dialog box lets you establish ACT!'s default settings the way you like them.

■   You can adjust the color and font ACT! uses to display your data to make it easier to read.

■   You can configure the dialer to place your phone calls for you.

■   You can direct ACT! to open the same database every time you start ACT! with the layout you want.

■   You can configure your defaults for scheduling activities to make new entries as fast as possible.

14

Chapter 15

Working with Groups

How to...

- Work with groups and subgroups
- Create a new group
- Use lookups on groups
- Use grouping to synchronize data
- Create group membership rules
- Use reminders to update groups

Understanding Groups Versus ID/Status

One of the main fields in ACT! is the ID/Status field. By main, I mean that its use in your database should be considered judiciously. In Chapter 3, I stressed the importance of the ID/Status and its relation to groups. The key idea is that the ID/Status field can be used as the primary categorizing field. For example, if your firm is using ACT! as a sales tool, you might have four types of entries for ID/Status: Prospect, Suspect, Customer, and Inactive. With this system, you could look up all your customers and send them a special direct mail, fax, or e-mail on closeout pricing.

The use of groups can involve subsets of the ID/Status. For example, you could create a group of customers who only purchase a particular product or customers who only respond to closeout pricing offers. You could create a group that includes an ID/Status of Prospect that previously was a Suspect. The possibilities are endless because a contact record can be a member of as many groups as you want, and you can add an unlimited number of groups. In addition, you can create subgroups, which means you can have a main group identified as widget customers and subgroups of those same widget customers sorted by geographic territory.

You can also think of group records as a master record for a particular company. If you have 45 contacts who work for BIG Company, you can create a group record that includes the main address and phone and other pertinent company information and then add the individual records to the group. (If the 45 folks all worked at the same location, it would be redundant to create a group record.) With a group record, you can add notes and history that are pertinent to the company, and not have to add notes on individual contact records that are superfluous.

After a group is created, you can access it by two means. You can click the Groups icon at the left of the contact record window and from the list that appears in the group window, click the group. Or you can click the Group button at the bottom right of the contact record window and select the group from that list.

TIP *An important point about groups is that the contact records do not have to have any relationship before being assigned to the group.*

Creating a New Group

The ACT! 2000 demo database, ACT5demo, has several groups already. Use the demonstration database or your own to follow these steps to make a new group.

1. Click the Groups icon. The Groups window opens, as shown in Figure 15-1. (You can have different layouts for a group window, as discussed in Chapter 16. This layout is the Group Layout 2000.)

FIGURE 15-1   The Groups window looks like this.

2. Open the Group menu and select New Group. The menu closes and ACT! presents a blank group record screen.

3. Enter a name for the group in the Group Name field.

15

4. In the Description field, enter a description for the group. This is important. As the number of groups increases, the description helps to eliminate the problem of people creating duplicate groups.

5. Open the Group menu again and select Group Membership.

6. Select Add/Remove Contacts. The Add/Remove Contacts dialog box appears, as shown in Figure 15-2.

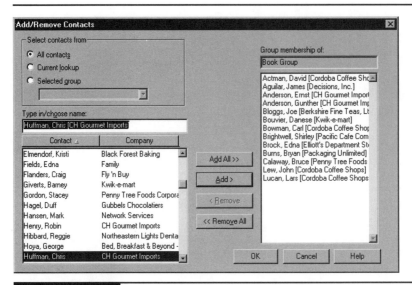

FIGURE 15-2 The Add/Remove Contacts dialog box is one way to add contacts to a group.

7. Select the radio button for All Contacts, Current Lookup, or Selected Group.

8. Click the name or company that you want to include in the group, and then click the Add button.

9. After selecting all the contacts that are to be members of the group, click OK. ACT! creates the group, and the group members are shown on the Contacts tab.

After you add contact records to the group and click OK to finish, do not be alarmed if ACT! seems as if it has stopped responding. It is working hard creating the group. On a database with several thousand records shared on a network, this is coffee break time.

Selecting a Group from the Contact Record Window

To see how the group is selected, close the Groups window, or change to the contact record window by clicking the Contacts icon at the left. At the bottom right of the contact record window, there are two long buttons, one for selecting groups (labeled No Group in Figure 15-3) and the second for selecting layouts. The default layout is Contact Layout 2000r.

Click the group button and ACT! displays a list of all groups in the database, as shown in Figure 15-3. If you have many groups, you might have to scroll through the list. Click the name of the group you want to select.

After you select the group, the name of the group appears on the group button to alert you that you are working within a group. Once you have selected a group, you can scroll the records within the group, add or delete contact records, run reports, or use this set of records to print labels.

TIP

If you want to print labels or run reports, the Run Report dialog box choice of Current Lookup is the same as the group selected.

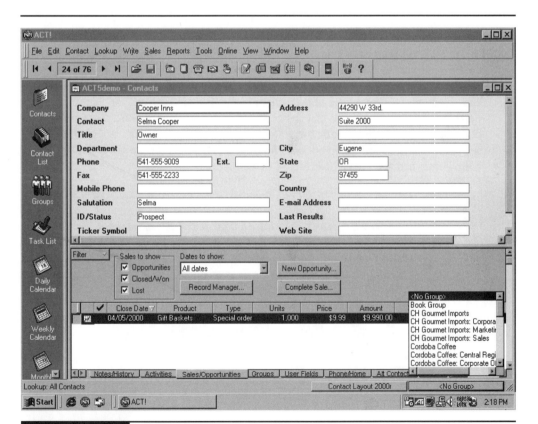

FIGURE 15-3   When you point the cursor to the group button, the list of groups appears.

Grouping and Its Effect on Lookups

When you are working in a group, you can always create a new lookup that considers all contact records for the lookup, but you can't use the Add To The Lookup option. You can use the Narrow option while in a group, but ACT! is only going to use the group members in its search. So if you have a group active, and you want to look up contact records in that group that have an ID/Status of Customer, you can do so by opening the Lookup menu, selecting ID/Status and selecting Customer, and then clicking the Narrow radio button.

Adding New Members to a Group Using a Lookup

You do not have to add members to a group upon its creation. You can simply go as far as creating the group by giving it a name and stop. Suppose that you have a large database and you want to use groups. I recommend that you decide on the groups you want and create them. Next, create a lookup that finds most (or all) of the members of the group. At that point, you can open the Groups window, select the group to which you want to add the contact records, and select the Current Lookup as the records from which to choose the new members.

But what if the group you want to create has nothing in common, making it difficult to create a lookup? In Chapter 6, you were introduced to the concept of working in a List view of the contact records. Create the lookup by opening the List view, opening the Lookup menu, and selecting All Contacts, and then changing to Tag mode. Now you can scroll the entire database and click the records that are to be members of the new group. After tagging the records, click the Lookup Tagged button, open the Groups window, and then open the Group menu and select the Group Membership option. From the dialog box, you can select the Current Lookup radio button and add the tagged records to the group.

> **TIP**
> *If you work on a shared database, you can create private groups, such as your bridge team or golfing buddies. The only person who can see the group is the person who created the group and access is based on the login name of the user. Not even an administrator can see the group. Before you create the group, open the Edit menu, select Preferences, and click the Startup tab. Click the radio button for Make New Groups Private.*

Adding an Existing Contact Record to a Group

After you have created a group and added some members to it, as you add new contact records you may wish to add the record to a particular group. Let's look at the manual way first.

1. Look up the contact record that you want to add to a group.

2. Click the Groups tab (between the Sales/Opportunities and the User Fields tabs) at the bottom of the contact record window (be sure you click the Groups tab, not the group button). Check the results against Figure 15-4 to make sure the correct tab is selected.

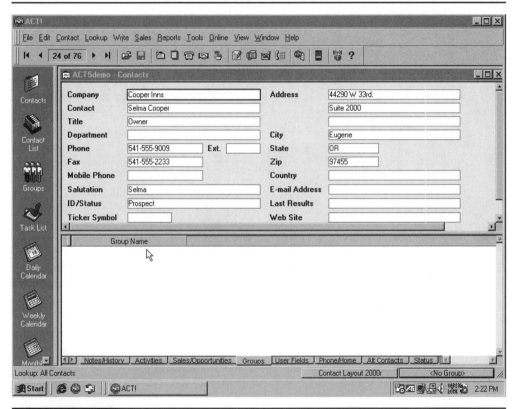

FIGURE 15-4   Your contact record looks like this with the Groups tab selected.

3. Right-click in the tab space to open the shortcut menu shown in Figure 15-5.

4. Select Group Membership. The Group Membership dialog box appears, as shown in Figure 15-6. This dialog box is the reverse of the Group Membership dialog box that you see when you are adding members. Only a single contact record is available, but all the existing groups are listed.

15

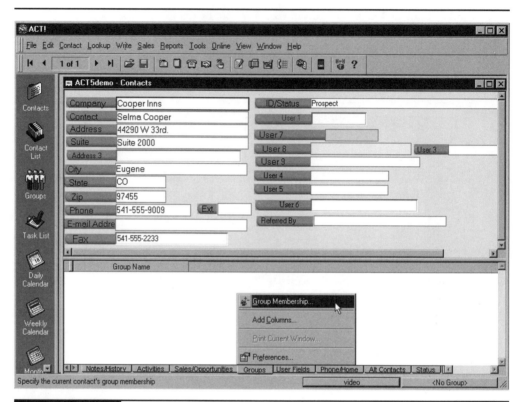

FIGURE 15-5 Right-click to open this shortcut menu in the Groups tab.

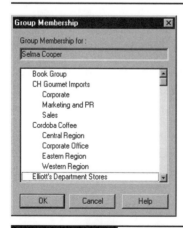

FIGURE 15-6 This Group Membership dialog box appears when you select Group Membership from the shortcut menu.

5. Scroll through the list and click the group name you want to add. A check mark appears in front of the group name, indicating that the record has been added to that group. Click as many groups as you want.

6. Click OK. The group name(s) appears in the Groups tab, as shown in Figure 15-7.

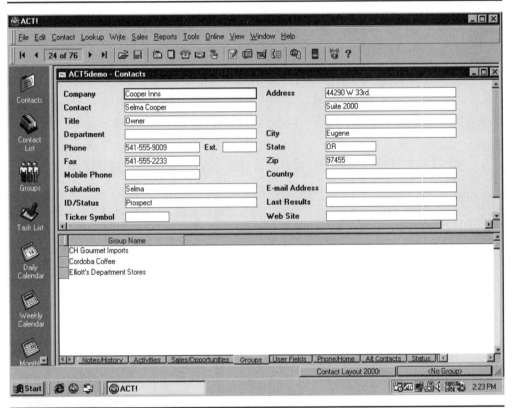

FIGURE 15-7   A contact record has been added to several groups.

Adding a New Contact Record to a Group

15

If you know that you are going to enter a new contact record, and you know that the contact record belongs in a certain group, you can add the record to the group at the same time. Select the group to which you want to add the contact record by clicking the group button. Then click the New Contact button and create the record. Because you selected the group before making the entry, ACT! assumes that the record belongs to that group. This can work the wrong way too, so make sure that the group button either reads No Group or has the group name you intend.

Removing a Contact Record from a Group

In the same way you added a contact record to a group, you can remove a record by clicking the Groups tab, right-clicking to open the shortcut menu, selecting Group Membership, and then clicking on a group name. The check mark is removed, removing the contact from that group.

Associating Activities with a Group

When you schedule an activity, one of the fields in the Schedule Activity dialog box is Associate With Group. By pulling down the list, you can select the group. What this does is add the activity to the group via its Activity tab. But, it does not schedule an activity with all members of that group. By associating an activity with a group, group reports reflect that activity.

Understanding Grouping and Synchronization

Another aspect of grouping is its use in synchronization. Generally, a company has a large database in its office and sales representatives with laptops in the field. If the company database has 20,000 records, it is not practical to synchronize all 20,000 records with each salesperson, especially when it is highly unlikely that a single salesperson is going to work with all 20,000 contact records. So ACT! uses groups to split the database into smaller pieces. What most companies do is create a lookup by state (or states) or Zip code (or codes) and then create the group. The group is then synched to the salesperson via e-mail or shared folders. As the salesperson makes changes, ACT! tracks the dates of the changes, creating a log. When the salesperson executes the synchronization process, only the changed records are sent to the company database. Likewise, the company database tracks changes and sends the changed records for that group to the salesperson. Chapter 24 covers the record tracking process in more detail.

Creating Subgroups of Groups

Refining the concept of grouping records even further, you can create subgroups of an existing group. In the ACT5demo database, there are several excellent examples of how this can be put to use. One of the groups is named Cordoba Coffee. When you open the Groups window, at the left is a list of the existing groups. A minus (-) or plus (+) sign preceding the group name indicates that there are subgroups under the parent group. To see the subgroup, click the minus or plus sign and the list is expanded. You can see an example of an expanded list in Figure 15-8.

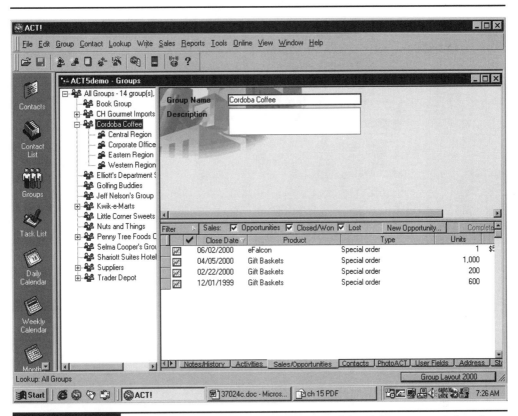

FIGURE 15-8 You've selected and expanded the Cordoba Coffee group to show its subgroups.

To create a subgroup:

1. Right-click the parent group. The shortcut menu appears, as shown in Figure 15-9.

2. Select New Subgroup.

3. The Group Name field now has the word "Untitled" in it. Enter a name for the new subgroup.

4. Add a description if the name does not make it obvious.

5. Open the Group menu and select Group Membership.

6. Add the members to the group.

7. Click OK.

15

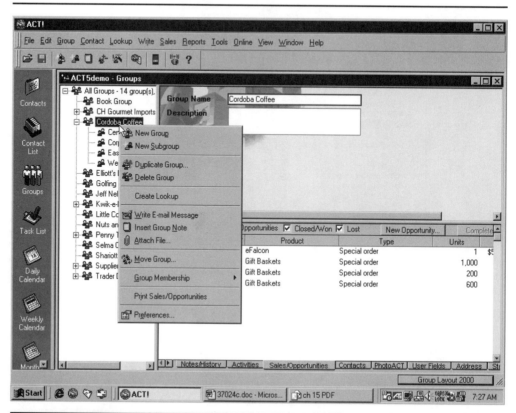

FIGURE 15-9 This shortcut menu appears after you right-click the parent group name.

Looking at Group Layouts

To fire your imagination in using groups, several layouts are included. Layouts are discussed in detail in Chapter 16. For the moment, take a look at the Account layout shown in Figure 15-10.

To see the layout, click the button at the bottom of the window labeled Group Layout 2000. Select Account Layout from the list.

As you can see, this layout reveals a great many more fields. The new fields provide a place to enter information that is more relevant to a group of contact records than it would be to a single contact. The idea is that you might have dozens of individuals in your database who all work for the same company and even in the same location. You can group those individuals and then have a place to enter information that applies to them all in a general way.

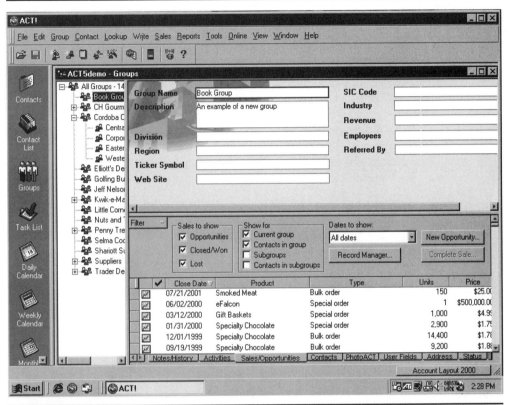

FIGURE 15-10 You can invoke this Account layout alternative to the default layout.

Adding New Group Fields

The steps to adding new fields to a group layout are nearly identical to adding fields to the contact record layouts. For the details, see Chapter 17.

Creating Group Membership Rules

This aspect of groups is particularly important to companies that synchronize databases. Consider a company with a home office database and 20 sales representatives with laptops who receive updates for their group of records via e-mail synchronization. If the home office is

15

generating new contact records as leads and inputting those leads into ACT!, very strong input discipline must be exercised by the home office so that every new lead is correctly assigned to the appropriate group. For example, salesperson Tim Kelly in Le Center, Minnesota, covers Minnesota, North and South Dakota, Iowa, and Wisconsin. The home office generates new sales leads via direct mail and prospects calling their toll-free number. Once a week, Tim synchronizes his database and receives the new leads, while sending his activities to the home office database. Many companies are good at generating new leads, but not very good at getting them to the sales force in a timely and effective manner. In this case, when the lead is added to ACT!, the home office person doing so has to know which salesperson covers which territory and make sure that the lead is identified as being part of his group. You can see the problem. ACT! 2000 automates the process of adding new contact records to the correct group, so the only thing the home office has to do is execute the process, as follows:

1. The manner in which contacts are going to be grouped must be determined: by state, Zip code, or an entry in an ACT! field.

2. Click the Groups icon to open the Groups window.

3. Select the group to which you want to add a membership rule.

4. Open the Group menu and select Group Membership.

5. Select Define Rules. The Group Membership Rules Wizard opens, as shown in Figure 15-11.

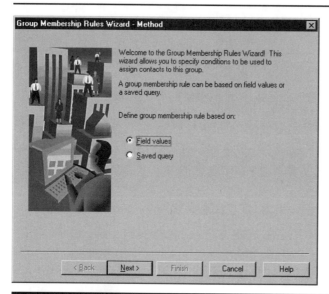

FIGURE 15-11   The Group Membership Rules Wizard guides you through creating rules for adding contact records to groups.

6. As you can see, creation of the membership rule begins by identifying how the contact record is added to a group: because of an entry in a particular field (Field Values) or as a result of a query (Saved Query). Remember, a query is an advanced form of a lookup and can be saved for reuse. (For more information on queries, see Chapter 5.) In the scenario outlined previously, Tim Kelly has several states in his territory, so looking at a field value might be the easiest rule to create. For this example, select Field Values and click Next.

7. The Rule 1 page appears. Select the contact field that you want ACT! to check when following the rule. In this example, shown in Figure 15-12, the State field is selected.

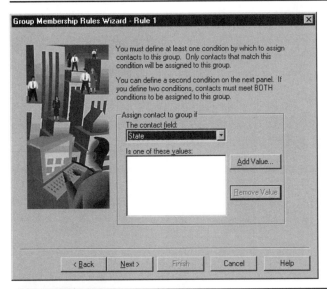

FIGURE 15-12   The State field is the field evaluated in this rule.

8. Click the Add Value button. ACT! opens the list of entries from the field selected. In this case, a list of the state name abbreviations is shown, as shown in Figure 15-13.

FIGURE 15-13   In the Add Value dialog box, you've selected the State field and opened the list of states.

15

9. Click the first value that matches your rule, such as state equals Minnesota.

10. Click OK. The value is added.

11. Repeat the process until all values are selected. The value does not have to be in the list to be entered. If you are building a new database and have not added any records or drop-down field lists, you can still proceed to create the rule.

12. Click Next.

13. If you want, add a second condition just as you did with the first. Be careful though, because when you entered the first condition, the field values to match on used the "or" as the criteria. To define the sales territory for Tim Kelly, you would include all four states in the first condition. Adding a second condition means that the record must have one of the first conditions (that is, it must be in one of the states) and meet the second condition. So, you could have one of several states as the first condition and the second condition could be an ID/Status of customer.

14. Click Next. The Group Membership Wizard Finish page appears, as shown in Figure 15-14.

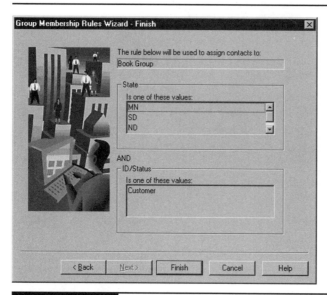

FIGURE 15-14   The final Group Membership Wizard page displays the rule you have designed.

15. Click Finish. ACT! records the new rule, and then prompts you with a dialog box asking if you want to execute the new rule right away. If you have more rules to add, or have more pressing business in ACT!, click No. Otherwise, run the new rule to see if it accurately identifies the contact records. Figure 15-15 is an example of a dialog box that ACT! displays after running rules.

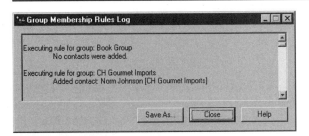

FIGURE 15-15   Here's an example of the information that appears as a result of executing group rules.

If the contact record was already a member of the group, it is not added again. If no records are identified that match your rule, ACT! displays that in the dialog box.

Viewing and Deleting Existing Rules

Before creating new rules, or if you want to delete an existing rule, you can easily see the current rules in place. Here's how:

1. Click the Groups icon to open the Groups window.

2. Open the Group menu.

3. Select Group Membership and, from the submenu, choose View Rules. The Group Membership Rules dialog box appears, as shown in Figure 15-16.

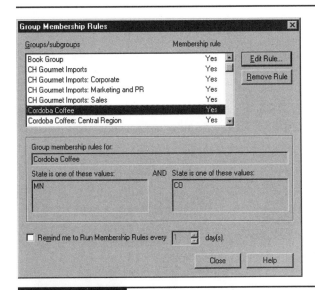

FIGURE 15-16   This is the Group Membership Rules dialog box from the demonstration database.

15

From this dialog box you can change an existing rule, by selecting the rule and clicking Edit Rule. You can delete an existing rule by selecting it and clicking Remove Rule.

Setting Reminder Options for Group Rules

The ACT! philosophy has always been to let the user decide when an action in ACT! is to be taken. If you have created group rules and want to be sure they run often enough to keep your records current, set a reminder that appears on startup to run the rules. Here's how:

1. Open the File menu and select Reminders. The Set Reminders dialog box appears, as shown in Figure 15-17.

FIGURE 15-17 The Set Reminders dialog box enables you to set prompts for housekeeping chores

2. Select Run Group Membership Rules from the Reminder drop-down list.

3. Set the time interval under Display Reminder.

4. Click OK.

If you are working on a shared database and you are not responsible for the actions listed in the Set Reminders dialog box, select each reminder and then select Don't Remind Me Again.

Using Lookups in Groups

There is no limit to the number of groups you can create in ACT!, so you could get to the point where scrolling through the list to find the group you want is not efficient or you may wish to search on a particular field. To understand how lookups work in groups:

1. Open the Lookup menu.

2. Select Other Fields. The Lookup dialog box appears, as shown in Figure 15-18.

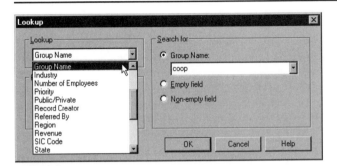

FIGURE 15-18   The Lookup dialog box shows the list of searchable fields.

3. Use the Lookup drop-down list to see a list of searchable fields. The default field that ACT! searches is the Group Name field. But, you can open the list of fields under Lookup and select a different field to search.

4. Enter the value you want to locate in the Search For field.

5. Click OK. ACT! locates the group records that match your search value.

    The lookup process here works identically to the contact record lookup process that was covered in Chapters 4 and 5. If needed, after selecting a field in which to search, use the switches, such as Empty Field or Non-Empty Field. You can also use the Narrow lookup and/or Add to lookup to further refine the search process.

If you perform a lookup on a group that you know is somewhere as a subgroup, and the group record you are looking for does not appear, the record must be added to the group.

Moving Groups

You can promote groups from a subgroup to a group, or move a group so that it is a subgroup of another group. That may be confusing to read, but it will make sense when you start working with groups. You cannot move a group that contains subgroups. If you select a group and then try to move it, ACT! prompts you with a message that indicates you cannot move the group because it has subgroups. In that case, you must first move or delete all the subgroups.

1. Select the group or subgroup you want to promote or demote.

2. Open the Group menu and select Move Group. The Move Group dialog box appears, as shown in Figure 15-19.

15

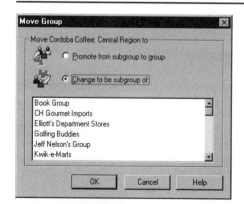

FIGURE 15-19   The Move Group dialog box lets you promote or demote groups.

3. Click the group or subgroup name you wish to move.

4. Select either Promote From Subgroup To Group or Change To Be A Subgroup Of.

5. Click OK. The group/subgroup is moved to the position you chose.

Deleting Groups

Deleting a group is easy, but slow, and that sometimes scares users. Do not jump to the erroneous conclusion that you have accidentally deleted the *records* that were added to the group. Not to worry, only the group is deleted. ACT! must check every record in the database to see if that particular record is in the group and with thousands of records, it is time consuming.

1. Open the Groups window by clicking the Groups icon.

2. Right-click the group you want to delete, and select Delete Group from the shortcut menu that appears. ACT! opens a warning dialog box that tells you that you cannot undo this process.

3. Click OK.

Again, this is a slow process as ACT! deletes the group by removing the group attribute from each of the selected records.

 *If you create and use groups to a great extent, you may have groups with hundreds if not thousands of contact records and their concomitant notes, histories, and attachments. If this is the case, ACT! will slow considerably when you switch from the contact record window to the Groups window. To enhance performance, make a group that is first in the list but has no contact records associated with it. Because ACT! sorts the names of the groups in ascending alphabetic order, create a group named AAAA. That is the first group that is open when you switch to the group window and it will be very fast.*

Summary

- Use groups to create permanent lookups or subsets of the ID/Status field. To have ACT! automatically add records to groups, create rules that define which records belong in the group.

- A contact record can be a member of as many groups as you need, and there is no limit to the number of groups you can create.

- Further refine your groups by creating subgroups.

- Groups are crucial to synchronization! Learn how to use groups and synchronization in Chapter 25.

15

Chapter 16

Customizing Layouts, Toolbars, and Macros

How to...

- Switch layouts
- Customize layout fields and background
- Share layouts over a network
- Customize toolbars and menus
- Create and run macros
- Assign shortcut keys to commands

Because ACT! is a general-purpose contact management tool with a heavy nod toward sales, it has a number of user-definable fields that you can customize for your enterprise. In this chapter, I outline the tools that ACT! provides for this task.

Working with Layouts

The first thing to understand about ACT! and its layout capabilities is this: An ACT! database can have 1,000 fields, but if you're using a layout that is designed to display only 20 fields, those are the only fields you will ever see. So, the layout acts as a mask over the database fields—only the fields you choose to display are seen.

To understand this potential, it is necessary that you look at the different layouts that come with ACT!. Follow these steps to explore layouts with the demonstration database:

1. Open the ACT5demo database.

2. At the bottom-right corner of the ACT! record window, next to the Groups button, is the Layout button. When you click the Layout button, you'll see an opened layout list next to the mouse pointer, as shown in Figure 16-1.

3. The default layout is named Contact Layout 2000r. But you have many more layouts to choose from! Click the layout named Modern. The interface changes appearance dramatically, as you can see in Figure 16-2.

 *It is important to recognize that none of the data in any of the fields is affected by changing the layout. Changing layouts affects only how the fields appear and which fields are visible.*

4. Open the Layout list again, and select Rotary Index. Figure 16-3 shows the result.

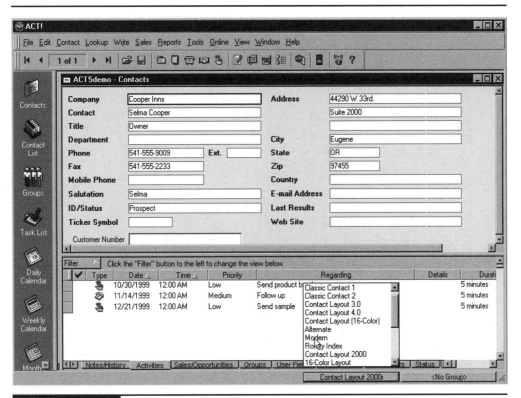

FIGURE 16-1   The Layout button, clicked open in the lower-right corner, lists the available layouts.

This layout is a dramatic departure from the previous two layouts. Its design imitates an actual rotary index file card. More dramatic is the change in which tabs appear at the bottom of the window. Gone are the User Fields, Phone/Home, Alt Contacts, and Status tabs. To repeat, the data in the database is not affected and the fields are still there—they are just not visible in this layout.

5. Click the Layout tab again and select the Contact Layout 2000r layout.

The view bar that appears to the left of the contact window can be adjusted so that the view icons appear on the bottom right of the contact window or are downsized. To adjust the view bar's appearance, move your mouse pointer over it and right-click. Select one of the shortcut menu options and see whether you prefer that view.

16

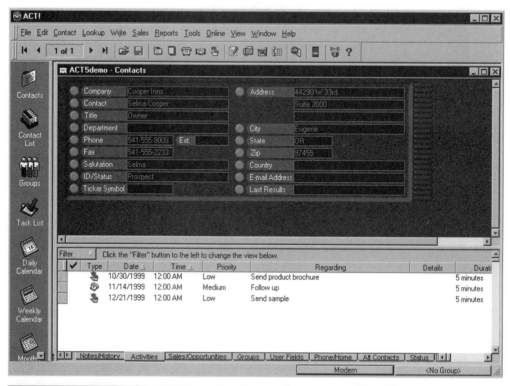

FIGURE 16-2   You can view your contact records in the Modern layout.

Customizing Layouts

ACT! is a general purpose contact manager; therefore, it's designed to be customized for your business. The customization can be extensive or minimal. It's up to you to decide how much tweaking you want to do. In this chapter, the focus is on changing the display of existing fields. In Chapter 17, I'll cover how you add new fields.

First, get a piece a paper and make a plan outlining which fields you think you want to modify, and how the data is going to be retrieved. Next, determine what type of data is going into each field: dates, characters, numeric data only, and so on. Finally, estimate the length of the longest field entry.

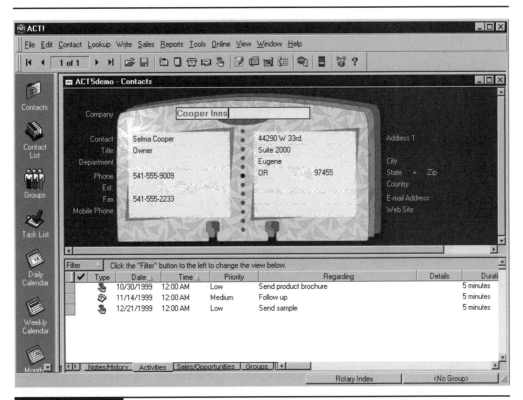

FIGURE 16-3   The Rotary Index layout is dramatically different from the other layouts.

A layout can be applied to any database you have. But, if in one database you added an entirely new field to the layout and then opened a second database that did not have that field as part of its structure, the field would not be visible. A further refinement is that if you modify an existing field—such as User 1—to a new name, that change will appear in every ACT! database that you open with that layout. It is confusing until you have made some changes to a layout and see the results.

Renaming Layout Files

Before making any changes to an existing layout, I recommend that you save it as a new file. To start creating your new layout by saving it as a new file, follow these steps:

1.   Open the database and select the layout that most nearly matches your desired layout. If you are making only minor changes, such as renaming the User fields, the default Contact Layout 2000r is fine.

16

2. Open the Tools menu and select Design Layouts. The window changes radically, as shown in Figure 16-4. You can see all the fields in the layout as well as the tool palette. To learn how to use the tool palette, see "Using the Tool Palette" later in this chapter.

3. Open the File menu and select Save As. The Save As dialog box appears, as shown in Figure 16-5.

    Note that the Layout folder is open and all the files have the extension .cly. Some of the filenames are recognizable—the Rotary Index layout is saved as rotary.cly, for example.

4. Enter a filename for this new layout. In this example type **Test**.

5. Click Save.

6. Click the Close button on the toolbar. (It's the third button from the right and looks like a small briefcase.)

    The Design Layout window closes and the Layout button reflects the new name. At this point it is identical to the layout you started with. So, in case the worst happens and you make a mess of your new layout, you can always delete the new one and return to the original.

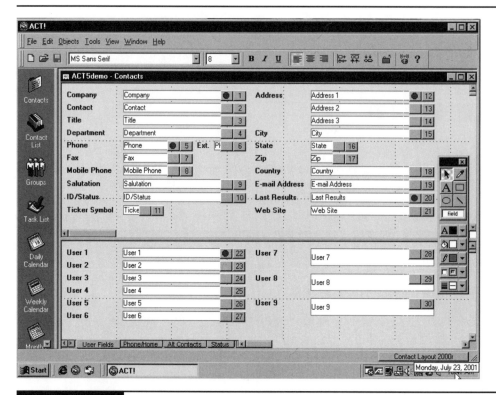

FIGURE 16-4   After you select the Design Layouts command from the Tools menu, the screen appears as shown here.

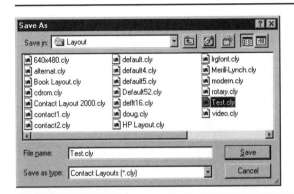

FIGURE 16-5   You can easily rename and save a custom layout with the Save As dialog box.

TIP

If ACT! hangs when you open the Design Layouts window, you can try several possible solutions. First, you will have to press CTRL-ALT-DELETE to select ACT! and End Task. Restart ACT! and open File | Administration | Database Maintenance | Compress And Reindex. Now try opening the Tools menu and selecting Design Layouts.

If ACT! dies again, before restarting, slow down the refresh rate on your video display card. On the desktop, right-click, select Properties from the shortcut menu, and click the Settings tab. Click the Advanced button and select the Performance tab. A slider bar appears. Move it to the left to slow down the refresh rate. Close the dialog box and try restarting ACT! again.

If that does not work, for designing only, try changing the color settings to 256 colors and switch back when finished.

Renaming User Fields

The easiest modification you can make to your layout is renaming one or more of the existing User fields. In many cases, this is all you will need to do. Suppose that in your plan, you decide that you need to have two fields that are not currently in your ACT! database. One is for entering a birth date and the second for a social security number. You can change the first two User fields to show that they contain those types of information.

Before you make changes, however, make a backup copy of the database, as described in Chapter 22, in case you inadvertently shorten an existing field, thereby losing data. Better yet, try the changes on the ACT5demo database before using your real data.

16

To rename User fields, follow these steps:

1. Open the database for which you want to change the layout.

2. Open the Edit menu and select Define Fields. The Define Fields dialog box appears, as shown in Figure 16-6.

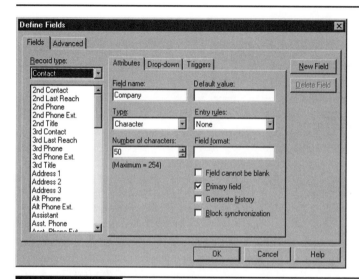

FIGURE 16-6   The Define Fields dialog box lets you rename existing fields, change field attributes, delete existing fields, or add new fields to your database.

3. Scroll the list at the left until you see the field named User 1. Click User 1 so that the name appears in the Field Name field on the Attributes tab. If you started with the default layout, the User 1 field will be a character field of up to 50 characters in length, as shown in the Type and Number Of Characters boxes.

4. Delete the name User 1 and type **Birth Date**, per our example.

5. Move to the Type box and pull down the list. Select Date.

   ACT! immediately alerts you that making this change, from a character field to a date field, might result in loss of data. Because the format of the field was characters and the length was 50, ACT! is warning you that any entries longer than what a date field allows, will be lost. If you are experimenting with the demo database, this restriction is not a problem because the User 1 field is empty in all the records. In your database, however, make sure before you change any field that valuable data is not going to be destroyed.

6. If you are certain that you are not destroying any data, click Yes to continue.

7. Click the User 2 field in the Define Fields dialog box.

8. Delete the field name User 2, and type **Social Security #**, per our example.

9. Because this field has a defined entry pattern, three numbers, a hyphen, two numbers, a hyphen, and four numbers, in the Field Format box type ###-##-####.

The pound sign (#) stands for a number. This means that the person making an entry into this field must enter nine numbers—no more, no less. ACT! automatically puts in the hyphens so that the entry looks like a standard social security number: 555-55-5555.

10. After you have modified the two fields, click OK.

ACT! processes the changes for a minute, and then you see a message that announces that ACT! is updating the database. Then the current record will appear with the changes visible, as shown in the Figure 16-7.

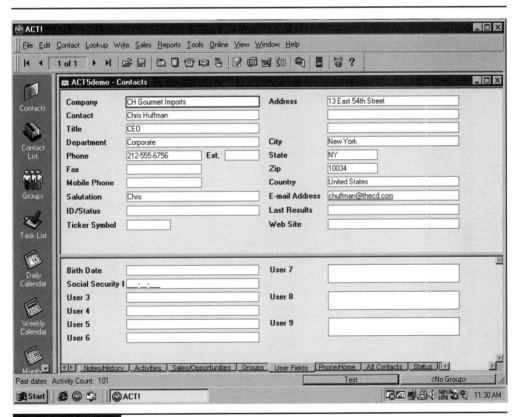

FIGURE 16-7   User fields 1 and 2 now are Birth Date and Social Security # fields.

16

If you are modifying a database that has thousands of records, it will take a while, perhaps 20 minutes, for ACT! to complete the task. DO NOT attempt to stop the process once it has begun.

If you made the modifications along with this exercise, you can test the fields.

1. Click the Birth Date field. A drop-down arrow should appear at the far right.

2. Click the drop-down arrow. A calendar will appear, as shown in Figure 16-8.

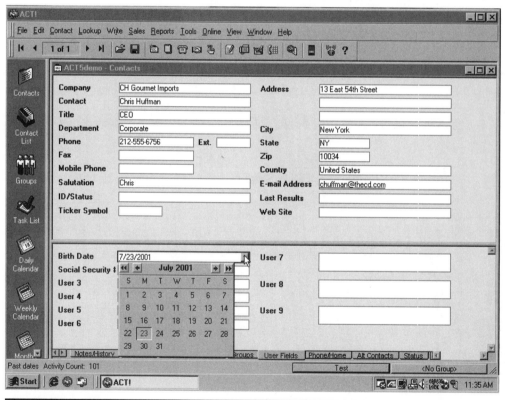

FIGURE 16-8   The Birth Date field appears complete with a drop-down calendar.

3. Click the Social Security # field and type any letter. ACT! ignores any entry that is not a number. Type a series of numbers to test the format. Even though the field definition for the Social Security # field was not changed from 50 characters, adding the Field Format restricted the number of entries ACT! would allow.

Creating a Lookup from the Renamed Fields

You can perform lookups based on the fields you rename. In our example, that means you can look up records based on the entries in the Birth Date and Social Security # fields. Follow these steps to do so:

1. Open the Lookup menu.

2. Select Other Fields; the Lookup dialog box appears.

3. In the Lookup field, pull down the list and select the field you want to use. In this example, select Birth Date.

4. Enter the birth date you want to find, exactly as entered into the field, or enter a partial date. For all the birth dates in June, you can enter 06.

5. Click OK. ACT! returns a lookup of records that match your entry. Now you know who needs to be sent a birthday card!

Modifying Fields with the Define Fields Dialog Box

There are many ways that you can modify fields using the options in the Define Fields dialog box (shown earlier, in Figure 16-6). Experiment with the following options:

Record Type   The first option is whether this field definition is for a Contact or a Group layout. To change a field in the Group window, pull down the list and select Group.

Field list   ACT! displays the fields that it finds in the database structure: either the contact fields or group fields, depending upon which option you selected under record type.

Attributes tab   The options on this tab include the following:

Field Name   The Field Name field is used to change the name that appears in the layout, but also changes the field name within ACT!.

Type   The Type field determines what type of data can be entered into the field. These are the choices:

Character   This is any type of entry.

Currency   This formats number entries into 19.2 places (19 numbers plus 2 decimals).

Date   This formats entries as MM/DD/YY and adds the drop-down calendar to the field.

Initial Capitals   This automatically formats text entries with a capital letter at the beginning of each word.

Lowercase   This formats the text as lowercase.

Uppercase   This makes all text uppercase.

16

Numeric   This allows only numbers to be entered.

Phone   This allows only numbers in the format XXX-XXX-XXXX.

Time   This allows M:SS entries and adds a Time drop-down box to the field.

URL   This makes the field an active web page address field allowing you to enter any web site address. When you click a field formatted as a URL, it starts your browser and tries to open the web site address.

Some Type options might not be available for all fields. The Company field cannot be changed into a date field, for example. All the User fields and any new fields you create can be any type of field.

Number Of Characters   The key idea for this field is saving space, although in the era of 80-gigabyte hard drives (soon to be terabytes!), this is not as important as it used to be. But, your database runs more efficiently if the field sizes are only as long as they need to be. A character field can be 254 characters in length, but to see all the characters, the field must be that long in the layout file as well.

Default Value   This attribute allows you to have ACT! enter a specific value every time you create a new record. This attribute does not affect existing records, only records created after this change is made. You might want to use this attribute if the vast majority of your contact records are geographically localized, for example. Let's say all your contacts are located in California. ACT! can enter CA into the State field for you in every new contact record. However, you can always enter a different value if the one ACT! inserts is not appropriate.

Entry Rules   If you want a field to be protected, that is, not modifiable by the user, select the Protected option. Another Entry Rules option is requiring that entries into the field come from the drop-down list that you supply.

Field Format   The Social Security # field we generated above is an example of a field whose format is restricted to a specific arrangement of numbers. You can also restrict a format to a certain arrangement of letters or a combination of letters and numbers. The pound sign (#) is the placeholder for numeric data, the at symbol (@) is the placeholder for alphabetic data, and the percent symbol (%) is used for alphanumeric data.

Field Cannot Be Blank   If the people who will be creating your database's new contact records are inexperienced (or if your salespeople are just a bit lazy), you can specify that a field must have an entry before they can go on to the next record by selecting this check box. My advice is to use this power judiciously, not making more than one or two required fields in your layout.

Primary Field   One of the options for creating a new contact record is the Duplicate Contact. When you select this option, a dialog box opens asking whether the entries from the primary fields or all fields should be duplicated from the current record. Making a field a primary field means that it is included when you create a duplicate record. The standard primary fields are Company, Address 1, Address 2, Address 3, City, State, Zip, Phone, and Fax.

Generate History   Select this check box if you want any changes made to the field to be recorded on the Notes/History tab. For example, if you created a field that recorded the customer's annual sales, and every year you updated the field, you could track the year-to-year changes in the Notes/History tab with this option.

Block Synchronization   When you synchronize data, ACT! sends changes in a record to the other database based on a time stamp. You might decide that a field in your database does not need to be updated when synchronizing. When this check box is selected, the field is not updated during synchronization. See Chapter 25 for more on synchronization.

Drop-Down tab   Click this tab to create a drop-down list for the current field. If you are adding new fields or modifying an existing field, you can add the entries you want for the field. To add a new item to the list, click New and type the name of the item. Add a description if necessary. Some companies use the description field to amplify the entry in the list. The list entry could be a part number and the description could identify that part, for example. The other options on this tab include the following:

Import button   Click this button, which opens the Import dialog box, to import a text file to create the drop-down list. You can use a file exported from a different ACT! database or from the current database. To import a list that was created in a different database, you must first create an export file from the originating ACT! database, using this same dialog box. ACT! formats the export file so that it imports properly.

Allow Editing   Selecting this check box allows anyone using ACT! to add or delete items on the drop-down list, while they are editing a contact record. Even if this option is not selected, anyone can type an entry in the field, they just cannot add it to the drop-down list. (Unless you have selected Only From Drop-Down as the option.)

Automatically Add New Items To The Drop-Down   When you select this check box, entries into the field that are not already on the drop-down list are added to the list automatically for next time. For example, if you select this option for the City field, each time you enter a new city into the field, that city name is added to the drop-down list. This also means that the next time you start typing that city name into a record, ACT! uses type-ahead to insert the city name for you.

Show Descriptions   Selecting this check box allows anyone who opens the drop-down list to see the concomitant description.

Use Drop-Down List From   When you are modifying an existing field or adding a new field and know that a separate field in the database already has the drop-down list you want, you can duplicate that existing list easily by selecting this option and then selecting the field from which to duplicate. ACT! copies the original list into the new drop-down and links the lists. In addition, when you use this capability, anytime a new entry is made to any of the linked drop-down lists, the new entry will automatically appear in all the lists.

16

Triggers tab ACT! can trigger an entirely different program to start either when a user enters the field by clicking in it or when the user enters a value and then exits the field. If you are ambitious, you can link ACT! to an accounting program or spreadsheet. There is even a software development kit (SDK) available from Interact.com for creating your own programs that work with ACT!. Appendix A for information on how to get your SDK.

Many of the third-party programs use the Trigger feature to activate their programs. For example, if you had a field called Birth Year and a second field called Age Next Birthday, one of the add-on programs reads the Birth Year entry and immediately enters the age in the Age Next Birthday field. Another program uses the entry in one field and calculates sales tax plus the price to enter a total in a different field.

After making the changes you want to a field or set of fields, click OK. If there are but a few records in the database, ACT! makes the changes quickly. With a large database, this can be a slow process because ACT! must modify each record, one at a time. A warning—be patient with this process. It might appear that ACT! has stopped responding to the system, but it is still working. This may be a good time to check out your favorite web sites or take a tea break. Never stop ACT! while this process is taking place.

Moving, Deleting, and Resizing Fields in the Contact Layout

Changing the position of fields in a layout does not modify any of the data in those fields—even if you modify the display length of the field! (Display length is not the same as field length, which is determined by the Number Of Characters attribute in the Define Fields dialog box.) Deleting fields from a layout does not modify the data either. The information is still part of your database; it just isn't displayed in the edited layout.

Moving Fields in the Layout

You can move a field by simply clicking and dragging. Remember, before you begin editing a layout, it's a good idea to save it as a new file (choose File | Save As).

To move a field using the drag method, open the demo database, or create a database on which you can experiment, and follow these steps:

1. Open the Tools menu and select Design Layouts. The window changes to resemble the one shown in Figure 16-9.

   A field in a layout consists of two main parts: the field display and the field label. In the Design Layout window, the name of the field appears in the field display. At the far right of each field are two gray boxes, which are used to set the tab entry order and the ENTER key entry order (this will be discussed more fully in Chapter 17).

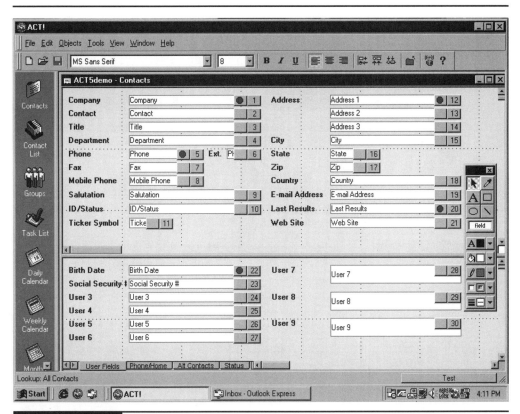

FIGURE 16-9   The Design Layout window lets you create your own custom design schemes.

2. Click the Ticker Symbol field so that the handles appear on the field.

3. Click the Ticker Symbol field again, this time holding down the mouse button, and drag the field underneath the Web Site field.

4. Release the mouse button to drop the field in its new position. The result appears as shown in Figure 16-10.

   Note that the field label did not automatically follow the moved field.

5. Click and hold the mouse button on the field label you want to move, in this example, the Ticker Symbol.

16

6. Drag the field label to its new position and release the mouse button.

After moving a field, you must save the change to the layout. Open the File menu and select Save—or Save As if you want to create a new layout file.

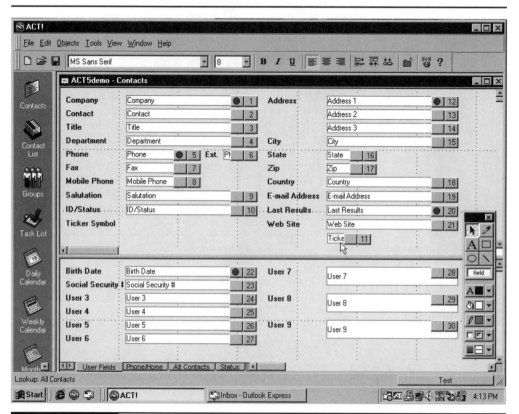

FIGURE 16-10   You've moved the Ticker symbol field to a new position.

TIP

Moving a field by dragging can be difficult if you are trying to move a field that is on one of the tabs to the top half of the window or vice versa. A better method is to select the field, right-click, and then select Cut from the shortcut menu. Move the mouse pointer to where you want the field to appear, right-click, and select Paste. If you have cut several fields, you can use the Field tool on the tool palette to select the fields you want to re-appear.

Deleting Fields from the Layout

Remember, removing a field from a layout does not affect the underlying field or any data that might have been entered into that field. One field that you might not need on the top half of the contact record is the Country field—especially if your business is strictly domestic.

Follow these steps to delete a field from the layout:

1.   Click the field you want to remove from the layout.

2.   Right-click to open the shortcut menu shown in Figure 16-11.

Undo text size

Cut
Copy
Clear
Select All

Move to Front
Move Forward
Move to Back
Move Backward

Align to Grid

✓ Align Text Left
Align Text Center
Align Text Right

File Description
Properties

FIGURE 16-11   This shortcut menu appears when you right-click a field.

3.   To remove the field and place it on the clipboard, so that you can paste it elsewhere in the layout, select Cut. To simply remove the field, select Clear. If you cut several fields, only the last field cut will remain on the Windows clipboard.

Follow the same procedure to delete the field label.

Deleting Fields and Labels Together

To remove a field and its label at the same time, click the field, press SHIFT, and then click the label. Then, right-click to access the shortcut menu, and choose the appropriate command to cut or clear the field.

16

Moving a Cut Field to a Different Location

Use the cut-and-paste method to move a field from the top portion of the contact record to one of the tabs or vice versa. After cutting a field, move the mouse pointer to the area of the layout where you want the field to appear. Right-click and select Paste. The field might not appear exactly where you want it to, so you might have to adjust its position by dragging.

Resizing Fields

The amount or length of data you can enter into a field is determined by the Number Of Characters attribute in the Define Fields dialog box. For example, if you modify a field and give it a two-character field length, no matter how large you make the field display in the layout, no more than two characters can be entered into the field. Conversely, you can set up a field display to be shorter than the actual field length. In this case, you can enter data that has more characters than are visible in the field display at one time. But don't worry, when you click the field, you can scroll the entry to see it all.

To resize a field, follow these steps:

1. Click the field so that the field handles appear.

2. Click and hold on a handle, and drag the outline of the field to the length/height desired.

3. Release the mouse button.

Moving or Aligning Multiple Objects Simultaneously

Clicking and dragging objects one at a time is okay for some modifications, but there are times when you want to move objects as a group or to align the objects. The trick is to click in an open space near the objects and then drag the mouse so that you can see the object handles appear on each. Once selected, you can then move the mouse pointer over the group of objects and click and drag the objects together. Figure 16-12 shows a group of objects, field names, and fields selected and ready to be moved, aligned with the alignment tools on the Edit menu, or cut from the layout.

Changing Field Properties

Each field has properties such as font, fill color, frame width, and fill pattern. You can modify these properties to highlight the field or otherwise suit your needs. You can use the tool palette or the procedure as described below to modify a field.

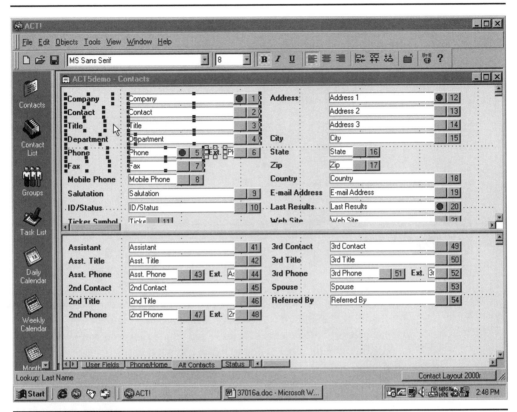

FIGURE 16-12   Once you've selected a set of objects, you can manipulate them as a group.

To change the property of a field you must be viewing the Design Layout window. Once there, follow these steps:

1. Right-click on the field and select Properties from the shortcut menu. The Object Properties dialog box appears, as shown in Figure 16-13.

   The Object Properties dialog box contains many options for changing the appearance of your fields. Use the following guidelines to make your selections:

   Style tab   As you make choices in the Style tab, the results are displayed in the Sample field, giving you a preview of the effect. This tab includes the following options:

   Fill Color   The fill color is the color that appears in the field. Use this property to highlight the field.

16

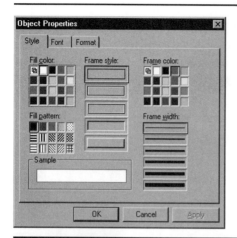

FIGURE 16-13 This Object Properties dialog box appears when you select Properties from a field's shortcut menu in the Design Layout window.

Fill Pattern   You can select the pattern that appears as you type an entry into the field. The pattern is seen only as you are making the entry—the purpose of this property is to make it easier to see which field you were working on when your significant other called to make a lunch date.

Frame Style   Use this property to set off a field from the others in the layout.

Frame Color   Use this property to further enhance a particular field or fields.

Frame Width   Draw a thicker border around a field by selecting a wider frame width.

Click the Apply button to save the modifications.

Font tab   When you change the font, say from 8 points to 14, and click the Apply button, the size of the field is adjusted on screen so you can see the effect before saving the change. Figure 16-14 shows the ID/Status field with the font changed to 14 points and a modified fill pattern and frame.

Format tab   The Format tab provides information about the field name the type of field. It has no attributes that you can change.

2. After you make any adjustments to the field, you have to save the layout for the changes to become permanent.

Changing a Layout's Background

The top half of the window and any of the information tabs can have a specific color or pattern as background. You might want to use this attribute to distinguish one tab from another.

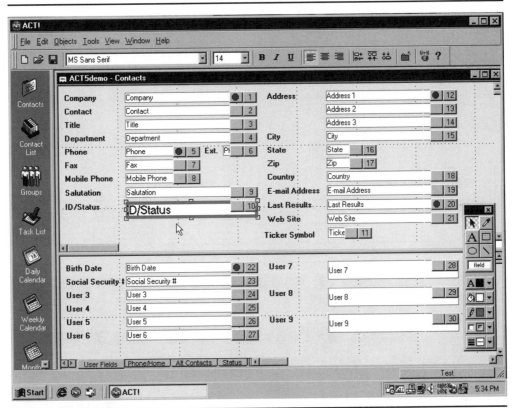

FIGURE 16-14 You've modified the Id/Status field with a new fill pattern, wider frame width, and larger font.

To change the background on a tab or the top of the contact record window, follow these steps:

1. In the Design Layout window, right-click in a blank place in the layout so that only the background is selected. The shortcut menu that appears, shown in Figure 16-15, has fewer choices than the shortcut menu you see when you right-click an object (shown in Figure 16-11, previously).

2. Select Properties. The Background Properties dialog box appears.

3. Select the color and pattern of the background or insert a background bitmap image.

   ACT! includes a bitmap image file called dflt5bg.bmp, which you see as the background to the Contact 2000r Layout. You can replace this image with one of your own choosing. Click the Browse button at the right of the Bitmap field and locate the file you want. You can display it as a single image or a tiled image. A tiled image means that the background is completely filled with the image. Figure 16-16 shows a handsome new tiled bitmap image added to the background.

16

4. After you add the bitmap, click OK. Save the layout if you like the change using the File menu.

This shortcut menu appears when you right-click a layout's background.

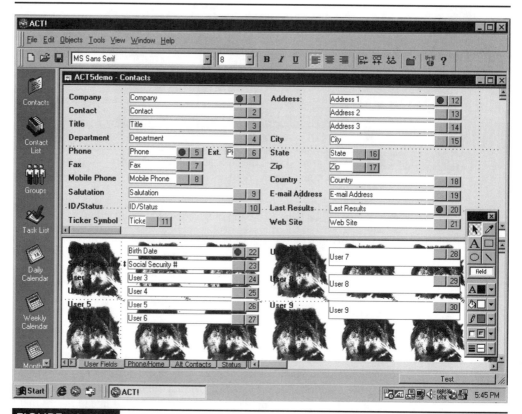

FIGURE 16-16   You can add a new background bitmap image to the ACT! layout.

Using the Tool Palette

When you switch to the Design Layout window, you should see the tool palette floating around the window. The palette has a set of tools that you can use to add shapes, highlights, colors, and borders to objects in the layout. If you don't see the tool palette when the Design Layout window appears, you can open the it manually. To do that, in the Design Layout window, open the View menu and select Tool Palette. It appears as shown in Figure 16-17.

FIGURE 16-17   You can use the tool palette to add design features to the layout.

The tool palette includes the following tools:

Pointer   You use the Pointer to select objects or the background. After you select something, click a design tool and make the change. Click this button to return to pointer mode.

Attribute   This tool may look like an eye dropper, but it is used to identify the attributes of the selected object. When you select this tool and then click on an object, the rest of the tools in the palette change to reflect the attributes of that object.

Text   Use the Text tool to add text anywhere on the layout or edit the name of a field. For example, if a field name is too long to be displayed next to the field display. Select the Text tool, click the field name, and edit the name. However, do not use this tool as a substitute for the Define Fields command (Edit | Define Fields) if you need to change a field's name completely. Use this menu command and make your change in the Define Fields dialog box.

Square   Use this tool to draw a square object in the layout.

Oval   Use this tool to draw an oval object in the layout.

Line   Use this tool to draw a line object in the layout.

Field   With this tool you can add a new field that is part of the database structure but is not currently part of the layout. Select the tool and draw a rectangular space for the new field. A dialog box opens that lists the database fields that are not visible in the layout. If you draw a single field and then select several names from the dialog box list, ACT! adds all of the fields in one operation.

16

Text Color   Use this tool to change the color of text.

Fill Color/Pattern   Use this tool to fill an object with a selected color or fill pattern.

Line/Border Color   Use this tool to modify the color of a line or the border of an object.

Border Style   Use this tool to select a border style for the object.

Line/Border Weight   Use this tool to modify the thickness of the object's border.

Closing the Design Layout Window

After making the changes you want, close the Design Layout window by clicking the Close File button (the third icon from the right on the toolbar). Even if you have saved the changes using the File menu and Save or Save As command, ACT! still checks with you on whether you want to save again. If you have really mucked up the layout and do not want to save changes, you can indicate that at this point.

Tips and Cautions on Layout Design

When you're designing a new layout, keep in mind these suggestions:

- Consider that the resolution of your computer monitor might be higher than that of other users and position fields so that all users can see them.

- The top half of the record window should contain the key fields that you want anyone who accesses the record to see.

- Don't drastically modify the fields that are listed on the Lookup menu, such as Company, Contact, and so on.

- When making changes to the layout, save often. There is no Undo button on the Edit menu in the Design Layout window in case you really make a mistake.

- Make changes in an empty database. If you have several thousand records and need to make multiple field changes, open the File menu and select Save As and then select Blank Copy. Create a new database name and then open that new database and make changes. To get the data into the new database, use the database-to-database synchronization method, as described in Chapter 25.

Customizing the Toolbars and Other Interface Elements

Customizing layouts is one aspect of changing the look and functionality of ACT!. Another related aspect is the interface of ACT!. The interface is the look of the program itself. Many of the aspects of the interface that you can customize are dependent upon the screen resolution you have selected in Windows. The higher the resolution, the more real estate that is visible on your screen. The size of the monitor is also a factor.

Changing the toolbar affects only your version of ACT!, not anyone else's on a network. Toolbars are not connected to the layout file.

Modifying the Toolbars

Two toolbars are visible in most ACT! views: the standard toolbar (along the top of the contact record window) and the view bar (to the left of the contact record window). To modify a toolbar, right-click it to open its shortcut menu, as shown in Figure 16-18.

The defaults for this toolbar are Large Icons and Large View Bar. The Mini View Bar option moves the icons to the lower-right corner of the window, à la ACT! 4.0. Try the various options to see what suits your work style. Whatever you choose, when you exit ACT! the settings are saved and appear the next time you open ACT!.

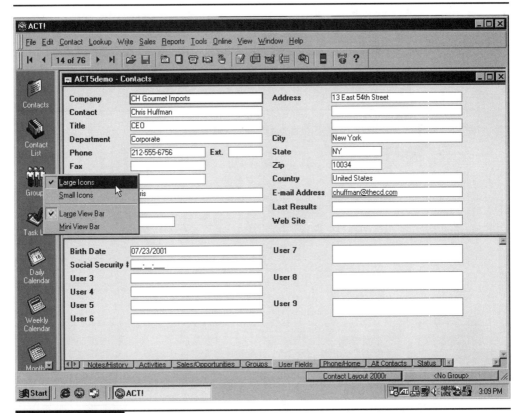

FIGURE 16-18   Use this shortcut menu to modify the view bar.

The standard toolbar, at the top of the window, can be modified in several ways, too. First, if you do not want to see the toolbar at all, right-click it at the far left to open the shortcut menu. Click Standard Toolbar to clear the check mark, and the toolbar disappears. Retrieve the toolbar by right-clicking the menu bar at the top of the window. The shortcut menu appears, and you can select Standard Toolbar again.

You can also grab the standard toolbar and drag it to a different position in the window. After moving the toolbar, you can resize it to a more square shape by selecting it and dragging a corner.

To return the toolbar to the top of the window, drag it to its original position and drop.

 *Windows will sometimes on its own decide to get rid of your toolbars and/or reposition one or more of the window positions so that they are unreadable. Chapter 21 explains how to handle this problem.*

Adding Buttons to Toolbars

If you find that you are using a particular ACT! process frequently, you might be able to add that process to a toolbar.

To add a button to a toolbar, follow these steps:

1. Open the Tools menu and select Customize Contacts Window. The Customize ACT! Contacts Window dialog box opens, as shown in Figure 16-19. You will see there that ACT! includes ready-made buttons for many processes.

FIGURE 16-19   You can use the Customize ACT! Contacts Window dialog box to add or remove buttons from the standard toolbar, create new toolbars, customize menus, create keyboard shortcuts, and more.

2. From the Categories list, select the name of the menu on which the command is likely to appear.

3. In the Commands list, scroll to find the command that represents the process you want to be able to access from the toolbar. Click the command icon and drag it to the position where you want the button to appear. If you can't find the command you want, look in the commands listed under a different category. If you can't find the command anywhere, you may have to create a macro to execute the command as described later in this chapter.

4. Release the mouse button. The new button should appear.

5. I suggest you test the button to see whether it runs the process you specified. If all goes well, click OK to close the dialog box.

If you really screw things up, you can reset the menus and toolbars to the ACT! defaults by clicking the Reset button.

One button that I always add to my toolbar is Run Macro. To add it to your toolbar, open the Categories list and select Tools. Scroll the list until Run Macro appears. Click the icon and drag it to the toolbar where you want it positioned. It must be in or to the left of the existing buttons—you cannot drag it to the right of the Help button. Release the mouse button and Run Macro appears on your toolbar.

Renaming a Menu Item

In addition to adding items to the toolbar, you can rename items that appear on the default menus. Let's say you have decided to use the ID/Status field to hold your customers' account numbers. You have modified the field to read Account Number, but the Lookup menu still reads ID/Status. Here is the way to modify the menu command to match the field name:

1. Open the Tools menu and select Customize Contacts Window. The Customize ACT! Contacts Window dialog box appears.

2. Click the Menus tab, as shown in Figure 16-20.

3. The menu trees are visible in the Menu box on the right side of the dialog box. Scroll to find the Lookup menu.

4. Click the plus sign (+) that precedes the Lookup menu listing. ACT! expands the tree to show the items that appear on the Lookup menu, as shown in Figure 16-21.

5. Scroll the list until you find the ID/Status command listing (&ID/Status…) and click it.

6. Click the Rename button. A smaller dialog box opens into which you can type the new command name. Make sure you add the three periods at the end of the entry so that the lookup works properly! See the tip below to add a hot key for your new item.

16

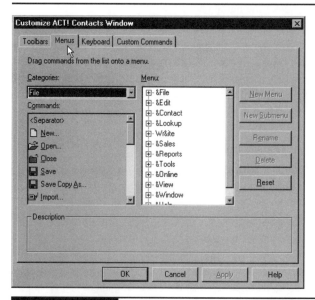

FIGURE 16-20   Use the Menus tab of this dialog box to customize menu items.

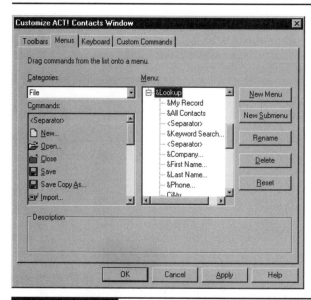

FIGURE 16-21   You can expand and collapse the menu trees in the Menu list to find the command you are looking for.

7. Click OK and then Apply and OK again to close the Customize ACT! Contacts Window dialog box.

8. Open the Lookup menu and see your new entry!

For your new menu item, you may want a hot key to work with ALT. *The hot key for ID/Status is I because an ampersand (&) precedes that letter in the name. You can use the ampersand to create a hot key for your new command too. In our example, the new item was Account Number; you can make N the hot key by typing* **Accou&nt Number.**....

Sharing the Layout on a Network

If you are sharing a database on a network and want everyone to see the same layout for that database, you have to make certain that everyone's copy of ACT! is pointed to the same layout file. On a network drive, I recommend that you create a folder in the same location as the folder that contains the database. Then follow these steps:

1. After creating a shared folder on the network, open the Tools menu and save the layout file to that network folder; Open the Tools menu and select Design Layouts. Open the File menu and select Save As. Enter a name for the layout and then browse to the Network folder and save it there.

2. Go to each of the computers of the people who are logging into the ACT! database. Open the Edit menu and select Preferences.

3. In the Preferences dialog box, the General tab is visible.

4. Pull down the list under Default Locations, File Type and select Layout.

5. Browse to the folder that contains the shared layout and select the folder.

6. Click Apply, and then OK.

7. Click the layout button at the bottom of the contact window and select the layout that you want the user to see.

Sharing a layout with users who synchronize from remote locations is a bit more work. You must send them the layout file either via e-mail or on a disk and they must save it to their ACT\Layout folder. Then they must select the layout using the Layout button.

16

There is no easy way to distribute changes to the toolbars or menus to other users on a network; you must change each user's computer individually.

Working with Macros

A macro is a series of keystrokes and/or mouse clicks that are stored in a file that can be replayed upon demand. A macro can be very simple, or it can involve a long series of steps. ACT! macros are not interactive, and they are not iterative. This first restriction means that you cannot create a macro that stops and waits for user input and then continues. The second means that a macro cannot be repeating. Macros that require mouse clicks are problematic, in that they rely on specific window positions to work properly, so I avoid using mouse clicks if at all possible.

Creating a Macro

What follows is an explanation of how to create a macro that opens the E-Mail window and Gets/Sends e-mail messages. (The E-Mail button on the view bar only opens the E-Mail window.) In this explanation I've assumed that you are already connected to your e-mail provider. To create this macro, start in the Contact Record window and follow these steps:

1. Press ALT-F5, which opens the Record Macro dialog box, shown in Figure 16-22.

FIGURE 16-22   Create a new macro with the Record Macro dialog box.

2. Enter the macro name as **View E-mail**.
3. In the Description box type **Opens and refreshes the e-mail inbox**.
4. Pull down the Record Events list and select Record Everything Except Mouse Events.
5. Click the Record button.
6. Press the ALT-V.
7. Type the letter **E**.
8. Press ALT-M.
9. Type the letter **G**.
10. Press ALT-F5 to stop the macro recorder.

The macro has been recorded, and you have, as a consequence of creating the macro, refreshed your e-mail inbox.

Running a Recorded Macro

You can test the macro recorded in the previous section (or run any macro) as follows:

1. Open the Tools menu and select Run Macro. Figure 16-23 shows the Run Macro dialog box, which contains a list of macros you have previously recorded.

2. Click the name of the macro you wish to run.

3. Click the Run button.

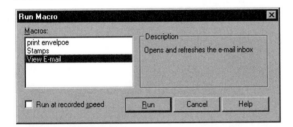

FIGURE 16-23   The Run Macro dialog box displays the macros you have recorded.

If the results of running the macro are not what you expected, run it again but this time select the Run At Recorded Speed check box. This slow play mode gives you the opportunity to see where you went off track. Once you figure out what went wrong, you can create a new macro. Unfortunately, there is no way to edit the macro; you must create an entirely new macro with corrections.

Creating a Toolbar Button for a Macro

You can attach a recorded macro to an icon and then add it to a toolbar. This makes running the macro a single-click affair. The first stage of this process is attaching the macro to an icon. The second stage is placing the new button on the toolbar. Assuming you have a macro ready to add to the toolbar, follow these steps to macro bliss:

1. Start in the window in which the macro was designed. This is important in that some macros will not run properly in a different window, as the menu commands you have captured are not available. If you recorded the View E-mail macro as described earlier, it works properly in the Contact Record view or the Contact List view.

16

2. Open the Tools menu and select Customize Contact Window.

3. Click the Custom Commands tab, shown in Figure 16-24.

   In the Custom Commands box you'll see that several custom commands have already been created, such as the one for printing to the Dymo label printer.

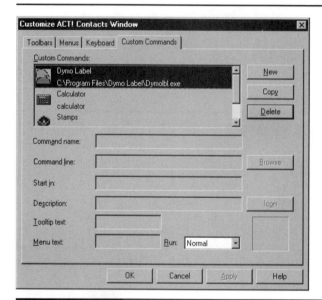

FIGURE 16-24   Use the Custom Commands tab of the Customize ACT! Contacts Window dialog box to create a new toolbar button.

4. Click the New button.

5. Click the Browse button, which opens the Macro folder in the Open dialog box.

6. At the bottom of the Open dialog box, pull down the Files Of Type list and select Macros (*.mpr).

7. Select the desired macro; in this example, View E-mail.

8. Click Open. The Open dialog box closes. The Command Line and the Start In fields are automatically completed.

9. In the Command Name field enter **View E-mail**.

10. In the Description field enter **View and Refresh E-mail Inbox**.

11. In the Tooltip Text field enter **View E-mail**, as shown in Figure 16-25.

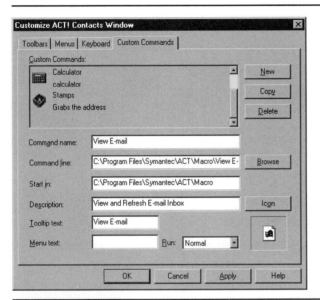

FIGURE 16-25   You've nearly completed your custom command.

12. Now, you need an icon to which to attach the macro. Many icons are available in a file that Microsoft provides. Click the Icon button to open the Select Icon dialog box.

13. Click the browse button to the far right of the Icon File field. The button is not labeled, but it appears as a square with three periods on the bottom. If you are successful, the Select File Containing Icons dialog box appears.

14. Change the file type by pulling down the list at the bottom of the dialog box and selecting Library Files (*.dll).

   At the top of the dialog box, use the navigation buttons to go to the C:\Windows folder for Windows 2000 (or for Windows NT users, go to C:\WinNT\System32). In the series of folders, scroll to the right and select the file named moreicons.dll.

15. Click Open and an abundance of icons fill the Select Icon dialog box, as shown in Figure 16-26.

16. Click the icon you wish to use for the macro, and then click OK.

17. Click Apply in the Customize ACT! Contacts Window dialog box. When you do, the command is added in the Custom Commands field at the top of the dialog box.

16

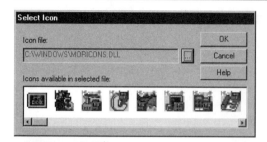

FIGURE 16-26   A series of icons are available via the moreicons.dll file.

All the information needed to attach the macro to an icon has been provided. The final series of steps involves actually placing the new button on the toolbar, as follows:

1. With the Customize ACT! Contacts Window dialog box open, click the Toolbars tab.

2. Under the Categories heading, scroll the list to the very bottom and select Custom Command. The View E-mail macro command appears in the Commands field, as shown in Figure 16-27.

3. Click and hold the left mouse button on the View E-mail command. Drag the mouse up to the toolbar where you want the button to appear.

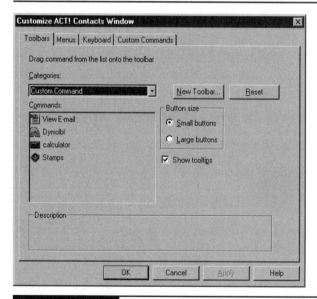

FIGURE 16-27   The Custom Command list shows the new command, View E-mail.

4. Release the mouse button and close the dialog box.

    The big moment has arrived. Click the new button and see whether the macro runs
    and performs its chore.

On paper the process of attaching a macro to a new toolbar button appears to be a lot of
work. In reality, it is easy once you have done it, and takes only moments to execute.

Assigning Shortcut Keys to Commands

It is great to be able to click a button and run a command or macro. But, you may be working on a
laptop or have other reasons for preferring keystrokes as a means of executing processes in ACT!.
To assign a keyboard shortcut, follow these steps:

1. Open the Tools menu and select Customize Contact Window.

2. In the Customize ACT! Contacts Window dialog box, click the Keyboard tab.

3. From the Categories list, select the menu containing the command to which you want
    to assign a shortcut key. To assign a shortcut key to a custom command that you
    created, such as a macro, select Custom Commands.

4. The Commands list displays the shortcut keys assigned to commands on the selected
    menu. In the Commands list, select the command and click Assign Shortcut. The
    Assign Shortcut dialog box opens, as shown in Figure 16-28.

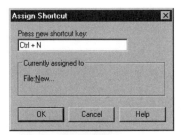

FIGURE 16-28   Use this dialog box to assign a new shortcut key combination.

5. Press the key combination that you want to assign to the command. If the key
    combination is assigned to another command, the command name is displayed in
    the Currently Assigned To box. To replace the current shortcut assignment with the
    new assignment, click OK. Or, press a different key combination and click OK.

6. Close the dialog box and try the new combination.

16

Summary

■ Different layouts can be used to show or hide fields as needed.

■ Rename the User fields to quickly customize the ACT! interface.

■ Customize layouts more thoroughly by modifying field properties and appearance.

■ On a shared network database, all users must be pointed to the correct layout.

■ Add commands to ACT! menus and toolbars with the Customize Contact Window option on the Tools menu.

■ Macros can easily be created to automate frequently used ACT! processes.

■ Reassign or assign new shortcut keystrokes to existing or new commands.

Chapter 17

Creating New Fields

How to...

- Create a new field
- Add a new field to a layout
- Create a an index for a field
- Create a new tab
- Arrange fields
- Set the data entry order

Even though ACT! has plenty of fields that you can modify to customize the database, you may find that you need even more. I recommend that you add new fields rather than modifying the fields you think you will never use, such as the Home Address field, and in this chapter, I will show you how to do this.

Creating a New Field

In ACT!, there are 15 user fields. If you need more, you have two choices. One is to change some of the existing fields, such as the 2nd Contact field, to what you want. Modifying existing user fields in ACT! by changing the field names and attributes was covered in Chapter 16. The second choice is to create new fields. I have found it more effective to add new fields because they are easier to track. If there are unwanted existing fields in ACT!, you can simply delete the field or, preferably, remove it from the layout, as I explained in Chapter 16.

Before you create any new fields, consider their purpose. What type of data will the field contain, and how will it be used in reports? Will the data be used for lookups? After you decide the purpose, the rest is easy. One caveat: If you have an existing database with thousands of records, the process of adding fields is very slow. Plan on doing this when you will not need to access the database for hours. If you are adding many fields, it might be better to design the database and then synchronize the existing database to the new structure, as explained in Chapter 25.

 *A field can be displayed only once in a database. If you need several fields that are very similar, such as birthdays, you must give them unique names such as Birthday1, Birthday2, and so on.*

To add a new field:

1. Open the database to which you want to add a new field. Select a layout to which you want to add the field by choosing the Layout button at the bottom of the screen and selecting the desired layout from the pop-up list.

2. Open the Edit menu and select Define Fields. The Define Fields dialog box opens, as shown in Figure 17-1.

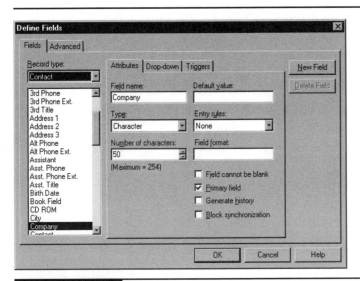

FIGURE 17-1 You add new fields to your database in the Define Fields dialog box.

3. Click the New Field button.

4. ACT! creates a generic field name New Field 1. Change the name to what is appropriate. In this example, I have named the field Customer Number.

5. Add any attributes to the field, such as data type, length, a default value, and any drop-downs that you want. The field attributes are described in Chapter 16.

6. Click OK. ACT! responds with a message that it is updating the database. When it is finished, you cannot see the new field because the layout doesn't include the new field. (This is discussed in the section that follows.)

7. Re-index the database by selecting File | Administration | Database Maintenance | Reindex.

Do not add more than one new field at a time. It is tempting, and seems logical, that you should be able to add multiple fields and then let ACT! add them to the database structure all in one process. But the chances of database corruption are very high if you add multiple fields, so stick to adding one at a time.

Deleting a Field

In addition to adding fields, you can easily delete a field using the Define Fields dialog box. Before you do so, be certain that the field does not contain any information that might be

17

critical at some later date. My advice is to simply remove the field from the layout. The data still exists if you should ever need it. In addition, make a backup copy of the database in case you delete the wrong field.

To delete a field:

1. Open the Edit menu and select Define Fields.

2. Scroll through the list of fields and click the one you want to delete.

3. Click the Delete Field button. ACT! checks with you before it executes the deletion. In a large database, this is a slow process, as the deletion process is executed one record at a time.

4. When the deletion is finished, reindex the database.

Adding a New Field to the Layout

When you modify an existing field, such as User 1, the change is apparent as soon as ACT! processes the update. When you create a new field, it is physically added to the database structure, but not to the layout. You have to manually add it to the layout. This makes sense, as you want the field to appear in a specific location.

To add a newly created field to a layout:

1. Open the Tools menu.

2. Select Design Layouts. If the tool palette is not visible, open the View menu and select Show Tool Palette. The tool palette appears, as shown in Figure 17-2.

FIGURE 17-2 The ACT! tool palette, with the field tool selected, is used to place newly created fields into the layout.

3. Click the Field button in the tool palette. When you move the mouse pointer into the design window, the pointer becomes a crosshair shape instead of an arrow.

4. Use the crosshairs to draw a rectangle for the location of the new field. To do this, click and hold the mouse button and draw a rectangle, releasing the mouse button when you have created the rectangle. When you release the button, the Fields dialog box appears, as shown in Figure 17-3.

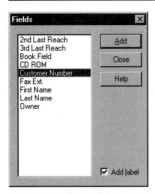

| **FIGURE 17-3** | The Fields dialog box lists the available fields you can add to the layout. |

5. Select the field you want to add to the layout. You have the option of including the field label.

6. Click Add.

7. The field is added to the layout. Figure 17-4 shows the example field, Customer Number, added to the layout. Close the Fields dialog box.

8. To save the layout, click the Close button on the toolbar (third from right). A dialog box appears asking if you want to save changes to the current layout. Click Yes.

The new field appears on the layout. If you switch to a different layout, the field is not visible. If you open a different database and keep the layout, the field will not appear because it has not been added to the database structure.

TIP   *If you plan to use multiple databases with differing layouts, it can get confusing as to which layout goes with which database. ACT! does not allow you to designate a specific layout as being attached to a specific database. However, you can purchase a third-party program that, with the click of a toolbar button, opens a different database and switches to the correct layout. The product is called dBrunner and can be had at www.cornerstonesolutions.com.*

17

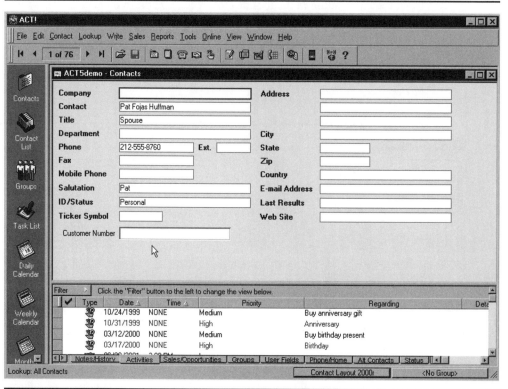

FIGURE 17-4   A new field is added to the layout.

Creating a New Indexed Field

Most databases use a feature called indexing to accelerate the process of locating records. ACT! does too, and several of the fields on the Lookup menu—Company through ID/Status—are indexed fields. It's a good idea to add an index to a field if you expect to be using the field for frequent lookups. For example, if you have modified a User field or created a new field that will contain the customer account number, and you plan to use that field for lookups, an index is essential. The process of adding an index to a database with thousands of contact records is time intensive. You might consider copying the database to a local drive for this process and upon completion, copying it back to the server.

To add an index to a new field:

1. Open the Edit menu and select Define Fields.

2. In the Define Fields dialog box, click the Advanced tab (shown in Figure 17-5).

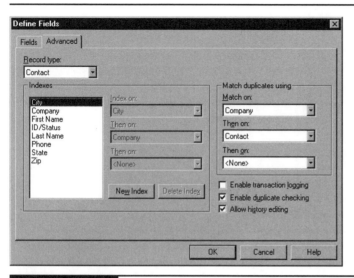

FIGURE 17-5   You've selected the Advanced tab in the Define Fields dialog box.

3. Click the New Index button.

4. Click the down arrow for the Index On field and scroll through the drop-down list to locate the field you want to index.

5. Add a second field as part of the index. It is irrelevant which field you choose, but ACT! requires a second field to be designated.

6. Click OK and be patient. In a large database, this process could run up to an hour.

Creating a New Tab

Adding a new field or multiple fields is now at your command. Taking this new skill a bit further, you can add several fields to the database and then put them all on a new tab that you also create. This is an efficacious way to group a series of related fields in the same physical location in ACT!.

To add a new tab:

1. Open the Tools menu and select Design Layouts.

2. Open the Edit menu, and select Tabs. The Define Tab Layouts dialog box appears, as shown in Figure 17-6.

3. Click Add. The Add Tab Layout dialog box appears, as shown in Figure 17-7.

4. Enter a name for the tab and click OK. The newly named tab is added to the list of tab layouts.

17

The tabs that are part of the current layout appear in the Define Tab Layouts dialog box.

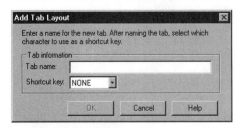

You can add tab layouts in this dialog box.

5. Before closing the Define Tab Layouts dialog box, you can adjust the display position of the tab by clicking the tab name and then the Move Up or Move Down button. You can delete or rename a tab at this point, too.

6. Click OK to close the Define Tab Layouts dialog box.

7. Finally, click your newly created tab and add the fields that you want to that tab. There is no limit to the number of tabs you can add, but from a practical standpoint, it is a good idea not to have so many tabs that the users are required to scroll the window to see them all.

Field-Arranging Tools

When you add a single field to the database, it is easy to align the field to existing fields. But you might want to add a series of fields, and in that case, aligning them so that their left edges are straight can be a challenge. The Objects menu in Design Layouts has several choices to assist you in this task.

To see the options, click a field so that it is selected (the handles appear), and then open the Objects menu. The options are as follows:

Move To Front   In ACT! you can layer objects such as bitmaps underneath the fields. This command moves any object so that it is on top of any others, making it visible.

Move Forward   If you stack several objects, use this command to move the selected object up one level in the stack.

Move To Back   If you paste a bitmap on the layout, it may cover up other objects. Selecting this option moves the object to the bottom layer.

Move Backward   This option moves the selected item one level down in any stacked objects.

Align   This option is active only if you have selected several objects before opening the Objects menu. The Align dialog box is shown in Figure 17-8.

Align To Grid   There is a set of squares that form a grid upon which the objects in the layout can be aligned. When you select the objects and then select this option, ACT! does its best to align the objects to the underlying grid. Open the View menu and select Ruler Settings to modify the grid size. In the Ruler Settings dialog box, select the Units, and then reduce or increase the divisions shown, which adjusts the grid size.

Make Same Height/Width   This option makes it easy to make all selected objects the same size.

Add Label   When you insert a field, you have the option of including a field label or not. If you neglected to add a label when you added a field to the layout, select the field, and then select this option to add the label.

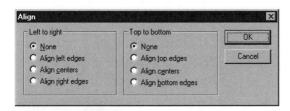

FIGURE 17-8   The Align dialog box contains options that allow for the correct alignment of multiple objects in a layout.

The options seen in Figure 17-8 are used when you have selected multiple objects and are trying to get them to line up, based on the various options. My advice is to open a layout and try the various aligning functions. If the alignment selected does not produce the result you expected, select Edit | Undo, and the most recent action is reversed.

TIP   *To select multiple objects, click the first object, and then hold down the SHIFT key and click the second object. Continuing to hold SHIFT, you can select as many objects as you want.*

17

Changing the Field Entry Order

In Chapter 14, one of the preferences that you learned to set was using either the ENTER key or the TAB key to move from field to field as you enter new information. But if you have added new fields or rearranged the fields, the order in which the TAB key moves you from field to field might not be what you want or expect. Also, ACT! includes a way to set the order in which the ENTER key moves among the fields.

When you are looking at the Design Layouts window, each field has two gray boxes at the far right. If the ENTER key is set to stop at a field, the first gray box has a red dot in it. The second gray box lists the order number for the TAB key stop. If you set your preferences so that the ENTER key moves the insertion point from field to field, the gray box at the far right relates to the entry order for that key.

To reorder the way the TAB and ENTER keys take you through the fields:

1. In Design Layouts, open the Edit menu.

2. Select the Field Entry Order option to see the submenu. Your options are to Hide, Clear, or Reset the order. I recommend that you select Clear, which removes all numbers.

3. Starting with the first field (that is, the field where you want the insertion point to go first), click the far-right gray box so that the number 1 appears.

4. Go to the next field and click so that the number 2 appears.

5. Repeat the process until all the fields that you want the insertion point to move to have a number on them. You are not required to add a number to every field. After the insertion reaches the last number field, it returns to the number 1 field.

6. If you want to set the order for the ENTER key, click the gray box that is the second from the right so that a red dot appears.

7. Click the Close button and save the changes.

Summary

■ You can create new fields in the database structure. This is preferable to modifying existing fields.

■ You must add a new field to a layout to make the field visible.

■ It is a good idea to index fields that will be frequently accessed.

■ Creating a new tab lets you pack even more information into a contact record.

■ You can set the field entry order by changing the TAB and ENTER stop settings.

Chapter 18

Tracking Sales Opportunities

How to...

- Add a new sales opportunity
- Create a sales funnel graph
- Forecast sales
- Set the sales stages
- Create sales reports

In business, nothing happens until a sale is made. The sales process has become much more sophisticated, and the means to measure progress of the sales force has evolved to a general standard. Most companies now use a sales funnel to graphically represent the stages of a salesperson's opportunities. ACT! has been designed to facilitate work with this model and to streamline the sales tracking process. ACT! provides a means to modify and then display the sales funnel, to represent the numbers as a chart, and to forecast sales. But, like all other aspects of ACT!, it is up to you to enter the data to make it work.

TIP

If you are synchronizing data, please be aware that entries to the drop-down lists for products and types DO NOT synchronize to the other users. In order for the list items to synch, each must be a component of a sales opportunity. The work-around is to create a series of faux sales opportunities using each list item and then synchronize with the remote users.

Adding a New Sales Opportunity to a Contact Record

A sales opportunity is just what it says it is; the probability of a sale being made to an existing or a new customer. The first step in creating a sales opportunity record is to look up the contact record to which you want to add a sales opportunity. After locating the contact record, follow these steps:

1. Open the Sales menu and select New Sales Opportunity. The Sales Opportunity dialog box appears, as shown in Figure 18-1.

2. Enter the opportunity using these guidelines:

    General tab This tab is selected when the dialog box opens. It includes the following options:

    Product This field includes an editable drop-down list of products/services that your company offers. When you enter a new product/service, ACT! automatically adds the product to the list.

    Type You can add details that might or might not be company specific in this field. For example, if you are offering a special price for orders over a certain dollar amount, you can enter that information here. When you enter a new type, ACT! automatically adds the type to the list.

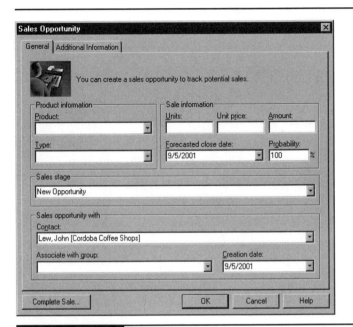

FIGURE 18-1 You can add a new sales opportunity to a record easily with the Sales Opportunity dialog box.

Units Enter the number of units that you anticipate the customer might buy.

Unit Price Enter the cost per unit.

Amount ACT! calculates the total based on the entries in the Units and Unit Price fields. But, you can override the field entry if necessary to reflect a discount or special deal.

Forecasted Close Date Enter the date you expect the customer to either take delivery of or pay for the product. Make sure the way the sales force enters this data is standardized or the data will be meaningless when analyzing the records of multiple salespeople.

Probability Every salesperson is an optimist. But, putting 100% in this field for every sale diminishes the utility of this tool. Enter a realistic estimate so that the probability report is accurate.

Sales Stage If you own your own company or are the sales manager, you should closely scrutinize this field's drop-down list and make sure all salespeople understand how to accurately categorize the state of the current opportunity. In addition, everyone must use the same list for the sales funnel model to work properly. The list that ACT! provides might be adequate for your firm and fit well, but you can also create a custom list.

Sales Opportunity With The default entry in this field is the current contact. However, you can select a different contact record by opening the drop-down list and typing the last name of the contact or by clicking the Company column and typing the company name.

Associate With Group Select the group to which you want to associate the sales opportunity.

Creation Date Enter the creation date, if it is different from the current date.

Complete Sale When your ship comes in, you can click this button and use the dialog box that appears to record the final disposition of the opportunity.

Additional Information tab Click this tab, shown in Figure 18-2, to continue adding information to the sale.

Main Competitor Enter the likely competitor for the sale, if known.

Record Manager The person managing the sale may be different from the person creating the sales opportunity. If so, you have the opportunity to indicate that here.

Details In the Details field, enter information that is relevant to the sale. For example, you might note that the buyer is new to the company or that he or she has a budget limit of $100K.

3. When you've finished entering all the data, click OK to close the dialog box.

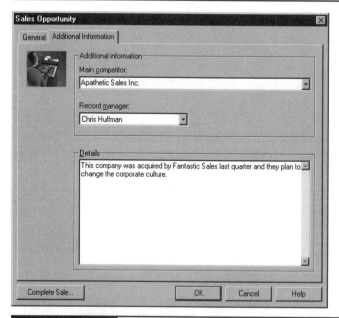

FIGURE 18-2 The Additional Information tab offers a location for including further information about the sale opportunity.

Working with the Sales/Opportunities Tab

After you record the information, the new sales opportunity appears, not unexpectedly, on the Sales/Opportunities tab. This tab is shown in Figure 18-3, with opportunities listed and the filter options visible.

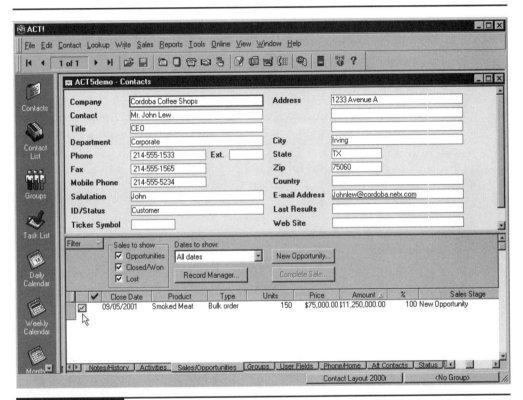

FIGURE 18-3   Sales opportunities information appears on this tab, shown here with the filter expanded to display the options.

It is important that a company set a policy as to the particulars of when and how a sales opportunity is added to a contact record. The salient point is consistency and regularity of data entry—something that salespeople hate to do but is necessary for meaningful analysis.

On the Sales/Opportunities tab are several filters that can be selected. For example, you can set the filter to see only pending opportunities and then select which record manager's opportunities you want to see. The opportunities themselves are completely editable by clicking on the data you want to change. For example, to change the entry in the Sales Stage column, click the current entry and select a new stage from the drop-down list. Sort the list by clicking the column header, the same way as other columnar lists in ACT!. Print the sales opportunity information for a single contact by opening the File menu and selecting Print Sales/Opportunities.

Modifying Columns

Also, the columns that are shown can be edited for size: Move the mouse pointer to the column border, and when the mouse pointer appears as a two-headed arrow, drag left or right as needed. The scroll bar in the bottom right of the window allows you to scroll left or right to see the other columns. If you right-click in the Sales/Opportunity tab, the shortcut menu appears, as shown in Figure 18-4.

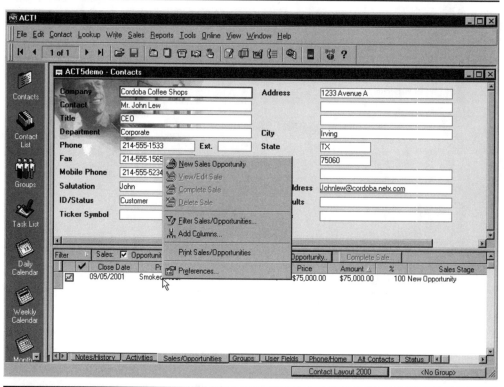

FIGURE 18-4   Use the shortcut menu on the Sales/Opportunities tab to edit the tab, print the sales opportunities information, and perform other functions.

Select an option from the shortcut menu such as Add Columns. When you do, the Add Columns dialog box appears, shown in Figure 18-5, with a list of fields that are not currently displayed on the tab. Select the field(s) you want and click Add. Click Close to finish. The new columns are added to the far right.

FIGURE 18-5   Add new columns to the Sales/Opportunities tab with this dialog box.

To delete columns in the view, click the column header, and while holding the mouse button down, drag toward the top of the window; the pointer is transformed into a tiny garbage can. Release the mouse button and the column (but not the data) is gone.

Locking the Column View

Because ACT! allows you to have enough columns so that you may have to scroll to see them all, you can lock the left edge of the tab to keep a specific column in view as you scroll, much as you might with a spreadsheet. To add a column lock, follow these steps:

1. Move the mouse pointer to the far left portion of the sales record and position it on the wider vertical bar.

2. Click and hold the mouse, and then drag it to the right edge of the column you want to keep in view.

3. Release the mouse button. Figure 18-6 shows the column lock to the right of the Product field.

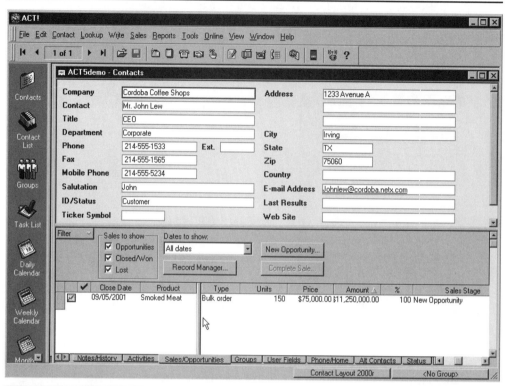

FIGURE 18-6   The lock bar appears to the right of the Product field in this view.

Editing a Sales Opportunity

You can edit an individual entry on a sales opportunity record by clicking directly on the affected field of the Sales/Opportunities tab. Or, you can begin editing by clicking the sales record on the far left of the row so that the entire sales record is highlighted. When you do, the following options on the Sales/Opportunities shortcut menu become available:

View/Edit Sale   Select this option to open the Sales Opportunity dialog box.

Complete Sale   Select this option to bring closure to the opportunity. Figure 18-7 shows the Complete Sale dialog box. Either the sale closed or it did not and entering a reason here helps you determine what is needed to procure future business. Add any modifications to the Product, Sale Information, Type, and Close Date fields as needed. Click the Additional Information tab to edit the information you entered here when the sales opportunity was created or to add new details.

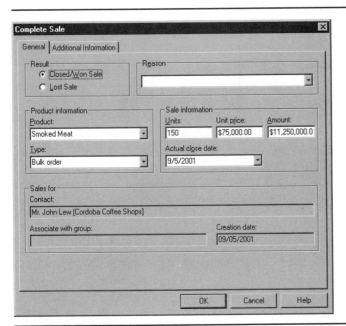

FIGURE 18-7 Use this dialog box to indicate the result of the sales opportunity and the reason for it.

Delete Sale Use this option only if the results of the opportunity do not fit into the normal parameters of a sales cycle. If the customer went out of business, for example, the sale was not won or lost—there was no sale to complete, and deleting the entire opportunity would be appropriate.

Working with Sales Funnels

The basic concept of the sales funnel is that you must make many initial contacts to result in a single sale. What percentage the number of completed sales will be of the number of initial contacts varies from industry to industry, but the general picture is the same: a funnel, with a wide mouth on one end and a narrow opening on the other.

Creating a New Sales Funnel

To learn how to create a sales funnel, let's first experiment with the ACT5demo database, which has a plethora of sales opportunities already. Open the database and then follow these steps:

1. Open the Sales menu and select Sales Funnel. The Sales Funnel Options dialog box appears, as shown in Figure 18-8.

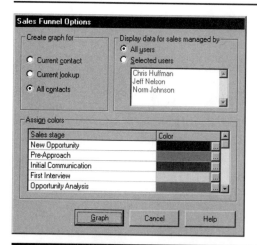

Use the Sales Funnel Options dialog box to create and modify a sales funnel.

2. Complete the options using the following guidelines:

Create Graph For Before opening this dialog box, you can create a lookup for the purpose of viewing the sales funnel for specific contact records. Select the appropriate option to create a graph for the current contact, the current lookup, or all contacts.

Display Data For Sales Managed By In a single user database the settings here are irrelevant, but on a multi-user database, you can select which salespeople's contacts are going to be included in the funnel. Combine this with the lookup capabilities in ACT! and you can fine-tune a funnel in a number of ways.

Assign Colors To modify the colors of each of the sales stages, click the small gray box with three tiny dots to the right of the color. The Color dialog box opens, shown in Figure 18-9, where you can select the color you want. If the standard colors are not cool enough, click the Define Custom Colors button and, in the resulting dialog box, adjust the color to the exact hue you want and then click Add To Custom Colors.

Unfortunately, changing the colors of the funnel slices is not sticky. That is, every time you want colors other than the defaults, you have to reset them.

3. After setting your options, click Graph.

The Sales Funnel window appears, displaying the funnel graph. The funnel itself is a series of graduated, stacked slices. Each slice corresponds to a step in the sales process. The funnel graph shows the number of sales opportunities by stage in the legend to the right of the funnel. Figure 18-10 presents an example.

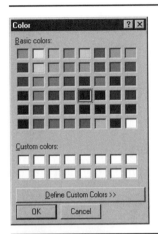

To change the color associated with a sales stage, select the stage, open the Color dialog box, and select a new color.

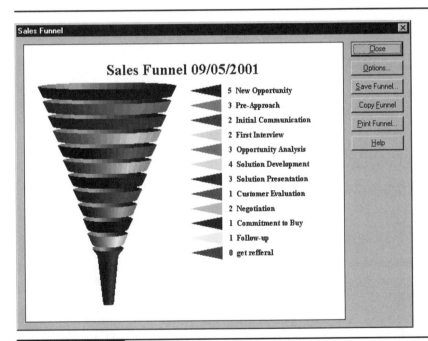

The sales funnel graph shows each sales stage with a number that corresponds to the contacts in that slice.

Saving a Funnel Graph

With the sales funnel displayed, click the Save Funnel button. ACT! opens the Save As dialog box so that you can create a filename. The graph is saved in bitmap format that is compatible with Microsoft PowerPoint and other graphing programs. You can attach the file to other records as well. Attach the file to a contact record of a salesperson, for example, and use it to track the performance of that salesperson.

Copying the Sales Funnel

In addition to saving the sales funnel to a file, you can copy the graph to another document. Click the Copy Funnel button, and a copy of the graph is placed on the Windows clipboard from which you can paste the graph into any compatible program.

Changing the Sales Funnel Display Options

With the graph displayed, click the Options button, which opens the Sales Funnel Options dialog box. Make the adjustments needed and click Apply and then click Graph to see the results.

Closing the Sales Funnel Window

Click the Close button to close the window. Any adjustments you made to the display properties while looking at the funnel must be reset if you want to use them again.

Creating a Sales Forecast Graph

The sales forecast graphing capability creates a visual representation of the sales opportunities that are in the company pipeline. This is a terrific tool for managers trying to calculate the income stream for the company. Obviously, the numbers generated are not set in stone and are only as good as the people entering the forecasts, but over time good managers can develop an intuitive sense of the accuracy of the data.

The ACT5demo database has a series of Sales Opportunities records already entered that can be used to generate a sales forecast graph and a sales funnel. To see how the graph looks, open that database and follow these steps:

1. Open the Sales menu and select Sales Graph. The Graph Options dialog box appears, as shown in Figure 18-11.

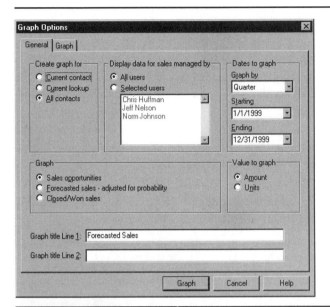

The Graph Options dialog box is used to refine the data used as the basis for the sales graph.

2. Adjust the settings in this dialog box, using the following guidelines:

General tab By default, this tab is selected when the dialog box opens. It includes these options:

> **Create Graph For** Select the set of contact records to be used in the graph. Create a lookup before opening the Graph Options dialog box if you want to graph data from specific contact records.

> **Display Data For Sales Managed By** In a single user database this setting is irrelevant, but on a multi-user database, you can select which salespeople's contacts are going to be included in the graph. Combine this with the lookup feature to fine-tune your graph.

> **Dates To Graph** To see the examples from the ACT5demo database you will have to enter a date range that corresponds to the sales opportunities in the database. In the Graph By box your choices are Day, Week, Month, Quarter, and Year. Select a value and enter the date range in the Starting and Ending boxes.

Graph Three options are presented for graphing the sales opportunities. Sales Opportunities shows all opportunities. Forecasted Sales - Adjusted For Probability creates a graph that reflects the total adjusted by the percentage. So, if the total sales opportunities are $50,000, factoring in a percentage reduces the total graphed. (Unless all opportunities had a 100 percent probability assigned.) Closed/Won Sales graphs those opportunities that were concluded successfully, based on your other settings.

Value To Graph Choose whether you want the graph to display the number of units or the dollar amount. You can combine this option with the Forecasted Sales setting, for example, to assist the manufacturing division in forecasting production runs.

Graph titles Enter one or two titles that reflect what is being graphed. For example, if you are graphing units, add that to the title.

Graph tab The Graph tab allows you to customize the graph, including graph style, size, scale, color, and other features. It includes the following options:

Bar/Line Graph Select the graph type which best represents your data.

Style A 3-D graph shows the data as a perspective drawing where objects are shaded to appear three-dimensional. The 2-D style is preferred for line charts.

Graph Size ACT! can display the graph in a window or so that the entire desktop is used.

Scale For the more detail oriented, you can set the parameters of the graph scale. This is useful if you have data that is widely disparate.

Horizontal/Vertical Lines Adding lines can clutter or enhance the display. If a graph is too busy, you defeat the purpose of the graph, which is to make the underlying data comprehensible at a glance.

Colors It is important to mix your colors carefully and consistently. For example, when graphing sales opportunities, be consistent with the colors used so that graphs from different time periods are easy to compare.

3. Click Graph to see the results.

   The Sales Forecast Graph window opens, displaying the graph according to the options you just selected. If you aren't satisfied with the graph, return to the dialog box and adjust the options. Figure 18-12 presents an example of a sales graph.

4. Save, copy, or print the graph using the buttons in the Sales Forecast Graph window. These buttons are identical in operation to those in the Sales Funnel window.

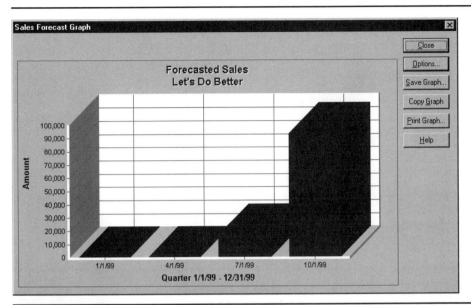

FIGURE 18-12   This 3-D sales forecast graph presents data by quarter and includes gridlines.

Modifying the Sales Stages

The sales stages that ACT! provides might be a perfect fit for your business, but I doubt it. Assuming that you know the stages of your own sales process, redefining is easy. To make changes, follow these steps:

1. Open the Sales menu and select Modify Sales Stages. The Edit Sales Stages dialog box appears, as shown in Figure 18-13.

2. Select the stage you want to change and click the Modify button. The Modify Sales Stage dialog box appears, as shown in Figure 18-14.

3. Type a new sales stage name and description.

4. Click OK.

5. In the Edit Sales Stages dialog box, reposition sales stages in the list or delete sales stages that you do not need using the Move Up, Move Down, or Delete button. Add a new sales stage by clicking the Add button and making the entry. The numbers that precede each stage are not modifiable, so to adjust the order of the sales stages, select the stage and use the Move Up or Move Down button to position it next to the correct number

6. After you've completed all your modifications, click OK to close the dialog box.

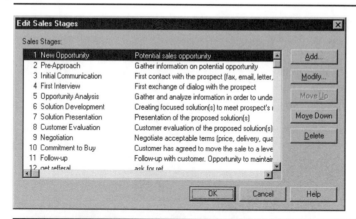

FIGURE 18-13   Use the Edit Sales Stages dialog box to customize sales stages.

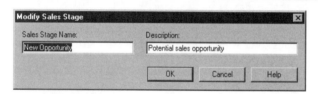

FIGURE 18-14   The Modify Sales Stage dialog box makes it easy to change one or all of the default sales stages in ACT!.

The sales stages are not attached to the layout but to the database, which means a remote user can get the new sales stages only by synchronizing and making certain that the database is not locked when doing so. See Chapter 25 for details.

Completing a Sale

Closing the loop on a sales opportunity is important and when the time comes to record the fact, you must do so to make the sales opportunity reports accurate (and perhaps, to get paid your commission). To complete a sale, follow these steps:

1. Look up the contact and select the Sales/Opportunities tab.

2. Select the sales opportunity from the list, and then click the Complete Sale button. The Complete Sale dialog box appears, as shown in Figure 18-15.

18

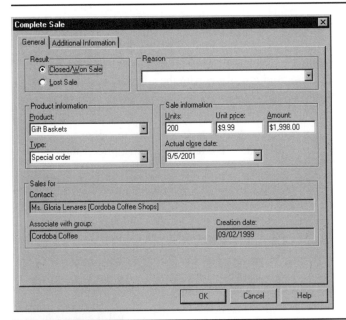

Use the Complete Sale dialog box to close the loop on a hot deal.

3. Enter the information requested, and then click OK.

The key to analyzing your sales data successfully is modifying the Reason drop-down list in the Complete Sale dialog box. Any good sales manager wants to track why sales are won or lost—not just the ratio of wins to losses. Create a custom list of reasons that reflects your business, and have your salespeople use this list as a standard. After analyzing the data, you can adjust marketing and sales strategies to focus on the most successful techniques.

Using Sales Reports

ACT! offers a plethora of reports that are derived from the information you have entered as sales opportunities, won/lost, and complete sales. To see the reports, open the Reports menu and select Sales Reports. The submenu displays a series of reports.

ACT! includes the following reports:

Sales Totals By Status   Generates a report that shows the total number of units and dollar amount in the report header. In the detail section of the report, each opportunity has the company, contact name, and phone number, plus the expected close date, the product, the type, the number of units, the price per unit, the probability of closing the sale, and the record manager.

Sales Totals With Probability   Generates a report that has the total forecasted units and dollars in the header. Each opportunity is listed with the contact, company, phone number, sales stage, expected close date, number of units, dollar amount, and probability. This report prints in landscape mode.

Sales List   Generates a report that has the contact, company, and phone number, followed by the status of the opportunity, close date, product, type, units, price, amount, probability, and record manager.

Sales Funnel   Generates a report by sales stages, with the name of the contact, company, phone number, close date, product, number of units, unit price, total sale, and probability of closing. In addition, you can sort the report by Closed/Won Sales and/or Lost Sales. You can also sort the report in many other ways, making this an extremely useful report.

Sales By Record Manager   Generates a report that lists the record manager in the report header. Each opportunity has the status, close date, product, type, units, price, amount, probability, and contact.

Sales By Contact   Generates a report that lists the name, company, and phone number; followed by the status, close date, product, type, units, price, amount, probability, and record manager.

 In a database with several thousand records, the report display is not fast. The first page of the report appears followed by any subsequent pages.

To create a sales report, follow these steps:

1. Open the Reports menu and select Sales Reports.

2. Select the type of report you want from the submenu. The Run Report dialog box opens with the Sales/Opportunities tab selected, as shown in Figure 18-16.

3. Set the options for the report. Report options are detailed in Chapter 19.

4. Click the General tab. Pull down the Send Output To list and select Preview to see the report in its own window.

5. Click OK. The preview window opens.

    At the lower-left corner of the report preview window a message appears letting you know the report is running or is completed. Figure 18-17 shows the preview window for a sales funnel report zoomed in to clearly display details.

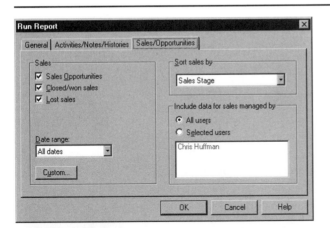

FIGURE 18-16   The Sales/Opportunities tab of the Run Report dialog box offers many options for refining your report.

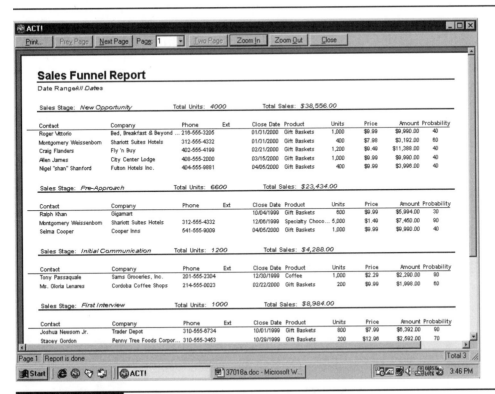

FIGURE 18-17   Zoomed in, you can see each entry in a sales report preview. Click Zoom Out to have the entire page displayed in the window.

Modifying a Report

Sales reports can be modified if you want to add or change the data presented. Chapter 19 is devoted to reports and the means to change existing reports or to create new reports.

Fine-Tuning Sales Reports

The standard reports for sales opportunities are limited in several important ways. Many do not allow a report that is filtered by a lookup. An example is the Sales Adjusted For Probability report, which most of my clients who have begun using the sales opportunities features of ACT! would like to run on a selected set of records, for example by product line. Fortunately, ACT! has such a large number of users that several third-party companies have produced products that allow you to either export the sales data to a spreadsheet such as Excel or to create reports with a product such as Crystal Reports.

Two companies offer products to export to Excel (www.jltechnical.com and www.nwoods.com). Both companies allow you to download and test the products they offer; you can decide from there. You can find information on Crystal Reports's reports tool at www.pinpointtools.com. For more details on these and several other products of this type, check Appendix A.

Accessing Dale Carnegie Techniques from the Web

ACT!'s deliberate orientation toward salespeople is extended with this link. The Dale Carnegie Corporation specializes in training folks for sales, leadership, time management, and other crucial life skills. If your life is perfect as it is, you have no need to check this web site. If, on the other hand, stress is an issue or you need specific skills for presentations, this is a good browse. The opening page presents a series of self-assessment tests for various areas of your life. They are fun to take, with the understanding that they are designed to lead you toward one of their courses.

Relationship Process

The Relationship process is not really a process in ACT!, rather, selecting this option triggers the appearance of an Adobe Acrobat document that describes the Dale Carnegie training course on managing the relationship process.

Summary

- Forecast sales accurately with ACT!'s new sales opportunities features.
- Add your sales model to ACT! by modifying the sales stages.
- See the progress of sales efforts in the Sales Funnel.
- Report on sales activity won or lost using sales reports.
- Extend the usefulness of sales reports with one of the third-party products.

Chapter 19

Working with Reports

How to...

- Look at the standard ACT! reports
- Customize an existing report
- Create a new report from scratch
- Add your customized report to the Reports menu

Running any type of organization requires reports, and ACT! has what might be considered an excessive amount of predefined reports. The reports run the gamut of targeted information from a contact record to the whole enchilada: every piece of data that is in the contact record. The best way to decide which report you want to run is to take a preview of the report and see if it contains the information you need.

Standard ACT! Reports

Each of the predesigned reports has evolved over time from feedback from ACT! users. They are accessed through the Reports menu. The following two sections describe the two kinds of reports you can generate: contact and group reports.

Contact Reports

Here's a synopsis of each report that you can generate from the contact records and the intent of the report:

Contact   This report prints everything that is in the contact record, which means that every standard field is included, and this includes all the information on the various tabs. The report can be quite lengthy; I would not recommend it for more than a single record at a time. Newly created custom fields do not automatically appear in this or any report. After creating a new field, you must add the field to the report just like you have to add the same field to the layout in order to see it.

Contact Directory   This report prints the company, contact, and address information, including the four phone fields. This comes in handy when you need to carry contact record information with you.

Phone List   This report has the company, contact, phone, phone extension, and mobile (cell) phone number.

Task List   This report prints the contact name, and the concomitant type of activity, its status (open or cleared), date, time, regarding, and the person for whom the activity is scheduled. This report overcomes one of the problems with the Task List you see in ACT!. The problem occurs when you schedule an activity for another person. It shows up on that person's Task List, but if you look at the Task List window, the Scheduled For column is nonexistent.

Notes/History   This report prints the company, contact name, and information on the Notes/History tab, such as what e-mail messages have been sent to the contact or what files are attached to a contact. The text of the e-mail messages and/or the attachments are not printed. You can set a filter for this report so that only the items you want to include print.

History Summary   This report prints the company and contact name with a total of the number of fields that were changed and the total number of calls, meetings, and letters sent.

History Summary Classic   This report disappeared for a time in ACT!, but the hue and cry from ACT! users brought it back. The report prints the total number of attempted calls, completed calls, meetings held, and letters sent.

Activities Time Spent   This report prints the activities that have been cleared and those activities that are still open. Each contact is listed with the status, type of activity, date and time, duration, and regarding information.

Contact Status   This report includes the name and company, phone number, last reached, last results, ID/Status, a section on activities, and the last meeting.

Source Of Referrals   This report is terrific for judging the results of marketing programs. The report lists the source of referrals and the total from that source, followed by the name and company, title, and phone number of the referred contact. Any contact that does not have a Referred By entry prints at the beginning of the report.

TIP   *I recommend to all my clients that they move the Referrals field from the Alt Contacts tab to the top of the contact record screen so that it is visible at all time and therefore reminds users to enter the source of the contact record. This information can also be pulled out and displayed in a meaningful format.*

Group Reports

The reports that appear as a submenu are generated from group records, not from contact records. Use these reports to determine which records are in which group and to generate a summary of the groups, a report of all information in the group record, and a list of existing groups.

Group Membership   This report lists the name of the group and its total number of members, followed by the name, company, phone, and title of each member. Also, each of the subgroups and their contacts are listed.

Groups Summary   This report is similar to a contact report with the group name and address information and all the user fields, plus some system fields such as the record creator, create date, and edit date. Subgroups are included with activities, notes, and history.

Groups Comprehensive   This report prints everything that is in the group record by group name.

Groups List   This report prints the name of each group, its description, names of subgroups, and number of subgroups.

Sales   Please refer to Chapter 18 to see details on Sales reports.

The standard reports cover 95 percent of what most ACT! users need, but you can enhance any report or create a new report if needed. ACT!'s report writer is limited in functionality, particularly in the area of calculations, so if you need more extensive reporting, see Appendix A for information on Crystal Reports, a software program for specifically creating reports from various databases.

Previewing a Report

You can view a report on your computer screen before printing it. This way, you can see if the report generates the information you want and if you have set the filters properly. To do so, follow these steps:

1. Open the Reports menu.

2. Select the report you would like to preview. The Run Report dialog box appears, as shown in Figure 19-1, with the General tab selected. The options in this dialog box are described in the following section.

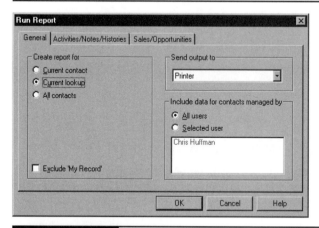

FIGURE 19-1   The Run Report dialog box with the General tab displayed

3. Change Send Output To from Printer to Preview by pulling down the list in the field.

4. Select the radio button that coincides with the scope of contact records you want included, and then select the users. The default is All Users, but you can see report data based on the entry in each record's Record Manager field.

When a contact record is created, two fields on the status tab—Record Creator and Record Manager—are automatically filled in, depending on the person creating the record. So, if Sally Jones creates the new record, her name is entered in both fields. In a shared database, the Record Manager field should reflect the person actually working with the contact record, so that the reports reflect the correct data. If the person working with the contact did not originally create the record, some data may not be reported. In order to change the entry in the Record Manager field, the user must have Administrative-level access.

5. Click OK. The report is shown in a window onscreen. Figure 19-2 shows a preview of the Contact report. To see the report in detail, click the Zoom In button to enlarge the report image.

6. Click Close to close the report window.

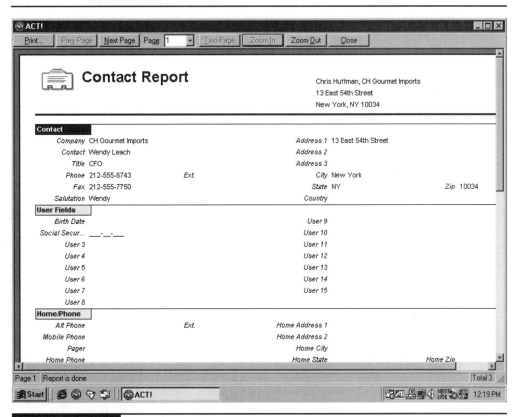

FIGURE 19-2   You can zoom your preview of the Contact report.

Run Report Options

Depending upon the report you select, you are presented with a series of options to fine-tune the results. After you select a report, the Run Report dialog box appears, as shown previously in Figure 19-1.

General Tab

The General tab has three sets of options: Create Report For, Send Output To, and Include Data For Contacts Managed By.

The Create Report For options determine the scope of the records that are to be included in the report. As you become more skilled with creating lookups, you will be able to target the report results, thereby gleaning better data from the database. They are described below:

Current Contact   Generates a report based on the contact record that you are viewing.

Current Lookup   Generates a report based upon the contact records that are included in the lookup.

All Contacts   Generates a report that includes every contact record in the database.

Exclude 'My Record'   Generally you do not want My Record included in the report, so be sure to click this check box.

The second option, Send Output To, is where to send the report output. The list of available destinations is described below:

Printer   Sends the report to the Windows Print Manager.

Preview   Sends the report to the screen in a window.

Fax   Sends the report to WinFax Pro, where you can send it to a fax recipient. This option is only available if you have installed WinFax Pro.

E-Mail   Creates the report, and then opens the E-Mail window and the report is attached as a file. At that point, you enter the details of the e-mail message. Note that the report will be in ACT! report format, and the recipient will need to have ACT! installed in order to view the report.

File-ACT! Report   Creates the report, and then opens the Save As dialog box so you can name the report and save it. You can open the report later if you want. The report is saved with an RPT extension.

File-Editable Text   Creates the report, opens the Save As dialog box, and assumes that you want to save the report in RTF (rich text format). After saving the report, ACT! opens a prompt asking if you want to open the report in the default word processor.

The third set of options—Include Data For Contacts Managed By—includes the following:

All Users and Selected User In a multi-user database, you have the situation where a contact record can be identified by the person who actually works with the contact record. (Check the Status tab for the Manager field.) So, when you create the report, you might want to see the report by a specific manager(s).

Any report you create in ACT! can easily be sent to and read by other ACT! users via e-mail. It is not editable.

Activities/Notes/Histories Tab

The Activities/Notes/Histories tab from the Run Report dialog box is shown in Figure 19-3. The options in this tab are further refinements of the report. Note that not all reports have these options available. Select the items you want included from the Notes/History section. If you include attachments, the attachment itself does not print, only the line item describing the attachment does. This is true for the e-mail, too.

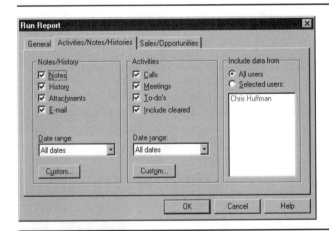

FIGURE 19-3 The Run Report dialog box Activities/Notes/Histories tab lets you include a variety of items in your report.

The Date Range drop-down list has many preset ranges. If they are not sufficient, you can select Custom, and ACT! opens a calendar. Click and hold the mouse button on the first date you want to include and then drag to select the other days, or press the SHIFT key and use the arrow keys to highlight. It is tricky to move the highlight from month to month. I recommend that you use the SHIFT key and the arrow keys. When you have to move to a different month, use the PAGE DOWN or PAGE UP keys.

The Activities setting works the same as the Notes/History setting. Select the type that you want to include and a date range for those items. You can have one date range for the Notes/History items and another for Activities.

The Include Data From setting allows another refinement. This is different from the Record Manager selection on the General tab. In this case, you can select which notes, histories, and activities you want by the person who added them to the contact record. So if you have a company where both salespeople and customer support people access the same contact records, you might want reports that isolate information by the person who added the information to the report.

Sales/Opportunities Tab

This tab is only active when one of the Sales reports has been selected. For more details on the individual Sales reports, see Chapter 18. One setting that you should look at is the Sorting options. Because Sales/Opportunities have unique data types, ACT! provides them as sort options. Pull down the list to select the order as the main sort order.

Customizing Reports

When you take on this task, it is usually because one of the predesigned reports does not exactly meet your needs. The logical starting point is to use one of the existing reports that is close to what you need. Alternatively, you can create a brand new report, which we'll cover later in this section.

Several of the ACT! reports are programmed to run certain procedures based on the name of the report. So, if you select an ACT! report because of some of the data it supplies, modify it, and then save it under a new name, the results may not be what you expect. The reports are Notes/History, History Summary, Sales By Contact, and Sales By Record Manager.

1. Open the Reports menu.

2. Select the Edit Report template option. The Open dialog box appears, as shown in Figure 19-4.

3. Select the report that is closest to what you want. Unfortunately, the filenames that ACT! provides are not very helpful in identifying what they do, so you might have to open a couple to get the one you want.

4. Click Open. The Contact Report template opens, as shown in Figure 19-5.

5. Before making any changes, save the report with a different filename so the original report is not lost. Open the File menu. Select Save As. The Save As dialog box appears.

19

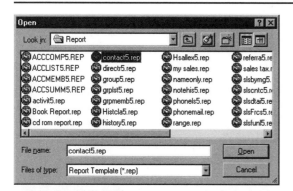

FIGURE 19-4 Select an existing report to edit from the Open dialog box.

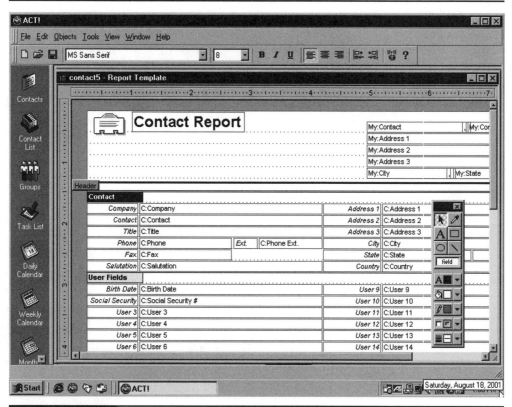

FIGURE 19-5 The Contact Report template is divided into sections that contain the individual fields from the database.

6. Type a new name. In this example, I typed **Book Report**.

7. Click Save. The newly named report is saved and the Contact Report template remains onscreen.

8. Close the Contact Report template by opening the File menu and selecting Close.

9. To open the newly renamed report, open the Reports menu and select Other Report. In the Open dialog box that appears, click Book Report (or whatever you have named the copy).

The new report name appears at the top of the report window, while in the body of the report, the header shows the original name.

All ACT! reports are divided by section. The sections are described here:

Header   The report header prints at the top of each page in the report and usually has the name of the report and the My Record information.

Primary Contact/Group   This section of the report has the details from the contact or group record. Every report has either a Primary Group or Contact section, but not both. However, a contact might have a group subsection, or a group might have a contact subsection.

Summary   This section of the report contains totals derived from formulas in the section, such as totals, counts, maximum, and so on.

Footer   This section of the report usually contains information such as the print date of the report.

One of the problems you might run into if you use an existing report is that some of the elements, such as the section name, cannot be removed. You might have to start with a brand new template, as described later in this chapter.

Adding and Deleting Fields from a Report

Any of the fields in the report can be removed very easily. Click the field you do not want, so that the window handles appear. Right-click to open the shortcut menu (see Figure 19-6) and select Cut.

To add a field, use the tool palette, as follows:

1. If the tool palette is not visible, open the View menu and select Show Tool Palette.

2. Click the Field button in the tool palette. When you do, the mouse pointer is modified to crosshairs, which you'll use to draw the field outline.

3. Click and hold the left mouse button to place the crosshairs at the beginning point where you want to start the field.

4. Drag the mouse to draw a rectangle.

FIGURE 19-6   You can access the shortcut editing menu in the report window.

5. Release the mouse button. When you do, the Field List dialog box appears, as shown in Figure 19-7. This dialog box offers many options for entering fields, which are outlined in the next section.

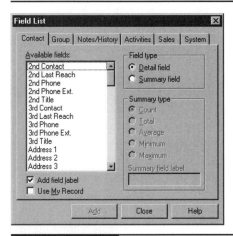

FIGURE 19-7   The Field List dialog box shows the information you can add to your report.

6. Click the name of the field you want to add to the report. The Add Field Label check box is selected by default.

7. Click the Add button. The field and its label are inserted into the report. You can add several fields at the same time by pressing and holding the CTRL key while selecting another field(s), then clicking Add.

8. Save the report by opening the File menu and selecting Save.

9. Test the report by opening the File menu and selecting Run. The Run Report dialog box appears. I suggest that you send the output to Preview, so you can look at the results on your monitor.

Field List Dialog Box

The Field List dialog box, as you just saw in the previous example, has many options. To better understand how the different options work, take a moment to read the following descriptions.

Contact tab   This tab entails all the fields in the particular database, the type, detail or summary and, if a summary, the type of summary and whether to use the My Record data.

Available Fields   ACT! lists the fields it has found in the database in alphabetical order. Unlike layouts, a report can have the same field used more than once. Generally, the information is pulled from the contact records, but you can pull information from My Record by clicking the Use My Record check box.

Field Type   Most of the time, you want a report to show the detail from the field in the contact record. The other choice is Summary Field, which can be used when you have a field that has numeric information, except for the Count summary type, which totals the number of entries in the field. For example, if you use the Count summary, and the range of the records in the report is 30 records and 20 of those records have entries in the field, the summary field would display the number 20. It is a good idea to add a field label to a summary field.

Summary Type   If you add a Summary field, you must then select a type of summary. The Count type calculates the number of entries from the records in the report. If the report has 30 records, and 20 have entries, the result is 20. The Total calculates a total value of all the entries from the selected field. So, if you had a field that contained the amount billed, the result would be the total of all the entries in that field for the records in the report. The Average calculates and displays the average of the values in the field selected for the records included in the report. The Minimum calculates and displays the smallest value in the field, and the Maximum calculates and displays the largest value in the field.

Group tab The Group tab options are identical to the Contact tab options. Select the field(s) you want to add to the report.

Notes/History, Activities, and Sales tabs These fields are very similar when added to reports. Select the field, and then determine if you want a detail or summary field.

System tab System fields are generated by ACT! or Windows. You can access them by clicking the Field List dialog box System tab, shown in Figure 19-8. As an example, the Date field information is gleaned from the Windows system clock. So, if the date shows up incorrectly, you have to reset the clock. The Activity, Notes/History, and Sales date ranges are derived from the settings you enter in the Run Report dialog box when you run the report. Add a field label, too, because you will likely forget what the value represents.

FIGURE 19-8   The Field List dialog box System tab gives you access to fields automatically generated by ACT! or Windows.

Testing a Report Template

After making modifications to a report template, you can run a test to see if the report generates the information you expect. If not, the template remains open and you can make further changes and try again.

1. Open the File menu and select Run. The Run Report dialog box appears.

2. Open the pull-down list in the Send Output To field and select Preview, which displays the report onscreen.

3. Select the range of contact records by clicking a radio button choice under Create Report For. I suggest that you limit the report to the current contact unless you need to see how the report breaks across several pages.

4. Click OK. The report appears in a full window that you can zoom.

5. Click Close to return to the report template.

 *If you select Print Preview from the File menu, you are not given a choice as to how many records to include. The default is All Records and the report is sent to the printer. In a large database, this could print for a very long time.*

Modifying the Phone List Report

The Phone List report is an easy one to modify and you can learn a few things by following the steps that follow. The important thing in this exercise, or any in which you are modifying an existing report is to save the report, with a new name so that you do not change the original.

1. Open the Reports menu and select the Edit Report Template option.

2. From the Open dialog box, select the report named phonels5.rep. The report template appears onscreen.

3. Scroll to the far right edge of the report so that you can see the Car Phone field.

4. Click the Car Phone field so that the handles appear.

5. Press the CTRL key and then click on the field label. The handles should appear on both the name and the field.

6. Right-click to open the shortcut menu and select Cut.

7. In the tool palette, click the Field button.

8. Draw a field where the Car Phone field was. The Field List dialog box appears.

9. On the Contacts tab, scroll the list of fields until you see the Fax field.

10. Click Fax. Uncheck the option Add Field Label.

11. Click Add. The Fax field is added, but there is no identifying label. ACT! would have placed the field label preceding the field itself, thereby pushing the field off the report template.

12. In the tool palette, click the button labeled A.

13. Above the Fax field, to the right of the Ext. label, draw a rectangle long enough to hold the label. When you release the mouse button, the insertion point is inside the rectangle you have drawn.

14. Type **Fax**.

15. Click the Bold button on the toolbar to add bolding to the label and then the Underline button to add underlining. The label matches the others in this template.

16. Open the File menu and select Save As and give the report a new name.

17. Test the report by opening the File menu and selecting Run. Try the report with a few contacts and see if you get what you expect.

Running a Newly Created Report

To run a report newly created or one you modified, you have to open the Reports menu and select Other Report because this is where reports are stored.

1. Open the Reports menu.

2. Select Other Report. The Open dialog box appears.

3. Click the report you want to run.

4. Click Open. The Run Report dialog box opens.

5. Select the options to fine-tune the report.

6. Click OK.

Starting from Scratch

If none of the existing reports that come with ACT! are remotely close to what you envision, or if they have too much formatting that cannot be removed, you can start with a blank report and add exactly what you need. Here's how:

1. Open the File menu from the contact record window.

2. Select New.

3. From the dialog box, select ACT! Report Template and click OK. As shown in Figure 19-9, a blank report template appears.

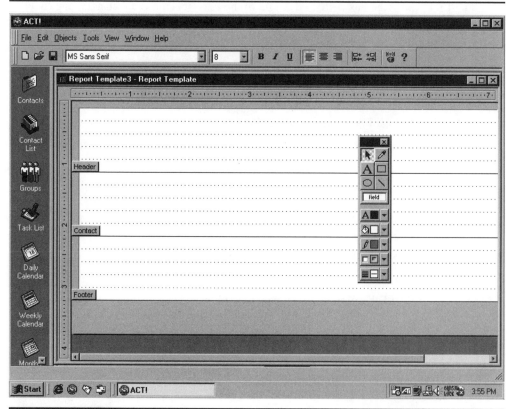

FIGURE 19-9 An ACT! new report template with three default sections is ready for editing.

At this point, you have to decide if the primary section is going to be a contact or group. By default, the template assumes that the report is going to have Contact as the primary section.

Adding and Deleting Sections

To add a new section, or to delete an existing section, right-click in the report and select the Define Sections option, or open the Edit menu and select Define Sections. The Define Sections dialog box appears, as shown in Figure 19-10.

If you want Group as the primary section, click the Contact section name and click Delete. To add Group as the primary section, click the Add button. The Add Section dialog box appears, as shown in Figure 19-11.

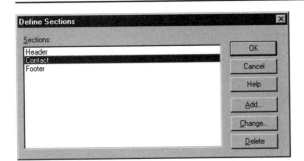

FIGURE 19-10   The Define Sections dialog box shows three section options.

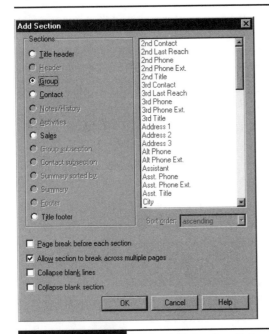

FIGURE 19-11   The Add Section dialog box lets you add Group as the primary section.

Select the section you want to add. Not all the section choices are active, depending upon where you want to add them. If you want to create summary information (which are fields that display results of a formula), you must add a Summary section in which to display the field. I'll describe each of the sections briefly:

Title Header   A Title Header is a section that prints once at the very beginning of the report. The normal header section appears on all other pages of the report.

Header   Add a Header section to print with every page of the report.

Group and Contact   Select Group or Contact as the primary section of the report. You cannot have both a Group section and a Contact section in a report.

Notes/History, Activities, and Sales   These sections contain information from that tab in the contact record. Although you can add fields from any of the tabs in other sections, adding these as sections makes it easy for the reader of the report to distinguish the information.

Group and Contact Subsections   You can add a subsection to the Group or Contact section by selecting one of these options. A subsection is used when you want to insert field information from either a Group or Contact tab. For instance, you might have a report with Contact as the primary section, but you may want certain fields from either the contact or group record to appear underneath.

Summary Sorted By   Add this section and not only can you add calculated fields, you can sort by the field you select.

Summary   Add this section to show the results of ACT! calculated fields.

Footer   Add this section if you have deleted the report footer from the report and want to add it back.

Title Footer   This section prints once on the first page of the report. The remaining pages have the normal footer.

Page Break Before Each Section   After a section prints, you can have the report print the next section on an entirely different page.

Allow Section To Break Across Multiple Pages   A single section might consume several pages. For example, if the section is Notes/History, it might be very long. This option allows the section to print from page to page without being interrupted by a header or footer.

Collapse Blank Lines   Some of the records might not contain information. With this option on, you save paper.

Collapse Blank Section   If the fields you insert into a section have no information, selecting this option makes the report print the section name, but no space is left blank.

Adding a Text Object

To add text to the report header, follow these steps:

1. Open the tool palette and click the Text tool (the letter A).

2. Draw a rectangle in the header by clicking and dragging. Release the mouse button and you can begin typing. In this example, shown in Figure 19-12, I typed **BOOK TITLE**.

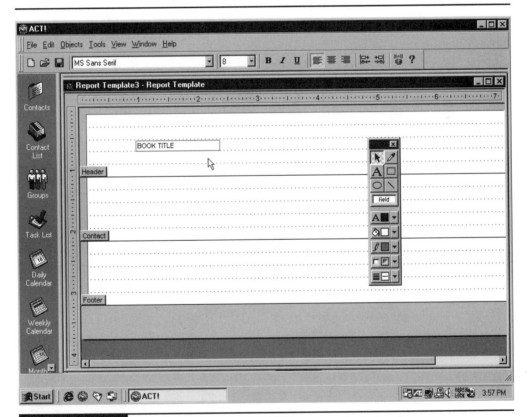

FIGURE 19-12   The new text, BOOK TITLE, appears in the header.

3. To add color to the text header background, click the tool palette and select the pointer tool.

4. Click the text you just added. With it selected, you can add color to the background.

5. The background coloring tool is the fourth one from the bottom of the tool palette. Click it and the color palette appears.

6. Click the color you want for the background.

The other tools can be used to add objects such as an ellipse or lines to the report or to add enhancements to fields.

Resizing a Section

If you need more room for fields in a section, you can easily add more space. The method is not obvious, and there is not a menu choice to do this. Use the following steps:

1. Click and hold the mouse button on the name of the section you want to enlarge or diminish.

2. Drag the name up to diminish, or down to enlarge.

ACT! allows you to change the size of the section within limits. In the predesigned reports, you have less sizing leeway.

Adding a Logo to the Report

To add a logo, you must have it saved in a bitmap (BMP) format. Then use the following steps:

1. Open the report template in ACT!.

2. Open the Windows Paint program by clicking the Windows Start button, and then selecting Programs | Accessories | Paint.

3. Once in the Paint program, open the logo file.

4. Use the Edit menu in the Paint program to select the logo image, then use the Edit menu again to select Copy. The logo image is now saved in memory on the Windows clipboard.

5. Return to the ACT! report template. Right-click to open the shortcut menu and select Paste. The logo image can be moved and resized as needed.

6. Save the report and try printing. If the design is not enchanting, simply repeat the editing steps and modify the design.

Adding Filters to a Report

This is a very desirable feature to add to your report. It makes it easy for a person not very familiar with ACT! to run the report with the data you expect. To add a filter, follow these steps:

1. Open the report template to which you want to add a filter.

2. Right-click the report template, and the shortcut menu appears.

3. Select Define Filters.

4. The only tab that is active is the General tab. You can select the range of contacts, the destination for the output, and the user data that is to be included.

5. Save the report template.

When you run the report, the Filter settings become the defaults for the report. But the Run Report dialog box still appears, at which point you can make choices other than the defaults.

 TIP   *Changing the destination for the output filter from the default Print to Preview makes it easy to see if the report is ready to be printed before actually doing so.*

Adding a Custom Report to the Reports Menu

After you spend the time and effort to design a report, make it easy to run. Here's how:

1. Open the Reports menu and select the Modify Menu option. The Modify Menu dialog box appears, as shown in Figure 19-13.

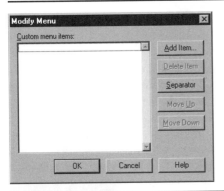

FIGURE 19-13   You can add a report to a menu via the Modify Menu dialog box.

2. Click the Add Item button. The Add Custom Menu Item dialog box appears, as shown in Figure 19-14.

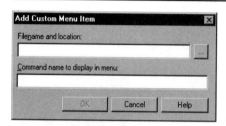

FIGURE 19-14 The Add Custom Menu Item dialog box lets you add your report to the menu of your choice.

3. Click the ellipsis button (the small button with three dots). The Open dialog box appears, from which you can select your custom report.

4. Click the report name and then click Open. Type the name that you want displayed on the Reports menu. (I entered **Book Report**.)

5. Click OK, and then click OK again. Figure 19-15 shows the new report added to the Reports menu.

Creating a Report that Totals Entries in a Field

The purpose of this report is to take the data from a single field in ACT! and generate the total for the range of records you select. The demonstration database that installs with ACT! does not include data that you can use to replicate this exercise. You can use a database of your own to try building this report or add data to the ACT! demonstration database and then see if you can get the report to work.

In my database, I have modified a field to read Amount Charged, and it is formatted as a currency field. In that field, I insert the dollar value I have charged each customer. You can easily duplicate this field in the demonstration database and then create the report as outlined in the steps that follow.

The report has the following sections: Header, Contact, Summary, and Footer. In order for ACT! to generate a total across records, you have to enter a totaling formula in the Contact section of the report and then insert a Summary section. Begin by starting with a new report.

1. Open the File menu and select New.

2. Select ACT! Report template and click OK. You see a blank report with three sections.

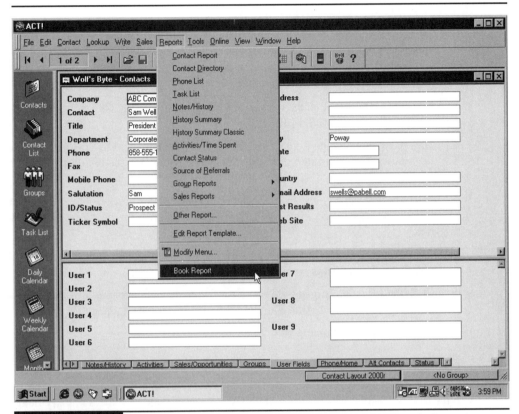

FIGURE 19-15   The new report is added to the Reports menu and ready for action.

3. Click the Contact section. This is an important step because the new section can only be placed before or after the section that is selected at this point.

4. Add the new Summary section by opening the Edit menu and selecting Define Sections. ACT! opens the Define Sections dialog box, which shows the three sections.

5. Click the Add button and the Add Section dialog box appears.

6. Click the radio button in front of Summary. ACT! prompts you with a dialog box that asks you to indicate where the Summary section should appear.

7. Click the Below button. Both dialog boxes close and you see the Define Sections dialog box. The section is added to the report.

8. Click OK to close the Define Sections dialog box.

Adding the Fields to the Report

This report requires very few fields. You need only the Company and the Amount charged fields in the Contact section. In fact, if you want, you do not have to have any fields in the Contact section, and then you can define the section with the Collapse Blank Section option. That way, a single page will print with only the Summary field.

1. Click the Field button on the tool palette. (If the tool palette is not visible, open the View menu and select Show Tool Palette.)

2. Draw a rectangle in the Contact section for the Company field by clicking and dragging the mouse from left to right. Release the mouse button and the Field List dialog box appears.

3. Click the Contact tab, and from the list of available fields, click Company. The defaults that should be selected are to add a field label and define the field type as a Detail field.

4. Click the Add button. The field and its label are added to the template, while the Field List dialog box remains open.

5. Click the Amount charged field name (or the name you have used in your database for this purpose) and click Add. The field is added under the Company field.

6. Close the Field List dialog box.

Adding the Summary Field

With the Contact section added and any fields you want inserted, add the Summary field that generates the total:

1. Click the Field button and draw a field in the Summary section of the report. The Field List dialog box appears.

2. In the Available Fields list, select Amount charged (or your substitute).

3. For the Field Type, click the Summary Field radio button.

4. In the Summary Type, click the Total radio button.

5. Add a Summary Field Label such as **Total Amount**.

6. Click Add. Your screen should look like the one shown in Figure 19-16.

7. Test the report by opening the File menu and selecting Run. Assuming that the current contact or the current lookup in your database has records with data, select the range and then select Preview as the output.

If you were careful following the steps, you should see one or more records with the total for each record, and in the last page of the report, the total for all records.

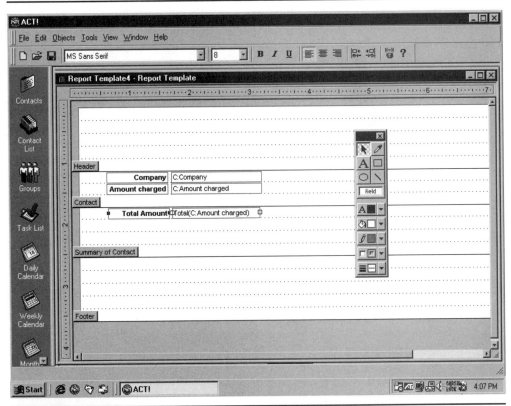

FIGURE 19-16   The completed report template generates a total for the Amount
charged field.

Summary

■ The standard reports that come with ACT! cover 95 percent of what most companies
need. Test them to see which is closest to your reporting needs.

■ You can modify any existing report and rename it, or create a new report from scratch.

■ After modifying or creating a report, if you use it frequently, add it to the Reports menu.

Chapter 20

Using SideACT!

How to...

- Understand and use SideACT!
- Enter tasks into SideACT!
- Move SideACT! tasks to ACT!
- Set preferences for SideACT!

One of the criticisms of ACT! that has been consistent since the initial DOS version in 1989 has been the lack of an easy way to record a task that was not necessarily related to a contact in the database. In other words, you basically had two courses of action if you wanted to be reminded to pick up your dry cleaning. One was to enter the dry cleaner as a contact record (a profile, back in the DOS days), and then, if on a network, make the record private so the boss did not see it while reviewing your weekly activity report. Or you could add the errand as a to-do attached to My Record. Either way was cumbersome, especially the latter, because your History file would become cluttered with effluvia.

In version 4.0, SideACT! was introduced and continues to be included as part of ACT!. This is a separate program that allows you to enter tasks within or (and this is the sexy part) without ACT!. This concept posed a considerable challenge to the software designers because almost since its inception, ACT! has had an official Task List (see Chapter 8) that combines the activities of all the records in the database. The challenge is twofold: how to get around the problem of adding what is in reality a second form of a task list, and how to connect the new task list to ACT! They also added a SideACT! icon to the ACT! toolbar, so that you could pop into SideACT! easily from within ACT!.

Starting SideACT!

When you install ACT!, an icon appears on your desktop and an entry is made to the Startup folder that will start SideACT! regardless of whether ACT! itself is running. To begin using this new attribute, you simply double-click the desktop icon or choose SideAct! from its Start menu folder. When you do, the SideACT! window appears, as shown in Figure 20-1.

At the top of the window is the title My Tasks. Although most users will likely use only one SideACT! file at a time, SideACT! allows you to create many unique files consisting of one or many tasks. You can only have one open at a time, but it's great to have the facility to create different files in case you have several projects going for which you want to keep separate lists.

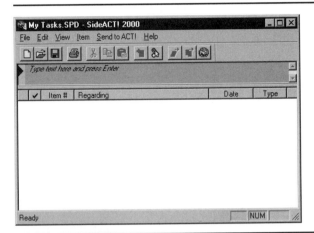

FIGURE 20-1 The SideACT! opening window appears when you launch the program.

Entering a Task

When SideACT! opens, the insertion point is automatically positioned so you can begin typing the task you want to record. To begin, type a task as I have done in Figure 20-2. (Because this book's obviously done, you might use a different task such as "Buy dog food.")

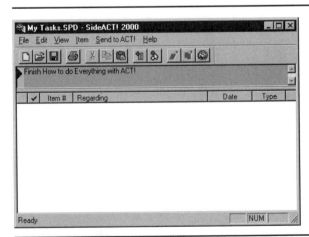

FIGURE 20-2 Entering an initial task into SideACT!

After typing the task, you add it to the SideACT! list by opening the Item menu and selecting Add Item To List or by pressing ENTER. The task is now listed in the bottom portion of the window, as shown in Figure 20-3.

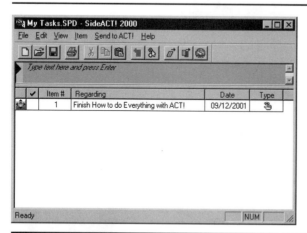

FIGURE 20-3   Your task is added to the SideACT! list.

That was easy enough! The advantage of being able to build a list of tasks without having to open ACT! is most apparent if you're like me. You have ideas popping into your head constantly and tend to scribble notes on pieces of paper, which have a nasty habit of disappearing about the time you need them. These tasks and ideas are not necessarily connected to any particular person—which is the ACT! paradigm. SideACT! gives you a convenient repository for those random thoughts.

When you are finished adding a task, you can minimize the SideACT! window, close the SideACT! application, or start ACT! and decide if you want to move or copy the task or tasks to ACT! itself. All tasks entered into SideACT! are assumed to be to-dos unless you change the default setting to another type of activity or change an individual task item after adding it to the list. To mark a task in SideACT! as being completed, right-click the mouse on the item and from the shortcut menu, select Mark As Completed. SideACT! draws a line through the item. This menu also allows you to delete, cut, or copy a task.

If you simply close SideACT!, all items are retained; you do not have to take any steps to save the list. This is true even for an entry in the text entry area above the list. Having added a series of tasks, let's move to the next step of connecting the tasks to ACT!.

Getting SideACT! Tasks into ACT!

The tasks in SideACT! can be moved or copied to ACT!. Moving a task removes it from the list in SideACT!, while copying duplicates the task to your ACT! database. You can move the list of tasks as a whole or select individual items.

To move or copy a task from SideACT! to ACT!:

1. Right-click anywhere on the item to open the shortcut menu, which is shown in Figure 20-4. Select Send To ACT!

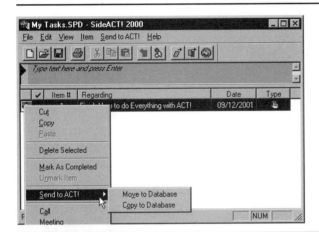

FIGURE 20-4   The shortcut menu is used to copy or move an item from the SideACT! list into an ACT! database.

2. Select either the Move or Copy option. When you do, a dialog box asks you to confirm the destination for the item, as shown in Figure 20-5.

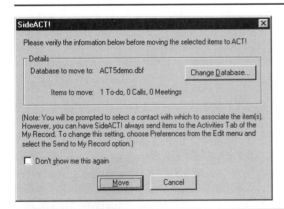

FIGURE 20-5   This dialog box checks with you for the correct destination for a SideACT! item.

3. If the database that ACT! suggests for the destination is correct, click Move (or Copy). If not, click the Change Database button to select the destination database.

4. After clicking Move or Copy, the destination database is opened and the Associate With Contact dialog box appears, as shown in Figure 20-6. ACT! assumes that you want to associate the item with My Record.

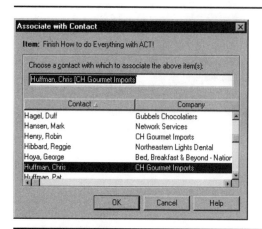

Item: Finish How to do Everything with ACT!

Choose a contact with which to associate the above item(s):

Huffman, Chris [CH Gourmet Imports]

Contact	Company
Hagel, Duff	Gubbels Chocolatiers
Hansen, Mark	Network Services
Henry, Robin	CH Gourmet Imports
Hibbard, Reggie	Northeastern Lights Dental
Hoya, George	Bed, Breakfast & Beyond - Natior
Huffman, Chris	CH Gourmet Imports
Huffman, Pat	

FIGURE 20-6   In the Associate With Contact dialog box, My Record is selected by default.

At this point, scroll through the window listing the contact names and their respective companies to locate a different target record. Alternatively, you can type the first letters of the last name of the contact and ACT! will list the matching name(s) in the field. Click OK to accept.

After being moved or copied to the database, the item appears in two places—on the Activities tab in the contact record and in the Task List—the same as any other activity.

Setting Preferences for SideACT!

To set the preferences, open SideACT!, then open the Edit menu and select Preferences. The Preferences dialog box (shown in Figure 20-7) offers options to make any new item a call, meeting, or to-do. You can sort the list so that any new item is added either to the top or bottom of the list or so that any items you mark as completed are moved to the bottom of the list or left in place. You can set the default to send all items directly to My Record. In addition, you can shut off the transfer confirmation window that appears when moving or copying items, and you can have ACT! display the SideACT! icon in the Windows taskbar at the bottom right of your computer screen.

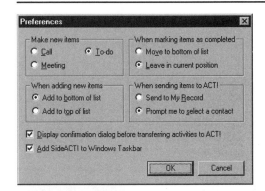

FIGURE 20-7 You can set your own Preferences for SideACT! in this dialog box.

Creating and Opening a Second SideACT! File

One of the uses of SideACT! is for personal goal setting. If you have educated yourself on goal setting, you know that goal setting should include financial, spiritual, physical, and emotional goals. SideACT! is an excellent place to store those goals, as they are readily accessible. But they are private, so you might not want your goal list to be on your desktop at all times. Plus, you might have several projects for which you would like to create lists, not as a detailed project manager, but as guideposts or check items.

To create a second SideACT! list:

1. Open the File menu and select New. A new SideACT! window appears with the word "Untitled" in the upper-left corner.

2. Open the File menu and select Save. The Save As dialog box appears. Type a name for the new SideACT! list.

To switch between lists, open the File menu and select Open. In the resulting dialog box, click the list you want to see.

Printing the SideACT! List of Tasks

The workday is over, and as you prepare to head for home, you can print your list of chores. For example, you might have entered your grocery list into SideACT! or you might have entered the names of the stores you need to visit: supermarket, dry cleaners, and cigar shop. With SideACT! open, simply click the Print button on the taskbar and the list is hard copy.

Summary

- SideACT! is a small program that lets you enter tasks without associating them with an ACT! contact.

- To add an activity to SideACT!, click the desktop icon or click the SideACT! icon in the ACT! toolbar, and start typing. Finish the new entry by pressing ENTER.

- You can move or copy SideACT! tasks to ACT!.

Chapter 21

Importing and Exporting Data

How to...

- Get data into ACT!
- Get data out of ACT!
- Check for duplicate records

Seamless data portability, that is moving data from one application to another easily, has been a dream for many years, and not only in the PC world. Even today, one needs look no further than the obstacles for sharing Macintosh and PC data files. This chapter is devoted to the movement of data into ACT! and out again. I'll show you how to avoid the nastier problems that you can encounter in this trial-and-error process.

Importing Files into ACT!

You won't have to abandon vital information that was stored in other software programs or re-type that information if you're adopting ACT! 2000 as your new database. Because most other programs allow you to export their data to standard formats, an ACT! database—with its ability to import data from a multitude of file types—can import the data, allowing you to make the transition without losing valuable data or creating redundant work for yourself. The sections that follow describe the various methods for getting data into ACT! from a number of sources.

Importing Files Created in Older Versions of ACT!

Before looking at importing data from other programs, a quick note on getting data from older versions of ACT!. When you install ACT!, it is supposed to check for a prior version of ACT! and for databases created by that version. If found, ACT! prompts you to convert the database to the current version. However, you might have an ACT! database on your hard drive that was created by an older version, but no longer have the old ACT! program. If this is the case, ACT! will not be able to identify the old database. Don't worry, you can convert the old database yourself, as follows:

1. Close any database that is open.
2. Open the File menu and select Open. The Open dialog box appears.
3. From the Files Of Type drop-down list, select the matching ACT! database type. You will probably have to browse to the folder that contains the older ACT! database.
4. Click the old database, and then click OK.

ACT! alerts you that the database was created by an older version of ACT! and that it will be converted. You also have the option of making a backup copy of the older database, which is always a good idea.

Importing Data from Other Programs

ACT! can import data from several file types. What that means is that if you have information in a different program, it can be converted into ACT!. The most common file type in use in creating databases is dBase. Now, dBase itself comes in several flavors, and not every flavor can be imported into ACT!, but the vast majority can. The second most common file type is called text-delimited (also known as ASCII). In some cases where a database cannot be imported as a dBase file, the program that created the database might be able to export its data into a text-delimited file, thereby allowing ACT! to import it. You will not know until you try to import the other database what the results will be. That is why I recommend that you first create a database that can act as a temporary holding place for the data. You can look at it and see if it is correct, or delete the imported records and try again.

Follow these steps to import data:

1. Create a new, blank ACT! database.

   If the database you are importing includes special fields that are not in ACT!, in the new blank ACT! database modify one or more of the User fields to accommodate those special fields. Or, if you have an existing ACT! database that has the fields you want, make a blank copy as follows: Open the File menu and select Save As | Create Empty Copy. Give this database a name like Import. Then, open this new database and proceed.

2. Open the File menu and select Data Exchange.

3. From the submenu, select Import to launch the Import Wizard, as shown in Figure 21-1.

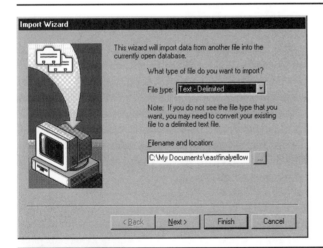

FIGURE 21-1   Use the Import Wizard to import files from other programs.

4. Open the drop-down list for file types and select the file type of the database you are trying to import. Check the source program documentation for help. In most cases, select dBASE or Text - Delimited.

5. In the Filename And Location field, type the name of the file, or click the Browse button (the gray box with three dots) to locate the file. dBase files have an extension such as .adb, .db, .dbf, or something very similar. Text-delimited files have a .txt, .csv, or .asc extension. After you have located the file, select it, and then click Open.

6. Click Next to move to the next page of the wizard, as shown in Figure 21-2.

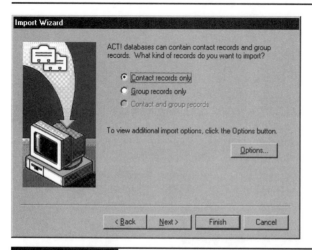

FIGURE 21-2   Select the kind of records you want to import on this page of the Import Wizard.

ACT! does not know whether the database you are trying to import has only contact or group records. If it is not an ACT! database, it will not have group records; so select Contact Records Only.

The Options button is important if you are merging an ACT! database into an existing ACT! database and you suspect that some of the records in both are alike—maybe not identical, but essentially the same record. Click Options and review the settings. For information about merge options, see "Setting Merge Options" later in this chapter.

7. Click Next. The Import Wizard CONTACT MAP page appears, as shown in Figure 21-3. (If you are importing from a database other than ACT!, the next wizard page will include map files for some other contact managers, such as GoldMine. Select Use Predefined Map, and choose the program from which you are importing from the list.)

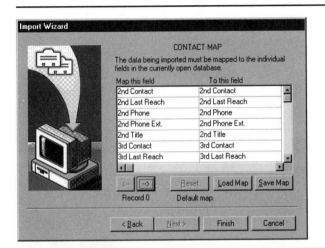

FIGURE 21-3   Use the Import Wizard CONTACT MAP page to match fields from the database you are importing to ACT! database fields.

This is where you physically map the data in the source database (the one you are importing) to the ACT! destination database.

On the left, under Map This Field, are the fields ACT! has read from the source database. On the right, under To This Field, are the fields into which ACT! thinks the data from the source database belongs.

It is very helpful to include the first record (Record 0) when you export data. This record usually consists of the field names, making it a bit easier to match them with ACT!'s field names.

ACT! reads the file information header from the source database and tries to match the fields in the source with its own fields, *mapping* one to the other. For example, say the source database contains a field called Company, which includes all the company names. ACT! matches the source database Company field with ACT!'s Company field. If ACT! cannot find a match among its fields for a field from the source, it leaves a blank for you to map.

8. Click the right arrow button above the caption Record 0, so that it reads Record 1. When you do, the field names on the left are replaced with information from the first real record in the source database, making it much easier for you to see if the data is going where it belongs. Scroll down the map to check all the fields. If the entries are matched with the correct fields in ACT!, you can finish the import.

If you think you might need the map at another time, save it by clicking the Save Map button. Plus, if the import was off just a little, you can reload the map, and tweak it, saving you the time of having to remap every field.

9. Click the Finish button.

If you have many records, say, in the thousands, now is the time for that latte break, as this will take time.

After ACT! has finished and the data is in the correct fields, you have to perform maintenance in order for ACT! to be able to work with the records.

1. Open the File menu and select Administration.

2. From the submenu, select Maintenance. The Database Maintenance dialog box appears, as shown in Figure 21-4.

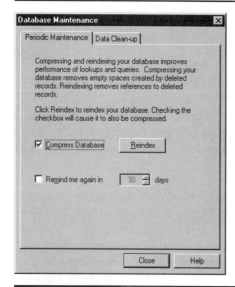

FIGURE 21-4   The Database Maintenance dialog box lets you reindex your imported records.

3. Click the Reindex button. This, too, can take some time, so go ahead and go back for some spumoni to go with your latte.

When ACT! is finished, your database is ready to go. If you look at the newly imported records and see that there are major problems, you have two choices: move the data from the wrong ACT! field to the correct field, or trash the database and start over. For details about deleting a database, see "Deleting a Database" later in this chapter.

Importing from Outlook

Importing from Outlook is pretty much the same as importing from any other program except the Import Wizard includes some custom options for Outlook. After completing steps 1 through 3 for importing, as described above, follow these steps to import data from Outlook:

1. Select Outlook from the Files Of Type list, and click Next.

   You do not need to specify the Outlook file; ACT! automatically locates it. If you are on a network, the Choose Profile dialog box appears.

2. Choose the user profile you want to use, and click OK.

3. Click Next, and click the Options button. The Import Options dialog box opens, as shown in Figure 21-5.

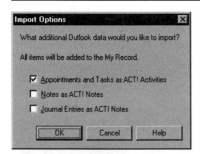

FIGURE 21-5   Specify the Outlook data you want to import in this dialog box.

4. Select the data you want to import, and click Next. The CONTACT MAP page of the wizard appears, customized for Outlook fields.

5. Map the fields from Outlook on the left to the fields in ACT! on the right.

6. Click Finish. Remember to reindex the database after completing the import.

Deleting a Database

To delete a database, you must be the administrator of the database. You cannot delete a database in which you are working.

1. Open a different database.

2. Open the File menu and select Administration.

3. From the submenu, select Delete Database. The Delete Database dialog box opens.

4. Select the database to be deleted and click the Delete button. ACT! checks to make certain you are the administrator before allowing the deletion.

5. Click OK. It is gone forever.

Data Cleanup after Importing

No matter how careful you are in executing an import, you may find that the data does not end up in the field that you expected, or the data is of a different type than you thought. In either case, you can solve those two problems easily with a couple of options that ACT! provides.

Copying Data from Field to Field

This subject is useful at more times than just importing, but this is where it seems to fit best. In the scenario where you have imported the data and reindexed the database, and find that some data that should have gone into one field has arrived in another, you can copy the data to the correct field, or swap the data in one field with data in another. Nifty.

To copy data in one field in ACT! to another, follow these steps:

1. Open the Edit menu and select Replace. ACT! displays a blank record.

2. Open the Replace menu and select Copy A Field. The Copy Field Contents dialog box appears, as shown in Figure 21-6.

3. Click the drop-down arrow in the Copy Contents Of list to see all the fields. Scroll the list and select the field in which the data is wrong (or type the first letter of that field name).

4. In the To field, select the destination for the data from the drop-down list.

5. Click OK. ACT! warns you that the action modifies all contacts in the lookup.

6. Click OK to finish. If the data was copied from or to a field on the Lookup menu—Company, First Name, or Last Name—perform a reindex, as described previously.

Swapping Data

If you want to switch the contents of two fields, that is, if you want the data in field A in field B and vice versa, you can use the Swap command. Swapping is very much like copying. Follow these steps:

1. Open the Replace menu and select Swap Fields. The Swap Field Contents dialog box appears.

2. Use the pull-down lists to select the two fields that have the data you want to move.

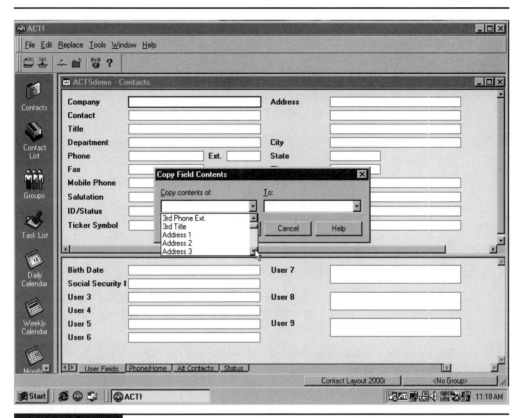

FIGURE 21-6   The Copy Field Contents dialog box contains a drop-down list of fields
to be copied.

3. Click OK. ACT! warns you that all the records in the lookup will be affected. Click
Yes to make the swap.

You cannot copy, move, or swap data in the E-Mail field.

To move, copy, or swap data in more than one field, first create a lookup of the records
that you wish to change. Then follow the steps as outlined previously for either copying or
swapping.

Erasing All Data in a Field

You can delete, or erase, the data in a field so that the field is blank in every record in your database or lookup. Note that this method does not work with all fields in ACT!. For example, it does not work with the Salutation field or Web Address field. To erase all the data in a field, follow these steps:

1. Open the Edit menu and select Replace.

2. Click the field that you want to make blank.

3. Press CTRL-F5, which inserts "<<BLANK>>" into the field.

4. Click the Apply button on the toolbar. ACT! alerts you that all records in the lookup are affected.

5. Click OK. The data in that field for all records in the lookup is erased.

Looking Up Newly Imported Records

Suppose that you have accidentally imported records into your working database instead of a blank database. ACT! allows you to modify records in a lookup, but how can you look up only the newly imported records? It's easy:

1. Open the Lookup menu and select By Example.

2. Click the Status tab.

3. In the Merge Date field, enter the date that matches the import date. If you want to, you can enter a modifier such as > or the Range command. See Chapter 5 for details.

4. Click the Run button on the toolbar.

   ACT! finds all the records that have been imported per your date entry. Now, you can use the Contact menu to delete the current lookup, or use the Edit menu to copy, swap, or erase the affected field(s).

 *If you imported two or more separate sets of data on the same day, there is no way to separate the two different sets of records.*

Mapping Fields That Do Not Match

It seldom works out that all the fields in your source database have the same names as the fields in your new database, so let's look at mapping strategies you can use to get the imported data into your database. On the CONTACT MAP page of the Import Wizard, you can select the destination (ACT!) field you want to match each source field. The destination fields are presented in a drop-down list on the right side of the page, as shown in Figure 21-7.

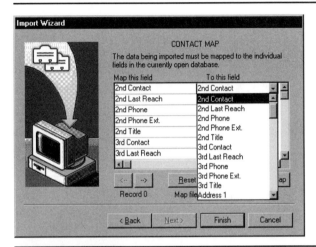

FIGURE 21-7   Select the destination field from this drop-down list.

You can scroll to select the correct field or type the first letter of the field name. So for ID/Status, for example, type **I**, and the field appears. Click the field to add it to the map.

For some imports, you might have a source database that uses two separate fields for First Name and Last Name. Because ACT! uses the single field Contact for both names, ACT! includes the mapping fields First Name and Last Name. Map your source database fields to these fields, and ACT! will put the incoming data into the Contact field correctly.

Your source database may contain fields that do not exist in your ACT! database. You have two choices. You can cancel the import process, add the required fields to the ACT! database, as described in Chapter 17, and then return to the import process and map the fields. Or, you can map the fields from the source database to one or more of ACT!'s User fields. If you choose the second method, take a moment to make a paper map, noting which source field was mapped to which User field. You can use this map later to rename these fields accordingly.

Finally, if the source database contains fields that you do not want to include in the import, select the first item in the To This Field list—Do Not Map.

Importing can present other challenges such as data that is all capitals, or data in which the city and state are in a single field and need to be separated when imported. Fortunately, a multitude of third-party software products have been created to solve these problems. Appendix A discusses them at length.

Setting Merge Options

If you followed my recommendation, you created an empty database into which you imported records. The newly created ACT! database, if the import has worked correctly, can then be imported into your working database. It is possible that some of the records in your working database match the records you are importing. That is, they might be identical based on the Company, Contact, and Phone fields, the fields ACT! uses to determine whether the records are duplicates. (You can change the fields ACT! uses for this purpose, as described in the following section.) You can merge the two ACT! databases so that duplicates are eliminated or so that new data is added to existing matching records. After opening the Import Wizard and selecting the ACT! database to import, clicking Next takes you to the next page and the Options button appears. Click the Options button and the Merge Options dialog box appears, as shown in Figure 21-8.

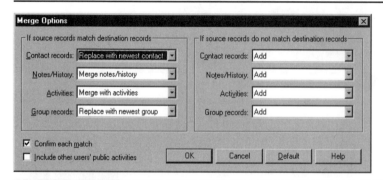

FIGURE 21-8   Use the Merge Options dialog box for merging databases.

The following list describes the available options. Keep in mind that the Source database is the one you are importing into the currently open database, which is called the Destination database. Configure the dialog box to best suit your needs. The options below determine what happens as the records are added to ACT!. Usually the default settings work very well, but you may occasionally want to make changes.

If Source Records Match Destination Records   The options under this heading apply to records from the imported database that ACT! designates as matches of records in the ACT! database. You have the following options:

Contact Records   Your options are Replace With Newest Contact, Replace With Source Contact, and Do Not Change. If you choose Replace With Newest Contact, ACT! looks at the edit dates of both records, source and destination, and keeps only the newest record. If you choose Replace With Source Contact, the incoming record overwrites the entire record in your database. If you select Do Not Change, nothing happens.

Notes/History   You can merge the notes and history, which combines the Notes/History of both records. Or, you can replace the notes in the destination record with the source record Notes/History. Or, you can choose to not make a change and no change occurs.

Activities   You can merge the activities, which combines the activities of both records. Or, you can replace the activities in the destination record with the source activities. Or, you can choose to not make a change.

Group Records   If the source group matches the destination group, you can replace with the newest group, replace with the source group, or make no change.

If Source Records Do Not Match Destination Records   On the right side are options for what ACT! does with source records that do not match any of the ACT! database records:

Contact Records   You can choose to add the record or not. You might want to merge only matching records in both databases without adding records that do not match.

Notes/History   If you add records that do not match destination records, you can decide whether to include the Notes/History.

Activities   If you add records that do not match destination records, you can decide whether to include the activities data.

Groups Records   If groups do not match, you can choose to add the group or not.

Two check boxes appear at the bottom of this dialog box—Confirm Each Match and Include Other Users' Public Activities. Selecting Confirm Each Match causes ACT! to stop the merge when it thinks it locates a matching record in the destination database. A dialog box appears at that point asking whether you want to merge the records (based on your settings), add the record as a new record, or skip the record (which means the record is not imported or merged). If you know your databases contain many matching records and you are confident in your merge settings, leave this check box cleared. Otherwise, you will have to sit in front of the computer and confirm every match—a very time-consuming practice.

The Include Other Users' Public Activities check box is cleared by default. I recommend that you select it; you can always delete activities later.

Checking for Duplicates

You don't have to wait until the next time you import data to check for duplicates. You can review your database at any time to seek out extraneous records. Simply open the Tools menu and select Scan For Duplicates.

If ACT! finds any suspected duplicates, the record counter will read "1 of X." At this point you can move from record to record to compare the records.

TIP

I prefer to change to the List view so that I can easily put the fields side by side to see which record is correct and then delete the incorrect record.

How ACT! Checks for Duplicates

ACT! can check for duplicates by reviewing the entries in *any* of three fields. The default fields are Company, Contact, and Phone. So, if you are importing into a database that includes a record with the entry Interact in the Company field, and the source database includes a record that also has the entry Interact in the Company field, ACT! thinks the second record might be a duplicate of the first. Another example: If a record has the company as Megatex, the contact as John Braun, and the phone number as 555-555-5555; and a second record has the company as Megatex, but with a different contact and phone number data, ACT! will interpret the second as a duplicate of the first.

Once ACT! has spotted a match, it appears in the Merge dialog box and prompts you to intervene and determine whether the record truly is a duplicate and should be merged with an existing record, whether it should be added as a new record, or whether it should be skipped, which means that it is not imported.

You can change the fields ACT! uses to check for duplicate/matches, as described in the next section.

Modifying the Criteria ACT! Uses to Check for Duplicates

Most of the time the fields ACT! uses by default to check for duplicates (and matches during import routines) is acceptable. But you might have modified your ACT! database in such a way, or are using fields in such a way, that you want to use a different field or fields to check for duplicates. An example of the latter case is the ID/Status field. Many companies use this field for the customer account number, which you do not want to be duplicated. Because ACT! does not include a feature for creating a rule so that only a unique number can be entered into a field, it is possible to enter the same number in two or more records. In that case, you would want ACT! to check the ID/Status field for duplication.

To change the field or fields that ACT! reviews when checking for duplicates or matches, follow these steps:

1. Open the Edit menu and select Define Fields. The Define Fields dialog box appears.

2. Select the Advanced tab at the top of the dialog box, as shown in Figure 21-9.

    ACT! uses three fields to check for matching records; for a match to be made, any of the three fields can match. See the "How ACT! Checks for Duplicates" sidebar prior to this section for details.

3. Change the fields you want ACT! to check for duplicates by opening the drop-down list for each one and clicking the field name. Make sure the Enable Duplicate Checking check box is selected.

4. Close the dialog box by clicking OK.

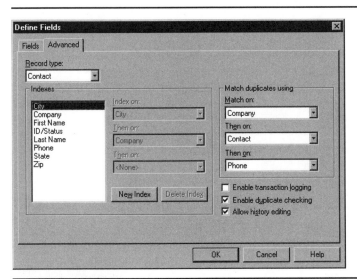

FIGURE 21-9   With the Define Fields dialog box you can change the criteria ACT! uses to check for duplicates.

   *When you change the fields that are used to check for duplicates, the change affects both the importing process and the routine for checking for duplicates already in the database.*

Exporting Records from ACT!

You can export records from ACT! in three formats: as text-delimited, as ACT! 2000, or as ACT! 2.01 for DOS. In the process of exporting, you can export only certain records, and in those exported records, the order of the fields and which fields are included is preserved. Let's take a look, using ACT!'s Export Wizard.

First, if you need to, create a lookup of the records that you want to export. Then follow these steps:

1. Open the File menu and select Data Exchange.

2. Select Export from the submenu to launch the Export Wizard, as shown in Figure 21-10.

3. Select the file type you are exporting to. If you are exporting to an ACT! database, it must already exist. If you are exporting to a text-delimited file, type a name for the file, and ACT! creates it for you, including the .txt extension.

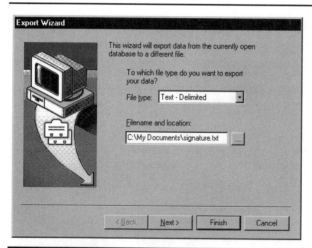

FIGURE 21-10   The Export Wizard lets you control how you export your contact records.

4. In the Filename And Location field, browse to locate the destination database. Or, for a new text-delimited file, browse to the folder and type a name for the file and click Save.

5. Click Next. Choose to export contact records or the group records.

   For a text-delimited export, click the Options button and choose the type of delimiter. You might have to ask the person who plans to import the records which delimiter is preferred. For imports to Excel, Tab works best as the delimiter. Also, ask the recipient whether to export field names with the records. Normally, the answer is yes.

   When exporting to an ACT! database, you can export contact records with or without groups. Click the Options button, and the Merge Options dialog box opens. See "Setting Merge Options" earlier in this chapter to determine the settings you need.

6. Click Next. You now can choose to export the current record, the current lookup, or all records.

7. Click Next. If you are exporting to an ACT! database, you must map the fields as explained earlier in this chapter. If you are exporting to a text-delimited file, the wizard page shown in Figure 21-11 appears, which has only one list of fields.

As you can see, you can arrange the order in which the fields are exported, starting from the top, which is the first field exported, and whether or not the field data is exported at all. To exclude a field from the export, open the drop-down list, scroll to the very top, which is a blank entry, and click. The field is eliminated from the list, giving you control over what information is sent to the delimited text file.

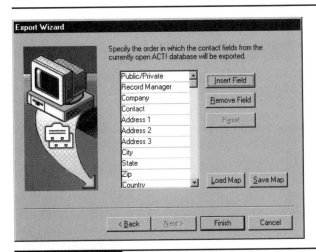

FIGURE 21-11   Use this page of the Export Wizard to select which fields to export to a text-delimited file and in what order.

ACT! does not support the export of Sales/Opportunities data. However, there are several third-party applications you can use to export this information. See Appendix A for details.

Summary

■ Getting data into ACT! is not necessarily an easy process, depending upon the source file structure. If it is an ACT!-to-ACT! import the process is easier, provided the fields are the same in both databases.

■ If you make a mistake when you import data, you can swap data between fields, copy data from one field to another, or delete all the data from a field.

■ Getting data out of ACT! is very straightforward. You can export all the data from every field or just the data from the fields you want, in the order you want.

■ ACT! performs a duplicate check using the fields you select as criteria. You can initiate a check for duplicates from the Tools menu.

■ For more complex imports, you may need to purchase a third-party product to assist in the process.

Chapter 22

Maintaining and Backing Up ACT! Data

How to...

- Back up your database
- Maintain your database
- Repair your database

Experience shows that ACT! users tend to not properly maintain or back up their data. The main reason seems to be that most ACT! users think that ACT! is like any other software program. It is not; ACT! is highly dynamic and complex and requires some basic maintenance. This chapter deals with the ease with which you can keep your business thriving with minimal effort and, if things do go wrong, the steps you can take to try and repair your database.

How to Go Out of Business

It is an unfortunate fact of life that nature is always in the process of creating and destroying at the same time. It would be great if computers never crashed, if backup tapes never broke, or if databases never became corrupted. But they do. You can't always prevent these kinds of problems, but you can prepare for them by backing up your data. Remember, the second most important asset a business has is its information. (Its people are first.) Why do users not maintain and back up their data? One reason is the lack of understanding that ACT! databases, unlike other computer files, are extremely dynamic and that, therefore, the possibility of data corruption from bad hard drives, file conflicts, viruses, and user error is high. Also people often do not value their access to data as they should. Consider the cost of each sales lead or the time it takes to recover from database disaster. Such procedures are not cheap, but are rarely calculated. The time invested in proper maintenance and backup yields a high return.

Backing Up Your Database

The most important aspect of keeping your prized database intact is by making backup copies regularly. Many customers wonder how often a backup should be made. The long answer is determined by the age of your database and the cost to you in lost business versus the cost of making the backup. The short answer is to back up your database at least once per day. It is even better to back up once at the beginning of the day and again at the end of the day. The end-of-day backup assures you that if a computer crashes at startup (the most likely time), you have lost nothing.

The end-of-day backup should be taken off site in case of computer theft or a disaster in the building. Or you can use a web-based service as the repository for your backup.

Network Backups

Many companies now have systems that back up data every evening. That might be sufficient, but if the server crashes, how long could you go without your ACT! data? It can take hours to repair a server and then replace the lost data files. Also, some network backup systems perform only incremental backups; that is, they copy only the files that have a later date than the current copy in the backup medium. Because ACT! databases consist of a series of files rather than one large file, and because these files are date sensitive, backing up files out of order, as will happen with an incremental backup, will corrupt the data. Therefore, you must perform a full backup, that is, you must make a copy of the entire data set when you back up your ACT! database.

Using the Backup Program

ACT! includes a backup program to help you perform the backup. Whether you are using ACT! over a network or on a standalone computer, I recommend you use this program to make your backup. To make a backup of your database, follow these steps:

1.   Open the database you want to back up.

2.   Open the File menu and select Backup. The Backup dialog box appears, as shown in Figure 22-1.

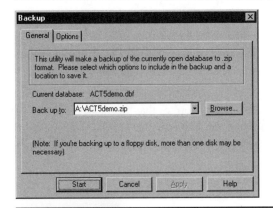

The Backup dialog box lets you back up an existing ACT! database.

The backup program in ACT! creates a compressed copy of the database and any other files you designate (more on this in the next step). A very large database can be stored on 3.5-inch disks because the compression program can create a series of disks that contain one large file. If you are on a network, you can send the compressed file to a different drive, as directed by your network administrator, by using the Browse button.

22

3. Click the Options tab, shown in Figure 22-2, to determine whether you want to include file types other than database.

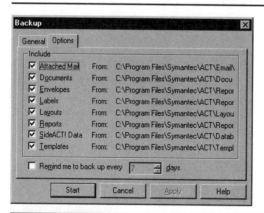

The Backup dialog box Options tab lists the other file types you can include in your backup.

4. Select the file types you want to include in the backup. The file locations are derived from the settings ACT! finds in the Preferences dialog box General tab. (Select Preferences from the Edit menu and click the General tab to see ACT!'s file types and locations.)

5. Set the time reminder for backing up your database. I recommend that you back up twice a day, but that isn't an option here, so set the reminder to every 1 day.

6. Click Start. If you are backing up to 3.5-inch disks and the database has several thousand records, you can't go to the coffee shop for that mocha because you must stand by and insert new disks as needed. ACT! overwrites any data on the disk, so be certain that the disk is not a backup of your accounting data or anything else important.

That's the process! After several minutes, the backup is completed, and you are good to go on your way.

If you use 3.5-inch disks to back up your database, make at least two sets of disks with every backup. That way, if a floppy disk dies, you have another set. It might take longer, but a 20-disk backup is no good if even one disk is lost, damaged, or corrupted.

 *Using an Iomega ZIP drive as a backup drive is not recommended by ACT!. More than one user has reported that the backup did not back up the latest version of their database.*

Restoring a Saved Database

In the unhappy event that your system does crash, you will need that backup to rescue your data from oblivion. You'll find that restoring your ACT! data is just as easy as backing it up. Just follow these steps:

1. Open the File menu and select Restore. The Restore dialog box opens, as shown in Figure 22-3.

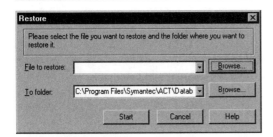

FIGURE 22-3   The Restore dialog box lets you recover a database that you have backed up.

2. To make an entry in the File To Restore field, click the Browse button. Assuming that you have backed up the database to floppy disks, select the A drive and if multiple disks were required, start with the last disk. If you have backed up to a different drive (such as a network drive), select that one instead.

3. In the To Folder field, accept the path that ACT! has selected, or use the Browse button to select the folder.

4. Click Start. ACT! displays a message alerting you that the currently open database will be closed and the restored database opened.

5. Click OK.

ACT! begins reading the data from the disk or location where you have stored the backup. If all goes well, the database will be restored.

 *The file format for backups is the common ZIP format. In case the Restore command does not open the files, try WinZip and extract the files to an empty folder. Then open the File menu, select Open, and browse to that folder to open the database.*

Maintaining Your Database

Proper maintenance of your ACT! database includes two activities: reindexing and data clean-up. If it's a shared database, only users with administrative access can perform the maintenance. If you are a remote user who synchronizes with a master database, you have administrative rights and should do the maintenance as described.

Reindexing Your Database

The ACT! database includes a series of indexes that it uses to locate contact records, notes, histories, and so on. These can become corrupted in several ways—ACT! might write data to a questionable portion of the hard drive, you could shut off the computer with an ACT! database open, the operating system might misbehave, or the moon could be aligned with Venus. Index corruption is indicated when ACT! shuts down when you are doing a lookup or trying to add a note, or when the record counter reads "125 of 14" (a larger number cannot precede a smaller one). Reindexing resets the indexes to where they should be.

 *On a network, you must be patient. Sometimes, it appears that ACT! is not running when in fact it is trying to complete an assignment. When users perceive ACT! to be moving too slowly, they often try CTRL-ALT-DELETE to end the task, and the Windows Task List shows ACT! as not responding, though in fact it is running. Give it more time and it should respond. However, if you do shut down ACT! in the middle of a process, reindex as soon as you start up.*

You should reindex a minimum of once per week. ACT! 2000 makes it easy to remember to do this by presenting a dialog box that lists such reminders when you start.

To reindex your database, follow these steps:

1. Open the File menu and select Administration.

2. From the Administration submenu, select Database Maintenance. The Database Maintenance dialog box appears, as shown in Figure 22-4.

    The Periodic Maintenance tab, which opens by default, contains two main options. You can compress and reindex, or simply reindex. Select the Compress Database check box when you have deleted records from the database.

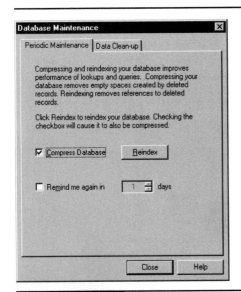

FIGURE 22-4   The Database Maintenance dialog box appears when you begin to reindex your database.

3. **Click Reindex.** If you are on a network, ACT! checks to see whether any other users are currently logged into the database. If they are, you, as the supreme administrator, can close them out at a certain time. They get a message on their computer screen that alerts them that they are going to be kicked out of ACT!, giving them an opportunity to finish what they are doing.

Depending on the size of your database and the speed of your computer, the reindexing operation is usually very fast.

TIP   *On a network database if you get a message, "Cannot reindex the database...," you must open the Edit menu and select Preferences and change the way that ACT! locates the shared database. You must select the folder where ACT! is sharing the database rather than use a Universal Naming Convention (UNC) pathname. UNC is a shortcut that MIS folks prefer for pointing to server locations. Instead, make sure the MIS folks map the drive where the ACT! database is located. They need to do this on each computer accessing the ACT! database on the server.*

Clearing Out Old Data

Large amounts of data can slow ACT! down. If your database includes many notes, attachments, cleared activities, and so forth, you should consider deleting the entries you no longer need. Such items are all stored in a single file. When this file becomes unwieldy, network performance can suffer. The Data Clean-Up tab of the Database Maintenance dialog box presents a host of options for removing these items, as shown in Figure 22-5.

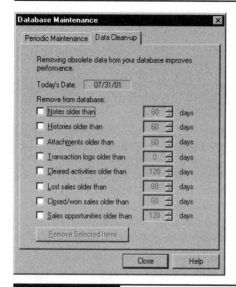

FIGURE 22-5 You can perform a variety of maintenance chores with the Data Clean-Up tab of the Database Maintenance dialog box.

When you select any of the Remove From Database options, entries fitting those parameters are removed from all records in the database. You can specify the age of items to be removed in the Days boxes. If you are hesitant to remove any of the listed items from the database, make an archive copy of the database and then remove what you wish. If you find that some important data is missing, you can retrieve it from the archive.

In the Task List, right-clicking to open the shortcut menu is slowed if you have many old, cleared activities as part of the database. Remove cleared activities that are more than a year old, and ACT! will open the shortcut menu much faster.

The current date shown in the Today's Date field comes from your computer system clock. Make sure it's correct. If it is wrong, you have to reset it via Windows.

Resetting Your Windows Clock

Here's how to reset your system clock:

1. Open the Start menu and select Settings.

2. Select Control Panel from the submenu.

3. In the Control Panel, double-click the Date Time icon.

4. Click the portion of the time that is incorrect, and then use the up or down arrows at the right of the field to adjust the time.

5. Click OK.

22

After you have selected the items you wish to remove and the time frame for each, click the Remove Selected Items button. ACT! then removes the items and reindexes and compresses the database.

Setting Reminders for Maintenance

It's all very well to intend to perform maintenance chores on a regular basis, but it helps if ACT! reminds you about these vital tasks. The File menu Set Reminders command is your key to having ACT! prompt you at regular intervals. The resulting dialog box offers the options for a series of maintenance options and some other ACT! actions:

Backup   Select this option to have ACT! remind you daily to back up. If you are connected to the network and are not the administrator, leave this option off.

Database Maintenance   Select this option if you are the administrator and open ACT! every day so that you see the reminder. Database maintenance should be done weekly.

Update ACT! And Outlook Calendars   If you are sharing calendar information with Outlook users, you can have ACT! automatically update the Outlook users.

Run Group Membership Rules   One of the most important uses of groups is for synchronizing the database with remote users. (For more information about groups, see Chapter 15.) In the past, when a new contact record was added to the main database, someone had to add that contact record to the correct group so that it was sent to the remote user via synchronization. ACT! 2000 ensures that the new contact record is added to the correct group by allowing you to create automatic group placement rules. On occasion, however, someone should run the rules checking procedure to ensure that every record is placed in the correct group. Select this option and ACT! will remind you to do so.

Synchronize ACT! has an automatic synchronization schedule in which you can program the time and dates to synchronize. However, you might not need a rigid schedule and only want to be reminded occasionally. This setting allows you to do that.

Roll Over Activities To Today's Calendar Activities that are not cleared can be rolled over automatically using the Scheduling tab of the Preferences dialog box (Edit | Preferences). If you have not set the activities to automatically roll over, ACT! can search for uncleared activities and roll them over with this option.

After making the settings you desire, click OK. The next time you start ACT!, it checks to see if any reminders are pending.

Creating a Copy of the Database

At times you might want an exact copy of the database, but not in the compressed format that is created by the backup program. To make an exact copy of the currently opened database, follow these steps:

1. Open the File menu and select Save Copy As. The Save Copy As dialog box appears, as shown in Figure 22-6.

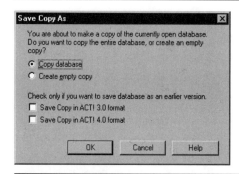

| FIGURE 22-6 | Use the Save Copy As dialog box to create a copy of your database complete with records or a blank copy. |

2. If you want a complete copy, select Copy Database. If you want to copy the fields, drop-downs, and other customizations of your database, but without any of the contact data, select Create Empty Copy. You can save the database in an earlier version of ACT! by selecting one of the check boxes.

3. Click OK. ACT! opens the Save As dialog box, in which you can browse to another drive or folder to save the copy and add a new name.

4. Click OK to close the Save As dialog box. ACT! creates the new file.

Troubleshooting Database Problems

There are some easy steps you can try if your ACT! database does not open, seems to be running very slowly, or keeps freezing whenever a certain procedure is attempted. If you cannot solve the problem yourself, the ACTDIAG program can give you information on your database that you can relay to ACT! product support or to your friendly neighborhood ACT! Certified Consultant and they may be able to assist in a repair.

The ACTDIAG Program

You might not be aware of it, but your ACT! installation includes a diagnostic program that can help iron out some system difficulties. (Though the program is called a diagnostic, it helps you resolve your problem, not just diagnose it.) This program is not supported by Interact for implementation by end users. It was written to help ACT! Certified Consultants fix client problems. But, if you are desperate because your database keeps crashing, give it a try. When you reindex the database from within ACT!, a limited repair takes place. When you use the diagnostic to remove indexes, ACT! completely rebuilds each index, which is a more thorough repair process. Besides the index fix outlined below, the program contains a plethora of tools for fixing ACT! problems. To remove the indexes, follow these steps:

1. Make a backup copy of the database.

2. Open the Windows Start menu and select Run.

3. In the Open field type **ACTDIAG** and click OK. The ACT! 2000 Data Diagnostic Tool window appears, as shown in Figure 22-7.

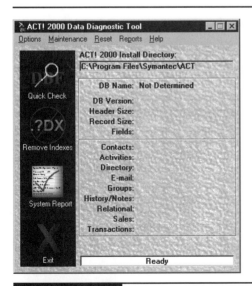

FIGURE 22-7   The ACT! 2000 Data Diagnostic Tool appears in its own window.

22

4. Click the Remove Indexes button. The Open dialog box appears.

5. Select the database that is broken.

6. Click the Open button. A warning message appears. Click Yes to complete the process.

7. Open ACT!. You might get a message that the database is in need of repair. Click Yes to finish the repair.

8. Open the Lookup menu, choose Company, and type **ACTDIAG**.

   ACT! responds with a record it created as part of the repair process that has "floating" data, such as notes and histories, that it found not connected to any record. Take a look at the Notes/History tab. If any of the data is of value, you can print it with the File | Print command or copy-paste it to the correct record.

9. Delete the ACTDIAG record.

This process should solve your database problem. If not, read "Synchronizing One Database to Another" later in this chapter for possible solutions.

ACTDIAG Options

It is important to understand that the Data Diagnostic Tool is not officially supported by ACT!. It was created by an employee who needed a set of programs to help carry out customer support. What follows is a brief run down on the menus and their respective items.

Options menu   This menu, shown in Figure 22-8, provides options to check the integrity of the database; delete index files, rogue synch files, and nasty Windows temp files; and help you with a conversion problem from an earlier version of ACT!.

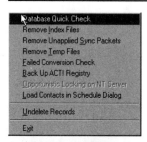

Database Quick Check
Remove Index Files
Remove Unapplied Sync Packets
Remove Temp Files
Failed Conversion Check
Back Up ACT! Registry
Opportunistic Locking on NT Server
Load Contacts in Schedule Dialog

Undelete Records

Exit

FIGURE 22-8   The Options menu

Database Quick Check   Use this item to see if a database is damaged in any way. The results of the check appear in the ACTDIAG window; you can report the information to ACT! technical support.

Remove Index Files   Removes all index files for the selected database.

Remove Unapplied Sync Packets   Deletes any synchronization packets that it finds for the local databases. Use this tool if ACT! crashes every time it tries to apply a specific synchronization file.

Remove Temp Files   If you are experiencing problems mail merging with MS Word, use this option to remove temporary files that may be interrupting the merge process.

Failed Conversion Check   If you try to convert an ACT! database that was created in a previous version of ACT! and ACT! keeps crashing, the program might be choking on a corrupt record in the old database. Use this tool to identify which record is causing the problem. (This can be tricky to resolve, so I advise a call to your friendly ACT! Certified Consultant.)

Back Up ACT! Registry   This tool is for ACT! Certified Consultants. It is used when the Windows Registry needs to be modified.

Opportunistic Locking On NT Server   Run this tool on the NT server if users of a shared database report cross-pollination of Notes. That is, when you enter a note on the Joe Smith record, Jane Doe's record gets the same note at the same time.

Load Contacts In Schedule Dialog   This option turns off or on one of ACT!'s activity scheduling features. When you open the Schedule Activity dialog box, ACT! loads the With drop-down list with all the contact record names. In a large database, this can be extremely slow. Clear the check box to turn off this feature.

Undelete Records   If you or a member of your team deleted a record or multiple records by mistake, and you have not reindexed the database, you can recover those records, but *only* the field information is retained. Any notes, histories, attachments, and so forth are gone.

Maintenance menu   This menu, shown in Figure 22-9, provides information on your database that you can relay to technical support and possibly effect a repair. Only critical files are backed up when the backup option in this menu is selected.

| FIGURE 22-9 | The Maintenance menu

Scan Database Integrity   This tool is used to determine where problems lie within the ACT! structure. ACT! Certified Consultants use this tool to determine whether they need to run the next tool.

Scan and Repair Database   This tool is used when the scan determines the database has been damaged.

Backup Database   This tool creates a ZIP file of only the core files of the database.

Reset menu   This menu, shown in Figure 22-10, helps you get back to square one without having to reinstall ACT!, solves a common e-mail problem, and has settings for an advanced user of ACT! to tinker with.

FIGURE 22-10   The Reset menu

Options And Window Positions   Because Windows occasionally decides that certain windows, such as the Alarm window, should be displayed where it cannot be seen, this menu item allows you to return it to its correct position. When you select this command, the dialog box shown in Figure 22-11 appears. The initial option, Default/Last Database, is a good tool when you are having problems with a corrupted database. Select this option, and ACT! will start without opening any database.

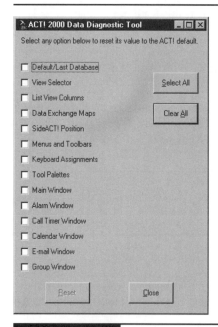

FIGURE 22-11   Choose from these options to reset window positions in ACT! and make other modifications.

Advanced Options   As its name implies, the settings in this dialog box are for those who understand the ramifications of the changes. Two options that are used by consultants regularly are the Outlook Folder To Ignore and Record Update. If you use Outlook as your primary e-mail software, what often happens is that hundreds of messages are stored in public folders on the network. So, when you try to see your Outlook e-mail messages via ACT!, it takes forever for the messages to appear. One solution is to move all the public folders under a master folder (except the Inbox folder) and then tell ACT! to ignore that master folder. It's also a good idea to keep the number of e-mail messages in your inbox as low as possible. Record Update is a function of network housekeeping. As the people log into the database, ACT! monitors users for alarms and refreshes the changes to the database as determined by the value in this field. To reduce network traffic, set this value higher. It is unlikely that the users will notice any difference.

22

Reports menu   This menu, shown in Figure 22-12, offers reports that can be used to identify problems in ACT!.

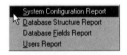

FIGURE 22-12   The Reports menu

System Configuration Report   Want to know everything there is to know about your workstation and the files that are pertinent to ACT!? Run this report, which will appear in Windows Notepad. This report is handy for network administrators who need to inventory their computers and can be used to diagnose hardware or software problems.

Database Structure Report   When you are trying to diagnose a problem with ACT!, this report is invaluable as it lists every field in the database with all attributes. It can also include all the shortcut menu commands.

Database Field Report   This report lists each field in the database by field number.

Users Report   Use this report to see who has access to the database, their user name, and whether they have created private records.

Synchronizing One Database to Another

If you have run the diagnostic program and tried everything else you can think of to resolve your database problem, you can try synchronizing the damaged database to another. (The details on synchronization are covered in Chapter 25.) This resolution depends on your being able to get into the damaged database. If the database is on a server, copy the damaged database to a workstation, and then execute this process on your local drive. After you have run the diagnostic, as outlined previously, follow these steps to synchronize:

1. Create a new, blank database and close it. Use a bogus name for the My Record, such as File Repair.

2. Open the damaged database, open the File menu, and select Synchronize. The Synchronize dialog box appears.

3. Select Send Updates, clear the Receive Updates check box, and select Database To Database.

4. Click the Setup button. The Synchronize Wizard starts.

5. In the Filename And Location field, click the Browse button to locate and select the new blank database.

6. Click Next.

7. Select all the options in the Types Of Data Wizard page.

8. Click Next.

9. Select All Groups And All Contacts.

10. Click Next.

11. Select Send And Receive Private Data.

12. Click Next.

13. Select the Send And Receive Database field definitions. Under Field Definitions, select Field Definitions From My Database.

14. Click Next.

15. Select Send All Records.

16. Click Finish. The wizard closes and you are returned to the Synchronize dialog box.

17. Click Synchronize.

ACT! sends all the data in the damaged database to the new blank copy, and in the process, filters and fixes information it deems damaged. Again, be patient with this process. A 6,000-record database can take several hours to synchronize depending upon the amount of information in each record. If you try to check with Windows via the Task Manager (CTRL-ALT-DELETE), it appears as though ACT! has stopped responding. It has not.

After the synchronization is finished, open the new database and see if the processes that caused problems before are still giving you trouble. On a multi-user database, make sure to add yourself as a new user and select the My Record from the database. *Do not create a new My Record!* Assign yourself administrative rights and delete the bogus record, moving all contacts associated with the bogus record to your record. Now, add the other log-in users, and assign their My Records from the database. Have one log-in user at a time open the database on his or her computer to make sure a particular machine is not causing the problem.

Interact Database Repair

If all else fails, you can send the damaged database to the folks at Interact, and they can repair it. They do not guarantee that all the records or all the information will be saved. But, they are impressive and have pulled many chestnuts out of the fire. To access this service, go to the Interact web site at www.act.com. Select ACT! as the product in which you are interested, and navigate to the technical support page. Or, if you can open another ACT! database, open the Internet Links menu and select Interact Commerce Corporation, and then Technical Support. Once there, you will find the link to the page that discusses the cost of and procedure for sending the database to Interact.

If you must go this route, it means that you will be without your database for at least a week. To mitigate the trauma, you can try several strategies. First, if you can get into the database, use it as a lookup-only tool. Do not add new records, schedule activities, write letters, or attempt anything beyond finding information. Revert to paper, and record everything that you normally would enter into ACT!, adding it later to the repaired database.

22

Summary

- Back up your database at least once a day.

- At least once a week, reindex your database and purge any information that is out of date.

- Use the Set Reminders option on the File menu to prompt you to do maintenance.

- If your database cannot be opened, try the ACT! Data Diagnostic tool to attempt a repair.

Chapter 23

Network Tricks and Traps

How to...

■ Use ACT! on a network

■ Install for multiple users

■ Edit user preferences

The proper way to run ACT! on a network is for the database to be stored on a file server and have all users log into that database. That way, as records are updated, everyone can see changes and the information resources of the company are effectively leveraged.

A Shared-File Application

ACT! is a shared-file application. That means the database is on a network file server—a computer that is designated to be the place where the network software resides. Most networks are controlled by Windows NT or Novell NetWare software. Fortunately, ACT! doesn't care which software runs your network. But you cannot network ACT! with more than two users via a peer-to-peer connection. It will open, but very quickly it will hang and corrupt your database.

ACT! is network-ready out of the box—that is, you do not have to buy a network version of ACT!. Not surprisingly, Interact insists that you own a copy of ACT! for every workstation that is accessing the ACT! database on the network.

For my clients, I recommend that they have as a minimum system configuration:

■ Windows NT Workstation on the computer that is the network file server.

■ At least 128 megabytes of RAM on the server.

■ For connections to the network file server, 100BaseT cards.

■ Ethernet switches instead of hubs.

■ 64 megabytes of RAM on each workstation (128 megabytes on Windows 2000 machines), especially if you want to use Microsoft Word instead of ACT!'s word processor. (Word is a notorious memory hog.)

■ Physically mapped drives to the server instead of using universal naming conventions.

TIP *Do not go cheap on server memory or Ethernet switches. Either will greatly diminish ACT! performance.*

Remember, if you get in over your head, want a network install to be painless, or have tried to set up synchronization and been less than successful, Interact has an online list of folks like yours truly—ACT! Certified Consultants—who can come to your office and do this for you. They will expect cash in exchange for this service! Visit www.iact.com and go to the ACT! page, then choose Support. Or open ACT! and click the Online menu, and then select ACT!, and then select ACT! Consulting Services. My favorite ACT! consultants are listed in the Introduction of this book.

Installing the Program for Multiple Users

You are not required to install ACT! on the server, but I recommend it as an easy way to do any required maintenance. However, installing ACT! on the server does require a license, so consider that in your planning.

If you do install a copy to the server, ACT! automatically creates folders for the database and for layouts. You can use these folders as the shared folders.

When you create the first database, the person who creates My Record is the default administrator—that cannot be changed. This fact presents no serious problems in that any login user can be given administrator privileges.

 *The initial release of ACT! 2000 (5.00) had a "feature" that was a huge mistake. The Company field was set up to include a drop-down list, and as you added new records, the list grew longer and longer. If you see a down arrow on the Company field, delete the entries in the list. Then open the Edit menu and select Define Fields. On the Drop-Down tab, turn off the Allow Editing attribute, then reindex the database. The speed of the database will increase dramatically.*

Adding Login Users

After creating the database, follow these steps from any workstation:

1. Open the File menu and select the Administration option. The submenu appears, assuming you have Administrator privileges.

2. Select Define Users. The Define Users dialog box appears, as shown in Figure 23-1.

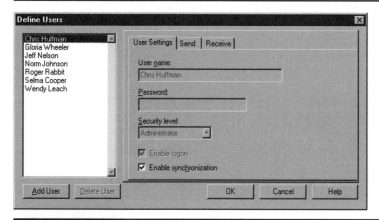

FIGURE 23-1   The Define Users dialog box lets you add network users to your ACT! system.

3. Click the Add User button.

4. Fill in the user name. It should match the name of the person as they are going to enter it into My Record.

5. The Password field is optional.

6. Set the security level. There are three levels:

   Administrator Allows the user to do anything to the database, including add or delete fields, set up new users, and so on

   Standard Allows the user to edit records and delete records, but not add or delete fields

   Browse Allows the user to use ACT! only for reference—no editing is allowed

7. Click OK. ACT! then prompts you for more information on the new user, as shown in Figure 23-2.

FIGURE 23-2 Because your new users have no My Record entries, the Assign My Records user dialog box appears.

You have two options at this point:

■ If the user already has a record in the database, click Assign Now. ACT! opens a dialog box in which you can click the Select button to locate that person's record, then click the record to use the information. If you are certain the person does not have a record, type the requisite information into the My Record dialog box.

■ If the user is not in the database, click Assign Later. When the new user tries to access the database, ACT! will ask them to complete their My Record.

Security is a concern with all company information, and ACT! is no exception. As it stands, it is possible for any user to make a copy of the database and e-mail it to an outsider or copy it to a floppy disk using the Backup command. Fortunately, you can purchase third-party software that encrypts the database so it is unreadable. The web address for this software is www.foreversecure.com.

Editing User Preferences

After adding a new user, you must stroll to their computer and set their preferences so that their copy of ACT! points to the correct place on the network for the shared folders.

1. Open the new user's copy of ACT!.

2. From the Edit menu, select Preferences.

3. In the Preferences dialog box, on the General tab, click the pull-down arrow to select the file type. For the database, select the database file type.

4. Click the Browse button. Navigate to the folder that has or will contain the matching file type. For example, if the file type is database and you created a folder on the network server named ACTDATABASE, navigate to that folder.

5. Click OK.

When the user opens the File menu and selects Open, ACT! begins looking in this folder for database files. Repeat the steps for each type of file that you want shared by all ACT! users on the network.

I recommend that you create network folders for templates, documents, and layouts at a minimum. That way, every user has the same letter and memo templates, a single repository for all saved documents, and a common layout.

ACT! is programmed to open the last accessed database every time you start. For instance, if you opened the SALES database on your C drive, and then shut down ACT!, the next time you start ACT! it opens the SALES database. In order for users to have ACT! open the shared database, the next step is to open the File menu and select Open. Because you have changed which folder ACT! is to look in when opening a database, the shared database should be available. Select the shared database and open it. Next, exit ACT!. Now reopen ACT! and the shared database is opened automatically.

You can override ACT!'s proclivity to open the last accessed database. In the Edit menu, open the Preferences dialog box and select Startup. Click Named Database and browse to the database you want to have open every time ACT! starts.

Tell your users to always display all items on Notes/History tab. If they turn any off (by unchecking the boxes), they will experience slow-motion ACT!. It is okay to switch the filter settings to simply look at the current record's data.

Deleting Login Users

The procedure for deleting a login user involves deciding if you are going to also delete the contact records that were managed by the user. In almost all cases, you do not delete the contact records. So when ACT! asks you if you want to reassign them to another user, select the person to whom the records will belong. If you are not certain, you can assign them to the administrator for safe keeping. It is best to have another user created before starting the deletion process. If you simply want to stop someone from accessing the database, you do not have to delete them as a user—simply shut off their login privileges.

If you decide to delete a user and reassign the contact records, be aware that this process is very slow. ACT! has to go through every record, every note, and so on, and reassign them one at a time. If you have several thousand records to be reassigned, do this at the end of the day, and run the process from the server, not a workstation. Back up the database before doing this procedure, just in case.

Windows NT/2000 Networks

There are a couple of server settings that you can adjust in ACT! to maximize its performance.

- If your network has no true client/server applications, open the Performance tab on the server in the System Control panel and set the slider bar to None.

- Set the Paging File size to 150.

- The shared folders must allow users to have read, write, and delete privileges.

- Make sure Opportunistic Locking is off. The ACTDIAG program will do that for you. See Chapter 22 for information on running ACTDIAG.

- Never have a screensaver running on the server.

- The best situation is to have ACT! hosted alone—that is, no other programs are shared on the server, such as Exchange or MAS 90.

Novell NetWare

ACT! 2000 functions under Novell networks, but with a few restrictions. Long filenames for ACT! databases will not work. They must be eight characters or less. The shared folders must have read, write, create, erase, modify, file scan, and access control. In addition:

Opportunistic Locking   Should be set to OFF. Note that this setting was removed from the Advanced Properties tab after the initial release of Client32 and is now set to OFF by default.

Cache Writes   Should be set to OFF.

File Cache Level   Should be set to 0 (zero).

True Commit   Should be set to ON.

Upgrade to the latest drivers at www.novell.com/download/ to make sure they are version 3.2 or later.

Summary

■   To run ACT! on a network, you'll need a license for everyone accessing the database.

■   The ACT! database must be hosted on a true server.

■   The file server must have at least one folder that is accessible by everyone on the network at the location of the shared database.

Chapter 24

Connecting to Handheld Devices

How to...

- Connect to your Palm handheld using ACT! Link software
- Synchronize your ACT! contacts with your Palm
- Use Windows CE linking software
- Synch to your cellular phone

Data portability is the ability to take your life with you electronically wherever you travel. ACT! has direct software links to the major portable devices. In this chapter, we take a look at the steps to connect to portable devices and some third-party software that improves the transfer of data.

ACT! Link

One thing you have to like about the ACT! Link 2.0 software is the price—free for the cost of a download. While there are several other products that can synchronize ACT! and the array of Palm products, I recommend that for 95 percent of ACT! users this is the way to go.

Before getting into specifics on how ACT! Link works, it is important to know that the operating system on the Palm is completely different than the Windows operating system. In fact, the basic system is based on the Macintosh. In addition, the strength of ACT! is that all the information regarding a contact is self-contained—that is, all data pertaining to a contact is available in the record. In the Palm, you have separate programs for the calendar, address book, to-do list, and memos. The difficulty of integrating the two systems is apparent. When data is sent from ACT! to the Palm, it must be directed into the relevant components, and conversely, when sent from the Palm to ACT!, it must be reassembled.

Setting Up the Process

I recommend to my clients that upon the first synch, they send the data one way—from ACT! to the Palm—and have the desktop overwrite everything on the Palm. If you have been synching already, make sure that all the data that is on your Palm is in ACT!, using whatever method you used previously. With that complete, if you previously installed any other third-party linking software, remove it by going to the Start menu and selecting Settings | Control Panel | Add/Remove Programs.

Get the ACT! Link software from the www.actsoftware.com/actlink web site. The download is a zipped file that you should put into an easily remembered folder. I have a folder named Downloads under the My Documents folder. Once the file is downloaded into the folder, double-click to install.

I recommend that you upgrade ACT! to at least version 5.03. Do not be confused by that number—if you are using ACT! 2000, to get the upgrade, start ACT! and open the Help menu and select the Check For Upgrades option. ACT! starts your Internet connection and, if the version you have is not current, instructs you on how to upgrade.

Also, you need version 3.0 of the Palm HotSync manager and Palm OS 3.0 or later. Get both at www.palm.com/support.

The official position of ACT! corporate is that the company does not support multiple user databases synching to Palm devices. The problem is that a record can be changed on the Palm and also changed on the network. When you try to synchronize, ACT! has no way of dealing with a record that has been changed in both the network and the Palm.

Processing the Initial Synchronization

Before you begin, reindex and back up your ACT! data. This seems obvious, but people seldom do this often enough. Open ACT! and then select File | Administration | Database Maintenance | Reindex. Next, open the File menu and select Backup.

The next step is to purge your Palm with a hard reset. On my Palm, that means I remove the batteries and use a paper clip to push the reset button. By doing this, I am assured that I have no lingering data. You may have to go through the Palm setup options after you perform the reset. I also delete all the records in the Palm desktop software. The reason is that when you synch from ACT! to the Palm, the Palm desktop software is still used as a pass-through for the data. In total, there are four pieces of software involved in the process: ACT!, the Palm desktop, ACT! Link, and the HotSync software.

In the following sections, I advise that you set the synch options to overwrite everything on the Palm. The quirk is that the Palm 2 Link software for the initial synch automatically forces an overwrite. This is okay for most users. If you are one of those people who owned a Palm before you bought ACT! and therefore all your important data is on the Palm, there is a workaround. Open the Start menu and select Find (or Search). In the dialog box that appears, enter the filename ACTCONFIG.DAT and click Find Now (or Search). After Windows locates the file, delete it from your computer. (Right-click the filename and select Delete.) Close the Find (or Search) dialog box. Now, start the ACT! Link 2.0 install program and set the contacts, activities, and to-dos to Palm Overwrites ACT!. Run HotSync and voilà, you are golden. Reset the settings afterwards to synch both ways or whatever setting you prefer.

Configuring the Link

When ACT! installs ACT! Link, it adds an icon to your desktop. Double-click it now to start the setup dialog box shown in Figure 24-1.

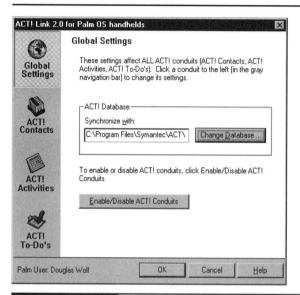

FIGURE 24-1 The ACT! Link opening dialog box

The first option to select is Global Settings. In this window, you choose the database with which you want to synchronize. The database selection process is easy. Simply click the Change Database button and locate the database on your computer or on the network. If you are required to enter a user name and password for a network database, you will be prompted to enter those items and ACT! Link will remember them for subsequent synchs. Now click the Enable/Disable ACT! Conduits button to determine which parts of the ACT! database are sent to the Palm. Figure 24-2 shows the Enable/Disable Conduits dialog box.

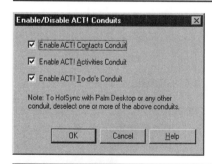

FIGURE 24-2   Enabling or disabling conduits from ACT! to the Palm

For a network database, you will have to configure the HotSync software to see the network. To get to the settings, start HotSync and right-click the HotSync icon in the toolbar. From the list that appears, select Setup and the Network tab. You may need your TCP/IP number from your system administrator.

This set of conduits determines if you are synching each type of information, not how the synch will work. The defaults are set to On, so unless you have a compelling reason not to send and receive any of the types of information listed here, leave these alone. Click OK to close the Enable/Disable Conduits dialog box. Move next to the settings for contacts, activities, and to-dos.

Synchronizing ACT! Contacts

Below the Global Settings button in the ACT! Link opening dialog box are three other buttons that allow you to configure specifically how data is handled for each part of the ACT! database. Click the ACT! Contacts button to configure how ACT! and the Palm synchronize contact data. The ACT! Contacts dialog box appears, as shown in Figure 24-3.

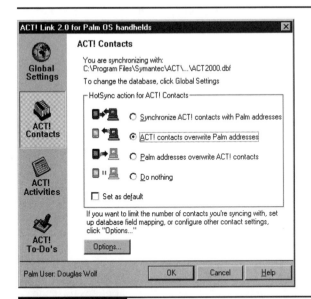

FIGURE 24-3 Settings for synchronizing Contact data

I switch this setting after the initial synch if the link is between a single user and his Palm. The default setting is to synch between the Palm and ACT!. I prefer to start with the second option, ACT! Contacts Overwrite Palm Addresses, where the ACT! database overwrites all the address data on the Palm. After the first synch, I reset this option to Synchronize ACT! Contacts With Palm Addresses—that is, changes at either location are sent back and forth. There are pitfalls of which you should be aware. If you change a particular record—such as the Wolf's Byte Productions record—in ACT! and then make a change on the Palm to the same record, when you run the synch process, you will get two records for the same contact—in this case, Wolf's Byte Productions. This happens because the synch is at the record level—not a field-by-field synch—so this is the only way ACT! can handle a dual change.

I have also been telling my clients who are linking to a network database to keep the ACT! Contacts Overwrite Palm Addresses setting selected so that data is only sent to the Palm. This may be inconvenient in that changes you make on the Palm are not sent to ACT!, but it maintains the integrity of the network database and still allows you to carry needed information with you. A workaround is to add notes to your own record on the Palm and then synch. You can then update the records in ACT! as per your notes, which will appear on My Record. An example might be that you have a meeting scheduled with a client. After the meeting, you locate your own record in the Palm and add a note as to the outcome of the meeting. Back at the office, you synch and, upon reading the new note on My Record, go to the contact record of the person with whom you met and clear the activity.

 *You cannot edit an ACT!-created note in the Palm and expect it to change in ACT!. Notes in ACT! have a unique identification number that the Palm cannot see and therefore cannot be edited.*

One of the options in the ACT! Contacts dialog box is labeled Do Nothing. Select this option if you do not want to synchronize ACT! contact data with Palm address book data. You can still synchronize other types of data without synchronizing contact data. This may be a viable option for you if you have many contacts in the Palm that are not in ACT! and you want to keep both sets of records.

After the initial synch to the Palm, choose the synching option that is correct for your system and then click the Set As Default check box to set the HotSync action you selected to be the default for future synchronizations.

More Options to Synchronize Contacts

Clicking the Options button opens a dialog box with more tabs to set options to synchronize contacts in selected groups only; map phone numbers and e-mail address between ACT! and your Palm handheld; map Palm custom fields with ACT! User fields; map Palm categories to an ACT! field; and specify the number of notes and histories to synchronize. Let's take a look at each of these. Click the Options button. The Options For ACT! Contacts dialog box that appears is shown in Figure 24-4. We'll go through the tabs one at a time.

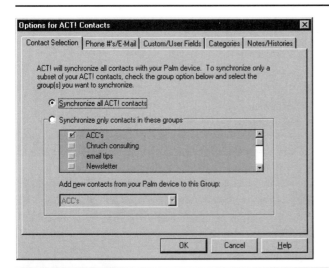

FIGURE 24-4   The Options For ACT! Contacts dialog box

Contact Selection Tab   The Contact Selection tab allows you to select a group of the database as the contacts you want to send to (and possibly from) the Palm. This is very useful in several ways. My ACT! database contains consulting clients, product clients, and my personal contacts. I only need the information for my personal and consulting clients, not from product clients. I created a group in ACT! named Palm Synch and added the records to that group that I want to make sure are on my Palm. I also created a group rule in ACT! that adds new contacts to the Palm group so I do not have to remember to do it every time I add a new client. Chapter 15 has more information on how to create a group.

If you are linking to a shared network database, I am certain that you will want only a portion of the database on your Palm, so create a group before the initial synch. Remember, synching to a shared database is not supported by Interact, the developer of ACT!.

You can also have new contact records added into the Palm automatically added to a specific group in ACT! by clicking the check box in front of Add New Contacts From Your Palm Device To This Group. This is an excellent way to track records that originated in the Palm.

Phone #'s/E-Mail Tab   The Phone #'s/E-Mail tab is pretty obvious. As you can see in Figure 24-5, you map the field in the Palm to the desired field in ACT!. You can change the mapping as needed.

TIP   *If you have modified the Alt Phone, Alt Phone Ext., or Home Phone field in ACT! by changing the data type, the data in the changed field will not synch.*

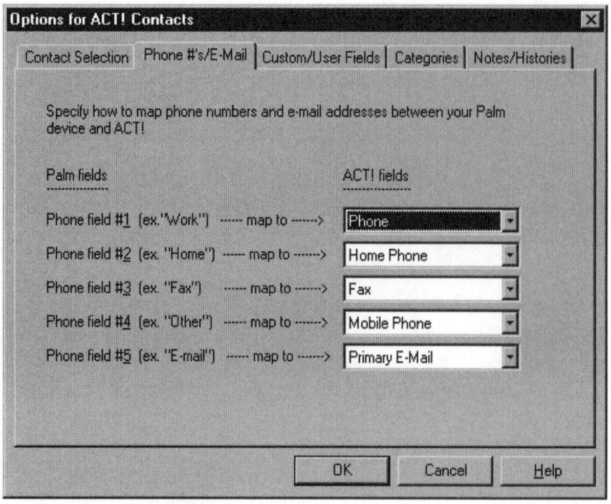

FIGURE 24-5   Mapped phone and e-mail fields

The Palm software allows for a single e-mail address, so when you synch, ACT! sends the default e-mail address to the Palm Phone Field #5. If you add a new e-mail address to a contact via the Palm, ACT! adds the prefix INTERNET to the address.

In order for ACT! to use the phone fields for the ACT! dialer, it formats the numbers. If you add a phone number in the Palm, therefore, it must be entered in a specific way for it to synch. Enter the number beginning with an open parenthesis or with a number, as follows:

(800…

800…

To add an extension, enter the number exactly as follows with no spacing until the letter x:

8004499653 x123

The number 123 is synched to the extension field for that phone number.

To add a phone number that requires a country code, type the number with a leading plus sign followed by the country code:

+676 5554444

The leading plus sign properly formats this phone number for the country of Tonga.

Custom/User Fields Tab   It is great that you can specify up to four ACT! user fields to synch to the Palm Custom 1–4 fields, as shown in Figure 24-6. However, the problem is that the fields in ACT! *must* remain in the default format. That is, if you renamed User 1 to Birth Date and then changed the field format (using Edit | Define Fields) to Date Format, that field will not synch. The workaround in this example would be to simply rename the field to Birth Date in the Design Layouts window, but forgo changing the field structure.

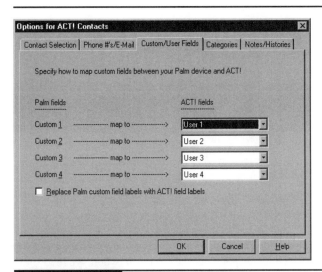

FIGURE 24-6   Custom/User Fields mapping tab

Categories Tab   The Palm software allows for a total of 15 types of categories. By contrast, ACT! can have unlimited types of entries in the ID/Status field, which is the default field to which categories are mapped. So, when you synch to the Palm, the first 14 unique ID/Status entries are accepted, but any subsequent records will appear with "Unfiled" in the ID/Status field. That means that you can have 2,000 records all with the ID/Status of "Customer" and that will work. Figure 24-7 shows the Categories tab where you can specify how to map categories on your Palm to ACT! fields.

A Palm category name can only be 15 characters in length. If you have an ID/Status entry that is longer, the Palm will recategorize the record as "Unfiled."

Notes/Histories Tab   This is one of the outstanding improvements added with this new Palm link. However, you are limited to sending the ten most recent notes per record to the Palm. If you have five years' worth of notes for a record, the most you will see are the ten most recent notes. The same is true for history entries—ten is the maximum—but you have more flexibility in that you can select the types of history entries you want to see on the Palm.

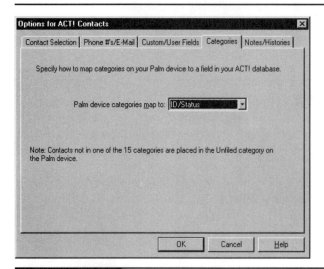

FIGURE 24-7   The Categories tab

Again, you cannot edit an ACT!-created note on the Palm and have the change sent to ACT!. But you can add a new Palm note, which appears as the first note when synched on the ACT! record.

If you have thousands of records and lots of notes/histories for each record, and you set the number for each to the maximum of ten, you will need lots of memory on the Palm device. Figure 24-8 shows the dialog box into which you can make the entries.

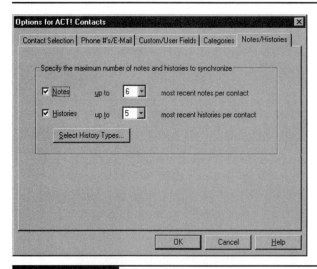

FIGURE 24-8   Use this dialog box to set the number of note or history entries that are sent to the Palm.

To get even more specific, you can determine which types of history entries are added to the Palm. Click the Select History Types button and select the types you want sent from the Select History Types dialog box shown in Figure 24-9.

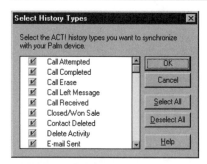

FIGURE 24-9   The Select History Types dialog box determines which history items are sent to the Palm.

Activities and To-Do Settings

There are two other sets of options worth noting regarding activities and to-dos, which are found on the Activities page (shown in Figure 24-10) and the To-Do page (shown in Figure 24-11). If you delete an ACT! activity on the Palm, it is then recorded as completed in ACT!. An ACT! to-do shows up as a history entry when completed on the Palm.

The ACT! Link software requires that you select a date as the starting point for sending activities and to-dos to the Palm. If you are a good ACT! user and have been clearing your activities like you should, this date setting should not present a problem. If you keep rolling over or never clear activities, be careful how far back you set the date. You might be surprised at how many activities and to-dos you find on your Palm that are not relevant. Finally, you can map the priority level of options and for To-dos between ACT! and the Palm, as shown in Figure 24-12.

As is true with the contacts, I recommend that on the initial synch, both the Activities and the To-do's setting is set to have ACT! overwrite anything on the Palm. Then, open these pages and select the Synchronize Activities for both.

The default setting for any to-dos that have an alarm or are timed (that is, they have a specified length) is that they are added to the date book rather than the Palm to-do list.

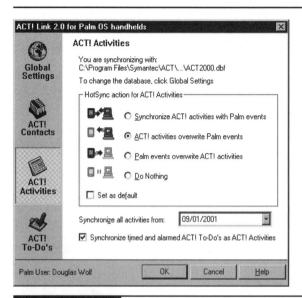

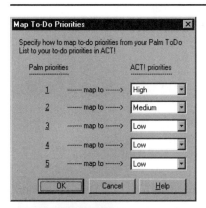

FIGURE 24-12   Map priorities between the Palm and ACT!

Synching to Windows CE

Windows CE devices (CE is the Compact Edition of Windows) are alleged to be the PDA (personal digital assistant) of today. Anywhere you go with your CE device and ACT!, you can add a new contact, schedule an activity, or add a note. Upon returning to your desktop computer, you can synchronize those changes with ACT!.

To connect to your CE device, you must purchase third-party software. There are several players in this market and you can test drive each yourself and decide which suits you. The suppliers are:

- CompanionLink Software (www.companionlink.com)

- Pumatech (www.pumatech.com)

- Extended Systems (www.extendedsystems.com)

- Advansys (www.advansyscorp.com)

Synching to Your Cellular Phone

Manufacturers of some newer cell phones have partnered with Palm to produce Palm-driven cell phones. The first several models were too large and did not sell well, but the Kyocera smartphone is small enough to carry comfortably and it flips open to reveal a Palm screen. The free ACT! Link software works flawlessly with this phone and all your data is now in your phone. You can connect to ACT! on the desktop with a cradle or using an infrared port.

On the installation disk for ACT! is a product that you can try that sends ACT! data to several models of cell phones, most notably Nokia models. Insert the ACT! installation disk and when the opening screen appears, select Related Software. From the menu that appears, select Paragon FoneSync. The software will be installed and you can use it to send ACT! contact names and phone numbers to your phone.

Summary

- You can send your ACT! data to any Palm device for free with the ACT! Link software.

- You can send your ACT! data to a Windows CE device by purchasing software from one of four vendors.

- You can add ACT! contact data to your cellular phone using Paragon FoneSync software.

Chapter 25

Synchronizing with Remote Users

How to...

- Understand how synchronization works
- Choose the right synchronization method
- Prepare for the initial synchronization
- Lock the database during synchronization
- Locate synchronized records
- Create a synchronization log
- Troubleshoot synching

Keeping everyone on the proverbial "same sheet of music" is the genesis of synchronization. The problem it attempts to solve is communication between the home office and the field salesperson, who both interact with the customer. In this chapter, I do my best to explain how it works and the procedure for creating synchronization users. However, the caveat is that an entire book could be written on synchronization alone, as there are many permutations to be considered. If you are intimidated by this process, ACT! Certified Consultants are adept at making this process work.

What Is Synchronization?

Synchronization is the process whereby two identical contact records are kept up to date in two different databases. For example, your company has a master ACT! database with all your customers and you have three salespeople who cover three distinct territories, each having a portion of the master database on a laptop. Suppose that a customer calls the main office and asks for service on a product. The office person who takes the call looks up the customer and then adds a note regarding the request. The salesperson, who has the same contact record, adds a new sales opportunity to the contact record. At this point, we have a contact record that is no longer synchronous. It is the same record, but the information in both versions is not identical. The process of synchronization updates both versions so that the main office and the field salesperson have the same information.

I am often asked why a product like LapLink cannot do the same thing as synchronization. Synchronization is an entirely different process from using products such as LapLink or Symantec's pcAnywhere, in which the older files are simply copied over by the newer ones. Inevitably, some data is lost, and that is never good.

When you execute synchronization, ACT! creates a computer file that contains the changed records and the information the receiving database needs in order to apply the changes. The file can be sent to a computer folder on a network drive or sent as an attachment to an e-mail message, which is the most common method.

Unique Identifications

When an ACT! database is created, a unique identification number is generated and assigned to the database. When a new contact record is created, it too gets a unique identification number. When synchronizing, ACT! first checks that the databases are not identical, by reading the unique database ID number. If the numbers are the same, ACT! will not allow the updated information to be copied to itself. Many new ACT! users are frustrated by synchronization because they make an exact copy of the main database using Windows Explorer and copy it to a laptop, and then wonder why it will not accept synchronizations. After the database unique ID test, ACT! matches the unique record IDs *of each record* to determine where updated information is to be recorded.

The update process is determined by the entries in the transaction log, which is not turned on until synchronization is enabled. The log tracks the unique ID of each contact record and when the date changes were made to the individual fields of the contact record. After the first synchronization, the only contact records that are included in the synch are the ones that have changed since the prior synchronization.

What Does Not Synchronize?

Not all of the data in ACT! synchronizes. The data that does not synch is as follows:

Target files of attachments   Suppose that you have created a contract in Word that is attached to the contact record. When you synchronize, the Notes/History tab for that record shows the name of the attachment and the entry you made in the Regarding field. But the underlying file itself is not sent. This is the case for attached e-mail messages, documents, or any other files that you may have attached to a contact record.

Contact and group layouts   As mentioned in Chapter 16, if you make modifications to the layout, such as adding a brand new field or inserting a background bitmap, the remote user will not get the change. You must attach the layout file to an e-mail message and send it to the remote user, who in turn must copy the layout file to the layout folder and apply it.

Preferences   Default file locations, activity settings, and calendar filters are all computer specific.

Custom menu items   New items added to the Write menu, for example, do not get to the remote users.

Custom commands   If you have added keyboard shortcuts, toolbar icons, or macros, they are not sent.

Letter, report, envelope, and label templates   As is true with layouts, these need to be sent separately.

Different Methods to Synchronize ACT!

Because the synchronization process creates a computer file, it can be sent from one database to another in one of four ways:

Shared folder   This method is used primarily when you have several users on a network who do not share a main ACT! database. An example might be an investment firm where each salesperson has their own client records and does not want other salespeople to see them. The sales manager needs to see everyone's records. With this method, each salesperson sends their changed records to the master database via a Windows folder. The master database sends any updates to each salesperson to a different Windows folder. The receiver's ACT! then looks in the folder for synch files and applies them to the currently open database.

Database to database   This method is used when you want to synch from one database to another on the same computer or on the same network. It can also be used to update a laptop to a network database. For example, if you are the owner of a business and take work home, you can synchronize using this method before you leave for home, make changes there, and then synchronize again to the network database upon returning to the office the next day. Then you would access the network database for the remainder of the workday, repeating the process at closing time.

> **TIP**   *The database-to-database method does not work with more than two databases. Therefore, you cannot synchronize two different databases on the network with one on a laptop. However, multiple salespeople can use database-to-database synchronization.*

E-mail   This is the most commonly used method to synch a master database with several remote databases. The office has a master database and several field salespeople have all or a subset (group) of the master database contact records on their laptops. The synch file is attached to an e-mail. When the remote user opens his e-mail, he sees the e-mail with an attachment, which can then be applied to the currently open ACT! database.

Modem to modem   This method has ACT! sending the synch file over a phone line directly to the remote ACT! database. The synchronization file is not immediately applied to the remote database, but is copied to the Drafts folder in ACT!'s e-mail. It is then applied after the connection is closed.

> **NOTE**   *If setting up synchronization sounds overwhelming, call an ACT! Certified Consultant. They can help you do this right the first time, thereby saving much time and grief.*

Getting Ready for the First Synchronization

Assuming that you are the person handed this hot potato, the first thing to do is decide how the synchronization is going to be set up for each user. You can have a mixed system—some users using e-mail while others use a shared folder, and still others using the database-to-database method.

Start with the master database. Even if it is new, purging the transaction log ensures a happy result.

1. Open the File menu and select Administration.

2. Select Database Maintenance.

3. Click the Data Clean-Up tab, shown in Figure 25-1.

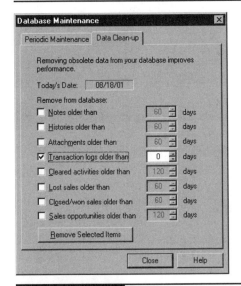

25

FIGURE 25-1   Database Maintenance dialog box with the Data Clean-Up tab selected

4. Select the Transaction Logs Older Than check box.

5. Select 0 (zero) as the number of days.

6. Click the Remove Selected Items button. ACT! asks you to confirm the removal. Click Yes.

The log is reset and the database is reindexed. As far as ACT! is concerned, this database has never synchronized with another database. This is important because you need to have a clean starting point for the process.

If you suspect that synchronization was tried before and failed, you need to make certain that no synchronization files are lurking on the computer with the master database. Open the ACT! Data Diagnostic Tool (see Chapter 22), then open the Options menu and select the Remove Unapplied Synch Packets option.

Creating the Remote Databases

There are two possible starting places for synchronization. The first scenario assumes that you are creating the database for each remote user and therefore they do not have any records. The second is that the remote users already have ACT! databases which contain contact records that you do not want to lose. The steps outlined below assume the first scenario.

In all cases, the remote databases must be copies—not exact duplicates—of the master database. That is, you cannot use Windows Explorer to copy the database files and send them to the remote users. Instead create an empty copy of the master database by clicking File | Save Copy As | Create Empty Copy for each remote user.

Before starting the process, make sure that you have entered all the remote users into the master database. Also, create the groups that are to be synched to each remote user. They do not have to be populated—that is, you do not have to add the contact records at this point, but create the group records as described in Chapter 15.

To make an empty copy of the master database that will synchronize, follow these steps:

1. Open the File menu and select Save Copy As. The Save As dialog box appears, as shown in Figure 25-2.

2. Select Create Empty Copy and click OK.

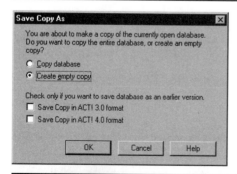

FIGURE 25-2   The Save Copy As dialog box allows you to make a copy of the currently opened database.

3. The Save As dialog box appears. I counsel my clients to name the remote database by territory or region instead of by salesperson. That way, if the salesperson leaves, the name can remain the same. Also, because this new remote database is destined for another computer, save it to a floppy disk or to an empty folder where you can easily copy all the files.

4. Click Save. The My Record dialog box appears. If the remote user has a contact record in the master database, click Select and locate that record. ACT! then fills in the fields for you. Otherwise, enter the data that is appropriate for each remote user. The most important fields are Company, Contact, and Phone.

5. Click OK.

ACT! creates the remote database with a single record and saves it to the disk or folder that you have directed.

Installing the Synchronization Settings for the Remote User

In my experience, the best practice is to prepare the synchronization process for the remote user before giving him the database. That way, you can be certain that the settings were correct before the remote database left your hands.

1. From the remote user's computer, open the newly created remote database.

2. Open the File menu and select Synchronization Setup. The initial page for the Synchronization Wizard appears. You are not required to input anything here.

3. Click Next and you'll see the wizard page shown in Figure 25-3.

4. In this scenario, the remote user will be synchronizing with another user, which is you, the master database administrator. Click the With Other Users radio button.

5. Click Next to see the page shown in Figure 25-4.

6. Select all five options in the What Data? wizard page by checking their check boxes, unless you have made the decision to not synchronize all aspects of your ACT! records.

7. Click Next. The With Whom? wizard page appears, as shown in Figure 25-5, where you can enter the person with whom the remote user will synchronize.

8. The remote user is only going to synchronize with you, the administrator, so click the New User button. The dialog box shown in Figure 25-6 appears. Enter *your* name (your user name) exactly as you log into the master database and click OK. Click Next in the With Whom? page and the Synchronization Wizard's How? page appears, as shown in Figure 25-7.

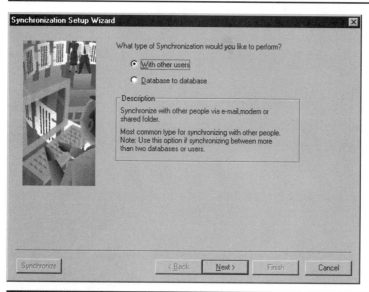

FIGURE 25-3   The wizard page determines the type of synchronization that is to take place.

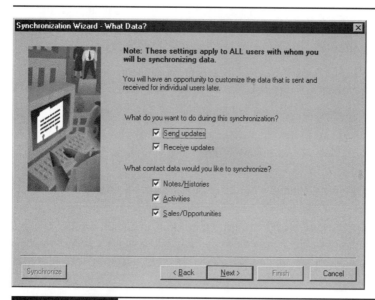

FIGURE 25-4   This wizard page determines which data will be sent and received from the remote user.

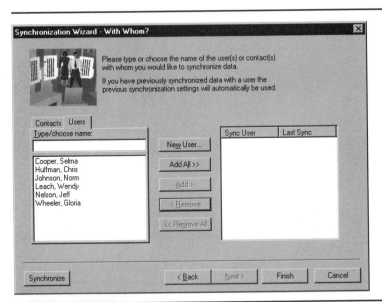

FIGURE 25-5 The With Whom? page sets up the person with whom this user will synchronize.

FIGURE 25-6 The New User dialog box appears allowing you to enter your name.

9. The How? page is for selecting the connection method for synchronization files. At this point, you have a multitude of connection choices. In our scenario, the e-mail method is used. The shared folder and modem methods are discussed in separate sections of this chapter.

10. Enter *your* e-mail address. (Remember, you are entering the settings for the remote user!) Click Next. The Receive What Data? page opens, as shown in Figure 25-8.

11. It is not likely that you will need to send private data to the remote user, but you might want to send field definitions (click the Field Definitions check box). That way, if you add a new field, or change field sizes or field types, the changes are sent and applied to the remote user's database.

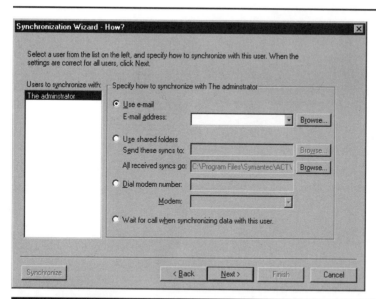

FIGURE 25-7   This wizard page is where you enter the means by which you will send and receive synchronization files.

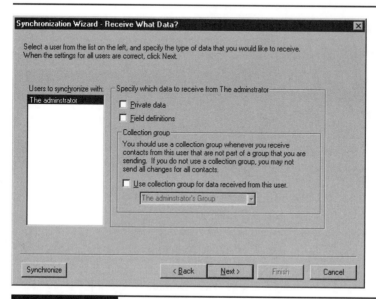

FIGURE 25-8   This wizard page lets you determine what data you want to send to the remote user.

 *If you add a new field and synch it to the remote users, they cannot see the field until you send the layout file, which is not part of the synchronization process. You must send the layout file separately to the remote users as an e-mail file attachment and have them copy it to the ACT\LAYOUT folder on their computer.*

12. The next option on this page is whether to use a collection group. This setting is not important for remote users and should not be selected. When you are finished making your option selections, click Next. The Send What Data? page appears, as shown in Figure 25-9.

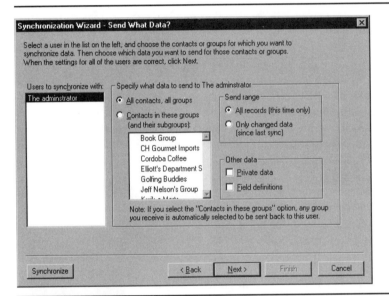

FIGURE 25-9   This wizard page determines what data the remote user should send to the master database.

13. The remote user, in most cases, sends all contacts and all groups, so select the All Contacts, All Groups radio button. The send range is going to be All Records (This Time Only). ACT! automatically switches the setting to Only Changed Data after the initial synchronization.

    The Private Data setting is determined by the company policy. Generally, the remote users do not send private data. But if the company needs to have the exact schedule of the remote user—including doctor visits—this button should be selected. Click Next.

14. The final wizard page is for creating an automatic synching schedule. In order for this to work, ACT! must be running at the scheduled time. The options for this are covered

in a separate section. For the moment, click No, then click Next, and then click Finish. The Synchronize dialog box appears. You cannot synchronize at this point, so click Cancel.

15. Finally, close this remote database. Now you have to copy the remote database to the remote user's computer. Hand the floppy disk on which his database is saved to him and he can copy all the files to his ACT\DATABASE folder. Alternatively, if you saved the database to a folder, create an e-mail with *all* the files attached and he can copy the files from the e-mail attachment to the ACT\DATABASE folder.

Repeat the process as described for every remote user. It may be tedious, but I have discovered that the synchronization settings are more likely to work properly for each user if each user is added separately.

What the Remote User Does with the New Database

The remote user should start ACT! and open the database that was sent/given to him by the administrator. If opened from a floppy, the database must be saved to the hard drive. After opening the database, if the synchronization is being done by e-mail, the remote user must open the Edit menu and select Preferences | E-mail to set up e-mail. Next, the remote user sends the initial synchronization file to the administrator, with the option to receive turned off. The initial synchronization file consists of one record: My Record. The administrator receives the initial synchronization file from the remote user, and ACT! confirms the settings for that user with a series of prompts. The remote user is now ready and able to receive his set of records from the administrator. After the administrator sends the initial synchronization file, the remote user should follow these steps:

1. Open ACT!.

2. Open the File menu and select Synchronize.

3. In the Synchronize dialog box, turn on the Receive setting.

4. Click the Synchronize button. ACT! looks for synchronization files as per the setup. If not connected to your e-mail system (such as with a dial-up connection), ACT! activates your connection to locate any synchronization files. In a moment, you will get the message that a synchronization file was found, who it is from, and whether it should be applied to the currently opened database.

5. Click Yes and then Yes again when prompted about the user name (the administrator who sent the file to you) as being the correct name. If the synchronization file is large, this will take time and you will see the message "Merging data." When the process is complete, you can see exactly what you received by going to My Record and looking at Notes/History. ACT! then deletes the e-mail synch file so as not to interfere with subsequent synchronizations.

Creating the Master Database Synchronization Settings

The remote user's settings are different from the master database. The key differences are what data is being sent and received. Open the master database and follow these steps:

1. Open the File menu and select Synchronization Setup. The Synchronization Wizard opens. Click Next in the initial wizard page.

2. Select all the radio buttons in the What Data? page, if that is your determination, and click Next. The With Whom? page appears.

3. Click the Contacts tab. The remote users are entered into the master database. Click the name of the remote user you're synchronizing with, click the Add button, and repeat until all remote users are selected. Click Next. The How? page appears.

4. On the left is the list of remote users. Click a remote user's name. At this point, you can enter the connection method for that remote user. Click the appropriate connection method—for this example, click e-mail. Then enter the e-mail address for the recipient. After entering the connection method for each remote user, click Next. The Receive What Data? page opens.

25

NOTE
The e-mail system you employ determines the correct e-mail address. If everyone connects via Internet mail, you simply enter their e-mail address. If you are using a more esoteric system such as cc:Mail, you will need assistance from your system administrator to make sure you have the correct e-mail address.

CAUTION
You cannot use America Online e-mail to send and receive synchronizations, unless you have added software from www.enebot.com.

5. All the remote users are listed at the left. Select a remote user and enter his settings. Again, there is a decision to be made about receiving private data from the remote users. Next, the default setting is *not* to receive field definitions from remote users, which is my recommendation. It is not likely that you want the remote users to add fields or field definitions to the master database.

6. The Collection Group setting is important for this reason: if the remote user creates a new record, it is sent on the next synchronization to the master database. However, at that point it might not be identified as a contact record that belongs to a particular remote user. So, to make sure new records are sent back and forth to the correct user, click the Collection Group button.

7. From the drop-down list, select the group that pertains to the remote user selected. ACT! creates a group name for you by using the name of the contacts, such as the Northeastern Region or John Smith group. Click Next.

8. In the Send What Data? page, select a remote user, and then click the Contacts In These Groups radio button.

9. Click the group for that remote user.

10. The All Records (This Time Only) radio button should be selected. This will switch to the Only Changed Data setting automatically after the initial synch is sent.

11. Under the Other Data section, the important setting is Field Definitions. If it is on, changes you make to the drop-down lists, new fields, or field attributes are sent to the remote user. You can also elect to send private data, which means that the remote user can better judge the schedules of other users—even though he cannot see with whom the activity is scheduled.

Remember, if you create a new field, it is sent to the remote user, but he will not see the new field in his layout until you send an updated layout file.

12. Click Next, and the When? page appears. Here, you can decide Yes or No as to whether you want ACT! to automatically run the synching process. If you select Yes, the When? page shown in Figure 25-10 appears. This wizard page is for creating a schedule of synching to each of the remote users. Remember that ACT! always checks for incoming synch files first before doing a send (unless you have Receive Updates shut off), applies the changes it receives, and then sends changes. Click the days you want the process to run, and then click the times. Automatic synchronization is optional, so you can skip this part of the setup entirely.

    (If you select No, you see the Finish page. Click Finish, and the Synchronize dialog box appears, as shown in Figure 25-11. Skip the next step for further instructions.)

CAUTION *If you choose to set up an automatic synchronization schedule, ACT! must be running and be able to connect to e-mail. By having ACT! running, you may conflict with the backup process that your network administrator has enacted.*

13. Click Next, and then Finish to complete the setup. The Synchronize dialog box appears.

At this point, if the remote users have their databases, you are ready to send them your initial synchronization. When you execute the synchronization, the remote user must open his e-mail-in ACT!. A message should alert him that a synchronization file is attached to the e-mail and ask him if he wants to apply it to the currently open database. Assuming that the correct database is open, he can click Yes and away we go—sort of. Because it is an initial synchronization, ACT! wants to confirm that the sender is correct. The user then should confirm the link to you as the sender. A few more OKs and the changes are added to the database. To check what has been received, the remote user can go to his My Record and check the Notes/History tab. It should read "Initial synchronization received from *XXXX*, 500 contacts, 300 notes" and so on.

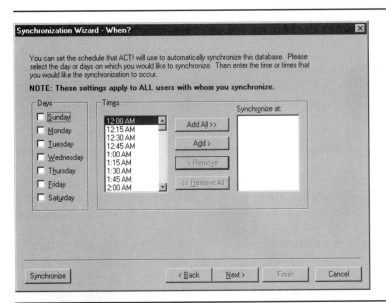

FIGURE 25-10   The Synchronization Wizard's When? page lets you schedule synchronization to occur at regular intervals.

25

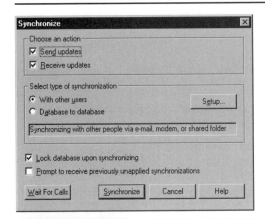

FIGURE 25-11   You can use this Synchronize dialog box to manually execute synchronization.

NOTE

After a synchronization received via e-mail is applied, the file is automatically deleted by ACT!.

Locking the Database During Synchronization

In previous versions of ACT!, the database had to be locked. In other words, on a shared database, no one except the administrator could be in the database during the process of synchronization. Because users can change the structure of the database, and synchronization sends and receives those changes, the lock prevents the database from being corrupted. In addition, ACT! locks a record when a person is looking at it and does not allow any changes to be made to that record by anyone else. Database locking is accomplished via the Synchronize dialog box.

In ACT! 2000, database locking was made optional so that an administrator of the master database could run the synchronization process while users were working. With that in mind, suppose that you are on a network looking at a record, the administrator decides to run synchronization, and the synchronization file received has changes for the same record with which you are working. Because you are working on the record, ACT! locks it so that only one person can change the record at a time. Therefore, the change that came with the synchronization file is *not* applied. ACT! creates a temporary file and, with the next synchronization, checks to see if the record can be modified. If so, ACT! applies the update.

Database structural changes are not handled this way. If the synchronization file has structural changes and the database is not locked when the synchronization process is run, the changes are not applied.

Because of this, remote users should always lock their database when synching, and the master database administrator needs to decide if the lock should be on all the time (meaning that the network users will have to exit ACT!) or only when changes are made to the database structure.

Shared Folder Synchronization

This method is used when users are attached to a local area network, but because of the security desired, they are not allowed access to a master database. The procedure to set up this type of synchronization is to create multiple folders. One folder is used by the master database to gather all synchronization files sent to the master, and another set of folders—one for each remote user—serves as the place ACT! sends updates to each of the remotes. The remote users access the network from their workstations, or if they are remote, via dial-up or high-speed connection. When they start the synchronization process, ACT! sends changes to the master database inbox folder and retrieves changes via their individual inbox folders. Before creating the copies of the main database, if necessary, create the groups that will be used by each of the shared folder users. In other words, if the individual users are not going to get all records in the master database, you should create groups of records for each user, as described in Chapter 15.

This scenario assumes that the remote users do not have contact records in an ACT! database that need to be added to a master database and that each user needs to have a database created for him. To set this up, follow the procedure outlined next.

Create the empty databases for each user as follows:

1. Open the master database.

2. Open the File menu and select Save Copy As.

3. Select the option to create an empty copy of the database. You might want to save the database to the drive/folder of the shared folder user.

4. When prompted, enter the My Record for the shared folder user.

5. Click OK. ACT! creates the database for the remote user. The remote user has to be able to get the newly created database in some way, either by accessing the database via a folder on the network or by having it sent to him via an e-mail.

Next, as the administrator, create an inbox folder for each of the shared folder users somewhere on the network. A naming convention for the folders might be Northern Territory, Southern Territory, and so on. The location of the folders is not important as long as the shared folder user has access to it. You might need to have the system administrator create these and set the access permissions. The remote users need all rights to the synch folders in order for the synchronization process to work properly.

 The steps to set up shared folder synchronization differ from the e-mail setup only in the way the synchronization files are sent and received from the master database to a remote user. The How? page of the Synchronization Wizard holds the key settings. Review the section on e-mail synchronization for the other pages of the synchronization setup.

25

In the master database, open the File menu and select Synchronization Setup. Enter the settings in the Synchronization Wizard as:

- With Other Users

- Send Updates, Receive Updates, Notes/Histories, Activities, Sales Opportunities

- Select the names of the shared folder users

In the How? dialog box, select Use Shared Folders. Click the Browse button to locate the folder to which master database synchronization files are to be sent for that user. Each shared folder user must have a unique inbox folder.

In the master database, ACT! receives all synchronizations from all users to the same folder. The default folder is C:\Program Files\ACT\Synchronization, but you should change that location to a folder on the server with a name, for example, "Master Folder."

Finish the Synchronization Wizard pages and add the settings you need as described in the e-mail section of this chapter.

Remote Users Using Shared Folder Synchronization

Before synchronization files can be sent and received, the remote user has to designate the locations of the folders. This *must* be done from the laptop or desktop of the remote user. To set up shared folder synchronization, use the following steps:

1. Open ACT!.

2. Open the File menu and select Synchronization Setup. The Synchronization Wizard opens.

3. Click Next to skip the first wizard page. In the next page, select With Other Users. Click Next.

4. In the What Data? page, all options should be selected unless you have decided otherwise. Click Next.

5. In the With Whom? page, click the New User button. Type the user name of the administrator in the New User dialog box that opens, then click OK to return to the With Whom? page. Click Next.

6. In the How? page, click the Use Shared Folders radio button. For the Send These Syncs To field, click the Browse button to navigate to the folder that has been created for all synchronization files that are being sent to the master database. For the All Received Syncs Go field, click the Browse button to navigate to the folder that has been created for synchronization files being sent to you (remember, *you* are the remote user when setting up the remote user's computer) and click OK. ACT! warns that you are changing the location for receiving synch files; click OK. The folders and their respective paths should appear in the fields. Click Next.

7. In the Receive What Data? page, select the Field Definitions item. You do not need to receive private data or a collection group. Click Next.

8. In the Send What Data? page, the most common setting for remote users is All Contacts, All Groups. That means that all the records that are sent from the master database by the administrator and all the records you create will be sent back and forth as needed. Because this is the initial synchronization in the Send Range section, ACT! automatically selects the All Records (This Time Only) setting and, after the initial synch, reverts to the Only Changed Data setting. Finally, if you wish, you can send private records and activities to the master database. Click Next.

9. In the When? page, you can set up a schedule for ACT! to synchronize without you. ACT! must be running and connected to an e-mail system for this to work. Click Finish.

Starting the Synchronization Process

At this point, as the remote user, you are ready to receive your first synchronization from the master database. Assuming it has been sent, do the following:

1. In ACT!, open the File menu.

2. Select Synchronize.

3. In the Synchronize dialog box, click the Synchronize button.

   ACT! will search for synchronization files in the folder that has been designated as your inbox. When it does, on the initial synchronization, it prompts you by saying a synchronization file has been found sent by the administrator and questions whether to apply it to the currently opened database. Select Yes, and ACT! should confirm your synchronization settings. Also, ACT! will ask if you want the synchronization to link to an existing user and will preselect the name for you. If the linked user name is correct, you can click Finish. The records are added to your database. Depending on the number of records, this process could be very fast or take some time. Be patient. After this initial synchronization, the process will happen very quickly. To see what has been synchronized, click the Notes/History tab on My Record.

Locating Synchronized Records

After you receive and send records via synchronization, you can create a lookup of those records. Doing so gives you an opportunity to decide what you should do with each of the records. To create this lookup, select Lookup | Synchronized Records | Select Last Synchronized. ACT! creates a lookup of the records. This lookup remains intact until the next synchronization occurs.

Modem-to-Modem Synchronization

The modem-to-modem method of synchronization requires both the master and remote ACT! databases to be open at the same time. The synchronization file is transferred between the two computers in real time. The master database dials via the modem and tries to connect with the remote computer. If the remote computer is on, the ACT! database opens. The file is sent to the ACT\Briefcase folder. After receiving the file, the remote user can apply the update by manually running the synchronization process.

25

In the master database, open the File menu and select Synchronization Setup. Enter the settings in the Synchronization Wizard as:

- With Other Users
- Send Updates, Receive Updates, Notes/Histories, Activities, Sales Opportunities

In the How? dialog box, select the names of the modem-to-modem users. In the Dial Modem Number and Modem fields, you must enter complete numbers, including any number to access an outside line.

The final setting in this dialog box is whether to wait for calls when synchronizing with this user. In most cases, as the master database, you will want to wait for the calls from the remote users. Otherwise, if you are synchronizing with multiple remote users, they will have to leave ACT! running and wait for the master ACT! database to dial them and send the synchronization file. If the situation exists where it is more efficient to send to them at a specified time, do not check this box.

Finish the Synchronization Wizard and add the settings you need as described under the e-mail section of this chapter.

When you are ready to synchronize, arrange with the remote users the times you can send or receive the synchronization files. After you've connected and the files have been exchanged, open the File menu and select Synchronize. In the Synchronize dialog box, click the Synchronize button.

Deleting Records

Remote users cannot permanently delete records from the master database, but they can delete contact records from their remote ACT! database. The contact records are marked for deletion and when remote users synchronize to the master database, ACT! creates a lookup of those records. To see the records at the master database, open the Lookup menu and select Synchronized Records | Deleted By Remote Users. Once the record is marked for deletion, it is excluded from the transaction log and is not sent back to the remote user. If you want the record(s) deleted, go to each record via the Lookup menu and then open the Contact Menu and select Delete Contact. For any records that you want to keep in the master database, you must open the Lookup menu and select Synchronized Records | Deleted By Remote Users. Figure 25-12 shows the dialog box.

NOTE   *If you are the administrator, and you decide that a record should not go back to the remote user, make certain that you immediately remove the record from that person's synchronization group. If, however, everyone is getting all records, ACT! will send the record back to all the remote users as soon as any edits are made to the record.*

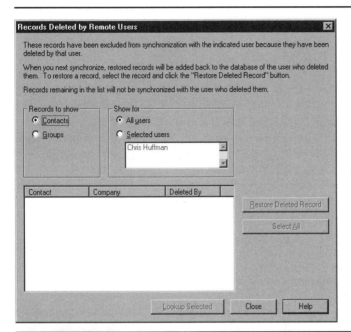

FIGURE 25-12   The Records Deleted By Remote Users dialog box has options to
restore records or groups deleted by a remote user.

Database-to-Database Synchronization

This method of synchronization works between two databases only. That means you cannot synch
database A with database B and database C. In my experience, this method is used primarily
when a user has a desktop database at an office and a laptop that they use for ACT! work at
home. The process is to synch between the laptop and the network before leaving for home
and then synch again when returning to the office. The laptop must be able to connect to the
network. Here is how to set up this process:

1. With the laptop connected to the network, open the ACT! database that you want to
    use for synchronization.

2. Open the File menu and select Save Copy As. The dialog box shown in Figure 25-13
    opens.

3. Select Create Empty Copy and click OK.

4. In the next Save As dialog box that opens, enter a name for the new database, such as
    HOME. Then navigate to the laptop and select a folder on the laptop into which you
    want to save the database.

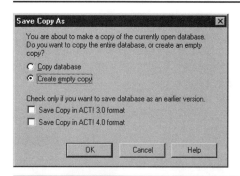

FIGURE 25-13   In the Save Copy As dialog box, you can create an empty copy of the database or make a duplicate.

5. Click Save. At this juncture, you have a database to which you can send the synchronization.

6. Open the File menu and select Synchronize.

7. In the Synchronize dialog box, select the Database To Database option and uncheck the Receive Updates check box. Because this is the first synchronization to the laptop, there is no data to receive. Your dialog box should match that in Figure 25-14.

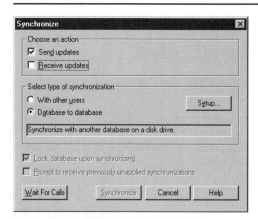

FIGURE 25-14   The Synchronize dialog box is set for database-to-database synchronization.

8. Click the Setup button. The next page of the wizard appears, as shown in Figure 25-15, and you are asked to select the database with which to synchronize.

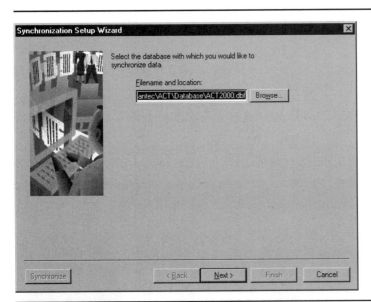

Synchronization Setup Wizard

Select the database with which you would like to synchronize data.

Filename and location:

antec\ACT\Database\ACT2000.dbf   Browse...

Synchronize   < Back   Next >   Finish   Cancel

FIGURE 25-15   Use the Browse button to locate the database to synchronize with.

25

9. Click the Browse button and navigate to the folder on the laptop in which you saved the empty database.

10. Click on the name of the empty database and click Open. You are returned to the dialog box.

11. Click Next and the wizard page shown in Figure 25-16 appears, listing the types of data you can synchronize. Click the data you want and then click Next.

12. In the next wizard page that appears, shown in Figure 25-17, select which sets of records to synchronize. You may need only a subset (a group) of the master database. If you are a remote user synchronizing with a master database, it is likely that you are only going to synchronize a group. Click Next.

13. The next wizard page that appears, shown in Figure 25-18, has the settings for sending and receive private data if needed. Remember, the login user name determines what data is private, so you will get only the data that is private to you. However, if you are synchronizing with yourself, this setting is irrelevant. If you are synchronizing to a master database, you may not want to send any private data. Click Next.

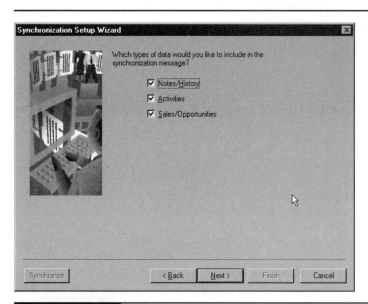

Choose whether or not to send and receive Notes/History, Activities, and/or Sales/Opportunities.

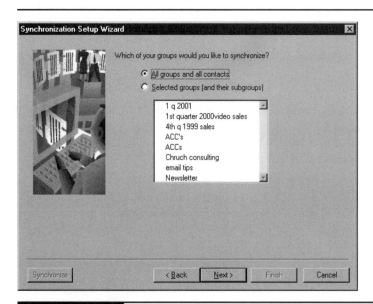

Choose which groups you wish to send and receive.

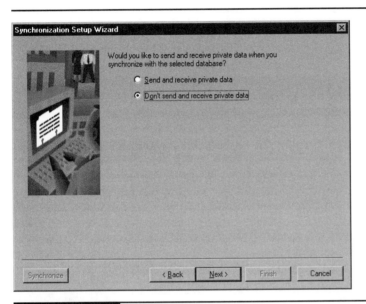

FIGURE 25-18 Sending and receiving private data options

14. The next page of the wizard, shown in Figure 25-19, requires a bit of thinking. If you are synchronizing with yourself and plan to make modifications to field drop-down lists or to fields themselves and want those in both databases, you must make a choice here. The safest choice is the Newest Field Definitions From Either Database setting. That way you do not have to worry about which database to make the changes in, as they will be sent to each database. However, if you are a remote user synchronizing to a master database, the best setting is to select Field Definitions From Other Database. That way, you will receive the changes the administrator of the master database makes. Click Next.

15. The next wizard page presents options for automatic synchronization. The automatic synchronization choices are not appropriate for this type of synchronization. Skip it by clicking Next.

16. Figure 25-20 shows the next wizard page. Because this is the initial synchronization to the empty database, the Send All Records (This Update Only) option must be selected. Click Finish. The Synchronize dialog box reappears.

17. Click Synchronize, and ACT! will start sending the records to the laptop database. The next time you want to update a laptop to desktop/master ACT! database, all you have to do is connect to the network, open the File menu and select Synchronize and in the Synchronize dialog box make sure Send and Receive are both on, and then click synchronize. The other settings remain in effect, and ACT! only sends changed records from this point forward.

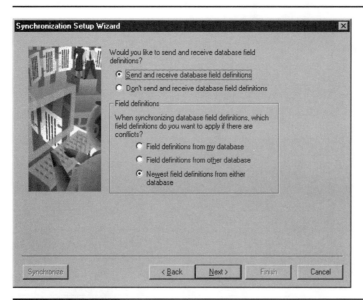

FIGURE 25-19   Make certain changes to the database structure are congruent with the manner in which you are synchronizing.

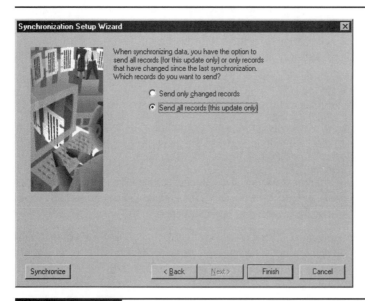

FIGURE 25-20   Choose to synch all records or only those that have changed.

When a database-to-database synchronization is in progress, no other users can be logged into either database.

The database-to-database synchronization process may also be used by several itinerant salespeople who occasionally travel. You might think that I am contradicting what I said about database-to-database being used only between two databases; what is actually happening is there is a single master database with which multiple remote users synchronize on occasion. The key in this scenario is what options, such as field definitions or private data, are sent and received.

Using Database-to-Database Synchronization for Repairs

Say you try to open ACT! and it either refuses to open or gives you an error message and then crashes. If you've tried the repair procedures using ACTDIAG, you can try using database-to-database synchronization to resurrect the dead data. Create a new database and then open the File menu and select Synchronize. In the Synchronize dialog box, uncheck the Send Updates check box, as you want to just receive the contact records from the corrupted database. Follow the steps outlined above to get all the data from the corrupted database. When the process is taking place, ACT! attempts to rebuild each record and the concomitant links to Notes/History. If it encounters a corrupted record that it cannot rebuild, it skips the record.

Synchronization Logs

Not only does the process of synchronization create a history entry on My Record, but ACT! can also generate a detailed report of each synchronization. These reports show which contact record or group record aspect of that record was altered and how. My advice is to turn this option on so that you can monitor the process and, if necessary, troubleshoot. Also, if your troubleshooting efforts don't work, you have a path that can be examined by an ACT! Certified Consultant. To set up ACT! to create the report, follow these steps:

1. Open the Edit menu and select Preferences.
2. Click the Synchronization tab.
3. At the bottom left, select the Generate Synchronization Report check box.
4. Click OK.

After the initial synchronization, changes made to the contact records and group records are duly recorded in an ordinary text file. To read the text file, you can open it with Microsoft Word or Notepad. The file has an extension .log, so you might have to adjust the settings in your word processor in order to access the file. There are two types of synchronization reports: the master log, which is appended at its beginning with every synchronization, and the individual logs for each individual synchronization. By opening either, you may be able to determine what is happening, but the report may only be decipherable by an ACT! Certified Consultant.

 *If you are adding new contact records to the master database, and they need to be added to specific groups so that they are sent via synchronization to remote users, read the section in Chapter 15 on creating group rules.*

Troubleshooting Synchronization

With all computer systems and software, things can and do fail or become corrupted. Synchronization is no different in that regard, so here are some tips on keeping the process as trouble-free as possible.

- Reindex on a regular basis. Not only the master database, but all remote users, should be doing this at least once a week.
- Delete temporary files often, especially if you are using Microsoft Word.
- Defragment the hard drive monthly.
- Make certain that the hard drive is not close to being filled. If it is, the synchronization could fail by not having enough memory.
- Do not use auto-rollover of activities. This great feature on a standalone system causes major problems for ACT! when synched.

Recovering from a Last Synchronization File

The very nature of sending files over computer networks creates a risk of corruption. So it may happen that a synchronization file sent to a remote user or sent to the master database arrives in less than pristine condition. You can recover by sending all records again, or by trying this method:

1. Open the File menu and select Administration.
2. Select Define Users.
3. In the Define Users dialog box, select the user to which you need recover data.
4. Click the Send tab, as shown in Figure 25-21.
5. In the Last Sent field, there should be a date (the field is empty in Figure 25-21). This date indicates the last synchronization that was sent. Reset the date to the day before the date in the Last Sent field.
6. Close the dialog box. Open the File menu and select Synchronize and then click the Synchronize button.

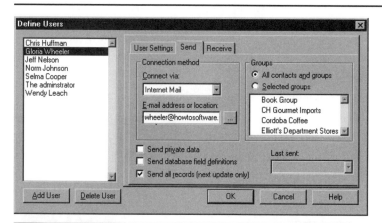

FIGURE 25-21   In this dialog box you can reset the date of the last synchronization for one or several users.

If you are synchronizing with multiple users, everyone will get a synchronization file, but those other files will not be affected by this change. The person who had the problem should now have the correct data based on the date you entered, as the date entry resets the log file for that user. If your database is small, you could have selected Send All Records (Next Update Only) in the Define Users dialog box to accomplish the same thing.

Ridding the Database of an Evil Twin

An evil twin is a record that is a duplicate My Record. It appears in the Define Users dialog box as Doug Wolf (1). This happens when you have a remote user defined in the Define Users dialog box (which creates a My Record in the master database), then you synchronize with that user and his My Record is different in one or more of the following fields: Company, Contact, or Phone. For example, suppose the master database record has the information:

 Beaver Productions

 June Cleaver

 555-555-1212

and the remote user has entered:

 Beaver Productions Inc.

 June Cleaver

 555-555-1212

Before the ink is dry, you will have two Cleavers in the master and the remote database. This is not always a major problem, but it can be if the wrong My Record is used accidentally. To fix this problem, get on the phone and compare the three field entries. Even an inadvertent space at the end of the company name can cause this to happen. After confirming an exact match, clean it up using the following steps:

1. In both the master and remote database, open the File menu and select Administration.

2. Select Define Users.

3. Click the name of the evil twin and then click the Delete User button. ACT! responds with the Delete User dialog box, shown in Figure 25-22. To be safe, select the Reassign To Another User option and then select the correct user.

FIGURE 25-22   Deleting a user's evil twin

4. Click OK and ACT! goes to work reassigning. After it is finished, perform a lookup by last name for the remote user. You should get at least one or two records (maybe more depending on the how common the last name is). Then delete the bad My Record.

5. Reindex the database (File | Administration | Database Maintenance | Reindex).

If All Else Fails, Ground Zero!

Ground zero is the term that Interact employs when a synchronization process is not working properly. The idea is that you consider the next synchronization to be the same as the very first synchronization—in essence, you are starting from scratch. Run the ACTDIAG program on the master database, recreate the database for each remote user, and start over.

Summary

- There are several methods for synchronizing databases, such as e-mail, shared folder, and modem to modem.

- If you are responsible for the setup of this process, the salient point to keep in mind is whether you are in the master database or in a remote database.

- If your database is corrupted, try database-to-database synchronization to effect a repair.

- A lost synchronization file can be resent by opening the File menu and selecting Define Users and resetting the date a synchronization file was sent.

- ACT! Certified Consultants can make the initial setup process and maintenance much easier.

25

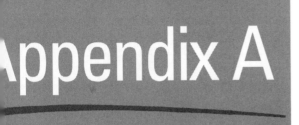

Appendix A

Enhance the Things You Can Do with ACT!

How to...
- Get help
- Get trained

This appendix lets you know about the many tools that can be used with ACT! for specific business needs or to solve a perceived shortcoming of ACT!. I use the word "perceived" because many of the products are vertical market specific, so while one ACT! user might see a shortcoming, another might think ACT! is great as it is. I have not included all the products that are available, only those that I think would be useful to my readers. I have also included a topic or two that did not fit anywhere else.

ACT! and Outlook Calendar Items

In many companies, people use Outlook as their address book, e-mail program, and calendar because they do not need the contact management aspects that ACT! provides. These same people want to be able to have a shared calendar with the ACT! users. Fortunately, it's possible to connect ACT! and Outlook activities. The way it works is ACT! sends activities to the Outlook calendar and, in turn, Outlook sends activities to the ACT! calendar. After an ACT! activity appears in Outlook, it may be modified, but that change is not reflected in the ACT! activity. Also, you can modify an Outlook activity in ACT!, but that change is not reflected in Outlook. To execute this process, open the Tools menu in ACT!, select Outlook Activities, and from the submenu, select Update. The Update Calendars dialog box opens.

In the Update options choose one of the following:

ACT! Calendar With Outlook Activities   Sends Outlook activities to ACT!.

Outlook Calendar With ACT! Activities   Sends ACT! activities to Outlook.

ACT! And Outlook Calendars   Sends activities both ways.

In the For These Dates group box, select one of the following options:
All Dates   Updates the selected calendar with activities scheduled for the past, today, and the future.

Today   Updates the selected calendar with activities scheduled for today only.

Today and Future   Updates the selected calendar with activities scheduled for today and all future dates.

Date Range   Updates the selected calendar with activities scheduled for a selected date range. Type or select the starting and ending dates of the date range.

Click Update and the process is executed and the dialog box closes.

Training Help

Buying this book is the best start you can make to get yourself trained to use ACT!. If you need more help, you can order training videos or CDs from my company, Wolf's Byte Productions, at http://www.howtosoftware.com/. As a bonus, all my customers get free phone or e-mail support.

The ACT! Buzz

When you install ACT!, your next step should be to check for updates to be certain you have the latest version of ACT!. The second thing you should do is subscribe to the free ezine *The ACT! Buzz*, which arrives in your e-mail once a week. It includes tips and tutorials that keep up with new ways to use ACT!, and it is edited by the author of this book. The web site is http://www.theactbuzz.com/.

Software Programs that Enhance ACT!

All the tools listed below can be found at ACT! Add-Ons (http://www.actaddons.com/) and purchased immediately via a download. Most have a 30-day money-back guarantee and are reasonably priced.

Q. How do I link my Palm handheld to ACT!?

Go to the http://www.act.com/ web site and download the Palm Link 2 software. Read Chapter 24 to get the inside scoop on the best configuration.

Q. How do I save money on direct mail campaigns using ACT!?

AccuMail   This product can dramatically improve your ACT! database accuracy and mail deliverability. It corrects addresses and appends ZIP+4 Zip codes, which virtually eliminates the high cost of undeliverable mail. AccuMail is CASS-certified and even prints a facsimile of Postal Form 3553.

OAK!Zip!   This software provides Zip code validation for the United States.

Master Delivery Series   This software provides accurate postal codes for Canadian addresses, as well as a number of other mail management features.

Q. How do I get data into ACT! or out to other programs without having to retype?

AddressGrabber Business   This product transfers ACT! contacts to QuickBooks, Peachtree, UPS, FedEx, and other applications. You can create invoices and shipping labels faster, plus it does everything that AddressGrabber Deluxe does.

ListGrabber   This program can capture any list from online yellow pages, e-mail, scanned documents web pages, Word, and so on. You can then easily transfer the entire address list into ACT!.

Q. We need to import new contact data from only a limited number of fields into ACT!, without affecting existing contact records.

OAK!Merge!   This software provides a field-by-field merge of ASCII data into ACT!, updating only the fields you specify. All other ACT! data remains unchanged.

Q. How can I print labels using those new online postage services?

LabelWriter   With this product, you can print professional labels directly from ACT!. Different versions allow you to print various sizes and types of labels.

Q. How can I create a lookup based on the distance from a specific point?

Proximity   Using this program, you can create an ACT! group with contact records all within a specific geographic proximity.

Q. I want to have a field filled with the result of a mathematical formula using numbers from two other ACT! fields.

OAK!Check!   This product will do this, as well as update area codes in your ACT! database, change uppercase entries in a field to lowercase, and much more.

Q. I am a software developer and I want to write custom applications for ACT!.

Sanscript for ACT!   This product lets you add features to ACT! just by dragging components onto a canvas. You can manipulate any data stored in your database, customizing it in any way you want.

Q. I have more than 5,000 records in ACT! and need a faster way to create complex lookups.

TurboLookup for ACT! 2000   You can search for contacts in your ACT! database with TurboLookup's easy-to-use queries.

Q. How can I look up records that have or have not been modified in a specific timeframe, including the Notes/History entries?

Touched Wizard   This product lets you create a group of contacts that have had any of their data modified in a timeframe you select.

Untouched Wizard   The complement to the Touched Wizard product, this software will create a group of contacts that have *not* had modifications in the timeframe you select.

Q. We have a company database that is not in ACT! and we need to keep it current with our shared ACT! database.

USI SYNCMaster v4.0   This product bridges two databases in any direction. You can create a data bridge between your favorite contact manager and another database, to synchronize in any direction. It eliminates tedious data entry via field-by-field synchronization and automatic processing. USI SYNCMaster is intelligent software that recognizes updates on either end and appends records as needed. If USI SYNCMaster sees an error, a report is generated to let you know. You can synchronize your data as often as you wish by setting your own parameters.

Q. We need to have a customer number entered for us automatically when a new ACT! record is created.

Account Number Wizard   The Account Number Wizard will generate unique numbers for your contacts based on data in their fields and the drop-down descriptions. It includes a run-once utility that allows you to set up the database and assign numbers to existing contacts. Also included is a utility that allows users to add new IDs for new contacts they create.

Q. We need a way to highlight data that cannot be missed in an ACT! record field.

ACT!Alert   When you set up ACT!Alert for a database, you will be prompted to select the ACT!Alert field. ACT!Alert will display an alert message when you scroll to contacts that have data in the field you select. For example, if a database has a field called User 1, you can run the ACT!Alert Configuration Wizard and set User 1 to be an alert field. Once done, whenever you scroll to a contact that has a value in the User 1 field, an alert message will appear that contains the data from that field.

Q. We need to move our shared ACT! database from one server to another. Can we preserve all the attachment links? Can we add attachments without opening ACT!?

Attachment Migration Wizard   This product changes the path of attachments stored within ACT!. If you have moved the folder containing your attachments or remapped your server, the Attachment Migration Wizard will reconnect the paths from ACT! to these attachments.

ShellACT   This product lets you quickly add attachments to an ACT! contact without ACT! running. You can also quickly and easily copy ACT! contact info into a WORD document.

Q. We need a way to automate ACT! maintenance and synchronization.

AutoAdmin   Allows you to specify the database and login information. You can choose to compress and reindex your database, or to back up the database before or after synchronization and/or compress and reindex.

Q. ACT! e-mail merge is great, but is there a way to send HTML or attachments?

3D FortuneFlow   Offers HTML e-mail merge, text and Word document e-mail merge, fax and mail merge, by address priority, including fax and e-mail attachments, auto scheduling, updating, and much more.

Mail Merge Mania   Allows you to attach PDF, ZIP, and other file formats plus send the e-mail in HTML format.

Q. I like the ACT! activity series, but I am lazy and want ACT! to process and complete the activities for me.

Action!   On a daily basis, your computer will automatically check every contact and group in your database to produce letters on the scheduled date. After sending the document, your Action! program will update your contact's history and schedule the next document to be sent.

Q. ACT! can send lots of faxes via WinFax, but I need to send hundreds at a time.

BroadFax   Quickly, effectively, and economically delivers attractive advertisements to thousands of contacts within minutes.

FaxNow!   Sends a cover page and attachments to the current contact, selected contacts, groups, or all contacts. Every user on the network can access these functions.

Q. We need customer support software that works with ACT!.

FrontSupport   Client/server version FrontSupport is Windows-based customer support software that enables your customer support personnel to store information for your customer support issues. Tracks the issues from the time they are reported to the time they are resolved.

FrontSupportWeb   Web-based version of the software above.

HelpDesk   Tracks and measures inquiries from start to resolution.

Q. I have a large Access database that I want to connect to ACT! records.

ACTAccess   Associates an MS Access database with any contact in ACT!. Transfers information between ACT! and Access with a few mouse clicks.

Q. I want to associate files with a contact record and be able to edit them without leaving ACT!.

ActiveACT   Allows you to view and edit Excel spreadsheets, Word documents, and Adobe Acrobat (PDF) files without leaving ACT!.

Q. ACT! is too easy to copy, and our database has lots of confidential information that cannot leave our office. How do we prevent theft?

ACT!Secure   ACT!Secure 2.0 is software that is easy to install and use. It simplifies control procedures and satisfies security requirements. All you need to do is create your unique user account and place files under ACT!Secure 2.0 for encryption.

Q. How can I export all the data in ACT!, including Notes/History?

Exporter for ACT!   Exports data into comma-delimited, standard dBase .dbf files and/or a Visual Foxpro .dbc file.

ExportPro   ACT! to Access converter preserves relationships between tables.

Q. The reports that ACT! has for sales opportunities are limited, and we need more ways to view the data.

Export Sales & Opportunities   Pivot Tables and Pivot Charts are easy-to-use, flexible tools for sales and opportunity reporting and analysis.

Sales2TXT   Exports all the data from ACT!'s Sales/Opportunities records into a comma-delimited .txt file. This allows you to use applications such as Excel to create summary reports and tables which are not possible with ACT!'s standard report writer. Includes two additional fields (quarter close and month close) which allow you to create summaries without the use of complex formulas.

Q. Is there a customized version of ACT! for financial planners?

Act4Advisors   Offers customized contact, client, and office management for financial advisors.

Q. Is there an easy way to add major holidays into ACT! automatically?

Holiday Calendar for ACT!   Adds U.S. and major religious holidays to your ACT! monthly calendar from 2001 through 2003. Can be synchronized with your Palm.

Q. Is there a customized version of ACT! for insurance offices?

TABs Insurance   Offers complete commission management, addressing unlimited hierarchy designs, both internal and external. Complies with various NAILBA and Olife formats.

Q. How can ACT! be enabled to do instant messaging on our network?

TextNow!   Enables network users to communicate instantly with any mobile or SMS enabled device.

Q. What software can we use with ACT! to spruce up our direct mail?

DAZzle Designer   Designs and prints any mail piece, including business reply mail, with built-in visual alarms for compliance with USPS regulations. Also features Dial-A-ZIP and POSTNET barcoding.

DAZzle Express   Easy-to-use wizard interface guides the user through bulk mailings. First-class or standard mail, nonprofit, and carrier route discounts are possible.

Envelope Manager PAVE   Full-featured mail management program. CASS- and PAVE-certified sorting for first-class and standard mail automation mailings. Includes a built-in address book and DAZzle Designer.

Envelope Manager LE   "Light" version of Envelope Manager PAVE. (No sorting for discount mailings.)

eReturn Detective   Identifies which contacts generate returned/bounced e-mail. Flags, removes, or schedules events to fix the problem.

Acxiom Print & Electronic Distribution   Print and mail promotions/campaigns from your ACT! database.

ProSort   Performs first class, ZIP+4, barcoded automation, and carrier route presorts. Also performs third-class 3/5 digit basic, carrier route, and automation presorts. Prints appropriate USPS 5-digit, ZIP+4, and delivery point POSTNET. Designed to work with AccuMail (see earlier in this appendix).

SmartAddresser   Ensures your company mail contains a correct Canadian address. Carries Canadian SERP Level A recognition. Works with any size list or ACT! database. Contains every postal code and its corresponding address in Canada.

SmartSort   Presorts your mail to Canada Post specifications. Designed to work with SmartAddresser (discussed previously).

Q. Can I create high quality maps of my ACT! records?

BusinessMAP PRO   Converts records from spreadsheets, contact managers, databases, and phone directories to symbols on a map. Allows you to perform color-code analysis, geographic searches, and territory design.

Street Wizard   Creates a route to your contact and copies the directions back into your ACT! database. Click on a dot on the map to access your ACT! contact record.

Q. Is there a customized version of ACT! for the construction business?

BetterACT!   Enters job track info; search, sort, and report on leads, clients, vendors, subcontractors, and associates. Produces quick and easy correspondence (documents, envelopes, mailing labels).

Q. I am a mortgage broker and need help generating new loan originations.

Mortgage Quest   This is a database marketing software program designed specifically for the mortgage industry. Contains automated marketing strategies and 78 sales letters to generate referrals from customers, realtors, builders, attorneys, and others.

Trans/ACT! Mortgage Banking   Offers custom-designed databases and layouts for the mortgage banking industry. Includes a scheduler and mail features, financial calculators, buyer/seller tools, and more.

A

Q. I purchased a Window CE device. Is there software to link it to ACT!?

XTNDConnect PC   Allows mobile devices, including Palm, Windows CE, and Casio Pocket Viewer devices, to synchronize with ACT! 3.05/4.0/2000. Users can synchronize contacts, calendars, tasks, and e-mail. Also supports other popular PC applications such as Microsoft Outlook, Lotus Notes, Organizer, and GoldMine. Users can keep two or more PC applications synchronized (such as ACT! and Outlook).

CompanionLink   Supports dozens of handheld organizers, including all Palm, Handspring, Pocket PC, and Psion units. Offers one-button synchronization of contacts, appointments, to-do lists, and memos.

Q. How do I print my calendars and address books to specific size paper formats?

OrganizerPaper.com   Prints your calendars (daily, weekly, or monthly) and address books from within ACT! on prepunched paper that fits existing organizers, including Day Runner, Day-Timer, Franklin Day Planner, Rolodex, and Filofax.

Q. Is there a product that will help us keep track of leads we have given to the sales team?

Lost Leads   Generates a graphical report showing who you haven't contacted in a while. You can quickly scan the generated bar chart and call those contacts you may have forgotten about.

Q. Can I access my ACT! database via my mobile phone?

UnwiredContact!   Offers real-time access to ACT! through your web phone.

Q. How can we easily generate and save sales quotes via ACT?

OAK!Quote!   Creates, saves, and edits individual and/or master quotations. Automatically calculates discounts based on customer code, product line, and quantity. Calculates discount at the line item level.

ProposalMaster   Creates complete proposals, letter proposals, and sales letters. Searches through the library of corporate information, using key words and phrases to answer Requests for Proposals.

QwikQuote   Uses ACT! contact information in combination with your catalog to generate quotes. Custom layouts, including logos and graphics.

QuoteWerks   Attaches quote under your ACT! contact's Notes/History tab, enabling you to launch your quote directly from ACT!. Sales opportunity and activity records are automatically created. Links to product databases. Integrated e-mail client allows you to e-mail quotes from within the program.

RFPMaster   Automatically reads a Request for Proposal, separates it into questions, and searches your database of existing content for the best answers.

Q. Are there customized versions of ACT! for residential and/or commercial real estate?

ACTive Agent   Offers customer tasking and calendar management for real estate. Schedule and manipulate multiple tasks and contacts in the included ACT! Real Estate Management Database through customized and openly definable "campaigns." Campaigns can contain tasks to do, meetings to schedule, calls to make, and form letters and brochure correspondence.

BetterACT!   Remodelers can easily enter meaningful job track info; search, sort, and report on leads, clients, vendors, subcontractors, associates, and so on.

REALHOUND   Tracks and analyzes your apartment and commercial properties.

Trans/ACT! Commercial Agent   Commercial real estate package including property database and customized layouts.

Trans/ACT! Home Builder   Complete home builder sales system using ACT!.

Trans/ACT! Residential Agent   Complete package for real estate agents who want increased productivity with ACT!.

Q. Is there reporting software that I can use on my ACT! database?

Crystal Reports   Creates virtually any report you can imagine, including subreports, conditional, summary, cross-tab, form, drill down, OLAP, Top N, multiple details, and mailing labels. Customizes your reports with logos, pictures, shapes and colors. A good reference book is *Crystal Reports for Dummies* by Douglas J. Wolf.

ExACT History   Uses the Notes/History information within ACT! to provide comprehensive per user and/or per contact activity analysis.

Q. ACT! used to have a link to Hot Data. Is there a new service like that?

zapdata.com   Provides customized, one-click access to targeted sales leads, company profiles, industry reports, prospect lists, and more.

Clickdata.com   Provides profit-generating sales leads, prospect lists and contact lists.

ThinkDirectMarketing   Offers demographic and geographic search capabilities to create the perfect prospect list. Designed to work seamlessly with ACT!, the lists you create will provide you with the names, numbers and addresses of the people you want to target.

Q. Can I easily attach scanned documents to contact records?

ACTScan   Scans documents directly into your ACT! contact records right from the ACT! toolbar. Files hardcopy client documentation along with other contact information, without ever leaving ACT!.

Q. I returned from a trade show and have hundreds of business cards that I want to enter into ACT! How can I do this without typing?

CardScan Executive for ACT!   With CardScan Executive, simply feed a business card into the scanner. The software accurately organizes all the information into the correct fields. You can add searchable notes, assign categories, and scan the back of a card to capture an image of your handwritten notes.

Q. I use ACT! to keep track of my employees, and I would like to attach a picture of each to their contact record.

PhotoAct   Associates and displays unlimited images with each contact in your ACT! database. Unlimited images can be associated with each contact. Tab settings control thumbnail size and arrangement along with background graphics.

Q. How can I attach telemarketing scripts to contact records?

OAK!Script!   Builds scripts as a series of screens that can branch, display text from ACT!, or collect data for updating ACT!. Uses hypertext links to navigate through a scenario—for example, a telemarketer clicks on hypertext keywords to continue the script according to the responses received.

Persuader   Creates an unlimited number of logical scripts to provide your agents with a sales-map, taking them from the greeting, through the objections, and finally to the close. As each step is completed, the information gathered is stored for future use.

Q. How do I get my ACT! names and phone numbers into my cell phone?

FoneSync   Allows you to simply drag and drop names and numbers from ACT! to your phone. Supports most makes of digital wireless phones, including Ericsson, Nokia, and Panasonic.

Q. I know I attached a document to an ACT! contact record that has important information, but I cannot find it. Help!

DocFindIt   DocFindIt searches documents attached to your ACT! contact records. Just enter a word or a phrase, and DocFindIt will track down the attachment (and contact record) that has it. Works with virtually any type of attached document, including Word documents, e-mail attachments, text files, and Excel spreadsheets.

Q. How can I grab information from company web sites and get into it with a single mouse click?

NetLinkIt   Retrieves a page from your web browser, stores it in a dedicated directory, and creates a linked document record in ACT!. Also fixes broken hyperlink documents so the web page is saved in its entirety.

Q. I need more prospects. Is there a way to search the Web and have the information added to ACT!?

Net Prospector 2000   Queries the leading Internet search engines and researches the results, finding e-mail addresses, phone numbers, and fax numbers of businesses whose web sites contain keywords that you provide. Matching web sites are also browsed automatically for your review.

A

Free Stuff

Freebee of the Month   From Northwoods Software (http://www.nwoods.com/). Sign up for e-mail notification when Freebees are published. Freebees include: ACT2Excel, MultiLookup, Copy2Clipboard, TimeZone, and more.

Index

N

INTERNATIONAL CONTACT INFORMATION

AUSTRALIA
McGraw-Hill Book Company Australia Pty. Ltd.
TEL +61-2-9417-9899
FAX +61-2-9417-5687
http://www.mcgraw-hill.com.au
books-it_sydney@mcgraw-hill.com

CANADA
McGraw-Hill Ryerson Ltd.
TEL +905-430-5000
FAX +905-430-5020
http://www.mcgrawhill.ca

GREECE, MIDDLE EAST,
NORTHERN AFRICA
McGraw-Hill Hellas
TEL +30-1-656-0990-3-4
FAX +30-1-654-5525

MEXICO (Also serving Latin America)
McGraw-Hill Interamericana Editores S.A. de C.V.
TEL +525-117-1583
FAX +525-117-1589
http://www.mcgraw-hill.com.mx
fernando_castellanos@mcgraw-hill.com

SINGAPORE (Serving Asia)
McGraw-Hill Book Company
TEL +65-863-1580
FAX +65-862-3354
http://www.mcgraw-hill.com.sg
mghasia@mcgraw-hill.com

SOUTH AFRICA
McGraw-Hill South Africa
TEL +27-11-622-7512
FAX +27-11-622-9045
robyn_swanepoel@mcgraw-hill.com

UNITED KINGDOM & EUROPE
(Excluding Southern Europe)
McGraw-Hill Publishing Company
TEL +44-1-628-502500
FAX +44-1-628-770224
http://www.mcgraw-hill.co.uk
computing_neurope@mcgraw-hill.com

ALL OTHER INQUIRIES Contact:
Osborne/McGraw-Hill
TEL +1-510-549-6600
FAX +1-510-883-7600
http://www.osborne.com
omg_international@mcgraw-hill.com